TWENTY YEARS
OF
CRISES:
The Cold War Era

When written in Chinese,
the word CRISIS is composed
of two characters:

 one represents danger

 and one represents opportunity.

—*John F. Kennedy*

TWENTY YEARS
OF
CRISES:
The Cold War Era

EDITED, WITH INTRODUCTIONS, BY

YOUNG HUM KIM

CALIFORNIA WESTERN UNIVERSITY

Prentice-Hall, Inc., *Englewood Cliffs, N.J.*

Library of Congress Catalog Card Number: 68-11552.

Printed in the United States of America.

Current printing (first digit)

1   2   3   4   5   6   7   8   9   10

Prentice-Hall International, Inc.
LONDON

Prentice-Hall of Australia, Pty. Ltd.
SYDNEY

Prentice-Hall of Canada, Ltd.
TORONTO

Prentice-Hall of India Private Ltd.
NEW DELHI

Prentice-Hall of Japan, Inc.
TOKYO

to
Susan
and
Miep

Preface

THOUGH THE TERM "Cold War" defies precise definition, it may be described as the international environment characterized by persistent tensions and conflict between the free world and the Communist camp in general, and between the United States and the Soviet Union in particular. This new *war* of *cold* realities in international politics has been waged in every conceivable field of international life, especially in national defense, economic growth, diplomacy, and ideology.

The date of origin of the Cold War varies with the opinions of different writers. Some scholars place it as far back as the Bolshevik Revolution in 1917, whence the Communists set out to control and dominate the world through a series of Marxist revolutions. Others maintain that the geneses of the Cold War are to be found in the period of the Grand Alliance of World War II. They claim that wartime cooperation among the Allies was often marred by the differences of opinions and attitudes over such issues as the treatment of anti-Nazi resistance forces in Poland and Yugoslavia, the establishment of the Second Front, the coordination of military strategy, and the postwar reconstruction of a new world. Still others assert that the Cold War was crystallized in 1947 when the West and the Soviet Union intensified and formalized the differences in interpretation of the provisions of the Yalta and Potsdam Agreements.

For the purpose of this study, however, it is assumed that the Cold War began shortly after World War II ended, granting that the former was not a continuation of the latter. At the war's end, the basic incompatibility between Soviet Communism and Western democracy in terms of ideology and security took a new turn toward higher intensity as Stalin reverted from the policy of wartime expediency (alliance with the West) to the policy of prewar orthodoxy (hard line dogmatism).

After the defeat of the Axis Powers, the world needed a respite from the carnage and devastation of the war, and continued cooperation among the victors was attempted. Limited agreements were reached in such issues as: 1) the seat of the United Nations headquarters in New York, 2) Soviet consent to the trusteeship by the United States of the strategic islands in the Pacific, 3) the establishment of the Far Eastern Commission and the Allied Control Council for Japan, and 4) the opening of a peace conference in Paris before May 1, 1946.

But the nature of power politics would not allow the kind of power vacuum created by the outcome of World War II to remain unaffected. Between the world wars the power structure had been one of multipolarity. The leading Powers were Great Britain, France, Germany, and Italy in Europe; the Soviet Union in Eurasia; Japan in the Far East; and the United States in North America. By mid-August, 1945, however, both Germany and Japan were vanquished, Great Britain was exhausted after the gallant struggle in her "finest hour," France having been defeated was still torn by political and economic chaos, and Italy was reduced to insignificance, although these Powers still remained factors to be reckoned with in subsequent world affairs. The only nations in a position to assume leadership were the United States and the Soviet Union. The world thus came to witness the phenomenon of bi-polarization. For the time being there was no third power strong enough to transform the precarious American-Soviet bipolar rivalry into multi-polar balance of power, even though it was a cardinal principle of British foreign policy to play the role of bridging the gap.

The Cold War in the past twenty years has been marked by a series of crises, alternated with heightened tensions and guarded relaxations. Part One of this book is devoted primarily to five crises during the period from Soviet resumption of the "hard line" policy vis-à-vis the West at the end of World War II to the signing of the Korean Armistice Agreement in July, 1953. This period was characterized by the militant, expansionist policy of the Soviet Union, and the United States' "containment policy." The inauguration of the Truman Doctrine, the implementation of the Marshall Plan, the massive airlift in response to the Soviet blockade of Berlin, and the resolute American action in the Korean War were the events of prime importance arising from the crisis struggles. In this respect the United States achieved a qualified success in blunting Soviet expansion, but she failed to stem the rising tide of Chinese communism in the heart of the Asian continent. The rise in power and influence of Communist China posed a formidable challenge to United States leadership in the Far East and somewhat began to change the nature, direction, and emphasis of the Cold War.

Part Two deals with seven crises during the period from the establishment of the Kremlin's collective leadership in the wake of

Stalin's death to the suppression of the Congo crisis. The unique feature
of this period was the conspicuous change in Soviet strategy in world
affairs—from the rigid, inflexible Stalinist tactics to the subtle, flexible
Khrushchevian policy of "peaceful coexistence." This period was
paralleled in the United States by the Republican Administration under
President Eisenhower, whose Secretary of State, John Foster Dulles, was
often accused of conducting American foreign policy by "slogans" such as
"massive retaliation," "brink of war," "liberation of Soviet satellites," and
"rolling-back Communism."

The prospect of thermonuclear destructive power capable of annihi-
lating civilization in an all-out nuclear war between the United States
and the Soviet Union has compelled the two superpowers to adhere
cautiously to the unwritten law of *coexistence.* Any one of such crises as
the Taiwan issue, the Suez invasion, the Hungarian Revolution, the
Middle Eastern tension, the Laotian conflict, the U-2 incident, and the
Congo strife might have escalated into an unthinkable war. But they
consciously and conscientiously pursued the course of nonconfrontation
in an effort to keep the sword of Damocles from falling.

Finally, Part Three of this volume is devoted to the period from the
Cuban missile crisis to the present. Two significant phenomena have
occurred in this stage. First, both the United States and the Soviet Union
have shown signs of political maturity and have resorted to reason and
moderation in the conduct of their policies toward each other. The incomprehensible destructive power of modern weapons in the hands of
both nations has made a total war a conceivably self-defeating instrument
of policy. Indeed the *balance of sanity* of the leaders of major Powers is
the only hope for the survival of mankind which is confronted with the
possibility of virtual self-annihilation.

Second, a multi-polar balance of power has re-emerged in the sixties.
Due to idealogical as well as political controversies, the monolithic
Communist solidarity has irrefutably broken into tri-centricism—Peking
orthodoxy, Moscow eclecticism, and Belgrade revisionism. The power
rivalry between the Soviet Union and Communist China is no less
vehement than that between the Soviet Union and the United States. In
the Western Alliance the undisputed leadership of the United States is
seriously challenged by France under President De Gaulle. The unprecedented economic prosperity of Western Europe has enabled Great
Britain, France, and West Germany to restore their power status of great
significance. In the Far East the power position of Communist China,
especially since its successful development of the atomic bomb, has
become a crucial factor in world affairs. Communist China's relentless
pursuit of universal recognition as a great power and the unceasing effort
to reestablish her hegemony in Asia, which the past Imperial dynasties of
China had held for centuries, have added new elements and dimension
to the Cold War. Japan likewise is playing an increasingly important

role. Although her voice in the international arena has been relatively weak, her industrial and technological capacities may well qualify her as a great power. Moreover, the growing number, power, prestige, and moral force of the so-called "nonaligned" or "uncommitted" nations of Asia, Africa, and the Middle East have come to constitute a preponderant weight on the international scale of the multi-polar balance.

Against this background a series of crises—the Cuban missile confrontation, Communist China's attack on India, the Cyprus issue, the United Nations' financial difficulties, and China's explosion of atomic bombs—have been overcome without upsetting the new power structure in the Cold War. As for the war in Vietnam, it has been a struggle between the United States, which was determined to contain Communist expansion in Southeast Asia, and the Communists, who were equally determined to eliminate American influence in that region.

This book is designed as a supplementary reader for such college courses as International Relations, American Foreign Policy, World Politics, Soviet Foreign Policy, Contemporary World Affairs, Contemporary History, and other related fields. Each of its three parts contains an *Introduction* by the editor designed to thread together various segments of the book, to describe general backgrounds of the crises, and to show where and how each of the collections fits into the overall pattern of the Cold War. The crises selected are further divided into twenty chapters—one crisis per chapter—and arranged in chronological order. The readings in each chapter are chosen with a view to presenting a balanced picture of the crises concerned; therefore, two diametrically opposing interpretations are often juxtaposed. The book has a list of Selected Bibliography for further studies.

I wish to extend my sincere gratitude to the following scholars and literati who have granted me their personal permission to reprint from their works in this volume: Professor Chalmers Johnson, Professor Weiner Levi, Mr. George Lichtheim, Mr. Walter Lippmann, Dr. Robert T. Oliver, Dr. Harry J. Psomiades, Dr. Robert A. Scalapino, Professor Arthur Schlesinger, Jr., Professor Hugh Seton-Watson, Mr. K. S. Shelvanker, Professor Telford Taylor, and Dr. Arnold Wolfers.

I am also grateful to the following publishers and organizations whose generous permission to reprint copyright materials made this volume possible: The American Academy of Political and Social Science, The American Academy of Political Science, The American Jewish Committee, The American Society of International Law, The Bulletin of the Atomic Scientists, Contemporary Co., Ltd., The Cornell University Press, The Council for Middle Eastern Affairs, The Council on Foreign Relations, Current History, Doubleday and Co., Foreign Policy Association–World Affairs Center, Foreign Policy Research Institute (University of Pennsylvania), Frederick A. Praeger, Inc., Institute of Government (University of Utah), The Joint Committee on Slavic Studies (Columbia

University), Nation Co., Inc., The New Republic, The New York Times
Co., The Oxford University Press, The Philosophical Library, Princeton
University Press, The Royal Institute of International Affairs (London),
United States Information Agency, and the Wall Street Journal.

Finally, I am deeply indebted to William C. Olson and the late
Charles D. Lerche, Dean of the School of International Service at
American University, for their valuable suggestions; to my colleagues,
Dr. Leigh Rhett and Professor Stanley S. Newcomb, for their unselfish
assistance; to Miss Elizabeth Armstrong and her Ryan Library staff for
their cooperation in search of materials; to Mr. James J. Murray, III, of
Prentice-Hall for his valuable advice; to Miss Judith L. Johnson for her
most helpful work in the preparation of the manuscript; and to my wife,
Susan, for her unceasing encouragement and understanding.

Y.H.K.

Contents

TWENTY YEARS
OF
CRISES:
The Cold War Era

part One

From Iran to Korea

INTRODUCTION

IN MAY, 1945, Hitler's Third Reich toppled in the ruins of World War II; three months later the Empire of Japan surrendered to the Allied Powers to terminate the "Great Tragedy" of our time.

However, the military victory of the Allies over the Axis Powers failed to establish genuine peace. Conflict and tensions among the victors replaced the wartime cooperation and assistance, and with the gradual dissipation of the spirit of the "Grand Alliance," the Cold War became crystallized.

The basic causes of the Cold War are numerous and varied. Among them, four key factors must be scrutinized, two from each side. From the viewpoint of the West, specifically of the United States, one of the principal causes was the aggressive, expansionist policy of the Soviet Union. Soviet Russia with its imperialistic ambitions, combined with its quest for security, sought to establish Soviet hegemony over the Eurasian Continent from the heart of Europe to the Pacific and from the Arctic zone to the Afghan border. Its relentless pursuit of territorial and political aggrandizement not only resulted in absorbing such areas as the ice-free port of Petsamo in Finland, the eastern region of Poland, Ruthenia from Czechoslovakia, Bessarabia from Rumania, and Sakhalin and the Kurils from Japan, but also succeeded in bringing into the Soviet sphere of influence such nations as Poland, East Germany, Czechoslovakia, Hungary, Austria, Yugoslavia, Rumania, Albania, and Outer Mongolia. Continued aggression and penetration in this fashion would obviously pose a grave and lasting threat to the security interests of the Western Powers.

Another conviction held by the West was that the Cold War had its roots in the morbid xenophobia of Russia itself. The age-old suspicion of the West, nurtured in Russian history and tradition and further remolded by the Marxist–Leninist doctrine, had driven Soviet leaders to regard their former allies as unavoidable foes, once the common enemies had been vanquished.

1

The legacy of Russian distrust of foreigners had found a valid conclusion in a statement that only countries as fully sovietized as Russia itself could be regarded as safe neighbors and reliable friends.

On the other hand, viewed from the Soviet Union, the capitalist West led by the United States was bent on the destruction of the Soviet socialist state. To Western democracies, fascism and communism were equally an anathema; World War II was a capitalist war in which fascism—the worse of the two evils—was defeated by capitalism in collaboration with communism. Now that the fascism in Europe and the militarism in East Asia had been beaten, so reasoned the Soviets, the capitalist democracies had embarked upon the task of bringing about the ultimate demise of communism, which had set firm roots in Soviet political, social, and economic systems. For instance, one of the immediate postwar manifestations of this Western "conspiracy" was the sudden United States decision, in August, 1945, to terminate all lend-lease and economic aid to the Soviet Union, while in subsequent months Washington extended loans to Great Britain and France of $4.4 billion and $1.4 billion, respectively. The Soviets had hoped to rehabilitate their ruined economy and reconstruct their devastated nation to some extent through continued American aid.

The other view held by the Soviet leaders was that American imperialism was responsible for the Cold War. Reared under Marxism–Leninism and adhering to the doctrine of dialectic materialism, the Soviets examined the postwar conditions of the United States through the prism of their logic: Of all the capitalist nations, only the United States emerged from World War II not only unweakened but even considerably stronger militarily and economically. In fact the American capitalists had been benefited and enriched by the war, although they were confronted with various problems at its end. The capitalist monopolies did their best to maintain their profits at the former high level; consequently, they sought to prevent a reduction of the wartime volume of deliveries. For this reason, they tried not only to retain the foreign markets which had absorbed their products during the war, but also to acquire new markets to supplement possible losses resulting from the weakened purchasing power of most of the countries. The United States, therefore, had taken a new aggressive, expansionist course leading to the world supremacy of American imperialism, which is, after all, "the highest stage of capitalism."

By early 1946, relations between the United States and the Soviet Union had deteriorated noticeably and become clouded with distrust, dissension, suspicion, apprehension, and frustration. On February 7, 1946, in the midst of this unsavory international atmosphere, Stalin delivered a pre-election speech to the Russian people, setting forth domestic and foreign policies and calling for greater efforts toward national reconstruction to meet the challenge of the West.

Nearly a month later, on March 5 at Fulton, Missouri, Stalin's speech was followed by the famous "iron curtain" speech of Sir Winston Churchill. His terse statement—"From Stettin in the Baltic to Triest in the Adriatic, an iron curtain has descended across the Continent"—was both a stark recognition and a succinct summation of the *fait accompli* of Soviet expansion into the heart of Europe.

Having entrenched themselves in Eastern Europe and drawn the "curtain" against the West, the Soviets directed their penetration into the Middle East, especially Iran. During World War II, Iran was occupied by the Allies—the north by the Soviet Union and the south by Great Britain—for the purpose of safeguarding the flow of arms supplies to the Soviet Union through that country. The United States also sent troops to Iran in order to render assistance and cooperation in this joint undertaking.

As the war progressed, the Soviets attempted to establish a satellite state in the territory they occupied. They increased the number of troops stationed in northern Iran and encouraged subversive activities of the local Communist (Tudeh) Party. In the fall of 1944, the Soviet Union also demanded Iranian oil concessions for a period of 25 years. The Iranian government rejected the demand, stating that so long as Iran was occupied by foreign troops no concessions would be granted to foreign powers. But the Soviet Union continued to press the issue.

When the war came to a close the Tudeh Party, with the blessing of Soviet occupation authorities, sought increased autonomy for Azerbaijan, a province in northwestern Iran bordering on the Soviet Union. As the central government refused this demand, the Tudeh Party changed its name to "Democratic Party" and took over the governmental machinery in the province, creating a state of insurgency. When the Teheran government dispatched troops to the troubled area, Soviet armed forces intercepted them and denied them access to the province.

In November, 1945, the Democratic Party unilaterally proclaimed the complete autonomy of Azerbaijan and began to form a "National Assembly" through "elections." Meeting in the city of Tabriz, the National Assembly announced the creation of the Autonomous Republic of Azerbaijan headed by Jafar Pishevari, a veteran Communist.

On January 19, 1946, the government of Iran informed the Security Council of the United Nations under Article 35 of the Charter that Soviet interference in Iranian domestic affairs might endanger international peace and security. After discussion, the Security Council adopted a resolution calling for negotiations among the parties concerned. The subsequent negotiations produced no visible results, and on March 18 Iran again drew the Council's attention to the continued presence and interference in Iran of Soviet troops and officials, which was likely to jeopardize international peace. The Soviet armed forces should have been withdrawn by March 2, 1946, in accordance with the terms of the Iranian–British–Soviet treaty of January 29, 1942, which had provided for the withdrawal of foreign troops from Iran six months after the end of hostilities with Germany. It should be noted that by that date British and American troops had evacuated Iran.

Meanwhile, in Moscow, bilateral negotiations were carried out between the Iranian Premier, Qavam Saltaneh, and the Soviet leaders. Although the Soviet delegation at the United Nations had walked out of the Security Council meeting, Premier Qavam was successful in his negotiations. The Soviet Union agreed to evacuate Iran in return for Iranian concessions such as the recognition of autonomy for Azerbaijan and the formation of a joint Soviet–Iranian oil company, subject to ratification of the Majlis (Iranian Parliament). However, when the Soviet Union completed its troop withdrawal in May, 1946, the Majlis refused to ratify the draft agreement. By the end of that year, with the noticeable dissipation of the Communist threat, Azerbaijan was brought back under the authority of the Teheran government. The significance of the Iranian issue was that in the first contest with the West in the Cold War, the Soviet Union ultimately failed in its attempt to make a satellite out of Iran.

During the one-year period from March, 1946, when world attention was focused on the Iranian controversy, to March, 1947, when the Truman Doctrine was proclaimed, the Cold War strategy of the Soviet Union was manifested in the form of an uncompromising, hostile attitude *vis-à-vis* the West. The Soviet Union tightened the rein of control over all its Eastern European satellites and sought to minimize their contact with non-Communist countries. The Soviets cast frequent vetoes in the U. N. Security Council against the admission of new members; when a proposal was made to amend the U. N. Charter to abolish the veto, they advocated continuing that right:

> The principle of veto demands that all the Great Powers display attention with regard to their common interests and the interests of universal peace, hindering the creation of narrow blocs and groups of some Powers against other Powers, and still more hampering opportunity for anyone's bargaining with an aggressor behind the backs and contrary to the interests of peace-loving countries.[1]

The Soviet government demonstrated neither willingness nor readiness to cooperate with the West in convening a peace conference to settle the outstanding issues of postwar Europe. In January, 1947, the Soviet authorities had the Polish elections rigged and manipulated for the Communists, who inevitably emerged as "winners." The United States and Great Britain lodged protests on the basis of the provisions of the Yalta and Potsdam Agreements which had stipulated:

> The Provisional Government which is now functioning in Poland should therefore be reorganized on a broader democratic basis with the inclusion of democratic leaders from Poland itself and from Poles abroad. This new Gov-

[1]Address by V. M. Molotov, September 14, 1946, to the session of the Paris Peace Conference for Italy.

ernment should then be called the Polish Provisional Government of National Unity. . . . [This Government] shall be pledged to the holding of free and unfettered elections as soon as possible on the basis of universal suffrage and secret ballot. In these elections all democratic and anti-Nazi parties shall have the right to take part and to put forward candidates.[2]

But the protests proved futile.

The first resolute response of the United States to the continued threat of Soviet expansion was the announcement of the Truman Doctrine on March 12, 1947. In Greece, as in Iran, the Soviets had strengthened the local Communists during the war, by exploiting the fight against National Socialism. The Communist "Liberation Front" and other Greek nationalists cooperated in their fight against the Italian and German occupation troops. But after November 2, 1944, when the German Army evacuated Greece, the nation was torn by factional and guerrilla struggles. The Greek government-in-exile returned to Athens from London, but it was unable to establish complete control throughout the country; only where British troops could render substantial assistance did its authority prevail. When the Communists threatened to capture Athens by force, clashes took place between them and British units. In the ensuing instability and turmoil, an armistice and other agreements were reached with the rebels, but the authority of the Greek government under the leadership of Archbishop Damaskinos remained limited to the cities. What was actually taking place was the restaging of the Azerbaijan drama with different casts in a different setting. Yet in January, 1946, the Soviet government submitted to the Security Council that the continued presence of British troops in Greece constituted unlawful interference in Greek internal affairs and would endanger international peace.

Throughout 1946, Communist guerrilla activities continued. Late in the year the Greek government requested the Security Council to consider the situation in northern Greece, where Communist guerrillas were aided by the Greeks' northern neighbors. In response the Security Council established the Commission of Investigation, whose subsequent report on its findings placed full responsibility for the disorders on Albania, Bulgaria, and Yugoslavia. On the basis of this report, the Security Council sought to adopt measures to protect Greece and to restore order, but its effort was thwarted by a Soviet veto.

The progressively deteriorating situation in Greece, coupled with the expressed inability of either the United Nations or Great Britain to maintain peace and order, prompted the United States to assume the burden and responsibility for the defense of that part of the free world. In March, 1947, President Truman announced in a message to Congress the United States policy which later became known as the Truman Doctrine:

One of the primary objectives of the foreign policy of the United States is the creation of conditions in which we and other nations of the world will be able

[2]U. S. Department of State, *Press Release No. 239,* March 24, 1947.

to work out a way of life free from coercion. . . . We shall not realize our objectives, however, unless we are willing to help free people to maintain their free institutions and their national integrity against the aggressive movements that seek to impose upon them totalitarian regimes. This is no more than a frank recognition that totalitarian regimes imposed on free peoples, by direct or indirect aggression, undermine the foundations of international peace and hence the security of the United States. . . . I believe that it must be the policy of the United States to support peoples who are resisting attempted subjugation by armed minorities or by outside pressure. . . . Should we fail to aid Greece and Turkey in this fateful hour, the effect will be far-reaching to the West as well as to the East.[3]

Congress acted immediately. It voted $400 million for assistance to Greece and Turkey; the latter was under Soviet pressure to cede certain territory and bases at the entrance to the Black Sea.

Soviet reaction to the Truman Doctrine was prompt and pungent. The Kremlin labeled it an instrument of American imperialism aimed at putting these countries under United States control, and said that the aid could not be recognized as being consistent with the purposes of the United Nations Organization.

The Truman Doctrine was supplemented by a more imaginative and grand program of American economic aid to the European nations. On June 5, 1947, the then-Secretary of State, George C. Marshall, in an address at Harvard University, said:

It is logical that the United States should do whatever it is able to do to assist in the return of normal economic health in the world, without which there can be no political stability and no assured peace. Our policy is directed not against any country or doctrine but against hunger, poverty, desperation, and chaos. Its purpose should be the revival of a working economy in the world so as to permit the emergence of political and social conditions in which free institutions can exist. Such assistance, I am convinced, must not be on a piecemeal basis as various crises develop. Any assistance that this Government may render in the future should provide a cure rather than a mere palliative.[4]

This was an invitation to all European countries, including the Soviet Union and its satellites, to join in a plan for European recovery with American assistance and on the basis of permanent economic cooperation among themselves. The Marshall Plan, as it became known, required the participants to supply economic statistics and allowed some American control over their internal budgets. After having participated in the initial conference in Paris, the Soviet Union refused to join the plan; it clarified its view as follows:

The U. S. A. is also interested in making use of its credit possibilities for expanding its external markets, especially in view of the approaching crisis. . . . Hitherto it has been taken for granted that each nation should decide for itself how best to secure the rehabilitation and development of its economy. . . .

[3]For the complete text, see *Congressional Record,* **93** (March 12, 1947), 1999–2000.
[4]For the complete text of the speech, see *The New York Times,* June 6, 1947.

If this is true, then attempts to compel the conference to engage in drawing up an all-embracing economic program for the European countries, which will inevitably entail intervention on the part of some states in the affairs of other states, cannot be accepted as a basis for cooperation among European countries. Certain Powers are at present making such attempts, which are doomed to failure and will only undermine their international prestige.[5]

In September, 1947, the Soviet representative to the United Nations, Andrei Vishinsky, attacked the Marshall Plan in his speech to the U. N. General Assembly:

> As is now clear, the Marshall Plan constitutes in essence merely a variant of the Truman Doctrine adapted to the conditions of postwar Europe. . . . The United States also counted on making all these countries directly dependent on the interests of American monopolies, which are striving to avert the approaching depression by an accelerated export of commodities and capital to Europe. . . . The implementation of the Marshall Plan will mean placing European countries under the economic and political control of the United States and direct interference by the latter in the internal affairs of those countries.[6]

The Soviet reply in kind to the Marshall Plan was the formation in September, 1947, of the Cominform (Communist Information Bureau). This organization, made up of the Soviet Union and its satellites, was the successor to the Comintern (the Communist International or the Third International), which had been "dissolved" in 1943, during the Grand Alliance. The Cominform indicated the direction and tone of the Cold War. Andrei Zhadanov, then a leading figure in the Soviet hierarchy, addressing the founding conference of the Cominform, bluntly accused the United States of imperialism:

> The fundamental changes caused by the war on the international scene and in the positions of individual countries have entirely changed the political landscape of the world. A new alignment of political forces has arisen. The more the war recedes into the past, the more distinct become two major trends in postwar international policy, corresponding to the division of the political forces operating on the international arena into two major camps: the imperialist and antidemocratic camp, on the one hand, and the anti-imperialist and democratic camp, on the other. The principal driving force of the imperialist camp is the U. S. A. Allied with it are Great Britain and France. . . . The cardinal purpose of the imperialist camp is to strengthen imperialism, to hatch a new imperialist war, to combat Socialism and democracy, and to support reactionary and antidemocratic pro-fascist regimes and movements everywhere.[7]

The intensification and institutionalization of the Cold War brought about two major events of great importance in 1948. One was the Communist

[5]*Soviet News*, March 15, 1947.

[6]U. N. General Assembly, *Official Records*, Plenary Meetings, Verbatim Record, September 18, 1947, p. 87.

[7]Andrei Zhadanov, *The International Situation* (Moscow: Foreign Language Publishing House, 1947), p. 5.

coup d'état in Prague, which totally eliminated the possibility of the continued existence of a democratic regime in Czechoslovakia. The lingering hope that Czechoslovakia would form a buffer between the Soviet Union and the West was shattered and the lines of struggle between the two camps were distinctly drawn. The other event, of even greater significance, was the Berlin blockade.

> On June 21, 1948, a United States military train No. 20. . . left Helmstedt en route to Berlin. Despite the fact that it had complied with all required regulations, the train was stopped at the Russian control point. There were three days of argument during which Russian demands were frequently altered. . . . Two American guards were forced off the U. S. engine by a Russian colonel and two armed Russian guards. Other Russian guards with automatic guns were placed beside the train in various spots. Soviet guards rode the train to the border point where they alighted and the train proceeded back to Helmstedt.[8]

Thus began the Berlin blockade. Prior to this event, to be sure, Soviet authorities had frequently interfered with communications between the Western zones of occupation and Berlin. But the total stoppage of all railroad, freight, and barge traffic into Berlin, which completely shut that city off from the West by land and water, was a surprising and unexpected move. What had motivated the Soviets to take such a drastic step, fraught with the grave danger of igniting another world conflagration? The Soviet government maintained that it was compelled "to adopt urgent measures to safeguard the interest of the population as well as the economy of the Soviet zone of occupation" and to cope with the difficulties "caused by the activities of the Governments of the United States, Great Britain, and France and, above all, by their separate actions in introducing a new currency in the Western zones of Germany and a special currency in the Western sectors of Berlin."[9] It was true that the Western Powers had announced the invalidation of the inflated Reichsmark in their zones and the introduction of the Deutschmark, or D-Mark, at a value of one-tenth of the Reichsmark.

In contrast, the Western Powers officially accused the Soviet Union of threatening "the Berlin population with starvation, disease, and economic ruin" in an attempt to secure political objectives "by illegal and coercive measures in disregard of its obligations." It may be added further that the blockade was designed: (1) to retaliate against the West for its insistence on treating Germany as a single economic unit as stipulated in the Potsdam Agreement, (2) to force the West out of Berlin in order to eliminate the Western "island" in the Socialist "sea," (3) to discredit the West if it chose to capitulate before the firm Soviet determination, (4) to demoralize the West and to create dissension and disunity among the Western nations, and (5) to test the will and courage of the West to meet the challenge of the Soviet Union.

[8]*Department of State Bulletin,* **19** (October 31, 1948), 543.
[9]*The New York Times,* July 15, 1948.

One of the specific responses of the West to the Soviet challenge was the formation of the North Atlantic Treaty Organization (NATO) in April, 1949. NATO was primarily a defense alliance based on the principle of collective self-defense recognized in the United Nations Charter. In the words of Ernest Bevin, the British Foreign Secretary at that time: "The Pact does not seek to interfere, but equally it does resist the right of any Powers with aggressive intentions to upset our institutions, to bring us into bondage, or to create a situation which will enable them to introduce the police state, or carry out devices which have been applied in so many other countries."

But the Soviet Union looked upon NATO as a military pact of the United States and other Western Powers designed to carry out extensive, aggressive military measures including "the increase in all types of armed forces, the drafting of a plan for the utilization of the atomic weapon, the stockpiling of atom bombs, which are purely an offensive weapon, the building of a network of air and naval bases, etc."[10] The Soviets concluded that NATO was an instrument of American foreign policy "designed to intimidate the states which do not agree to obey the dictate of the Anglo-American grouping of Powers that lay claim to world domination."

By the time the Berlin blockade was terminated, nearly a year later, the United States, Great Britain, and France, through the massive airlift, had supplied more than 2 million people in Berlin with food, fuel, and other necessities of life. This remarkable performance was an eloquent demonstration of the determination of the West not to yield to Soviet pressure or threats.

The Berlin blockade brought the East dangerously close to a direct confrontation with the West and constituted a grave threat to international peace and security. World attention was focused on Berlin. It was during this breathtaking period that a history-making event was also taking place in the Far East—the triumphant rise of Communist China.

When World War II ended, the flickering hope of peace in China was quickly extinguished and the nation was precipitated into a tragic civil war between the Nationalists and the Communists. The Marshall mission of 1946 which attempted to mediate the warring factions proved futile. With the mediation failure and an all-out offensive launched by the Communists, the fortunes of war turned against the Nationalists, who had lost the will to fight or resist. Throughout 1947–1948, the Nationalist forces were marked by inferior leadership, poor strategy, low morale, apathy, defeatism, and disunity. By early 1949, there was definitely nothing to sustain the crumbling Nationalist forces. They collapsed like sand castles. Manchuria had been totally lost to the Nationalist government, and Tientsin and Peiping fell into the hands of the Communists. In April the Communists crossed the Yangtze and occupied Nanking; in May they seized Hankow and Shanghai; and in November they reached Chungking, the wartime capital.

[10] *The New York Times*, April 1, 1949.

Flushed with victory, Mao Tse-tung and his lieutenants began the task of establishing a new regime which was based on the principle of "New Democracy." In July, 1949, Chairman Mao declared: "We must have the people's democratic dictatorship led by the working class and based upon the alliance of workers and peasants." The new regime, thenceforth to be called the People's Republic of China, was formally created on October 1, 1949, with its capital at Peking (formerly Peiping). Little was left for the Nationalists. In December, Chiang Kai-shek retreated to Formosa (Taiwan) with what was left of his Nationalist government and his troops who had managed to survive the Communist onslaught.

The Soviet Union immediately extended *de jure* recognition to the People's Republic of China, followed by most of the Communist satellites. The Soviet recognition, though premature, was a diplomatic gesture motivated by the desire both to render greater prestige and honor to the Peking government and to add heavier weight on the scale of the Cold War in favor of the Communist camp. Among the non-Communist nations which established formal diplomatic relations with the Peking regime within the first year of its establishment were: India, Burma, Afghanistan, Ceylon, Denmark, Finland, Israel, Indonesia, the Netherlands, Norway, Pakistan, Sweden, and Switzerland.

Great Britain was the first great Western Power to recognize the People's Republic of China. The British recognition was motivated by the desire: (1) to protect the British interests in China, including Hong Kong, (2) to facilitate trade with China, (3) to placate the militant anti-Western disposition of the Chinese Communists, (4) to help lessen the mounting tensions in the Cold War, and (5) to follow its traditional recognition policy.

The United States refused persistently to extend formal recognition to the Peking government or to approve its seating in the United Nations. From the United States's standpoint, the Chinese Communists deliberately disregarded the rules of international law which civilized nations respect and observe. The Communists had mistreated American citizens in China, including consular and diplomatic officials, seized American property without due process of law, accused the United States of imperialism, and launched unwarranted nationwide "hate-America" campaigns. Their alliance with the Soviet Union and international Communism, even though it was expected, further irritated the United States. The Sino-Soviet Agreements signed in February, 1950, which included a 30-year military alliance, provided that should "any state allied with Japan," meaning the United States, attack one of the contracting parties, the other would immediately render military and other assistance. Thus the growing antagonism and militancy between the United States and the Moscow–Peking axis began to cast a dark shadow over the world landscape.

The intensity of the Cold War reached a new height with the outbreak of the Korean War. The surprise attack by the North Korean armed forces on

South Korea was launched in the dawn of June 25, 1950. It was a calculated, coordinated attack prepared with secrecy, presumably in cooperation and consultation with the Soviets. The same day, the Security Council of the United Nations, meeting in an emergency session in which the Soviet delegate was absent, adopted a resolution calling for the immediate cessation of hostilities and requesting all member nations "to render every assistance to the United Nations in the execution of this resolution and to refrain from giving assistance to the North Korean authorities." Disregarding the Council's order, the invading forces continued to destroy South Korean resistance and, on June 27, occupied the capital city of Seoul. The Security Council thereupon adopted another resolution calling upon the member states to furnish necessary assistance to the Republic of Korea, "to repel the armed attack and to restore international peace and security in the area." President Truman concurrently ordered United States air and sea forces to give the South Korean troops cover and support.

During the first three months of hostilities, North Korea enjoyed all the military advantages—preparedness, initiative, manpower, firepower, and high morale. By the middle of September, the United Nations Forces in Korea were compressed into a small beachhead perimeter around Pusan, a southern port. But on September 15, 1950, the United Nations Forces under the command of General Douglas MacArthur executed a successful amphibious landing at Inchon, a port city on the west coast 25 miles from Seoul. This landing marked the beginning of the United Nations offensive, which cut the enemy's supply route in the middle, recaptured most of South Korea, and broke the backbone of the North Korean armed forces. When the United Nations Forces reached the 38th parallel, they were given the order to pursue the retreating enemy across the line. It appeared that they were seeking not only to destroy the aggressors but to unify all Korea by force of arms. Although the wisdom and legality of such an action remains debatable, it may be contended that this measure was implied in a General Assembly resolution of October 7, 1950, recommeding that "*all* appropriate steps be taken to ensure conditions of stability *throughout* Korea."[11]

On October 19, 1950, the United Nations Forces captured Pyongyang, the North Korean capital. As they continued to advance toward the Yalu and the Tuman on the Korean–Manchurian border, the enemy resistance became light and sporadic. Suddenly, however, the United Nations Forces came in contact with fresh new fighting forces—the Chinese Communist troops—whose intervention in the conflict created an entirely new war. Earlier, Communist China had warned that it would not tolerate an "invasion" by the United Nations Forces across the 38th parallel, but that warning had been taken as a bluff by the United Nations Command.

Confronted with this new situation, the United States, which had been

---

[11]U. S. Department of State Publication 4245, General Foreign Policy Series 53, released October, 1951, p. 78. Italics are mine.

carrying the major burden of the United Nations operations in terms of men, money, and matériel, agreed with Great Britain not to extend the hostilities beyond the Yalu into Manchuria or into the mainland of China. They feared that the Soviet Union might invoke the eight-month-old Sino-Soviet treaty of alliance to join the war, although Japan was not involved in the conflict. It is interesting to note that Chinese Communist propaganda at that time feverishly accused the United Nations Command of using "germ weapons" against the Communists, and at the same time attempted to spread the rumor of the presence of *Japanese* troops in Korea.

Some American officials came to believe that a full-scale war with Communist China in Korea would mean "the wrong war, at the wrong place, at the wrong time, and with the wrong enemy."[12] They seemed to have seen the ominous shadow of the "bear" behind the "dragon." As a result, only a series of seesaw battles, bitter and costly, were fought along the 38th parallel, and a stalemate developed.

By late spring of 1951 the Korean War was waged not so much in the military fields as on the political and diplomatic fronts. Military operations were controlled by political considerations. In other words, the Korean War was conducted with the tactics and strategies of the Cold War. For this reason, General MacArthur, who had advocated stern military measures including strategic bombing of Manchuria, a blockade of the entire China coast, and a Chinese Nationalist invasion of the mainland, was relieved of his command.

The nature of the "limited war" had made it impossible for either of the belligerents to achieve a complete military victory over the other. Moreover, the potential danger of triggering another world war by expanding the Korean conflict hung menacingly over both the free and communist worlds. It was in this dilemma that Jacob Malik, the Soviet Ambassador to the United Nations, proposed a cease-fire and an armistice. In response to this proposal, the representatives of both the United Nations and Communist Commands held their first meeting on July 9, 1951. This was the beginning of the tedious, protracted armistice negotiations, which put on trial a great deal of stamina, patience, pride, and passion on both sides. The Korean Armistice Agreement was finally signed July 27, 1953, at Panmunjom, a hitherto unknown farm village in the no-man's-land near the 38th parallel. The Armistice stopped the shooting war and at the same time marked the end of the first stage of the Cold War.

---

[12]Statement by General Omar N. Bradley, Chairman of the Joint Chiefs of Staff, before the Senate Armed Services and Foreign Relations Committees, May 15, 1951. See Richard Rovere and Arthur Schlesinger, Jr., *The General and the President*, (New York: Farrar, Straus & Young, 1951), pp. 282–287.

I

The Cold War

1

Strategy for the Immediate Future*

JOSEPH STALIN

. . .

And so, what are the results of the [Second World] war?

There is one chief result in which all other results have their source. This result is that in the upshot of the war our enemies were defeated and we, together with our Allies, emerged the victors. We concluded the war with complete victory over the enemies. That is the chief result of war. But that result is too general and we cannot stop at that. Of course, to crush an enemy in a war like the Second World War, for which the history of mankind knew no parallel, meant to achieve a world historic victory. All that is true. But still, it is only a general result and we cannot rest content with that. In order to grasp the great historic importance of our victory we must examine the thing more concretely.

And so, how is our victory over our enemies to be understood? What is the significance of this victory as regards the State and the development of the internal forces of our country?

Our victory means, first of all, that our Soviet social order has triumphed, that the Soviet social order has successfully passed the ordeal in the fire of war and has proved its unquestionable vitality. . . .

More than that, there is no longer any question today whether the Soviet social order is or is not capable of enduring, for after the object lessons of war none of the skeptics ventures any longer to voice doubts as to the vitality of the Soviet social order. The point now is that the Soviet social order has shown itself more stable and capable of enduring than a non-Soviet social order, that the Soviet social order is a form of organization, a society superior to any non-Soviet social order.

Second, our victory means that our Soviet state system has triumphed,

*U. S. House of Representatives, Committee on Foreign Affairs, The Strategy and Tactics of World Communism, House Document No. 619 (1948), pp. 168–178. Excerpts.

that our multinational Soviet State has stood all the trials of war and has proved its vitality. . . .

Today it is no longer a question of the vitality of the Soviet state system, for that vitality can no longer be doubted; the point now is that the Soviet state system has proved itself a model for a multinational state, has proved that the Soviet state system is a system of state organization in which the national question and the problem of collaboration among nations has been settled better than in any other multinational state.

Third, our victory means that the Soviet armed forces have triumphed, that our Red Army has triumphed, that the Red Army bore up heroically under all the trials of war, utterly routed the armies of our enemies and came out of the war as a victor. . . .

Today we can say that the war has refuted all such statements as unfounded and absurd. The war showed that the Red Army is not a "colossus with feet of clay," but a first-class contemporary army with fully modern armaments, highly experienced commanding personnel and high moral and fighting qualities. It must not be forgotten that the Red Army is the army that utterly routed the German army which but yesterday was striking terror into the armies of the European states. . . .

Such in the main are the results of the war.

It would be a mistake to think that such a historic victory could have been won if the whole country had not prepared beforehand for active defense. It would be no less mistaken to imagine that such preparations could be carried through in a short time—in the space of some three or four years. It would be a still greater mistake to say that we won only owing to the gallantry of our troops.

Of course, victory cannot be achieved without gallantry. But gallantry alone is not enough to vanquish an enemy who has a large army, first-class armaments, well-trained officer cadres, and a fairly good organization of supplies. To meet the blow of such an enemy, to repulse him and then to inflict utter defeat upon him required, in addition to the matchless gallantry of our troops, fully up-to-date armaments and adequate quantities of them as well as well-organized supplies in sufficient quantities.

But that, in turn, necessitated having—and in adequate amounts—such elementary things as metal for the manufacture of armaments, equipment and machinery for factories, fuel to keep the factories and transport going, cotton for the manufacture of uniforms, and grain for supplying the Army.

Can it be claimed that before entering the Second World War our country already commanded the necessary minimum material potentialities for satisfying all these requirements in the main? I think it can. In order to prepare for this tremendous job we had to carry out three Five-Year Plans of national economic development. It was precisely these three Five-Year Plans that helped us to create these material potentialities. At any rate, our country's position in this respect before the Second World War, in 1940, was several times better than it was before the First World War, in 1913. . . .

This historic transformation was accomplished in the course of three Five-Year Plan periods, beginning with 1928, the first year of the First Five-Year Plan. Up to that time we had to concern ourselves with rehabilitating our ravaged industry and healing the wounds received in the First World War and the Civil War. Moreover, if we bear in mind that the First Five-Year Plan was fulfilled in four years, and that the fulfillment of the Third Five-Year Plan was interrupted by war in its fourth year, we find that it took only about 13 years to transform our country from an agrarian into an industrial one.

It cannot but be admitted that 13 years is an incredibly short period for the accomplishment of such an immense task.

This it is that explains the storm of conflicting comment which the publication of these figures produced at the time in the foreign press. Our friends decided that a "miracle" had taken place, while our ill-wishers declared that the Five-Year Plans were "Bolshevik propaganda" and the "tricks of the Cheka." But since miracles do not happen, and the Cheka is not so powerful as to abolish the laws of social development, "public opinion" abroad had to accept facts. . . .

Now a few words about the Communist Party's plans of work for the immediate future. As is known these plans are set forth in the new Five-Year Plan which is shortly to be endorsed. The principal aims of the new Five-Year Plan are to rehabilitate the ravaged areas of the country, to restore the prewar level in industry and agriculture, and then to surpass this level in more or less substantial measure. To say nothing of the fact that the rationing system will shortly be abolished (*stormy, prolonged applause*), special attention will be devoted to extending the production of consumer goods, to raising the living standard of the working people by steadily lowering the prices of all goods (*stormy, prolonged applause*), and to the widespread construction of all manner of scientific research institutions (*applause*) that can give science the opportunity to develop its potentialities. (*Stormy applause.*)

I have no doubt that if we give our scientists proper assistance they will be able in the near future not only to overtake but to surpass the achievements of science beyond the boundaries of our country. (*Prolonged applause.*)

As regards the plans for a longer period ahead, the Party means to organize a new mighty upsurge in the national economy, which would allow us to increase our industrial production, for example, three times over as compared with the prewar period. We must achieve a situation where our industry can produce annually up to 50 million tons of pig iron (*prolonged applause*), up to 60 million tons of steel (*prolonged applause*), up to 500 million tons of coal (*prolonged applause*) and up to 60 million tons of oil (*prolonged applause*). Only under such conditions can we consider that our homeland will be guaranteed against all possible accidents. (*Stormy applause.*) That will take three more Five-Year Plans, I should think, if not more. But it can be done and we must do it. (*Stormy applause.*)

Such is my brief report on the Communist Party's work in the recent past and its plans of work for the future.

It is for you to judge how correctly the Party has been working and whether it could not have worked better. . . .

2

Iron Curtain*

WINSTON S. CHURCHILL

A shadow has fallen upon the scenes so lately lighted by the Allied victory. Nobody knows what Soviet Russia and its Communist international organization intends to do in the immediate future, or what are the limits, if any, to their expansive and proselytizing tendencies. I have a strong admiration and regard for the valiant Russian people and for my war-time comrade, Marshal Stalin. There is sympathy and good will in Britain—and I doubt not here also—toward the peoples of all the Russias and a resolve to persevere through many differences and rebuffs in establishing lasting friendships. We understand the Russians need to be secure on her western frontiers from all renewal of German aggression. We welcome her to her rightful place among the leading nations of the world. Above all we welcome constant, frequent and growing contacts between the Russian people and our own people on both sides of the Atlantic. It is my duty, however, to place before you certain facts about the present position in Europe—I am sure I do not wish to, but it is my duty, I feel, to present them to you.

From Stettin in the Baltic to Triest in the Adriatic, an iron curtain has descended across the Continent. Behind that line lie all the capitals of the ancient states of central and eastern Europe. Warsaw, Berlin, Prague, Vienna, Budapest, Belgrade, Bucharest and Sofia, all these famous cities and the populations around them lie in the Soviet sphere and all are subject in one form or another, not only to Soviet influence but to a very high and increasing measure of control from Moscow. Athens alone, with its immortal glories, is free to decide its future at an election under British, American and French observation. The Russian-dominated Polish government has been encouraged to make enormous and wrongful inroads upon Germany, and mass expulsions of millions of Germans on a scale grievous and undreamed of are now taking place. The Communist parties, which were very small in

Speech delivered at Westminster College, Fulton, Mo., March 5, 1946. Excerpts.

all these eastern states of Europe, have been raised to pre-eminence and power far beyond their numbers and are seeking everywhere to obtain totalitarian control. Police governments are prevailing in nearly every case, and so far, except in Czechoslovakia, there is no true democracy. Turkey and Persia are both profoundly alarmed and disturbed at the claims which are made upon them and at the pressure being exerted by the Moscow government. An attempt is being made by the Russians in Berlin to build up a quasi-Communist party in their zone of occupied Germany by showing special favors to groups of Left-Wing German leaders. At the end of the fighting last June, the American and British armies withdrew westward, in accordance with an earlier agreement, to a depth at some points 150 miles on a front of nearly 400 miles to allow the Russians to occupy this vast expanse of territory which the western democracies had conquered. If now the Soviet government tries, by separate action, to build up a pro-Communist Germany in their areas this will cause new serious difficulties in the British and American zones, and will give the defeated Germans the power of putting themselves up to auction between the Soviets and western democracies. Whatever conclusions may be drawn from these facts—and facts they are—this is certainly not the liberated Europe we fought to build up. Nor is it one which contains the essentials of permanent peace.

The safety of the world, ladies and gentlemen, requires a new unity in Europe from which no nation should be permanently outcast.

It is impossible not to comprehend—twice we have seen them drawn by irresistible forces in time to secure the victory but only after frightful slaughter and devastation have occurred. Twice the United States has had to send millions of its young men to fight a war, but now war can find any nation between dusk and dawn. Surely we should work within the structure of the United Nations and in accordance with our charter. That is an open course of policy.

In front of the iron curtain which lies across Europe are other causes for anxiety. In Italy the Communist party is seriously hampered by having to support the Communist-trained Marshal Tito's claims to former Italian territory at the head of the Adriatic. Nevertheless the future of Italy hangs in the balance. Again one cannot imagine a regenerated Europe without a strong France. All my public life I have worked for a strong France and I never lost faith in her destiny, even in the darkest hours. I will not lose faith now. However, in a great number of countries, far from the Russian frontiers and throughout the world, Communist fifth columns are established and work in complete unity and absolute obedience to the directions they receive from the Communist center. Except in the British Commonwealth and in this United States, where Communism is in its infancy, the Communist parties or fifth columns constitute a growing challenge and peril to Christian civilization. These are somber facts for any one to have to recite on the morrow of a victory gained by so much splendid comradeship in arms and in the cause of freedom and democracy, and we should be most unwise not to face them squarely while time remains.

The outlook is also anxious in the Far East and especially in Manchuria. The agreement which was made at Yalta, to which I was a party, was extremely favorable to Soviet Russia, but it was made at a time when no one could say that the German war might not extend all through the summer and autumn of 1945 and when the Japanese war was expected to last for a further eighteen months from the end of the German war. In this country you are all so well informed about the Far East, and such devoted friends of China, that I do not need to expatiate on the situation there.

I have felt bound to portray the shadow which, alike in the West and in the East, falls upon the world. I was a minister at the time of the Versailles treaty and a close friend of Mr. Lloyd George. I did not myself agree with many things that were done, but I have a very vague impression in my mind of that situation, and I find it painful to contrast it with that which prevails now. In those days there were high hopes and unbounded confidence that the wars were over, and that the League of Nations would become all-powerful. I do not see or feel the same confidence or even the same hopes in the haggard world at this time.

On the other hand I repulse the idea that a new war is inevitable; still more that it is imminent. It is because I am so sure that our fortunes are in our own hands and that we hold the power to save the future, that I feel the duty to speak out now that I have an occasion to do so. I do not believe that Soviet Russia desires war. What they desire is the fruits of war and the indefinite expansion of their power and doctrines. But what we have to consider here today while time remains, is the permanent prevention of war and the establishment of conditions of freedom and democracy as rapidly as possible in all countries. Our difficulties and dangers will not be removed by closing our eyes to them. They will not be removed by mere waiting to see what happens; nor will they be relieved by a policy of appeasement. What is needed is a settlement and the longer this is delayed the more difficult it will be and the greater our dangers will become. From what I have seen of our Russian friends and allies during the war, I am convinced that there is nothing they admire so much as strength, and there is nothing for which they have less respect than for military weakness. For that reason the old doctrine of a balance of power is unsound. We cannot afford, if we can help it, to work on narrow margins, offering temptations to a trial of strength. If the western democracies stand together in strict adherence to the principles of the United Nations Charter, their influence for furthering these principles will be immense and no one is likely to molest them. If, however, they become divided or falter in their duty, and if these all-important years are allowed to slip away, then indeed catastrophe may overwhelm us all.

Last time I saw it all coming, and cried aloud to my fellow countrymen and to the world, but no one paid any attention. Up till the year 1933 or even 1935, Germany might have been saved from the awful fate which has overtaken her and we might all have been spared the miseries Hitler let loose upon mankind. There never was a war in all history easier to prevent by timely action than the one which has just desolated such great areas of the globe. It could have been prevented without the firing of a single shot, and Germany might be powerful, prosperous and honored today, but no one would listen and one by one we were all sucked into the awful whirlpool. We surely must not let that happen again. This can only be achieved by reaching now, in 1946, a good understanding on all points with Russia under the general authority of the United Nations Organization and by the maintenance of that good understanding through many peaceful years, by the world instrument, supported by the whole strength of the English-speaking world and all its connections.

Let no man underrate the abiding power of the British Empire and Commonwealth. Because you see the forty-six millions in our island harassed about their food supply, of which they grew only one half, even in war time, or because we have difficulty in restarting our industries and export trade after six years of passionate war effort, do not suppose that we shall not come through these dark years of privation as we have come through the glorious years of agony, or that half a century from now you will not see seventy or eighty millions of Britons spread about the world and united in defense of our traditions, our way of life and of the world causes we and you espouse. If the population of the English-speaking commonwealth be added to that of the United States, with all that such co-operation implies in the air, on the sea and in science and industry, there will be no quivering, precarious balance of power to offer its temptation to ambition or adventure. On the contrary, there will be an overwhelming assurance of security. If we adhere faithfully to the charter of the United Nations and walk forward in sedate and sober strength, seeking no one's land or treasure, or seeking to lay no arbitrary control on the thoughts of men, if all British moral and material forces and convictions are joined with your own in fraternal association, the highroads of the future will be clear, not only for us but for all, not only for our time but for a century to come.

3

Introduction to the Cold War*

KENNETH INGRAM

Whatever the manner in which posterity interprets the years immediately following the second world war, there can be no doubt that this period will

From History of the Cold War, by Kenneth Ingram (New York: Philosophical Library, 1955), pp. 9–15. Reprinted by permission.

be recognised as a time of acute tension and of critical historical significance. The tension arose from, and was expressed in, the hostile relationship between the Western democracies and the Soviet Union, together with its Communist allies. Accordingly, this record will be concerned exclusively with that relationship, tracing its development and endeavouring to explain its causes. . . .

We shall presently be examining in greater detail these and other instances showing the attempt of Western statesmen to preserve alliance with the Soviet Union, even at the cost of assenting to Soviet claims to a fuller extent than they would otherwise have wished. What, however, needs at once to be emphasised is that suspicion of Soviet intentions was a consistent underlying factor in the minds of Western statesmen, and that this suspicion was never removed either during or since the war. The Soviet leaders were well aware of this attitude, and reacted by remaining correspondingly suspicious of the West. We are not here discussing whether Western suspicions and Soviet counter-suspicions were justified or not. All that needs to be stated is that this mutual distrust was dominant throughout. It is not enough, indeed, to attribute Soviet obstruction to a spirit of 'measureless ambition.' The 'measureless ambition' was due, in part at least, to a belief that the West was so intensely critical and hostile towards the Communist system as to induce the Soviet Union to safeguard its frontiers by extending its territorial influence, by maintaining its war strength, by isolating itself from any schemes which might compromise its independence, and in general by treating the West as a potential enemy rather than an ally. Distrust breeds distrust, and though we may deplore the Soviet attitude and regard it as unreasonable, we cannot afford to leave out of account the influences which helped to produce it.

That the Western distrust of Russian integrity and condemnation of the Soviet system never abated during the war years can be confirmed by many incidents. As early as September 1941 Mr. Churchill was writing to President Roosevelt expressing his fear that the Russians might be harbouring the idea of making a separate peace, although he admitted that "nothing in [the Soviet ambassador's] . . . language warranted the assumption."* In his famous broadcast on the day of the German invasion of Russia Mr. Churchill, while welcoming as allies and promising unstinted support to Russia and the Russian people in their struggle against a common foe, was frank enough to interject the remark that "the Nazi régime is indistinguishable from the worst features of Communism." Those who urged that the Second Front should be opened in mid-Europe rather than in France admitted that the purpose of such a campaign would be to prevent the spread of Soviet power westwards. Again, in 1945 Mr. Churchill was urging General Eisenhower to stack the arms taken from the Germans so that they could be issued again to German soldiers to use against the Russians in case the Soviet advanced

* *The Grand Alliance.* (Cassell.)

too far to the west. But the outstanding example of Western distrust—outstanding in the sense that it subsequently left a deeper impression on the Soviet mind than any other event—was the Western determination to confine the secret of the atom bomb to American and British laboratories. Whereas Great Britain could feel sufficient confidence in the United States to welcome the fact that it possessed this epoch-making weapon, both of them were determined not to assist the Soviet Union similarly to arm itself.

On the other hand it should be remembered that the Western Allies passed on to the Russians full information regarding radar and the invention of penicillin. Russian gratitude for penicillin was not very noticeably expressed. Indeed, the Russians subsequently claimed that penicillin was their own discovery!

Western fears of Soviet intentions were greatly intensified by the Moscow attitude regarding the Polish settlement. Sir Winston Churchill, writing about British–Soviet relations as early as 1941, stated that "the attitude of Russia to Poland lay at the root of our [British] relations with the Soviets."* It became evident after Yalta and before the Potsdam Conference that Moscow was determined that what became known as the 'Lublin Government' should be constituted as the Government of Poland with as little alteration in its constitution as possible. The Western Powers regarded this body as an entirely unrepresentative puppet instrument which Stalin intended to impose on the Polish people, in defiance of all democratic principles. In addition, they were dismayed by the fact that the Soviet Union had transferred German territory east of the Oder and Neisse to Polish administration, even before the Potsdam Conference had met. In the Western view these activities showed that Russia was prepared to act with unscrupulous disregard of agreements already reached, whenever her own interests were concerned. . . . At the moment it is only necessary to note that Western suspicions of Soviet designs before the end of the war were deepened more seriously over the Polish issue than on any other count.

The Soviet reaction to these suspicions and their consequences was that the West must be regarded as an enemy, once military hostilities had ceased. This conclusion was based not merely on incidents during the war but on memories of prewar Western policy—such as the Western support of anti-Soviet offensives by Czarist and Polish armies in the twenties, the exclusion of the Soviet Union from the Munich Conference, the refusals of Britain to agree to conferences of the anti-Fascist States in face of the Hitler menace, the readiness of Britain to declare war on the Soviet Union by sending an expeditionary force in 1940 to assist Finland. Moreover, the repeated Western expressions of detestation of the Communist system were accepted as proof that in its postwar relations with the West the Soviet Union would be dealing with Powers which would make use of any opportunity to weaken or

* *The Grand Alliance.*

destroy the Soviet régime. The Russians are extraordinarily sensitive to Western criticism, to the traditional Western view that the Russian Empire was, and the Soviet Union is, barbaric and semi-Asiatic. There has always been the element of an inferiority complex in the Russian attitude to European Powers. When Sir Stafford Cripps was Ambassador in Moscow he was continually writing home to urge that the utmost care should be taken by the B. B. C. not to offend Soviet susceptibilities by any disparaging remarks in reference to the Soviet conduct of the war. The very tone of voice of British announcers in recording events in the Russian theatre of operations was commented upon in Moscow circles and frequently resented.

The delay in opening the Second Front intensified Soviet suspicions of the West and led to bitter criticisms of Western strategy.* From the Western standpoint it was essential not to incur the disaster of another Dunkirk, and essential therefore not to launch the attack before preparations attending this gigantic undertaking were complete. The invasion had accordingly to be postponed until the summer of 1944, although at first Western assurances had allowed the Russians to suppose that it would take place at a much earlier date. From the Soviet standpoint the reasons advanced for this delay were only another way of saying that in the Western view it mattered comparatively little that Russia should continue to endure the full weight of the German divisions and that the colossal losses of the Red Army should be unrelieved, provided that American and British casualties were kept down to a minimum. This clash of interests would no doubt have occurred under any circumstances, but the bitterness of the Russians was fed by the belief that Western strategy desired to see the brunt of the fighting fall on the Soviet Union so that its strength in the postwar period might be diminished. Though we may consider this to be an unfair and ill-founded interpretation of Western motives, we must not forget that it was a point of view openly expressed in some quarters, and that Soviet statesmen were well aware of such utterances. Thus, two days after the German invasion of Russia, there appeared on the front page of the *New York Times* the following statement: "If we see that Germany is winning we ought to help Russia, and if Russia is winning we ought to help Germany, and that way let them kill as many as possible." The author of this article was at the time a comparatively inconspicuous senator, but its significance is that he subsequently became the American President—Harry S. Truman.

*The chief of the United States Military Mission to U. S. S. R., General John R. Deane, remarks in his book, *The Strange Alliance*: "In August 1942, after the decision was made to invade Africa, Prime Minister Churchill made a special trip to Moscow to break the news to Stalin. The interview was stormy, to say the least!" See also Mr. Churchill's own account of the interview in *The Hinge of Fate*.

Stalin, however, paid generous tribute to the Normandy invasion-operation, once it had commenced. In an interview on June 13th, 1944, he said that history "knows of no other similar undertaking in the breadth of its conception, in its giant dimensions and the mastery of its performance."

So strained had Soviet–Western relations become in the closing stages of the war that in March 1945 Stalin announced to Roosevelt by cable his belief that the Nazi commander, Marshal Kesselring, had "agreed to open the front and permit the Anglo-American troops to advance to the east," and that Britain and U. S. A. had promised in return "to ease for the Germans the peace terms." Churchill's reactions to this accusation were immediate. He "stressed the political importance of the capture of Berlin by Allied forces in order to counterbalance the prestige the Red Army was about to gain by capturing Vienna and overwhelming Austria. . . . Quite apart from the political advantage which the Russians would gain by capturing Berlin, Churchill feared that if priority were given to Bradley's drive for Dresden, Montgomery would not have the resources to reach the Baltic quickly and thus prevent the Russians 'liberating' Denmark, seizing the north German ports, and gaining an outlet to the Atlantic."*

We must rid ourselves altogether, therefore, of the impression that official relations between the West and the Soviet Union had become during the war wholly cordial, and that the subsequent Soviet attitude represented a sudden unexpected and unwarrantable change of policy. The misgivings of each of the parties towards the other had never subsided. So long as both the Soviet Union and the West were engaged in the task of overcoming a peril which mutually threatened them, this discord was expressed less openly than in former days. Once the war was at an end, the deep underlying estrangement was bound to be revealed more blatantly.

---

* *The Struggle for Europe*, by Chester Wilmot. (Collins.)

II

The Iranian Issue

1

Power Politics in the Near East*

HUSSEIN ALA

Iran, the country for which I have the honor of speaking, being situated in what is called the Middle East, the title of my talk should be slightly modified.

And first let us see what Power Politics means:

. . .

Today Power Politics, as I understand it, means the reprehensible method by which the Strong Powers deviate from the straight path of adherence to principles laid down in International Agreements and Law and resort to force or subtle means—such as infiltration, penetration, pressure, to gain working control of the Governments of weak States. Just as politicians seek to attain their ends by compromise, intimidation and bribery—sacrificing the principles they warmly advocated during the elections—so unscrupulous powers resort to the same means to achieve the end which the treaties and understandings subscribed to by them preclude. What was known in America as "dollar diplomacy," that is to say the use of money for political ends and not for economic well-being, is a kind of power politics still practised by certain countries of the old world.

The principles laid down by the Atlantic Charter, to which Iran adhered during the war, have unfortunately been progressively abandoned in favor of Power Politics. The Teheran, Yalta, and Potsdam agreements of December 1943, February 1945 and August 1945 involved possibilities of discord which have now grown to threatening proportions.

The Allied Powers had, during the war, pledged themselves to seek no territorial expansion; to respect the right of all peoples to choose their own form of Government; to avoid the use of the threat of force against other nations; to create democratic institutions of self-government based on the

*Speech of the Iranian Ambassador to the United States delivered at Princeton University, Princeton, N.J., June 11, 1946. Excerpts.

will of the people as manifested in free elections—yet once victory was achieved and the unity required for concerted and concentrated action against the common foe relaxed, Power Politics came into their own. One of the Big Three demanded special privileges of the other two, refusing to make reciprocal concessions to their point of view, and hastened to pocket his gains and to extend them by unilateral action without waiting for the sanction of either ally or a peace settlement. . . .

For you must remember that Iran was your loyal ally and that of Great Britain and the Soviet Union. She made substantial sacrifices in the common cause, having placed all her resources and man-power at the disposal of her friends, thus enabling the U. S. and Great Britain to transport over our roads and railways millions of tons of war material and supplies to the USSR in their hour of dire need. Iran indeed may claim to have contributed largely to the defeat of the Germans at Stalingrad. In spite of the services rendered and the sufferings endured, Iran found at the termination of hostilities that there was great procrastination in the withdrawal of the Red Army stationed in her territory during the war. The presence of these forces had served to encourage a so-called autonomous movement, by no means spontaneous, in our Northwestern province of Azerbaidjan—an integral part of Iran from the most ancient times. Every effort made by the Teheran Government to exercise its duties of sovereignty by sending reinforcements to maintain law and order in Azerbaidjan was opposed by the Soviet troops, whilst the insurgents enjoyed facility of movement and resorted to armed violence.

Russia's action constituted a flagrant breach of the pledges she had given us in the hour of need in the Tripartite Treaty of Alliance of January 1942 and the Declaration of Teheran of December 1943 which had also been signed by President Roosevelt and Mr. Churchill. In Article 1 of the Tripartite Treaty of Alliance of January 29th, 1942, Great Britain and the U. S. S. R. "jointly and severally undertake to respect the territorial integrity, sovereignty and political independence of Iran." They assure her in Article 4 of the same treaty that the presence of the British and Russian forces on Iranian territory "does not constitute a military occupation and will disturb as little as possible the administration and security forces of Iran, the economic life of the country, the normal movements of the population and the application of Iranian laws and regulations." In Article 5 of the Tripartite Treaty—the allied powers promise to withdraw their forces from Iranian territory "*not later* than six months after all hostilities between the allied powers and Germany and her associates have been suspended by the conclusion of an armistice or armistices or the conclusion of peace between them, whichever date is the earlier."

The Declaration of Teheran, signed by President Roosevelt, Mr. Churchill and Marshal Stalin on December 1st, 1943, "recognizes the assistance which Iran has given in the prosecution of the war against the common enemy, particularly by facilitating the transportation of supplies from overseas to the Soviet Union." "The three governments realize that the war has caused special economic difficulties for Iran and they are agreed that they will continue to make available to the Government of Iran such economic assistance as may be possible . . ." and they "are in accord with the Government of Iran that any economic problems confronting Iran at the close of hostilities should receive full consideration. . . ." Last but not least, the Declaration solemnly affirms that "the governments of the U. S., the USSR, and the United Kingdom are at one with the Government of Iran in their desire for the maintenance of the independence, sovereignty and territorial integrity of Iran. They count upon the participation of Iran, together with all other peace-loving nations, in the establishment of International Peace, Security, and Prosperity after the war, in accordance with the principles of the Atlantic Charter, to which all four governments have subscribed." It is curious how the Great Powers have a way of suffering from amnesia when it comes to fulfilling the pledges they had given to the small nations.

Having met with no success in our direct negotiations with the Soviet Embassy in Teheran, and with the Government at Moscow, we had no alternative but to bring the matter before the Security Council at its first meeting in London. This complaint, the first brought before the Council under Article 35 of the Charter, related to the interference of Soviet military and civilian authorities in Azerbaidjan who, in the violation of the Treaty of 1943, had prevented Persian security forces from moving into our northwestern province. In London, the Soviet Representative on the Council, Mr. Vishinsky, tried to prevent the Council from discussing the matter at all and finally suggested further direct negotiations between the two parties. This being agreed to by both sides, the Council passed a Resolution recommending such negotiations, but reserving the right to ask for a report and continue to concern itself with the matter.

Direct negotiations carried on by our Prime Minister himself at Moscow in February and March having failed, we again appealed to the Security Council at its second Session in New York City on March 25th. This time the dispute was two-fold: first the question of interference which had remained unsolved and, second, the continued presence of Soviet forces in the North of Iran after the 2nd of March, which was the deadline fixed by the Tripartite Treaty. On this occasion the Soviet Representative asked for a postponement of the session of the Council and of the discussion of the Iranian matter. When this was strenuously opposed by a large majority of the Members of the Council, and particularly by Secretary of State Byrnes, who took a very firm attitude in the defence of the rights of the small nations, the Russian Representative, Mr. Gromyko, boycotted the meetings of the Council, and did not put in an appearance as long as the Iranian question was discussed.

But undoubtedly the action taken by the Council, the determined attitude of the United States and the condemnation of the Soviet Government's breach of faith by world opinion had a chastening effect, and by May 6th the greater part of the Russian forces had evacuated the North of Iran. . . .

The Near and Middle East has become more than ever a critical point in international relations, the link between Europe and the vast continent of Asia; always a crucial spot in world history, the Middle East has today assumed tremendous importance. It is a region where the great powers have vital interests which unfortunately clash, where long-standing rivalries exist which today are greatly accentuated to the detriment of the weaker countries who only seek to be rid of foreign troops and foreign interference in their internal affairs and left alone to work out their own salvation. It is a part of the globe in which for the sake of security, justice and prosperity and the settling of acute differences it is imperative for the United States not only to take more interest but to exert greater influence as the leading world power.

We must at all costs make the United Nations a success if we do not want to relapse into Power Politics. Might must not any longer be allowed to prevail over right. And Power Politics exercised under the garb of the veto and of the extraordinary method of boycotting any disagreeable meetings of the Council must also cease. . . .

2

International Aspects*

GEORGE LENCZOWSKI

It was characteristic of the Iranian political situation that nothing that happened between Iran and the Soviet Union could remain of indifference to Great Britain. But even more characteristic was the fact that beginning with the fall of 1945 the United States was definitely drawn into the vortex of turbulent Iranian politics. On November 24, 1945, at the time when the Azerbaijan rebellion began, the United States delivered a note to the Soviet Union proposing the evacuation of Soviet, British, and American troops from Iran by January 1, 1946. A parallel British note was also delivered. Moscow's reply was negative. The Soviet note of November 29 to the United States rejected the American proposal, invoked earlier correspondence with the British government as providing for the withdrawal of troops by March 2, 1946, blamed "reactionary elements" for troubles in Azerbaijan and denied interference of Soviet military authorities in internal affairs of Iran. The note said further:

*From Russia and The West in Iran, 1918–1948, by George Lenczowski (Ithaca, N. Y.: Cornell University Press, 1949), pp. 292–300. Copyright 1949 by Cornell University. Used by permission of Cornell University Press.

The Soviet Government opposed the dispatch of new Iranian troops to northern districts of Iran and informed the Iranian Government that the dispatch of further Iranian forces to northern Iran could cause not the cessation, but the increase, of the disorders and likewise bloodshed, which would compel the Soviet Government to introduce into Iran further forces of its own for the purpose of preserving order and insuring the security of the Soviet garrison.

The note finally invoked the Soviet–Iranian Treaty of February 26, 1921, as giving the Soviet Union the "right of introduction of Soviet troops into the territory of Iran."

This exchange of notes did not exhaust diplomatic action. In the West it was hoped that Azerbaijan could be discussed during the second conference of Foreign Ministers to be held in Moscow in the middle of December, 1945. British Foreign Secretary Bevin and American Secretary of State Byrnes arrived in Moscow on December 15 hopeful that some solution might be reached, but Russia presented them with a *fait accompli* just prior to the opening of the conference for the Azerbaijan Republic was proclaimed three days before their arrival. Accompanied by their area experts, Sir Reader Bullard, British Ambassador to Iran, and John D. Jernegan, Second Secretary of the American Embassy at Teheran, both Foreign Secretaries tried in vain to settle the Iranian problem. In the course of the conference Bevin proposed that a three-Power commission of Britain, Russia, and the United States visit Iran to settle differences. Bevin also suggested, with a view to reaching a compromise between Russia's special interest in Azerbaijan and the principle of Iranian territorial integrity, a scheme for the creation of local governments in Iran. The Russians, who initially seemed amenable to such a solution, reversed their attitude at the end of the conference and rejected Bevin's scheme. It is not quite clear what caused them to change their views. It is possible that the Soviet side expected a firmer stand on the part of the West on many international issues on the agenda, but seeing the will of the Western ministers falter (due to their ardent desire to reach agreement with the Russians rather than to stick to their principles), it decided that it could afford to be uncompromising on the Iranian issue.

Whatever the reason, the fact remains that nothing was done to relieve Soviet pressure on Azerbaijan. Listing the unsettled questions at Moscow, Secretary Bevin declared on his return to London: "One of the most important of these is the Iranian question. It has been the subject of a protracted exchange of views between the Soviet Government and the Governments of the United States and Great Britain. Final agreement has not been reached, but discussions will continue through ordinary channels." Commenting on the British and American attitudes on the subject, the London correspondent of the *New York Times* wrote on January 1, 1946:

That was a principal reason that Mr. Bevin came back from the tri-power parley of Foreign Ministers far less happy about the Moscow agreement than Mr. Byrnes. It is felt here that Americans are inclined to overlook the vital importance of Iran and the whole Middle East to the British Empire.

What may have seemed to be a relatively minor question to Mr. Byrnes was a major one to Mr. Bevin.

The Moscow conference was a turning point in the development of the Soviet–Iranian dispute. The British, despite its failure, stuck to their idea that some compromise solution should be reached. That is why Sir Reader Bullard, upon his return to Teheran, was instructed to induce the Iranians to accept the Bevin scheme of a three-power investigating commission. Apparently the British hoped that Iranian readiness to accept such a commission would increase the chances of its being accepted by the Soviet. The Iranian government felt, however, that it had little to gain and much to lose if such a commission were dispatched and suspected some deal that would legalize Soviet encroachment upon its sovereignty. It complained in the first place that it had not been invited to present its views at the Moscow conference, and on January 10 Finance Minister Hazhir announced to the cheering Majlis that the government had rejected the British suggestion. Premier Hakimi confirmed the statement a few days later.

On January 19, 1946, the Iranian delegate to the newly formed United Nations, Seyyid Hasan Taqi-zadeh, formally requested the Security Council to investigate Soviet encroachments in Iran. . . .

The result of the Council's debate was to some degree disappointing to the Iranians since they were again left to their own devices. The only gain from their point of view, was that Soviet infiltration was now given world publicity and that the United Nations reserved for itself the right to request from the parties information on the progress of Soviet–Iranian talks.

In the meantime a cabinet crisis occurred in Iran. It was largely due to new Soviet pressure expressed by the severance of all trade between Azerbaijan and the rest of the country. The economic strain thus created was intolerable. Despairing of his ability to settle the quarrel with the Russians and yielding to persuasion, Premier Hakimi resigned on January 22 and the Shah asked Qavam Saltaneh, known for his flirtation with the Tudeh, to form a new cabinet. Qavam, appointed Prime Minister on January 27, began his official duties by dismissing General Ibrahim Arfa, who was of pro-British tendencies, from the post of Chief of Staff of the Army. Arfa was replaced by General Aghevli, an officer interned during the war because of his pro-German sympathies. This was interpreted as a desire on the part of Qavam to make the high personnel of his administration more acceptable to the Russians before entering into parleys with them. Then, following the Security Council's recommendation, Qavam at the head of a five-man mission left for Moscow. He stayed in the Soviet capital from February 19 till March 11 but failed to reach an agreement. During this two-and-a-half-week stay he saw Stalin twice and Molotov four times. . . .

On March 2, 1946, during Qavam's stay in Moscow, the deadline came for evacuation of all Allied troops. In practice the deadline referred only to British and Soviet troops, as the Americans had left Iran by January 1. The British forces were withdrawn by March 2, but there was no sign of Soviet evacuation, except for some military movements from one district to another inside Iran. The approach of March 2 was watched in Washington and London with growing uneasiness and tension. The failure of the Soviets to evacuate would place before the West a new violation of an international agreement by the Russians and thus complicate the whole matter. It would also call for more positive action on the part of the West, as nonevacuation, in contrast to internal interference, would be easy to ascertain.

Encouraged by the timidity of the Security Council in dealing with the situation in January, the Soviet government officially announced that it had decided to withdraw its forces from Khorasan, Shahrud, and Semnan as of March 2 but to retain them in other parts of northern Iran until the situation had been "clarified." This challenge did not remain unanswered. On March 4 Great Britain and on March 8 the United States addressed formal protests to the Soviet Union against the retention of its troops. In Moscow, Qavam lodged a similar protest with the Soviet Foreign Minister and with Stalin personally. Refusing to accept the Soviet demands, he then left for Teheran. . . .

Despite all pessimistic prognostications, Qavam showed himself an astute statesman and diplomat. Following his instruction, Ambassador Ala appealed for the second time to the United Nations. This time he accused the Soviets of keeping their troops in Iran despite their March 2 deadline for withdrawal and of continued interference "through the medium of Soviet agents, officials and armed forces." Ala's accusation made sensational news in the United States where the Security Council was then meeting. A prolonged debate was characterized by extreme frankness on the part of the Iranian delegate, whose testimony was impressive for its legalistic precision. The Soviets procrastinated and through procedural devices tried to stop the hearing of the case and to keep the Iranian delegate from speaking. At one time the Soviet delegate Andrei Gromyko walked dramatically out of the conference room. During this debate the American government took upon itself the burden of defending the principles of international intercourse. Secretary Byrnes, who appeared in person before the Council, boldly led the American delegation and gave clear signs that the United States assumed responsibility and leadership in international affairs.

For the Soviets the publicity of an international gathering in which they stood in the defendant's box was obviously most inconvenient. Their only hope lay in continuance of direct negotiations with the Iranian Premier, which might result in an agreement favoring their interests. This is probably the explanation why on March 26 Gromyko suddenly announced that his government had reached an agreement with Iran providing for the evacuation of Soviet troops within six weeks after March 24 "if no unforeseen circumstances occur." Steady Soviet pressure on Qavam caused him to instruct Ambassador Ala to demand the removal of the dispute from the Council's agenda. With truly patriotic intransigence Ala declined to follow this instruction, making it clear that his government must have acted under duress.

This was undoubtedly true. In fact, the instructions given by Qavam during this nerve-racking period were largely conditioned by his alternating conversations with the Soviet and the American Ambassadors in Teheran. Unfortunately for Iran, the American Ambassador, Mr. Murray, was at this juncture confined to bed at his doctor's orders. As a result, the Soviet Ambassador's calls on the Premier were more frequent and his insistence on a solution satisfactory to Moscow stronger. At this point the American delegation to the United Nations seemed to waver in its resolve to pursue the matter energetically and appeared inclined again to leave Iran to face her formidable neighbor alone. On Secretary Byrnes's suggestion the Security Council decided on April 4 to accept the Soviet statement and "to defer further proceedings on the Iranian appeal until May 6th, at which date the Soviet government and the Iranian government are requested to report to the Council whether the withdrawal of all Soviet troops from the whole of Iran has been completed and at which time the Council shall consider what, if any, further proceedings on the Iranian appeal are required."*

The Soviet promise of evacuation was well calculated. On one hand it caused the temporary removal of the dispute from the Council; on the other it served as an inducement to Qavam to comply with the Russian demands. In both points Russia succeeded. On April 4, the day of the Council's decision to defer further proceedings, the Soviet Union and Iran concluded an agreement that comprised the following provisions:

1. The Red Army was to be evacuated within one month and a half after March 24, 1946.
2. A joint stock Irano-Soviet oil company was to be established and ratified by the Fifteenth Majlis within seven months after March 24.
3. "With regard to Azerbaijan, since it is an internal Iranian affair, peaceful arrangements will be made between the Government and the people of Azerbaijan for the carrying out of improvements in accordance with existing laws and in benevolent spirit toward the people of Azerbaijan.". . .

3

The Cold War in Iran†

DENNA F. FLEMING

Russia contained. An agreement between Iran and the Soviet Union had been signed giving the Russians an oil concession in North Iran on a 51 to 49

---

*New York Times, April 5, 1946.
†From The Cold War and its Origins, 1917–1960, by D.F. Fleming, Vol. I (New York: Doubleday & Company, Inc., 1961), pp. 345–348. Reprinted by permission of Doubleday & Company, Inc.

division of the profits, a basis highly embarrassing to the British who turned over to Iran only about 20 per cent of their oil gains. The agreement was, however, conditional since the Iranian Parliament had passed a law forbidding the giving of any oil concessions while foreign troops remained in Iran. All that Quavam could do accordingly was to promise to bring the Russian oil concession before Parliament for ratification. When he did so it was rejected, over his protest, on October 22, 1947, and he resigned, on December 10. The pro-British Hakimi became Prime Minister again.

Lacking confidence in the strength of the Iranian army, Quavam had not ventured to send troops against Azerbaijan until December 1946. Then the Russian-sponsored government collapsed, though the province did succeed in retaining somewhat more autonomy than before.

In May 1947 American Brigadier General Schwartzkopf, head of the Iranian gendarmerie, came to the United States to secure equipment for his force and for the army of Iran. In June Iran was given $25,000,000 worth of military supplies on credit, but no heavy weapons.

Russia had been defeated, temporarily at least, all alone the line. She was forced to withdraw from Iran and she got no oil.

After March 2, 1946, the date before which she had agreed to withdraw her troops, she was legally in the wrong. It was upon this point that Secretary Byrnes kept attention focused throughout the dispute. He went to New York to conduct the case himself and did so with complete firmness. A real victory for the position of small nations in the United Nations was won.

Russia was also "contained," forced back even, in a region where her interests were vital and where she felt them to be urgent. The AP correspondent in Moscow reported that foreign observers were almost unanimous in agreeing that the Russians could not understand: (a) that the point of legality justified the expulsion of Russian troops from Iran while British and American troops remained in a dozen far-flung places over the world; (b) why Russia could have no oil in Iran while the British and Americans did; and (c) why the Security Council should be used to embarrass the Soviet Union before the world. On May 6, as the Iran case ebbed, *Pravda* attacked the British–American policy "in the bluntest and most smashing criticism of that program" that had appeared in the Soviet press.

In the United States there was general agreement that Russia's tactics had been provocative and offensive to the other members of the Council. She had: (a) denied its right to deal with the controversy and Iran's right to be heard; (b) insisted on postponement and walked out when it was not granted; (c) put the severest diplomatic pressure on Iran and then argued that the Council was denying Iran's sovereignty when it refused to drop the the case; and (d) kept troops in Iran beyond the deadline and then failed to report to the Council when they were out. The impression made upon the British *New Statesman and Nation* was "not that of a Machiavellian Power pursuing a calculated course of aggrandizement, but rather of a blundering and suspicious giant, throwing its weight around and hurting itself and everyone else."

Impasse. In the Security Council there was considerable sympathy for Soviet objectives in Iran. It was understood that war damage had reduced Russia's oil output by 5,000,000 tons annually and that Soviet officials were deeply worried about the future, building synthetic oil plants and urging conservation. It was appreciated also that Moscow had reason for being concerned about the internal situation in Iran, which lay only an hour's flight from the Baku region—Russia's jugular vein—notoriously corrupt, long under British influence and now submitting its army and police to American training. The United States had become very agitated when conditions were bad in Mexico and would become more so if the Russians monopolized the oil concessions there, backed by a ring of air bases below Mexico.

There was real tragedy in the situation, or so it seemed to me after observing most of the Security Council sessions. On the merits of the case there was much to be said for Russia's concern about Azerbaijan. Yet the merits were never presented or considered. All of the controversy turned on points of procedure. Here the Russians either were wrong, or they put themselves there. The whole affair humiliated and embittered them and created a permanent grievance. There could be no doubt that they would await a favorable day for ending Anglo-American dominance in Iran, and the Middle East, especially since "a large section" of the American press continued to breathe "continuous hatred and threats of war" against Russia.

On the other hand, Byrnes had tried to negotiate the issue in Moscow and had been rebuffed. Iran had a right to appeal to UN and it was essential that she be heard. Russia's conduct was illegal and it was difficult to see any alternative except to oppose it and insist upon the right of the Security Council to consider the case.

Yet there was no legal way for Russia to gain any of her objectives in Iran. The great landlords in the Iranian parliament would never willingly grant an oil concession to Russia, since that would bring Communist influence into the zone of the concession. They had good reason to believe also that the Russians would not be satisfied with less than real control of the region concerned, as well as of Azerbaijan. They were certain therefore to keep the Russians out and to rely on the British and Americans to back them. The Westerners might exploit Iran's resources on less favorable terms, but they would leave the landlords in control of Iran, especially since the latter were supported by American arms and military instructors.

Their rule could only be preserved by British and American support. The correspondent of the *Chicago Daily News* telegraphed that the leftist Tudeh party, allegedly Russian inspired, was the only strong political group in Iran. He had talked with many of its leaders, mostly professional people, and found them full of love for their wretched country and fed up with British domination, a sentiment in which the Iranian workers fully joined. They wanted a government "friendly" to Russia both in Tabriz and Teheran.

One thing was certain. The long series of public fights in the Security Council from January to May 1946, touched off by Iran's appeal, left the three Great Powers embittered and estranged. Russia had been stopped, and the formal authority of UN upheld, but no way had been found for UN to tackle the basic problems in Iran, its dangerous social unrest, and the clash of Britain and Russia for oil and control. In his address to the Overseas Press Club in New York, early in March, Byrnes had opposed "unilateral gnawing away at the status quo" and disclaimed that it was sacrosanct anywhere. It was "not in our tradition to defend the dead hand of reaction or the tyranny of privilege." Our diplomacy "must not be negative and inert," but "marked by creative ideas, constructive proposals, practical and forward looking suggestions."

This was eminently sound doctrine, and it is to be regretted that some way was not found to apply it to Iran.

We stop Russia.   Instead, Secretary Byrnes felt compelled by Russia's acts and by the American–British pressures upon him to concentrate all his energies on forcing Russian troops out of Iran. In the process the United States became the leader of a stop-Russia coalition.

A turning-point came in early 1946, when very heavy pressure was concentrated on Secretary Byrnes from three directions, the President, the Congress and the British Government. Lord Vansittart cried out angrily that to pursue the mediator's role was "self righteous abstention" and when Byrnes changed his course sharply Vansittart commented that he had "evolved into a statesman." Byrnes was much more popular in Washington also when he became the tough prosecutor of the Soviet Union.

During all these months the British Labor Government followed the Churchill policy toward Russia without the slightest deviation. It was not until after the United States had also accepted it and moved out in front that cautionary British voices began to be heard. Late in May Field-Marshal Smuts, elder statesman and Premier of South Africa, made a speech in London advocating that the British Commonwealth group should assume the mediator's role between the two behemoths, interpreting one to the other and thus preventing war. This would surely accord with the interests of the British Dominions, whose greatest interest is to avoid another war.

By this time a great British leader could aspire to take up the mediator's role, but the United States could hardly regain that strategic situation.

III

The Truman Doctrine

1

Our Near Eastern Policy in the Making*

WALTER L. WRIGHT, JR.

RUSSIAN INTENTIONS

Russian intentions, as evidenced by threats and acts, have been to use every means short of open war to make Turkey accept Soviet domination and to become a satellite like Yugoslavia or Bulgaria: the size and strength of the doomed country were to be reduced by the cession of territory, its present rulers were to be discredited by propaganda in press and radio, and its military security was to be reduced to zero by the presence on its soil of Soviet troops. If the nerve of the Turks had not been tough, the "iron curtain" would today run along the northern frontiers of Syria and Iraq, and Greece and Iran would both be outflanked.

Would this mean anything serious to the Government and people of the United States? Would Russia's swallowing of another small independent nation make any difference to our security and welfare?

Our Government answered these questions in the affirmative. At the Potsdam Conference we took the position that the Montreux Convention should be modified appreciably but not radically in Russia's favor. We stipulated that the revision must be made by all the interested states, including all the existing great powers—not by a small group of Russian-controlled states. This was the position taken by the Turks also. We gave the Turks a limited credit to buy surplus war material and railway rolling stock. This was all, until developments in Greece reached so critical a point that a complete revision of our responsibilities and policies in the Near East became imperative.

*From The Annals of The American Academy of Political and Social Science, Vol. 255 (January, 1948), pp. 93–104. Reprinted by permission of The American Academy of Political and Social Science.

PLIGHT OF GREECE

Failure of the Communist-directed effort of December 1944 to destroy domestic rivals and force the British out of Greece had not brought peace to the Hellenes. British reinforcements and hastily organized Greek government troops had broken up the larger revolutionary concentrations and had driven the remnants into the high mountains or across the northern boundaries. But guerrilla warfare continued wherever there were inaccessible fastnesses or conveniently friendly frontiers. To the ravages of the Fascists and the Nazis had been added the destruction of civil war and sabotage. Greece was bankrupt in almost every sense: politically, economically, socially, and morally. The help supplied to the Greek Government by the British, who gave more than they could afford, was entirely inadequate to bring order and security out of the existing chaos.

Disintegration of society and debasement of human character reached an extreme which Greece had not known since the later stages of the Peloponnesian War in the fifth century before Christ. Passages from the classical historian Thucydides describing the factions, revolutions, foreign interventions, atrocities, and utter lack of every kind of honor or security can be used almost verbatim to describe conditions in 1945. The greatest obstacle to recovery then, as in Thucydides' time, was the disappearance of the moderate group in politics and society. As he writes, "Moderation was held to be a cloak for unmanliness; ability to see all sides of a question [was regarded as] inaptness to act on [any side of it]. . . . Even blood became weaker than party. . . . The moderate part of the citizens perished."*

As though this domestic ruin were not enough, the guerrillas were provided with arms for their raids and safe retreats in the countries to the north. Where the Greek Government succeeded in establishing its control and some sort of public order, extreme royalists perpetrated acts of vengeance which raised up new enemies of the regime, even if they did not always make new Communists. The calm tempers and regular procedures essential to orderly democratic government existed nowhere in the country. No leader capable of uniting the distracted people made his appearance. The Government accomplished little with the aid which Britain was supplying at the cost of privation to her home islands.

The British economic crisis of the winter of 1946–47 at length convinced His Majesty's Government that it would have to end its support of Greece. The decision was made with the utmost reluctance, for it was clear that the well-organized and foreign-guided Communist minority would use its arms to seize control. This would mean effective Soviet control, with airfields on Crete and other islands within easy range of the Suez Canal. It would also

*Thucydides, *History of the Peloponnesian War*. Done into English by Richard Crawley. Everyman Edition (New York: Dutton, 1929), pp. 82–83. Compare this account with William Hardy McNeill: *The Greek Dilemma, War and Aftermath* (Philadelphia: Lippincott, 1947), Chaps. VII and VIII.

mean Russian pressure on Turkey from still another frontier, where the great valleys of the Aegean coast offer the easiest access to the mountain-girt fortress of Anatolia. But there was no alternative for Britain; she simply did not have the strength to continue aiding Greece.

SIGNIFICANCE TO UNITED STATES

Events had developed to this point when President Truman read his message of March 12, 1947 to the Congress of the United States. He outlined very clearly the reasons for his proposal that the United States should take up the responsibility which had proved too heavy for the British. Rightly he laid much emphasis on the moral issues involved. The fate of our whole concept of a better world, a world of power and justice, not of power alone, was at stake. We could not stand aside and let the Soviet Union cold-bloodedly use force, or threat of war, or armed Communist minorities to deprive Greece and Turkey of their independence. "I believe," he said, "that we must assist free peoples to work out their own destinies in their own way." And he continued, "Totalitarian regimes imposed on free peoples by direct or indirect aggression undermine the foundations of international peace and hence the security of the United States."

This last somewhat elliptical statement I wish to elaborate. How could the security of the United States be undermined by the disappearance of Greece and Turkey behind the "iron curtain"? To anyone familiar with the elements of modern strategy, it is clear that a great military power established in Greece and Turkey would have at the mercy of its air and ground forces the sea routes of the eastern Mediterranean as well as the open plains of interior Syria, of Iraq, and of Arabia. The vast oil fields of the Persian Gulf area, 40 per cent of the world's estimated reserves, could swiftly be overrun and access to them by sea could be cut off. Deprived of access to these fuel supplies, Britain would cease to be a great power. During the recent war she relied principally on oil from the Western Hemisphere. Her domestic fuel resources are depleted. Even with the free access to Near Eastern fuel which she at present enjoys, she is in desperate straits to keep her factories working, her ships at sea, and her airplanes in the skies.

If Britain becomes another Netherlands, what can she contribute to the building of the world of free and cooperating nations which the British and American peoples long for? Today the United States has only Britain as a seriously useful helper in the effort to stem the advance of those "totalitarian regimes imposed on free peoples by direct or indirect aggression" which "undermine the foundations of international peace and hence the security of the United States." If we Americans were to permit Greece and Turkey to succumb and Britain to decline into insignificance as a power, other free peoples would inevitably conclude that we had no concern for their fate. Italy, Germany, France, the Low Countries, Scandinavia, and eventually even countries outside Europe would begin resigning themselves to a Communist future. In a power-conscious world, what friends or allies would we have? What moral leadership would there be to stir the minds and hearts of free men?

Happily, these questions have already been answered, for the Government and people of the United States have responded to the challenge. Congress has approved the aid to Greece and Turkey which was asked by the President. Secretary Marshall has roused the enthusiasm of the whole non-Communist world by pointing out that Greece and Turkey are not the only free peoples remaining, that western Europe also needs the economic and financial aid which, as President Truman said, "is essential to economic stability and orderly political processes." The response of the American people and the Congress to these constructively and far-sightedly self-interested policies has been greatly heartening to every believer in democracy. . . .

OUR ATTITUDE

Certain shrill voices have been proclaiming over the American radio that the policy of the United States should be to give aid only to "truly democratic" foreign governments. One wonders whether these speakers would define the word "democratic" in the pre-Yalta or in the post-Yalta sense, in Jeffersonian or Stalinesque terms. President Truman has wisely held that our concern is to support "free peoples," implying that we should not be finicky over their degree of democracy. It is sound policy for the United States, I believe, to leave to another great power its existing monopoly on the setting up of regimes duplicating its own. Democracy as we understand it is not a thing which can be established by foreign power. Its success depends on the development of a special kind of political climate—a climate in which the losers can accept without dishonor the verdict of a majority at the polls.

The whole world is going to be watching what we do in Greece and Turkey, watching to see whether our financial and technical strength is used to enslave or to free, whether we leave these countries when their peoples and the United Nations tell us that our job is done. We shall be asked to leave very soon indeed if we appear to be working exclusively for American advantage or if we mix in local politics beyond the obvious requirements of our task. No one expects us to be disinterested, for all the world knows that we would not be there if we had no interests there. One of our most important objectives should be to show that we are as concerned for the interests of the Greeks and Turks as for our own.

If a complete pattern of what not to do is needed, it is easily found. In Iran, in the Balkans, in eastern Europe, in faraway Korea, the Soviet Government has provided a pattern of principles and practices for us to avoid like the plague. Moscow has also pointed out and exploited with complete selfishness the economic and social injustices which we should aid free nations to remove. We have quite recently arrived at the status of superpower, and are not, I hope, too proud to learn both positive and negative lessons from our chief competitor. Our own experience in Latin America has taught us the extremely important lesson that the good-neighbor policy is the necessary companion of the Monroe Doctrine.

OUR WORLD-WIDE RESPONSIBILITY

For the second time in the history of the United States a government of Russia has unintentionally done us a great service. In the early days of our Republic a consistent and world-wide Russian policy touched the American continents and stimulated the formulation of the Monroe Doctrine. Our reaction to current Soviet Russian policy toward Greece and Turkey has produced the Truman Doctrine of aid to free peoples whose independence is threatened. But Russia's policy in the Near East is only part of a larger policy threatening free peoples everywhere, on every continent. So the Truman Doctrine must be extended to meet the threat. Secretary Marshall's proposals for the reconstruction of Europe are such an extension. The Truman Doctrine and the Marshall policy are, therefore, global developments of familiar principles, the principles of the Monroe Doctrine and the good-neighbor policy. We have the men of the Kremlin to thank for opening our eyes to our inescapable responsibility to see that government of the people, by the people, for the people does not perish from the earth.

2

On the Truman Doctrine*

IZVESTIA

On March 12, President Truman addressed a message to the U. S. Congress asking for 400 million dollars to be assigned for urgent aid to Greece and Turkey, and for authority to send to those countries American civil and military personnel, and to provide for the training by Americans of specially picked Greek and Turkish personnel.

Greece, said Truman, was in a desperate economic and political situation. Britain was no longer able to act as trustee for the Greeks. Turkey had requested speedy American aid. Turkey, unlike Greece, had not suffered from the Second World War, but she needed financial aid from Britain and from the U. S. A. in order to carry out that modernisation necessary for maintaining her national integrity. Since the British Government, on

*Soviet News, *March 15, 1947.*

account of its own difficulties, was not capable of offering financial or other aid to the Turks, this aid must be furnished by the U. S. A.

Thus Congress was asked to do two 'good deeds' at once—to save Greece from internal disorders and to pay for the cost of 'modernising' Turkey.

The pathetic appeal of the Tsaldaris Government to the U. S. A. is clear evidence of the bankruptcy of the political regime in Greece. But the matter does not lie solely with the Greek Monarchists and their friends, now cracked up to American Congressmen as the direct descendants of the heroes of Thermopylae: it is well known that the real masters of Greece have been and are the British military authorities.

British troops have been on Greek territory since 1944. On Churchill's initiative, Britain took on herself the responsibility for 'stabilising' political conditions in Greece. The British authorities did not confine themselves to perpetuating the rule of the reactionary, anti-democratic forces in Greece, making no scruple in supporting ex-collaborators with the Germans. The entire political and economic activities under a number of short-lived Greek Governments have been carried on under close British control and direction.

To-day we can see the results of this policy—complete bankruptcy. British troops failed to bring peace and tranquillity to tormented Greece. The Greek people have been plunged into the abyss of new sufferings, of hunger and poverty. Civil war takes on ever fiercer forms.

Was not the presence of foreign troops on Greek territory instrumental in bringing about this state of affairs? Does not Britain, who proclaimed herself the guardian of Greece, bear responsibility for the bankruptcy of her charge?

The American President's message completely glosses over these questions. The U. S. A. does not wish to criticise Britain, since she herself intends to follow the British example. Truman's statement makes it clear that the U. S. A. does not intend to deviate from the course of British policy in Greece. So one cannot expect better results.

The U. S. Government has no intention of acting in the Greek question as one might have expected a member of UNO, concerned about the fate of another member, to act. It is obvious that in Washington they do not wish to take into account the obligations assumed by the U. S. Government regarding UNO. Truman did not even consider it necessary to wait for the findings of the Security Council Commission specially sent to Greece to investigate the situation on the spot.

Truman, indeed, failed to reckon either with the international organisation or with the sovereignty of Greece. What will be left of Greek sovereignty when the 'American military and civilian personnel' gets to work in Greece by means of the 250 million dollars brought into that country? The sovereignty and independence of Greece will be the first victims of such singular 'defence.'

The American arguments for assisting Turkey base themselves on the existence of a threat to the integrity of Turkish territory—though no-one and nothing actually threatens Turkey's integrity. This 'assistance' is evidently aimed at putting this country also under U. S. control.

Some American commentators admit this quite openly. Walter Lippmann, for example, frankly points out in the *Herald Tribune* that an American alliance with Turkey would give the U. S. A. a strategic position, incomparably more advantageous than any other, from which power could be wielded over the Middle East.

Commenting on Truman's message to Congress, the *New York Times* proclaims the advent of 'the age of American responsibility.' Yet what is this responsibility but a smokescreen for expansion? The cry of saving Greece and Turkey from the expansion of the so-called 'totalitarian states' is not new. Hitler used to refer to the Bolsheviks when he wanted to open the road for his own conquests. Now they want to take Greece and Turkey under their control, they raise a din about 'totalitarian states.' This seems all the more attractive since, in elbowing in itself, the U. S. A. is pushing non-totalitarian Britain out of yet another country or two.

One cannot say that Truman's declaration has not met with serious criticism even in the U. S. Congress. A group of thirteen Congressmen tried to dissuade him from making his statement.

Senator Taylor expressed disgust at the proposal to vote financial aid to the Greek Monarchist Government, which was persecuting those who fought against Nazism. Senator Johnson said he approved aid in foodstuffs, without political aims, with all his heart, but that the President had not made a distinction between foodstuffs and bullets. The Senator said he did not approve the sending of American military personnel to Greece and Turkey, even as advisers. Military aid to Turkey and Greece could lead to military interference in other parts of the world. He was ready to give millions to aid hungry people, but not a cent to help decaying Monarchies.

Senator Pepper said that Truman's recommendations, put forward completely without consultation with the United Nations, created a threat to UNO and would place unknown obligations upon the United States.

The Chairman of the Budget Commission of the House of Representatives said that supporters of Truman's programme apparently would not be satisfied until the United States was made bankrupt.

Henry Wallace and several other leading American figures came out with a sharply negative response to Truman's message.

We are now witnessing a fresh intrusion of the U. S. A. into the affairs of other states. American claims to leadership in international affairs grow parallel with the growing appetite of the American quarters concerned. But the American leaders, in the new historical circumstances, fail to reckon with the fact that the old methods of the colonisers and diehard politicians have out-lived their time and are doomed to failure. In this lies the chief weakness of Truman's message.

3

The Truman Doctrine and the Marshall Plan*

EDWIN BORCHARD

While the Marshall proposal for aid by the United States toward European recovery is often called a corollary of the Truman Doctrine, they differ essentially in their aims. While both are directed against the expansion of Soviet Russia the Truman Doctrine looks to military aid to Greece and Turkey, and the outcome is unknown. The Marshall proposal, on the other hand, looks purely to economic aid for the countries of Western Europe and professes to disregard political considerations.

The so-called Truman Doctrine is often called an extension of the Monroe Doctrine. But this is surely an error. The Monroe Doctrine was limited geographically to this continent. It announced that American arms would protect the Continent against any effort of Europe to extend its system across the Atlantic. Several efforts at European intervention were made during the nineteenth century, efforts which always failed. The Truman Doctrine has no geographical limits and promises American intervention in places where the United States has little or no interest. One of the major premises of the Monroe Doctrine was the traditional American policy of not intervening in European feuds. The bottom has, therefore, been taken out of the Monroe Doctrine by American intervention abroad, so that the United States has now little moral claim to ask Europe to refrain from extending its political philosophy to this continent. Moreover the Truman Doctrine is not a self-denying ordinance but a promise to use American dollars, if not more, to stop Communism. Apart from the fact that Soviet Russia exemplifies not Communism but National Socialism—the Communist Utopia not having yet arrived—it remains to be proved that dollars can stem the advance of a doctrine which finds its major source and soil in poverty and misery. President Truman recently announced, in describing the Potsdam Declaration, that chaos had been brought to Germany by the Nazi Party. Regardless of the accuracy of his ascription, the fact is that chaos prevails in most of Europe and that American money, which European peoples naturally are delighted to spend, can hardly shore up countries that surrender to the inevitable. It shows how fantastic was the half-truth of the idea of "One World." As Senator Root said to Senator Bacon of Georgia in a famous debate on Mexico, many ideas, like world government, are logical, but not practical.

*From The American Journal of International Law, 41 (October, 1947), 885–888. Reprinted by permission of the American Society of International Law.

One of the primary interests of the founders of this country, who are entitled to be heard in such a dilemma as now confronts the United States, is that European ideology must not be imported into this heterogeneous population. The founders' warning was prophetic. The major opposition to the Italian Treaty comes from Italian–American societies who resent the fate meted out to Italy. In that opposition they have a good ground for protest, but it seems pitiful to transfer European problems to this soil in the alleged interests of an unachievable Utopia.

THE MARSHALL PROPOSAL

The so-called Marshall Plan is no plan at all but merely undertakes to finance some plan satisfactory to Secretary Marshall and the United States Congress if the European countries can come to agreement. Russia and her satellites have already declined American aid and profess to see in it danger to the aided. They promise to defeat the proposal.

If we should advance any money to Europe in addition to the twenty billions already devoted to relief and other purposes it will show that the United States is the only country really paying reparations in addition to what Russia has looted out of Germany and Austria and her satellites, mostly private property. It may be questioned why the United States should pay reparations, but it is a result of failing to think about what will happen after a war. The psychology of merely defeating the enemy is manifestly inadequate. Yet the mores of war forbid thought beyond this point. First we spend billions, not, it is true, with a view to destroying Europe but having that effect. Now we are to spend new billions to restore Europe with the promise that it will be interpreted as American imperialism. It may also have that result, since Secretary Marshall promises to supervise the expenditure of any funds which Congress may advance. But that is not the initial intention. The Russians are wrong in charging that it positively will have that result. We can accept Secretary Marshall's statement that he, at least, has no such intention. He may, however, find himself in the position of the British in Egypt after 1882; then the United States, already a Balkan power, will become an imperialist power. It is simply too early to forecast all future developments. The chances are not weak that the reparations of Italy and other countries payable to Russia and her satellites may be siphoned off from American loans to Italy and other reparation-paying countries.

The Marshall Plan seems particularly to lack consideration because no one can tell what it may cost the United States. We have seen figures mentioned of three billions for three years, five billions for four years, and seven billions for ten years. The President states that we have already contributed twenty billions to Europe since the end of hostilities in 1945. Europe is now based on the unsound political plan of Potsdam, and no amount of American money can change that fact. So long as that basis stands any American money raised, as it must be on credit, will be the sheerest palliative and can serve no purpose of recovery.

There are other dilemmas that must be faced. Europe's condition is not only due to the unfortunate features of the Potsdam agreement, of which Russia seems to have taken full advantage, but Eastern Europe has also been separated from the West to a considerable extent by the so-called Iron Curtain. Eastern Europe normally exports foodstuffs and raw materials, as does Russia, but they are not getting in exchange industrial goods from the West, goods which they badly need. Although Russia hurries to make agreements with her satellites, they can hardly make good the deficiency. Eastern Europe, therefore, seems likely to suffer an industrial famine, although the Marshall proposal does not contemplate a termination of the bilateral treaties made between Eastern countries and the West.

The Marshall proposal seems more likely to finance state socialism, although the word "recovery" is frequently employed. At this writing (September, 1947), it is unsafe to predict developments, but since Russia and her satellites have declared war on the plan, the financing of Western Europe might turn into a military measure, leaving recovery an unachieved aim.

We now learn that France objects to increasing the German output, though the joint chiefs-of-staff have already issued a directive to that effect. Great Britain is also said to protest against part of the program. Perhaps this is the most significant event of recent years, since it throws light on the origins of the war in 1914, however justified the protest. If Europe is not to be allowed full production, it seems idle to throw American money into the breach. The plan is stymied at the source.

The countries which possess the fifteen billion dollars of gold and foreign exchange that the National City Bank reports are not the countries with which the bulk of American trade is done, but some exchange is possessed by those countries. Should Secretary Marshall insist first on their spending their assets on American goods before receiving American bounty? Or will they say, as a British cabinet minister threatened the other day, that default in certain loans will follow or that the United States in its own interest must finance exports up to eight billions a year—the difference between exports and imports—since otherwise unemployment will result in the United States?

There are thus many obstacles which the Marshall proposal must overcome. Will the proposal founder on one or more of these obstacles? Only the future can give an answer.

IV

The Berlin Blockade

1

Rights of the United States in Berlin*

PHILIP C. JESSUP

The United States is in Berlin as of right. The rights of the United States as a joint occupying power in Berlin derive from the total defeat and unconditional surrender of Germany. Article I of protocol on zones of occupation in Germany agreed to by the Soviet Union in the European Advisory Commission on November 14, 1944 provides:

I. Germany, within frontiers as were on December 31, 1937, will, for purposes of occupation, be divided into three zones, one of which will be allotted to each of three powers, and a special Berlin area, which will be under joint occupation by the three powers.

This agreement (later amended to include France) established the area of Berlin as an international enclave to be jointly occupied and administered by four powers.

The representatives of commanders-in-chief adopted, on July 7, 1945, a resolution establishing the Allied Kommandatura for administration of Berlin. The Kommandatura was to be under the direction of the chief military commandant which post was to be held in rotation by each of four military commanders. The chief military commandant in consultation with the other commanders was to exercise administration of all Berlin sectors when a question of principle and problems common to all sectors arose. In order to exercise supervision of Berlin local government, one or two representatives from each Allied command were to be attached to each section of the local German government.

Implicit in these agreements is the right of each of the four powers to free access to and egress from the greater Berlin area. Not only has this right been clearly recognized and confirmed by the Soviet Union by practice and usage for almost three years, but it has been the subject of written agreements between the respective governments as well as by their repre-

*U. S. Department of State Press Release No. 821, October 8, 1948. Excerpts.

45

sentatives in the Allied Control Council for Germany. Rights of free access were directly specified in the message from President Truman to Premier Stalin on June 14, 1945, which agreed to withdraw back to the prescribed zonal boundaries those forces which in the course of the war had overrun part of the territory which later became the Soviet zone of occupation, provided satisfactory arrangements for free access by rail, road and air to the forces in Berlin could be entered into between the military commanders. I quote one sentence from the Truman message:

> . . . As to Germany, I am ready to have instructions issued to all American troops to begin withdrawal into their own zone on June 21 in accordance with arrangements between the respective commanders, including in these arrangements simultaneous movement of the national garrisons into greater Berlin and provision of free access by air, road and rail from Frankfurt and Bremen to Berlin for United States forces.

Premier Stalin replied on June 16, 1945, accepting this plan excepting for a change in date. Premier Stalin gave assurances that all necessary measures would be taken in accordance with the plan. Correspondence in a similar sense took place between Premier Stalin and Prime Minister Churchill. Premier Stalin thus agreed that the Western occupying powers should have "free access by air, road and rail" to Berlin. Even in the Russian language, "free access" does not mean "blockade."

The four zone commanders met in Berlin on June 29, 1945, to put the agreement of the Chiefs of States into force. At this meeting it was agreed that the Western Powers would withdraw their forces from the Soviet zone and would have the use of the Helmstedt–Berlin *Autobahn* and rail routes without restriction and subject only to the normal traffic regulations of the Soviet zone. In reply to a question from General Clay, Marshal Zhukov, the Soviet commander, stated: "It will be necessary for vehicles to be governed by Russian road signs, military police, document checking, but no inspection of cargo—the Soviets are not interested in what is being hauled, how much or how many trucks are moving." In accordance with this understanding, the United States, whose armed forces had penetrated deep into lands of Saxony and Thuringia, in the Soviet zone, withdrew its forces to its zone. Simultaneously, United States garrisoning forces took up their position in Berlin.

The right of the United States to be in Berlin thus stems from the same source as the right of the Soviet Union. Rights of occupying powers are co-equal as to freedom of access, occupation and administration of the area.

It clearly results from these undertakings that Berlin is not a part of the Soviet zone of occupation, but is, by express agreement, an international enclave. Commitments entered into in good faith by the commanders of the four zones of occupation, agreements reached by the Allied Control Authority in Germany, as well as uncontested usage, have recognized basic rights of the United States in the joint administration of Berlin and rights of freedom of access thereto for the purpose of fulfilling United States obligations and responsibilities as an occupying power.

Since July 7, 1945, it agreed that supplies necessary for the welfare of the people of Berlin were a joint responsibility of the four powers. There have been a series of quadripartite agreements entered into between July 1945 and April 1948 for the join provision of food, solid fuels and electric power, and medical supplies.

All agreements, of course, carried with them the right of access to permit the Western occupying powers to bring their share of supplies to Berlin.

Pursuant to agreement in the Control Council establishing train paths, military trains regularly traversed the Helmstedt–Berlin train route. There was no inspection by Soviet authorities and no Soviet permit was required for outgoing shipments from the Berlin area. Proof of identity through proper documentation was sufficient to comply with traffic regulations, which during this period were reasonable and were fully accepted by the Western Powers. Similarly, personnel of the United States Military Forces and other United States officials traveled freely by train or motorcar over the rail and *Autobahn* routes from Berlin to Helmstedt without Soviet visa.

Air corridors were established between the Western zones and Berlin with unrestricted flight, subject, of course, to safety regulations. Three such corridors were established in November 1945 by Four Power agreement in the Allied Control Council to augment the single provisional corridor agreed to in the meeting of the Allied Commanders-in-Chief on July 7, 1945. In December 1945 uniform safety regulations were adopted in these corridors, under which aircraft have operated continuously since that date. These regulations were reaffirmed by publication on October 22, 1946, of the agreed second revision of these flight rules. In practice, military and civilian airline aircraft of the three Western Powers used the corridors for unlimited flight without notification to Soviet authorities.

Bilateral agreements were made by British and Soviet authorities concerning barge traffic between their two zones. Quadripartite arrangements concerning postal traffic, telecommunications and movement of Germans between the Western zones and Berlin were concurred in, and carried out satisfactorily, prior to institution by the Soviet Union of blockade measures.

There can thus be no question of the legal basis for United States rights to free access to Berlin or of recognition of these rights by the Soviet Union.

The United States maintains its basic juridical rights of free access to Berlin. These are clearly established and recognized by the Soviet Government. As every reasonable and practical person knows, rail, road, barge and air traffic must be subject to some degree of regulation. Let me repeat the statement of Marshal Zhukov on June 29, 1945:

> It will be necessary for vehicles to be governed by Russian road-signs, military police, and documents checking, but no inspection of cargo—Soviets not interested in what is being hauled, how much or how many trucks are moving.

The United States agreed to this position and we still agree. We do not assert freedom of access means absence of reasonable regulations, but precaution cannot be distorted to mean imposition of restrictions to the point where the principle of free access is completely strangled. The United States will not permit the Soviet Government to use the agreed principle of reasonable regulation as a measure to cloak the threat of force designed to force the United States to abandon Berlin to single domination and rule by the Soviet Union.

2

Soviet Position on the Dispute*

ANDREI VISHINSKY

The Government of the U. S. S. R. considers that the proposal of the three governments, the United States of America, the United Kingdom and France, to include in the agenda of the Security Council the question of the situation which has arisen in Berlin is devoid of any grounds inasmuch as this question does not fall within the scope of competence of the Security Council and cannot therefore be subjected to discussion in the Security Council.

Measures taken by U. S. S. R. authorities against which the complaints are directed by the governments of the United States of America, the United Kingdom and France are very responsible measures which the Government of the U. S. S. R. has to take in view of the measures taken by the three governments in respect of currency reforms in the Western zones of Germany, reforms which have placed Berlin and the whole Soviet zone of occupation in the position of being threatened by a new currency coming into Berlin and the Soviet zone of occupation from the Western zones. It was necessary to defend the Soviet zone of occupation in Germany against collapse which threatened it pursuant to measures taken by the governments of the United States of America, the United Kingdom and France. These governments did not take into account the economic interests of the Soviet zone and the interests of its population. Measures undertaken by U. S. S. R. authorities in the Soviet occupation zone of Germany in this connection are of a defensive character against aggressive actions of the three governments, which governments must bear responsibility for the situation which has arisen in Berlin. If these aggressive measures of the governments of the United States of Amer-

* *The statement of Soviet Deputy Foreign Minister Andrei Y. Vishinsky, on October 4, 1948, to the Security Council of the United Nations in Paris. Excerpts.*

ica, United Kingdom and France had not taken place, then the Berlin question would not have arisen because there would not have been any necessity for the above-mentioned measures of defensive character.

There can be no question of fact that this question of the situation in Germany as a whole and that separation of the Berlin question from the general German problem would bear an utterly artificial character and would only be calculated to lead to decisions which would be incorrect and which would not meet the necessity of the situation.

Admission of the Berlin question for consideration of the Security Council would be a violation of Article 107 of the Charter of the United Nations. It is well known that Article 107 of the Charter states:

"Nothing in the present Charter shall invalidate or preclude action in relation to any state which during the second World War has been an enemy of any signatory to the present Charter, taken or authorized as a result of that war by the governments having responsibility for such action."

Thus the Berlin question, which is part and parcel of the question of Germany as a whole pursuant to Article 107 of the Charter of the United Nations, is subject to solution by agreement of those governments that bear responsibility for occupation of Germany. Therefore, solution of this question is not within the purview of the Security Council and is not subject to decision of the Security Council.

In fact, with respect to Germany in general and Berlin in particular, there is a whole series of rather important international treaties and agreements which were concluded among four powers—the Union of Soviet Socialist Republics, United States of America, United Kingdom and France. Most important of these international agreements are agreements of the great powers concluded at Yalta and Potsdam, agreements which set forth the economic and political principles which were to govern actions of the governments with respect to Germany. Among these agreements there are such important documents as the declaration of surrender of Germany and an agreement for a quadripartite control mechanism for control of Germany. These documents represent international agreements or treaties. All these documents entered into force after having been signed for the period of carrying out by Germany of the basic requirements of unconditional surrender.

We have several agreements of the above-mentioned powers with regard to the division of Germany into zones of occupation and with regard to the government of Berlin and so on. There are also important decisions of the Potsdam Conference of three powers which were subsequently adhered to by China and France, such as the decision for establishment of the Council of Foreign Ministers, which council also received the task of having the appropriate drafted treaty for Germany adopted and accepted by a democratic government of Germany if and when such democratic government of Germany were established.

Thus, the whole question of Germany, including the Berlin question, pursuant to special international agreements and treaties of the great powers, is subject to solution by the governments which bear responsibility for the occupation of Germany.

Therefore, this question cannot be subject to consideration under any other procedure or any procedure which was not provided for in international agreements which have been signed by the great powers. That is a position of principle which is taken care of by terms of Article 107 of the Charter, terms which make it perfectly clear that responsibility for the situation in enemy countries where the governments are bearing responsibilities of government, is borne by those very governments.

Therefore, any questions arising from carrying out of the control of Germany, including the question as to the situation in Berlin, has to be settled through direct negotiations by the powers concerned, which powers according to international agreements bear responsibility for the state of things in Germany as a whole and in any sector or part of Germany and in particular in the capital of Germany, Berlin. For solution of such questions, international agreements which I have already mentioned have established a special control mechanism for Germany, namely a quadripartite Allied Council for Germany.

Furthermore, the Potsdam Agreement set up the Council of Foreign Ministers. The Council of Foreign Ministers received the specific task of preparing the work for the peace settlement in general, including the peace settlement with Germany. This settlement was supposed to be prepared through agreement of the four powers represented in the Council of Foreign Ministers.

If we are to stay upon the ground of international agreements which I have just quoted and if the signatures which are appended to these agreements are to be respected, then we cannot consider it to be either legal or acceptable to transmit to the Security Council for its consideration any question relevant to the question of Germany—and that includes the question of Berlin. A decision to transmit this question to the Security Council would be an overt violation of the Charter of the United Nations and of the above-mentioned international agreements. It would, in the first place, be a violation of the Yalta and Potsdam agreements, pursuant to which the question of Germany is solely within the competence of the four powers which bear responsibility for the occupation of Germany. There can be no doubt that the questions of Germany are questions which have to be considered only within the framework of procedure established in the above-mentioned international agreements which were concluded among the four powers bearing primary responsibility for the occupation of Germany.

The governments of the United States, United Kingdom and France have at their disposal legal means in order to satisfy their claims. They have at their disposal every means to see to it that the treaties are carried out and that all questions connected with Germany are settled according to legal procedure. For that, however, it is necessary to respect one's own signature to international agreements. It is necessary to carry out obligations which have been agreed upon and which are contained in international agreements. It is impossible under the screen of the Security Council to refuse carrying out of obligations which were freely assumed by governments with respect to such important questions—obligations, incidentally, which have been set forth not in one but in several international treaties or agreements. It is impossible, thus, to give up the carrying out of obligations and of responsibilities which are set forth in these conventions and international treaties. It is unacceptable to eschew responsibility for the violation of obligations assumed in those instruments.

Therefore the governments of the United States, United Kingdom and France should take the legal way, the one chartered by international agreements signed by those powers and by powers that adhere thereto subsequently. That is the legal way. That is the way which does not violate the Charter of the United Nations, which does not violate international agreements under which one may read the signatures of representatives of the appropriate states.

As is well known to the other three governments from a note of the U. S. S. R. Government dated October 3, the U. S. S. R. Government has proposed the convocation of the Council of Foreign Ministers within whose competence the regulation of the Berlin question falls. Is it not strange that the organ created by virtue of international agreement, the body which has been functioning or which did function, by foregathering in periodic sessions—is it not strange that when a complicated and difficult situation has arisen which requires action by that body, which requires authoritative intervention under these very circumstances, it is deemed that this organ should be left out, should be frozen out? The Council of Foreign Ministers was set up in order to settle the German question, was set up by the Potsdam Conference in order to deal with these questions, in order to deal in concert with any questions including the question for which the council was created with regard to a peaceful settlement of conditions in Germany which are, of course, connected with all problems which have been raised now—problems which are so important and which the Secretary General, Mr. Trygve Lie, says are of such grave significance. This Council of Foreign Ministers which was set up by us, by three, then by four, and then by five governments—because France and China subsequently adhered to the decision—this council which was set up by us especially to settle German questions is frozen out, it left out, is ignored. It is being circumvented; it remains outside; it is not being used by the countries which established it, which assumed certain obligations for the settlement of the German question. That very council is being ignored.

This legal way of consideration of the German question, the way which leads through the Council of Foreign Ministers—the only legal way—is the one which is in accordance with the Charter of the United Nations. It is the one way in which to reconcile the Charter with existing international agreements because Article 2 of the Charter requires respect for international agreements previously assumed on the part of those states which assumed those obligations. *Pacta sunt servanda;* treaties must be saved. That is a basic principle of international law and of international co-operation. Please be kind enough to carry out this basic requirement of international law. Turn to the organ which was established for this purpose by virtue of the treaty which you yourselves signed. Go ahead and carry out the obligations which you have assumed by virtue of that very treaty.

The governments of three powers—the United States of America, United Kingdom and France—in a note addressed to the Secretary General of the United Nations, assert that the situation that has arisen in Berlin represents a grave threat to international peace and security. The notification says that the above mentioned governments have decided to transmit the Berlin question to the Security Council for consideration so that international peace and security may not be threatened in the future. They allege international peace and security now are in danger. However, such statements are absurd and devoid of any foundation. As has already been indicated in the note of the U. S. S. R. Government dated October 3—the note dated yesterday—the statement of the Government of the United States to the effect that a situation has arisen which threatens international peace and security does not correspond to the truth of the situation and amounts to nothing but means of pressure, to nothing but an attempt to utilize the United Nations for the achievement of the aggressive ends of that Government. Such absurd allegations are designed to raise a hubbub around the question of the so-called blockade of Berlin, although in reality no such blockade exists. Statements about the threat of hunger and epidemics in Berlin are also empty allegations and are mere propaganda maneuvers.

The U. S. S. R. Government, upon representations of Soviet military authorities in Germany, adopted decisions according to which it expressed its readiness to assume responsibility for supplying of food to all of Berlin. Marshal Sokolovsky told press correspondents that the U. S. S. R. Government could supply thousands of tons of grain and fats to the Western zone. According to incomplete data, those people in Western Berlin are daily recipients of about 900 tons of various products such as coal and others. However, there would be no obstacle to the supply of occupation troops.

Therefore, all accusations which have been made against the U. S. S. R. do not stand criticism, and all these rumors are merely being spread in order to worsen the state of fear and war hysteria. The spreading of these rumors is not actuated by any desire to effect a peaceful solution of the Berlin situation.

In the note of September 26 there is an allegation to the effect that U. S.

S. R. authorities in Berlin had permitted an attempt by a minority of the Berlin population to put down by force the Berlin ministerial government. The Government of U. S. S. R. in its reply, addressed to the governments of France, the United States and the United Kingdom, officially rejected these empty accusations and allegations. U. S. S. R. authorities in Berlin have received firm instructions from the U. S. S. R. Government that, despite the discontent of the Berlin population because of the present situation, the U. S. S. R. military authorities should insure calm conditions for the work of local organs of government.

These instructions were confirmed by the Minister of Foreign Affairs of the U. S. S. R., Mr. Molotov, on August 30 when he had his conversation with representatives of the United States, the United Kingdom and France. The ludicrous charactor of the above-mentioned allegations made against U. S. S. R. authorities also is evident from the fact that the disorders which are complained about by the three governments took place within those sectors of Berlin which are not within the competence of the U. S. S. R. military command.

Those were events for which the responsibility should not be borne by the U. S. S. R. military government, but by the military authorities of the three other occupation forces. Therefore, this allegation of the Western powers does not also correspond to the truth. It does not describe the true situation. This argument, therefore, about the fact that the situation which had arisen in Berlin is allegedly due to actions of the U. S. S. R. forces and is a threat to peace and security and an argument in favor of the necessity of having the Security Council consider the Berlin question also falls and must be considered illogical, and therefore must be rejected as not corresponding to the reality of the situation. . . .

3

Behind the Blockade Settlement *

PHILLIPS DAVISON

The Soviet decision to lift the blockade has usually been ascribed to a combination of factors. Ambassador Smith wrote that it was based in part on the fact that the counterblockade was hurting the East far more than the blockade was hurting the West. J. P. Nettl, a student of the east zone economy, also maintained that East Germany suffered more severely from the economic

*From The Berlin Blockade (*Princeton, N. J.: Princeton University Press, 1958*), pp. 275–280. Copyright 1958. Reprinted by permission of Princeton University Press.*

effects of the crisis than did West Germany. General Clay expressed the opinion that it was not only pressure on the East German economy but also the revival in West Germany that led the Soviets to change their plans.

Others, in seeking to explain the Soviet action, have placed the stress elsewhere. U. N. Secretary General Trygve Lie believed that the propaganda effects of the triumphant airlift, possibly combined with the force of world public opinion, played a large role, in addition to the counterblockade. He also pointed to the fact that the blockade had led to a tremendous increase of Allied air power in Western Europe. British and American diplomatic officials have added the theory that the Soviets, feeling themselves excluded from all means by which they might influence developments in Western Europe, had wanted to rejoin the "diplomatic club" and had therefore proposed the meeting of the Council of Foreign Ministers. Another factor that was believed to have prompted the Soviet decision was the loss of prestige to communist parties throughout Europe, caused in part by the dramatic success of the airlift.

All these considerations probably entered into the Soviet decision. In the light of broader Soviet policies, however, Moscow's reasons for ending the crisis when it did appear in a somewhat different perspective. The blockade had been imposed originally as one phase of an effort to ensure the continuance of a European balance of power favorable to the Soviets. At first, the Soviets demanded that the Western powers either sacrifice all of Berlin (and with it much of their prestige in Europe) or else give up their plans for a West German government. When the airlift showed that the Allies would do neither, the Soviets decided to consolidate their position in East Berlin. Having completed that process, they found that what advantages could thenceforth be derived from the continuation of the blockade were relatively modest. One advantage was that the airlift constituted an appreciable financial drain on Germany and the Western powers; another, that it effectively tied up the bulk of Western military air transport in Berlin.*

The disadvantages of continuing the blockade, on the other hand, were substantial. Far from weighting the balance of power in favor of the Soviets, it was producing the opposite effect. The Western powers were united in their stand on Berlin. So were the West German states. As long as the Soviets were cast in the aggressive role of blockaders of more than two million

*Some observers of international relations have advanced the thesis that one purpose of the Berlin blockade was to occupy the attention of the Western powers in Europe while Chinese communist armies were advancing in Asia. The communist conquest of China proceeded during much of the Berlin blockade, and Shanghai was occupied on May 25.

The writer is not inclined to include this "diversion of attention" tactic among the causes of the blockade. All the available information indicates that the Soviets at first expected the blockade to be concluded successfully in a relatively short space of time, and that they certainly did not foresee the massive airlift. Nevertheless, the possibility cannot be completely discounted that Soviet delay in lifting the blockade was due in part to the war in China. By ensuring that Western air transport was fully occupied in Germany, Stalin could guard against the possibility that last-minute logistic aid might be extended to Chiang Kai-shek.

civilians, they were in a poor position to interfere with formation of the North Atlantic Treaty Organization, the functioning of the Marshall Plan, and the establishment of a West German government. Local communists in West Germany and West Europe were equally hampered in their opposition to these Western moves. The blockade was thus furthering the very developments in Western Europe that it had been intended to block.

In casting about for some other instrument with which to oppose Western consolidation, the Soviets, it appears, decided to promote the growth of a "peace" or "neutralist" sentiment in Western Europe. By this tactic, they hoped to encourage divisions among the Western powers that would prevent their forming an effective military counterweight to Soviet power. France, in particular, had already shown herself extremely suspicious of plans for a West German state, and might be pried loose from the Western alliance, once the Berlin tension had been eased. Through the campaign for German unity and withdrawal of occupation troops, the Soviets also hoped to promote divisions of opinion within West Germany. Even if these might not be sufficient to stop the creation of a government, perhaps they would at least prevent the new government from cooperating in Western defense.

Viewed in this broader perspective, then, the blockade can be said to have been withdrawn in order to clear the way for other tactics: a peace offensive and a campaign for German unity. The end of the blockade signified a change in Soviet strategy, but not in Soviet aims.

In this interpretation, the counterblockade assumes only very limited importance. For one thing, its full effects were not felt until February or March of 1949, by which time the Soviets must have made at least a tentative decision to restore land communications to Berlin. For another, though the counterblockade caused definite hardships to certain branches of East German industry by depriving them of critical materials, it did not affect a very large volume of trade. Soviet efforts, all along, had been directed toward making the Eastern bloc economically independent of the West. Before World War II, according to a study of the Economic Commission for Europe, the annual interchange of goods between what are now East and West Germany was valued at some 2.7 billion marks. In 1947 the value of this trade was calculated at 496 million marks. During 1948 and 1949, both of which years were affected by the blockade, the value dropped to 357 and 432 million marks, respectively. In 1950 the figure jumped to 807 million "payment units,"* but it sank again to 365 million payment units in 1951 and 293 in 1952. Despite the obvious difficulties of comparing values expressed in different kinds of marks and in payment units, it is clear that postwar trade between East and West Germany was relatively small, irrespective of the blockade. The *Deutschland-Jahrbuch* for 1949 observed that in 1947, the last "normal" year before the blockade, trade between East and

---

*A device used because of the difference in value between east and west marks.

West Germany amounted to scarcely the volume of one of the larger prewar department stores. It is difficult to believe, therefore, that economic considerations played more than a minor role in the Soviet decision to lift the blockade.*

The Soviets themselves seemed anxious to have their action ascribed to economic motives. This was pointed out by newsmen at the time. The repeated communist requests to West German and West Berlin authorities, in early 1949, for a reopening of interzonal trade were certainly made in the knowledge that they would be rejected as long as the blockade continued. The purpose of these overtures, therefore, must have been chiefly propagandistic. They not only put the Western authorities in the position of saying "no" to a suggestion that seemed to favor the economy in both East and West Germany, but they also made it appear that the Soviets were taking the interests of the Germans into account when they decided to lift the blockade.

Moscow's desire for a meeting of the Council of Foreign Ministers also seems to have been an excuse, rather than a reason, for lifting the blockade. The meeting, which convened in Paris on May 23, settled nothing. Indeed, a leading student of the period observed that this session "produced no clear-cut indication of what the U. S. S. R. was driving at: If Soviet policy was a mystery . . . on May 23, it was scarcely less so when the conference adjourned four weeks later." The major Soviet political moves during this period were made not in diplomatic discussions but at the peace congresses in New York and Paris.

Whether Western tactics during the negotiations that led to the lifting of the blockade had any effect on Soviet behavior is impossible to determine. Certainly, Western behavior at the time of these negotiations was very different from what it had been during the previous, unfruitful talks. Whereas in 1948 the Western powers had been willing to bargain, and anxious not to provoke the Soviets and thereby prejudice the situation, they now adopted a "take it or leave it" attitude. Some diplomatic officials have ascribed this to the Allies' thorough disillusionment as a result of the previous negotiations, which made them inclined to sit back and wait for the Soviets to show evidence of good faith.

While this may have been part of it, there were additional reasons for the Allied attitude. As newsmen repeatedly pointed out at the time, many Western diplomats felt that the blockade was working in favor of the West. On March 30 a *New York Times* report from Frankfurt described Allied officials as believing that new negotiations with the Soviets should be undertaken only after the bargaining position of the democracies had been strengthened by

---

*As far as the author could determine, no Allied agency ever attempted a systematic study of the actual or potential effects of the counterblockade while it was in progress or after it was over. Data are consequently extremely fragmentary.

the signing of the North Atlantic Pact and the establishment of a West German government. A few weeks later Drew Middleton reported from Berlin that "most United States and British officials in Berlin" believed that the German impetus to form a West German state would be lost if the blockade were lifted. Two days after that the *New York Herald Tribune* described officials in Washington as apprehensive that a softening in the Soviet attitude might delay both the ratification of the North Atlantic Pact and West Germany's acceptance of the proposed occupation statute. Once it was fairly certain that the Soviets were serious, Western officials pushed ahead with negotiations to end the blockade, but they did so without any sense of urgency or anxiety.

There is no way of determining whether the changed Western attitude hastened or retarded the negotiations. It was during the time of these final discussions that Allied policy in Germany was becoming noticeably firmer, as shown by the intensified airlift and counterblockade, and the second currency reform. The Soviets must have assumed that this posture was adopted in full knowledge of the Jessup–Malik talks, for they could not have known that Western military authorities were, in fact, unaware of the discussions. It may be significant that negotiations nevertheless did not break down.

There remains one puzzling question: Why did more than a month elapse between Stalin's famous statement to Kingsbury Smith and Malik's reply to Jessup that Stalin's failure to mention the currency question was "not accidental"?

There are various explanations, all of them conjectural. The idea that Stalin, on second thought, may have wished to keep Western air transport tied up in Germany until China had been overrun by communist armies has already been mentioned. There is also the possibility that the Soviets were waiting to see how the weather in Germany developed, before committing themselves to lifting the blockade. A period of very bad weather or intense cold during February might well have weakened the Western bargaining position. Then again, Stalin may have hoped to resume negotiations about Berlin in direct conference with President Truman, and may have had to recast his plans when the United States government turned down his proposal for a high-level conference.

Another possible explanation for the delay is that the Soviets did not wish to abandon their pressure on Berlin until they had developed a new form of pressure to take its place, and that they needed more time to prepare their peace campaign. The staff work for the New York and Paris peace congresses may have taken longer than originally expected.

A final possible interpretation is that it was a basic principle of Soviet diplomatic behavior always to have negotiations of one type or another in progress. Stalin's January 31 statement may have been indicative, at the time it was made, not of any serious wish to end the blockade, but only of a desire to ensure continuous negotiations.* It was by then clear that the efforts of the technical committee were about to break down, and Moscow may have been looking toward the establishment of a new forum for discussions.

Whatever the specific reasons that prompted the Soviets to end restrictions on traffic between Berlin and West Germany just when they did, it is clear that behind their decision to raise the blockade was the fact that it showed no prospect of achieving either of the gains to which they had apparently aspired in June 1948: incorporation of West Berlin into the Soviet zone, or further delay in the recovery of West Germany.

The course of events in West Germany, in particular, must have weighed heavily in convincing Stalin that the blockade was a liability and that a new policy was necessary if the balance of power were not to shift to the disadvantage of the Soviet Union. Indeed, one can say with a large measure of justice that the blockade was defeated in West Germany as much as in Berlin.
. . .

*One small shred of evidence tends to support this view. The TASS account of the Jessup–Malik conversations represents Jessup's question about Stalin's statement and Malik's reply as having occurred on the same day—February 15. In actuality, Malik's reply was not received until March 15. This change in date might mean that the Soviets wished to show that they were serious about entering into new negotiations one month earlier than they actually were. Or, it may simply have been an error. (Cf. The London *Times*, April 27, 1949.)

V

Rise of Communist China

1

Toward a New China Policy*

JOHN K. FAIRBANK

American policy toward any coalition regime that might succeed Chiang Kai-shek has been foreshadowed by Paul Hoffman's statement as E. C. A. administrator that our economic aid is for peoples, not governments, and that "if a de facto government of the people were set up that met all conditions for receiving our aid," we would probably continue that aid. This statement contains a big "if" which a Communist-dominated coalition in China might eventually have difficulty in satisfying. Yet an offer of aid conditional on the development of free institutions not only carries out the spirit of the Marshall Plan but also points the way toward a new and more constructive China policy.

The argument, based on the analogy of Eastern Europe, that a Communist-dominated coalition is bound to develop into a police state is too readily applied to a coalition in China. Unless we propose to turn our backs on China entirely, we have to assess the possibility of a Chinese coalition remaining for some time in a more malleable condition, less firmly in the Communist pattern, than might be expected in a smaller and more centralized country closer to Russia. In other words, we may have more time than we think to pursue a constructive policy designed to support freedom within China. This more constructive policy, however, requires us to make a distinction between the Chinese Communist movement and the Chinese social revolution.

Failure to distinguish these two aspects of change in the Chinese scene has left Americans bickering with one another for many months past. Partisans of Chennault and of Stilwell, supporters and critics of General Marshall's effort at mediation, denunciations of American aid to Chiang and protests that it was too small—all this babble of voices leading nowhere derives from the fundamental American failure to distinguish communism from social revolution in China and analyze the role of each in current developments.

*From The Nation, *Vol. 168* (*January 1, 1949*), pp. 5–8. Reprinted by permission.

As a result there has been a great deal of very sincere arguing on both sides of the question. Americans who approach China by way of Europe and international communism have stressed the genuinely Communist nature of the Chinese party's ideology and practice. Their analysis has tried to show that the Chinese Communist movement is not "mere agrarian reform" but contains all the evil potentialities of the Russian police state. On the other hand, Americans who approach the China problem primarily from a background of on-the-spot observation among the Chinese people have stressed the vitality of the new popular movements—the sincerity of the students, the awakening of the peasantry, the morale of Communist troops, and the idealism of Communist cadres of party organizers—in comparison with the sorry demoralization visible on every hand under the established regime. Tales of the Communist "liberation" movement to free the peasantry from illiteracy, disease, famine, and exploitation have been balanced by tales of its atrocities and ruthless violence and of lying Communist propaganda. From the flood of good and bad incidents Americans can pick the data to support their position, at whichever extreme it may be.

During the last year opinion in the United States has been largely influenced by those American observers who stress the pattern of international communism at work in China. They have been aided by the pro-Moscow declarations of Mao Tse-tung and his doctrinaire anti-American propaganda. At the same time the trend of popular opinion in China has been the other way, toward acquiescence in a Chinese Communist accession to power as the only escape from the deepening crisis of inflation, stoppage of production, scarcity, breakdown of services, and utter demoralization of the National Government, its armies, and its administrators. Thus the American and the Chinese people are in danger of drifting apart, and the Chinese Communist movement may be able to exacerbate the rift into a complete rupture. This makes it all the more urgent to distinguish the two components which have been contributing to Communist success in China.

The first of these components, the Chinese Communist movement, is easily identifiable. The Chinese Communist Party was formally organized in 1921. Mao Tse-tung, who rose as an organizer of peasant unions, has been the chief figure in the party's politburo for almost fifteen years. His "new democracy" line, in spite of its obvious originality in applying Leninism to China, has gone along with his consistent support of the Moscow line in international affairs. One of the most recent illustrations of the Chinese Communist puzzle has been Mao's orthodox denunciation of Tito and Titoism, at a time when Mao and his movement, with their own party, army, and self-sufficient territorial base far removed from the threat of Kremlin troops and apparently independent of Kremlin aid, appear to be far better situated to follow Tito's nationalist line than Tito himself. Mao's ideological subservience to Moscow may be a fancy cover for his de facto independence; but this is pure supposition. Thus in spite of the relative paucity of verified

Russian aid to Chinese communism, we have no basis for divorcing Chinese communism from international communism as a worldwide movement bent on the extension of its power.

This general view has been eloquently stated in the report on "Communism in China" prepared by a subcommittee of the House Committee on Foreign Affairs, as part of its series on "The Strategy and Tactics of World Communism" (Government Printing Office, 1948). The report summarizes the devices used to spread Communist influence in China and succeeds in laying—for the last time, I hope—the ghost of "mere agrarian reform." The House report continues by stating that "those who hold to it [the theory that the Chinese Communists are moderate agrarian reformers] have been or still are in official positions where they have shaped policies of the United States government on China." This seems to me untrue as applied to any American officials I can think of; and since it is vaguely stated, it seems irresponsible and mischievous.

What the House committee investigators have observed, I suggest, is not that American specialists, in or out of government, have tried to whitewash Chinese communism but that they have seen in the Chinese revolution other forces in addition to international communism, forces which I think can usefully be grouped under the heading of the Chinese social revolution. The game between us and the Russians is to see which side can use these forces to its own advantage; or, less cynically, which side can align itself with the long-term needs and aspirations of the Chinese masses and so find real allies among them. The House report on "Communism in China" makes many important and valid points as to the hollow promises and deceptive stratagems of Chinese communism, and yet it leaves one wondering where the Chinese people stand. If the Chinese Communists are thus manipulating an unsound land economics, a Russia-first foreign policy, a coercive "reform" movement, and a double-talking ideology, where do they get their popular support?

The usual answer to this is to deny that the Chinese Communists have genuine popular support. But if that is the case, we have before us the spectacle of some 150,000,000 peasants being unaccountably dragooned by a peasant-based party of 3,000,000 members and a peasant-fed army of 2,000,000. This explanation of Chinese Communist power as based purely on coercion and chicanery seems wholly inadequate. Actually, the strength of Chinese communism lies in its alignment with the forces of social revolution, which we should study and comprehend more thoroughly. The current social revolution in China began long before the Chinese ever heard of communism, and it has not by any means been confined to the Communist area of China. The great achievement of the Chinese Communist apparatus has been not so much to create this revolution as to capture its leadership and control it. The continued effort to control it is seen in the present Communist bid for the allegiance or cooperation of Chinese liberals both inside and outside the Kuomintang. Since the Kuomintang in its day, in the 1920's, acquired the leadership of social change and later lost it, we may well speculate as to how and when the Communists in their turn may lose it, and find themselves as power-holders arrayed against the very forces which brought them to power.

I call these forces "social revolution" because I think Americans too often overlook the "social" aspects of change in China in favor of the "economic," "political," and "military." No doubt this is because we can understand the intricacies of the Chinese farm economy and the material poverty of the peasant masses, the rivalry of political factions and the clash of armies, more easily than the long-term and less concrete changes in Chinese social structure and institutions. But the latter are fundamental, and a new China policy must encompass the problems of social change as well as the more immediate crises of poverty, propaganda, police control, and organized violence. . . .

The social changes which the Chinese Communists use with such history-making results are not in the main their invention or their monopoly. The student movement in modern China, which even now shows considerable independence of Communist manipulation, stems from the 1890's and succeeding decades, when modern scholars began to have an organized voice in politics. The modern Chinese press also dates from the 1890's; the *pai-bua* (written vernacular) movement, from 1917; mass education and the cooperative movement, from non-Communist projects in the 1920's; and Chinese patriotism, now increasingly inflamed against American aid to Chiang, from the last two generations of foreign aggression in China. Social movements of this type are revolutionary, but they are not necessarily made in Moscow. Many were sparked by Western missionaries. Few Americans would like to expend our resources in the effort to suppress them. Yet we must ruefully admit that Chinese communism on the whole has turned them to its uses, or organized their potentialities, more effectively than its rival the Kuomintang.

This means that American policy must be, as Mr. Hoffman's statement on the continuation of E. C. A. in China would imply, to align ourselves more positively and actively with social change in China of the type we really believe in, even though we find ourselves running parallel to or even "getting in bed with" Chinese communism. In its present phase of development the Chinese Communist movement must base its appeal in part on principles of "liberation" and mass welfare to which most Americans would subscribe— not, however, by calling the Chinese Communists "mere agrarian reformers." The nature of communism as an organized effort to acquire and keep power makes us doubt that its various promises can be realized in China any more than was the case in Russia. But in China, to a more obvious degree than in Eastern Europe, we are confronted by a genuine national and social revolution, not just a made-in-Moscow drive for the seizure of power. Our policy, therefore, to have any hope of success, must take into account the powerful social forces behind the Chinese revolution as well as its Communist ideology.

2

The Alliance and Stalin's Policies*

A. DOAK BARNETT

When the Chinese Communist government was formally established on October 1, 1949, the Soviet Union immediately recognized it, with the satellites following suit, and in the next few months the initial framework of Sino-Soviet relations was worked out in detail. In December Mao Tse-tung paid his first visit to the U. S. S. R., and during his nine-week stay a number of important Sino-Soviet agreements were concluded. Most important was the 30-year Treaty of Friendship, Alliance, and Mutual Assistance, signed in February 1950. In this political and military alliance the Chinese and Russians agreed that if either ally were "attacked by Japan or any state allied with it" (the latter phrase clearly referred to the United States), the other partner would "immediately render military and other assistance by all means at its disposal." This treaty gave Communist China strong, though not unqualified, military backing. By a separate agreement the Russians gave Communist China economic backing through a five-year 300 million dollar loan. During the same period important trade and other economic arrangements were also worked out.

In return for Soviet support, Communist China had to make major concessions. Stalin was still concerned about establishing Russia's "special rights" in China, even though China was now under Communist rule. An agreement signed in February 1950 provided for joint Sino-Soviet administration of the principal railways in Manchuria, as well as for joint use of the naval base at Port Arthur, either until a peace treaty with Japan could be concluded or, at the latest, until the end of 1952. Later agreements called for the establishment of several long-term joint stock companies, to operate mostly in China's borderlands, where the Russians had traditionally pressed for special rights. These included: two companies to exploit petroleum and nonferrous metals in Sinkiang, a company to build and repair ships in Dairen, and a civil aviation company to provide services between Communist China and the U. S. S. R. The Chinese Communists also agreed, in an exhange of notes in February, to accept the *status quo*—that is, Soviet-dominated "inde-

From Communist China and Asia (New York: Vintage Books, 1960), pp. 344–347. Reprinted by permission of the Council on Foreign Relations, Inc.

pendence"—in Outer Mongolia. At Moscow Stalin and Mao probably also discussed plans for bringing South Korea under Communist control— although there was no indication of this at the time.

The first real test of the Sino-Soviet alliance came less than a half-year later with the outbreak of the Korean War, and, whatever pullings and haulings may have taken place behind the scenes, the partnership weathered the test successfully. Entering the war to make good Soviet miscalculations and rescue the North Korean regime, the Chinese Communists did the bulk of the fighting to preserve the Communist bloc's interests. Peking's willingness to bear the brunt of the conflict enabled the Russians to avoid direct involvement, and in return Moscow poured in large amounts of military supplies and equipment, which helped the Chinese Communists not only to fight the war but also to modernize and build up their army and air force. Furthermore, Peking's alliance with the Soviet Union and the Russians' possession of atomic weapons were undoubtedly major factors which deterred the West from direct attacks against Communist bases in Manchuria, and the war remained a limited one. (The United States' desire to avoid an all-out war, and the unwillingness of its allies to support attacks beyond the Yalu, were other important factors, of course, which contributed to the decision to limit the war.) It is clear, however, that the major risks and costs of the war had to be borne primarily by the Chinese Communists, and this may have been less than wholly satisfactory to Peking.

In the autumn of 1952 Chinese Communist and Russian leaders again sat down together to discuss a wide range of problems, in their most important meeting since Mao's 1949–1950 visit. In September, while Premier Chou En-lai was in Moscow, the two governments announced that the Manchurian railways would be returned to sole Chinese management by the end of 1952, as agreed in 1950. They also revealed, however, that the Russians would stay on beyond 1952 in joint control of the naval base at Port Arthur, allegedly at Peking's "request." Because the Korean War was still going on and Communist China had no strong navy of its own, Peking may genuinely have wished the Russians to continue using and maintaining the base, but Chinese Communist leaders probably had mixed feelings about prolonging the special Russian rights on Chinese soil.

A large delegation of Chinese experts, whom Chou left behind in Moscow, continued negotiating with the Russians until mid-1953. Liu Shao-ch'i attended the 19th Congress of the Soviet Communist party in October 1952 and stayed on in Russia until January 1953, and he may also have taken part in the negotiations. Apparently, there was hard bargaining, particularly over economic matters, and the aid offered by the Russians may have fallen considerably short of what the Chinese Communists hoped for. Peking had formally launched its first Five Year Plan at the start of 1953, while the negotiations were still in progress, and it could not determine the scope of the Plan until it knew how much economic assistance would be forthcoming from the Russians. Finally, after the negotiations had dragged on for many months, the results were announced in the autumn of 1953. The Russians committed themselves to help the Chinese by providing equipment and technical assistance for a large number of key development projects, which made it possible for Peking to proceed with its Five Year Plan. But there was no announcement of any new financial aid to supplement the Soviet loan of 1950. (An agreement on the construction of a new railway linking China and the Soviet Union was also signed in this period, in late 1952, but it was not publicly announced until 1954.)

The Moscow discussions must also have dealt with the problem of terminating the Korean War. Later developments suggest that the Chinese Communists were probably more eager than Stalin to end the war and extricate themselves from it. Until Stalin's death in March 1953 the truce talks in Korea had remained deadlocked, but only four days after Stalin's death Chou En-lai put forth new proposals, very similar to the proposals previously advanced by India and rejected by the Communist powers, which made possible a solution of the main issues still outstanding.

Throughout Stalin's last years, although the alliance remained solid and a public posture of monolithic unity and enthusiastic cooperation was carefully maintained, there clearly must have been strains and frictions beneath the surface. Soviet primacy and superiority were highlighted at all times by both partners in the alliance. The Chinese Communists, on their part, engaged in enthusiastic adulation of Stalin and of almost everything about the Soviet Union, going to extraordinary lengths to indoctrinate their people in Stalinism and pro-Soviet feelings. At the same time, however, Peking was paying a sizable price for Soviet support, and apparently Stalin withheld both the level of assistance and the political status which the Chinese Communists wished for. According to Polish sources, Khrushchev, in a speech in Warsaw made after his decision to promote "de-Stalinization," specifically accused Stalin of having been responsible for serious strains in Sino-Soviet relations.

3

China and the Two Great Powers*

WERNER LEVI

What is the influence of the People's Republic of China upon the foreign policies of the United States and the Soviet Union? This question arouses considerable interest in all parts of the world—evidence of the phenomenally

*From Current History, **39** (*December, 1960*), 321–326. Reprinted by permission of the author and Current History.

rapid rise of China to the position of a world power. How did China achieve this position when only two decades ago she was essentially a pawn of the big powers? The likely answer is that the present leaders, by an effective exploitation of nationalism, resentments from the past, Communist ideology, and the craving for a better livelihood, combined with an intense devotion to their country according to their own lights, have been able successfully to conclude the work begun by preceding regimes over the last 100 years.

China's nationalism, the primary force behind Chinese international ambitions, is young and vigorous. As a mass movement it is less than half a century old. Even the Communists found it necessary, at times, to undertake a propaganda campaign to replace a lingering regional or cultural patriotism with a political national consciousness. The aim of Chinese nationalism, determined by grievances arising from foreign dominance long before the Communist regime, has always been to rid the country of foreign penetration and control, so that China could regain her place as an equal or superior partner among the nations and restore the political strength, imperial standing and leadership in Asia to which she felt entitled by rights of past grandeur and tradition. Mao Tse-tung surely expressed the feelings of patriots when he exclaimed in the fall of 1949: "Our nation will never again be an insulted nation."

The Communist government is inspired, like its predecessors, by the traditional concept of China as the Middle Kingdom, the central and superior power of the Asian world. . . . After achieving the initial goal of full sovereignty, Chinese nationalism, like all big-power nationalism, aims at imperial greatness, usually rationalized as a search for security, the fulfilment of a higher mission, or the restoration of historical rights. The resulting manifestations of Chinese foreign policy are therefore, in principle, neither peculiarly Chinese nor Communist, and, in the context of modern Chinese history, their main novelty is that they are now real while in pre-Communist days they remained mostly a dream and a plan. One of the reasons for this novelty is that success could only result from the effects of a cumulative effort in which successive Chinese governments participated. A second reason is the enthusiasm, determination and ruthlessness applied to Communist internal and foreign policy, due presumably to the fanatic certainty inspiring the Communist leaders in the pursuit of their goals. . . .

Immediately following the seizure of power in 1949, the Communist government's foreign policy was obviously influenced by the flush of victory and its endeavor, within the limits of its ability, to realize some major, primarily nationalistic goals. These included the demonstrative elimination of Western dominance (conceived to be maintained by the non-Russian Western nations) and the unification of the country, including many outlying territories, such as Tibet. Chinese support of North Korean aggression in 1950, followed by direct intervention, also was evidence of a nationalistic drive to restore and secure the empire. When Chou En-lai announced that his country could not permit the use of Korea as a springboard for the invasion of China, he expressed a Chinese policy of long standing: i.e., preventing Korea from falling into inimical hands (and China's original support of aggression may well have rested upon this consideration). Taiwan and Indochina policies are similarly part of the aggressive, nationalistic pattern. For, like Korea, these areas had belonged to the Chinese Empire and were separated from it by war only about 100 years ago or more recently. . . .

Chinese experience with Western imperialism has left a strong impression. Since before 1900, it has served as the main source of nationalist inspiration. For at least half a decade Chinese diplomacy was preoccupied with elimination of Western dominance. There was never much effort to make fine distinctions among the various Western powers according to the degree of their imperialism; otherwise the United States would have emerged with the cleanest record. As the strongest power in the world and therefore the only effective opponent to Chinese ambitions in Asia, in other words, for practical political reasons, the United States now is made to carry the onus of all Western imperialism of the past. By expediently identifying the United States with capitalism and imperialism, the Communist leaders can rally their people against this "enemy," make their people more receptive to their policies, arouse them against the Western world, and consolidate their regime.

For Communist purposes, making the United States China's greatest enemy was almost indispensable and the price was relatively small. The Communists were confronted, in 1949, by an inevitable choice between Russian imperialism in Manchuria and inner Asia and an American determination to stand by the Nationalists and prevent a Communist Chinese sweep across free Asia. Alone, China could not have realized her ambitions. She could hardly expect much aid from the United States, while the Soviet Union since 1945 had gradually added material assistance to her moral encouragement. When Mao Tse-tung decided to "lean to one side" (the Russian), he and his fellow leaders may have done so as a matter of course.

Yet the arguments they used to justify this step before the people indicate quite clearly that they had also calculated the interests involved, and that they expected very concrete returns from their friendship with the Soviet Union. On the other hand, the declaration of open hostility toward the United States has led to a struggle for power in the free parts of Asia which has predominantly influenced the political, economic and military policy of the United States in Asia.

When the United States abandoned hope, after 1947, that a strong Nationalist China could be used as a balance against the power of the Soviet Union in Asia, and turned to Japan instead, there prevailed the belief that China for some time to come would remain a power unable to affect significantly and actively the course of international events. In 1950, the American government announced that America's security required a defense perimeter passing from Alaska through the chain of islands off the China coast to the Philippines. Korea's fate was to be left to the United Nations. The colonial and independent states of Southeast and South Asia were to be immunized against communism by economic aid and, presumably, kept safe by their metropolitan powers.

The containment of Communist China was the basic goal of this strategy. The United States was obviously reluctant to become militarily committed in any area other than the perimeter. But the unexpectedly vigorous and aggressive Chinese foreign policy changed this reluctance into hesitant acquiescence when the United States needed the collaboration of some friendly powers in the Pacific for the success of her policy. The first extension of American commitments came in 1952 when a defense agreement was signed with the Philippines, Australia and New Zealand in return for their signatures on the Japanese Peace Treaty. While these nations were primarily concerned over the revival of Japan, the United States insisted upon the peace treaty and the accompanying defense agreement with Japan as a move to discourage Chinese aggression.

The growing success of the Communists in Southeast Asia destroyed American hopes that the colonial powers could cope with the guerillas. American military aid, especially to Indochina, increased, as did economic aid everywhere in Asia. The greater Chinese freedom of maneuver after the Korean war benefited the Communists in Indochina, leading to their victories there and to the Geneva Conference in 1954. Aware that the Chinese were not too weak to exploit Western weakness and conscious of great pressure from Australia, the United States decided to enter into a collective security agreement, SEATO, for southeast Asia. Thus the United States committed her power in Southeast Asia and closed the chain of collective defense arrangements around the Communist world, with India the only missing link among the important powers.

This evidence of American determination to fight, if necessary, presumably discouraged more outright Chinese aggression. (Except, significantly, in areas where the American commitment did not apply!) More important, China was given time to make mistakes. Chinese aggression in Tibet, India and other areas brought about a degree of disillusionment with communism that years of American information programs failed to produce. An opportunity has thus arisen for the free states of Asia to consolidate and strengthen themselves. But it is clear that in the foreseeable future, only American commitments in south and southeast Asia can succeed in keeping the area out of Communist control. This area turns out to be just one section of that vast Communist front stretching from the Elbe to the Pacific whose further advance neither the United States nor any other free power can tolerate.

The vastness of this front and the enormity of the power behind it have induced the wish in the West that somehow it might be broken up, preferably by a split between the Soviet Union and Communist China (although the increasing extremism of Peking has provoked second thoughts and the question has arisen whether it might not be a good thing for the world if a more moderate Moscow could keep its ally under control). Since both powers are totalitarian dictatorships, there is no certain way of knowing what the relations between them are. . . .

Since it is certain that both powers formulate their policies to suit their own interests, the safest way to guess the nature of their relations is to discover what they consider their interests to be and how these may conduce to cooperation or conflict. Within that framework, ideological affinity has its significance. But it would be risky to exaggerate this or even to assume that it could outweigh the reality of national interests. When the Chinese Communist theoreticians allowed for sovereignty of nations and its support by nationalism (called "proletarian patriotism") they allowed for the conduct of international relations according to the ambitions and practice of states over the past several hundred years.

Ideology may create sentimental bonds and a certain similarity in outlook and in interpretation of national interests. But it is only one of the factors shaping relations between China and the Soviet Union. And since neither of the two powers is engaged in abstract ideological crusade but is, rather, using ideology as one instrument of power, ideology may well become a cause of conflict. Indeed, the practice of interpreting Communist doctrine according to its political usefulness has led to more open differences between Moscow and Peking in the allegedly ideological sphere than in any other. The Russians and Chinese have disagreed on such matters as the possibility of "contradictions" between governors and governed in a Communist state; the need for and degree of dictatorship of the proletariat; the development of communes and the transition to communism; and, lately and especially, the possibility of peaceful co-existence between capitalist and socialist states.

In all these questions, China has taken an independent and, usually, a more fundamentalist and radical position. These differences can be explained as the result of individual tactics in the use of ideology for political purposes, internally and externally. In other words, although clothed in ideological terminology, these are political differences. The interests leading to these differences would, however, have to become very serious before the two parties would risk endangering the political usefulness of communism beyond the Communist bloc or the benefit which each tries to reap from close cooperation. . . .

The Soviet Union is interested in having on her borders a nation that is friendly and unable to challenge her security and hegemony. But since China interprets friendship according to the aid she can obtain to make her strong, Soviet and Chinese interests are fundamentally incompatible in the long run. Moscow must follow a difficult path, giving China enough aid to retain her good will and not so much as will make her a potential threat. That path is bound to end somewhere in the future. Where that point is will be decided by either China or the Soviet Union. . . .

It is in China's interest and also in the Soviet Union's interest to exploit, each for her own reasons, their cooperation and to leave undamaged the political usefulness of communism.

To the Chinese, the alliance with the Soviet Union has paid good dividends. Russian backing has enabled them to expand their influence aggressively in various parts of Asia. Russian aid in men and materials has been an indispensable factor in Chinese progress. It has, apparently, not been forthcoming in the desired quantities; yet, not a fraction of it could have been obtained from the West. In Manchuria, Sinkiang, Mongolia, where Russian and Chinese interests have traditionally clashed, the Chinese have been able to make some advances in restoring their influence.

This is part of the price the Soviet Union has to pay for Chinese friendship. But it may also have been the result of China's bargaining power which, at the moment, lies in her weakness rather than her strength. This power rests in the possibility that China might start a major war in which she would undoubtedly have less to lose than the Soviet Union or the United States. It may be this power which China is presently trying to apply to its maximum effect when she insists that peaceful co-existence with capitalist states is not possible. For the Soviet Union could not stay out of such a war; she would have to come to China's aid.

China also exerts pressure upon the Soviet Union by taking independent ideological positions, thereby not only creating precedents with political implications appealing to Russian satellites, but rivalling the Soviet Union as the "fatherland" of communism, in Asia, Africa and Europe. The respectful treatment Moscow granted China even in the days of Stalin indicates that the Russians have feared just such a development and have tried to avoid it.

Thus, the two most powerful nations in the world, the United States and the Soviet Union, are obliged to shape their foreign policies with due regard to the People's Republic of China. The Chinese government will presumably interpret this as an encouragement to continue its current course. To the Chinese people, this will be a matter of pride which enhances the value of the government in their eyes.

VI
The Korean War

1

Why War Came to Korea*

ROBERT T. OLIVER

Since the first armed clash between the Communist empire and the free world broke out in Korea, it seems pertinent to examine the question of why this relatively remote peninsula was selected as the area in which the cold war of subversion should be superseded by open and direct military attack. The reasons are many: some remote and some immediate; some obvious and some complex.

1. Traditionally and historically Korea occupies the heart of the strategic triangle of north Asia, with Siberia on one side, China on another, and Japan on the third. When Korea has been independent, north Asia has been at peace. When Korea has been held by a dominant military power, that same power has been able to subjugate all north Asia. The Mongol hordes first demonstrated this fact in the thirteenth century (being restrained then from conquering Japan only by just such a catastrophe to their fleet as happened to the Spanish Armada in the storm off England's coast in the sixteenth century). Hideyoshi, the great Japanese war lord, sought to conquer Korea in 1592–97, as a prelude to overrunning all Asia, and was beaten back through the invention of the first ironclad warship by the Korean Admiral Yi Soon-Sin. Japan and China fought over Korea's position in 1894–95. Then, in a crucial test of strength, Japan and Russia fought the war of 1904–05 to determine which should gain the strategic Korean peninsula. After Japan won, she was able to build rail lines and bases in Korea and proceed on to the conquest of Manchuria in 1931, the attack on China in 1937, and the descent on Pearl Harbor in 1941.

2. Russia has made possession of Korea a prime aim of its foreign policy for at least 75 years. In 1896, in 1903, and again in 1910 Russia and Japan engaged in secret negotiations regarding a possible division of Korea between

*From Current History, **19** (*September, 1950*), *139–143. Reprinted by permission of the* author and Current History.

them, along either the Thirty-eighth or Thirty-ninth Parallels. Prior to the Russo-Japanese War, Czar Nicholas II wrote to his foreign ministers, "Russia absolutely needs a port free and open throughout the whole year. This port must be located on the mainland (southeast Korea) and must certainly be connected with our possessions by a strip of land." Pursuing this same goal, Russia demanded admittance to Korea as part of its price for entering the war against Japan in August, 1945. This demand led to the "temporary" division of Korea along the Thirty-eighth Parallel, supposedly merely to permit disarming of Japanese troops north of that line by Russia and south of the line by United States troops.

3. Russia proceeded instantly to build a militarily and politically strong puppet regime in north Korea. She brought back to north Korea some 300,000 Koreans who had fled from Japanese tyranny (during the period 1905–45 while Japan ruled Korea) into Siberia, and who had there been communized. She also brought back another 2,000,000 who had fled into Manchuria and north China, and who there had allied themselves with Communist guerrillas in fighting troops. With this large nucleus, Russia established a Communist "People's Republic" and started building an army of upwards of 200,000 men. This army was equipped with tanks, artillery and planes, and some 100,000 of its troops were battle-hardened in warfare against the Nationalist forces in China. With a strict iron curtain around north Korea, Russia subjected the north Korean populace to five solid years of propaganda, along the basic line that "American imperialism was preventing the reunification of Korea for the purpose of maintaining a military base in south Korea." The fact that the United Nations voted in November, 1947, for an election in all Korea to reunite the country under a government of its own choice did not, of course, result in any qualification of this propaganda barrage. Consequently, the Soviets had in north Korea a dependable totalitarian puppet regime, with a strong army, well trained and equipped for battle, and indoctrinated to believe it was fighting for the reunification of its homeland.

4. In contrast to the north Korean strength, the Republic of Korea was militarily weak. This weakness was no accident, but was deliberately planned. United States policy in Korea consisted in part of "proving" to both Soviet Russia and the peoples of Asia that our government had no colonial or military designs of any sort upon south Korea. To the contrary, all we wished to do was withdraw at the earliest possible moment. For two and a half years, until September, 1947, the United States held south Korea under military occupation, refraining from building any Korean army and refusing to permit establishment of any Korean government, while we sought a joint agreement with Russia for withdrawal. This failing, the question was turned over to the United Nations. After the Republic of Korea was inaugurated, American policy again was to keep the Republic so weak that there would be no possibility of charges that we were attempting to build through it a

military base from which to attack Russia. The Republic was warned that any movement north of the Thirty-eighth Parallel, even to repel attacks, would lead instantly to a cessation of all American aid. The only weapons supplied to the army of the Republic were light arms sufficient to put down guerrilla uprisings within the country. Repeated pleas of President Syngman Rhee for tanks, artillery, and fighting planes were brushed aside. Thus, confronting the formidable fighting machine of north Korea was only an ill-armed force in south Korea. The last American troops (except for a 500-man military advisory force) were withdrawn on June 29, 1949.

5. The weakness of the position of the Republic of Korea was accentuated by official and unofficial indications from the United States that our government did not intend to defend the Republic. In January and February, 1950, Secretary Acheson informed Congressional committees that there was "no moral obligation" and "no commitment" to support Korea. Authoritative spokesmen made it clear that the American "defense line" in the Pacific ran down through the main islands of Japan, Okinawa, and the Philippines, thus leaving Korea outside. Underscoring this apparent fact was President Truman's decision in January of this year not to defend Formosa. To the Kremlin it must have appeared that the Republic of Korea was not only hopelessly weak militarily but also had been diplomatically abandoned.

6. Paradoxically, it was not only the weakness but also the strength of the Republic of Korea which led to the attack upon it. The Communist propaganda line in Asia has been that imperialistic, capitalistic democracy is dedicated to the enslavement of the masses for the benefit of a ruling class; whereas the people's democracy (communism) is dedicated to overthrowing the master class for the benefit of the farmers and workers. To this propaganda the remarkable democratic success achieved by the Republic of Korea was an effective and unanswerable refutation. The Republic of Korea, accordingly, had to be destroyed because it was (in Soviet opinion) intolerably successful. It was this success which led Paul Hoffman, Director of the E. C. A., in December, 1948, to call the Republic "a bastion of democracy in Asia;" and which led John Foster Dulles, in his speech on July 4, 1950, to explain the Communist attack by saying, "The society was so wholesome that it could not be overthrown from within."

The clearest fact in relation to the democratic–Communist struggle over Korea is that in five years of strenuous effort the Communists were not able to make any headway in winning over the 20 millions of south Koreans. Despite the mountainous terrain, they were not even able to stir up any considerable amount of guerrilla opposition to the government. Never did Communist guerrillas hold any large area in south Korea, as, for example, they were so notably able to do in Greece. The loyalty of the masses of south Koreans to their own elected democracy was never shaken. . . .

In summation, then, the reasonable presumption is that the Red army struck in force against the Republic of Korea for the following reasons: (1)

Korea is of great strategic military value in north Asia, providing a good base from which to launch an attack upon Japan; (2) Russian foreign policy long has aimed to secure possession of Korea; (3) the puppet regime in north Korea was militarily strong and well propagandized; (4) the Republic of Korea seemed too weak militarily to be able to resist an attack; (5) American authoritative statements indicated that we would not defend Korea; and (6) the success of democracy in south Korea constituted an intolerable refutation of the Communist propaganda line in Asia.

In view of American refusal to arm south Korea adequately and considering that our defense line excluded the Republic of Korea, why did President Truman so promptly and decisively order all-out American resistance to the Communist attack? The question mystified the Kremlin so much that its propaganda mills were silent for a full 36 hours after Truman's announcement. The answer lies in the nature of the attack itself and in the delicately balanced political and military position of all Asia.

The attack of June 25, 1950, will be recorded by historians as the great crystallizing event of these post-war years. This is the first time in its 30-year history that the Communist empire has deliberately challenged the free world by an armed assault. Since the Republic of Korea had been established under United Nations auspices, it was peculiarly a ward of the democratic world and the attack could only be interpreted as a decisive test of the ability and will of the democracies to unite in resistance to armed aggression. The shock caused by the attack is illustrated by the fact that within 24 hours after it occurred the Security Council of the United Nations was able to convene and its members already had instructions from their governments as to how to vote. The Communist empire (by the same kind of miscalculation that marked the Japanese and Nazi dictatorships) had issued a challenge which could not be ignored.

Aside from the world-wide implications of this appeal to force, the effect in Asia was crucial. The United States has been exercising moral suasion upon the peoples of Asia to resist communism and accept democracy. The big unanswered question was the degree to which the United States would help them to fend off communism if a crisis arose. The issuance of the White Paper on China, and the subsequent collapse of the Nationalist Government, was a disturbing indication to Asian peoples that perhaps the United States would resist Communist aggression only with complaints and excuses. When 11 members of Congress traveled through the Far East in October and November, 1949, they found political leaders everywhere asking them, "What will the United States do about Korea?" In Asian eyes, the United States was clearly committed to support the Republic of Korea, and if we had not done so, faith in our willingness or ability to check Communist expansion would have dissolved. The defense of Korea became directly a defense of democracy in all Asia and indirectly a defense of freedom all over the world. Faced with such conditions, the Joint Chiefs of Staff and the

State Department could not but advise President Truman that this was the time and place for a decisive stand. . . .

2

The U.S.S.R. Restates its Attitude on Korea*

DEPARTMENT OF PUBLIC INFORMATION, UNITED NATIONS

At the request of Yakov Malik, permanent representative of the U. S. S. R. to the United Nations, a statement made on July 4 by Andrei Gromyko, Deputy Foreign Minister of his Government, has been circulated as an official document of the Security Council.

"The events now taking place in Korea broke out on June 25 as the result of a provocative attack by the troops of the South Korean authorities on the frontier areas of the Korean People's Democratic Republic," Mr. Gromyko's statement said. "This attack was the outcome of a premeditated plan. From time to time, both Syngman Rhee himself and other representatives of the South Korean authorities had blurted out the fact that the South Korean Syngman Rhee clique had such a plan."

Such statements could have been made only because they felt they had American support, Mr. Gromyko continued. Only a few days before the Korean conflict began, Secretary of Defence Louis Johnson, General Omar Bradley, Chief of Staff of the United States Armed Forces, and John Foster Dulles, State Department adviser, arrived in Japan and had special conferences with General Douglas MacArthur. Afterwards, Mr. Dulles went to South Korea and visited the frontier areas along the thirty-eighth parallel. On June 19, only a week before events in Korea, Mr. Dulles declared in the "so-called 'National Assembly' of South Korea" that the United States was ready to give all necessary moral and material support to South Korea, which was fighting against Communism.

"*Aggressive plans in Korea*"   When events did not develop in favor of the South Korean authorities, when it became clear that the "terrorist regime of Syngman Rhee" was collapsing, the United States resorted to open intervention. "Thereby, the United States Government went over from a policy of preparing aggression to outright acts of aggression and embarked on a course of open intervention in Korea's domestic affairs, on a course of armed interven-

From United Nations Bulletin, **9** (*August 1, 1950*), *98–99.*

tion. Having taken this course, the United States Government violated peace, demonstrating thereby that, far from seeking to consolidate peace, it is on the contrary an enemy of peace."

The United States, continued Mr. Gromyko, is disclosing its aggressive plans in Korea only step by step—from shipment of war materials to operations by the United States Air Force against Pyongyang and other North Korean cities. "All this goes to show that the United States Government is drawing the United States more and more into war, but, compelled to reckon with the unwillingness of the American people to be involved in a new military venture, it is gradually impelling the country step by step towards open war."

"Charter violated"   The United States, said Mr. Gromyko, "tries to justify armed intervention against Korea by alleging that it has been undertaken on the authorization of the Security Council. The falsity of such an allegation strikes the eye. . . . It is known that the United States Government had started armed intervention in Korea before the convening of the Security Council on June 27, without taking into consideration what decision the Security Council might take. Thus the United States Government confronted the United Nations organization with a *fait accompli*, with a violation of peace. The Security Council merely rubber-stamped and back-dated the resolution proposed by the United States Government, approving the aggressive actions undertaken by that Government."

Charter violation charged   Furthermore, the American resolution was adopted in violation of the Charter, which stipulates that all Security Council decisions must be adopted by not less than seven affirmative votes. The American resolution was adopted by only six votes, the seventh being that of the "Kuomintangite Tsiang Ting-Fu, who unlawfully occupies China's seat in the Security Council." Second, the decision was taken in the absence of two permanent members, the U. S. S. R. and China, and the Charter provides that all major decisions in the Council must have the concurring votes of the five permanent members. This, then, deprived the resolution of June 27 "of any legal force."

In another respect, the Security Council decision violated a most important principle of the Charter, which "directly forbids the intervention of the United Nations organization in the domestic affairs of any state, when it is a matter of conflict between two groups of one state."

The "illegal" resolution of June 27, adopted under United States pressure, showed that the Council was "acting not as a body which is charged with the main responsibility for the maintenance of peace, but as a tool utilized by the ruling circles of the United States for the unleashing of war."

If the Council had "valued the cause of peace," said Mr. Gromyko, "it should have attempted to reconcile the fighting sides in Korea before it adopted such a scandalous resolution. Only the Security Council and the

United Nations Secretary-General could have done this. However, they did not make such an attempt, evidently knowing that such peaceful action contradicts the aggressor's plans."

Mr. Gromyko charged that the Secretary-General had played "an unseemly role." Far from fulfilling his direct duties to observe the exact fulfillment of the Charter, Mr. Lie had "obsequiously helped a gross violation of the Charter on the part of the United States Government and other members of the Security Council."

"Real American aim" President Truman had announced on June 29 that American military action in Korea was only "police action" in support of the United Nations and against a "group of bandits" from North Korea. It was well known, Mr. Gromyko continued, that an "aggressor usually resorts to this or that method of camouflaging his actions." Even the naive will not believe that General MacArthur with Flying Fortresses and jet planes, cruisers and aircraft carriers was carrying out "police action against bandits." Mr. Gromyko also said that the People's liberation army of China was described as bandits but it turned out eventually that the "bandits" constituted the Chinese people and represented the "fundamental national interests of China."

The real aims of American armed intervention in Korea, he declared, were "to deprive Korea of its national independence, to prevent the formation of a united democratic Korean State, and forcibly to establish in Korea an anti-popular regime which would allow the ruling circles of the United States to convert the country into their colony and use Korean territory as a military and strategic springboard in the Far East."

"Aggression against China" The action of President Truman in ordering the American Navy "to prevent an attack on Formosa," taken at the time he ordered armed forces, "to attack Korea," constituted "outright aggression against China" and was a "gross violation of the Cairo and Potsdam international agreements establishing Formosa as part of Chinese territory, agreements which bear the signature of the United States Government." It also violated President Truman's statement of January 5 "to the effect that the Americans would not intervene in the affairs of Formosa."

This, together with President Truman's instructions that American armed forces be increased in the Philippines and that "so-called 'military assistance'" to France in Indo-China be accelerated, showed that the United States Government was "assuming the role of gendarme of the peoples of Asia," Mr. Gromyko declared. It had "gone over from a policy of preparing aggression to direct acts of aggression simultaneously in a whole number of countries in Asia. Thereby, the Government of the United States has trampled underfoot its obligations to the United Nations in strengthening peace throughout the world, and has acted as a violator of peace."

There were many examples of outside intervention to throttle the will of a people for national unity and democratic rights—in the American Civil War and the Russian Revolution—but it was known how these interventionist adventures ended.

The Soviet Government, Mr. Gromyko concluded, "invariably adheres to a policy of strengthening peace throughout the world and to its traditional principle of non-interference in the domestic affairs of other states. The Soviet Government considers that the Koreans have the same right to arrange at their own discretion their internal affairs in the matter of the unification of South and North Korea into a single national state as the North Americans held and exercised in the '60s of the last century when they united the North and South of America into a single national state.

"It follows from the aforesaid that the Government of the United States of America has committed a hostile act against the peace, and that it bears the responsibility for the consequences of the armed aggression undertaken by it.

"The United Nations organization will fulfil its obligations to maintain peace only if the Security Council demands the unconditional cessation of American military intervention and the immediate withdrawal of American armed forces from Korea."

3

Collective Security and the War in Korea*

ARNOLD WOLFERS

The action taken by the United Nations in 1950 to halt the attack on South Korea has been heralded as the first experiment in collective security. The implication is that a radical break with the traditional foreign policy of nations has occurred; power politics, we are told, have been replaced by police action of the world community. It is quite likely that many who suffered in the Korean War on our side have been comforted by the thought that they have served the cause of law enforcement by community action, though others who believed that no vital interests of their country were at stake may have found the ordeal harder to bear. Whatever the emotional reaction, it is necessary to investigate dispassionately whether in fact a turning point in world politics was reached when the United Nations flag was unfurled in Korea. . . .

The attack by the North Koreans occurred on June 25. On the same day,

*From The Yale Review, **43** (*June, 1954*), *481–494. Reprinted by permission of the author.*

in the absence of the Soviet delegate, the Security Council determined that a breach of the peace had occurred. It called upon North Korea to withdraw its forces and proceeded to invite its members "to render every assistance to the United Nations in execution of this resolution." Some hours prior to the second meeting of the Council, on June 27, the United States Government announced that it had ordered American air and sea forces to go to the assistance of South Korea for the specific purpose of executing the June 25 resolution of the Security Council. If this was not enough to qualify American intervention as United Nations action, the Security Council identified itself with the action of the United States by voting on the same day that urgent military measures were required. The members were now called upon to furnish assistance of the kind necessary to repel the attack. From then on, the action of the United States and its associates was carried forward in the name of the United Nations, under the United Nations flag, and under a unified United Nations command set up by the United States in accordance with a resolution of the Security Council. Limited to recommendations, the United Nations continued to put what little pressure it could on its members to get them to participate or to make larger contributions; at the same time it sought to influence the United Nations command in the conduct and termination of the war, acting in this respect as a restraining factor.

Aside from this rather marginal though not unimportant role played by the United Nations itself, the character of the action in Korea must be judged by the decisions and acts of the United States and its associates. It would seem permissible, in fact, to concentrate on the conduct of the United States, because the other nations which made contributions to the defense of South Korea might conceivably have done so as friends and allies of the United States, whether this country was acting traditionally in what it considered to be its national interest and that of its friends or was conducting police action on the principle of collective security.

It is not a simple matter to discover whether or not United States intervention in Korea qualifies as collective security in the restricted sense in which the term is used here. The motivations of the chief architects of the policy are not decisive. The devotion of men like Mr. Truman and Mr. Acheson to the idea of collective security as they conceived it is not in doubt, any more than their desire to prevent the United Nations from suffering the same dismal fate which befell the League of Nations at the time of Italy's aggression against Ethiopia.

What is being asked is whether the United States, even if it believed itself to be engaging in police action in conformity with the concept of collective security, did in fact break with traditional national defense policy by accepting the kind of risks which such a break presupposes. If the aggressor had been South Korea rather than North Korea, the answer could not be in doubt. To take up arms against South Korea would have meant siding with this country's chief national enemy, the Soviet bloc, and strengthening the Com-

munist countries at the expense of a country on which the United States
could have relied as an ally in the Cold War. No more striking proof could
have been given of unqualified American support for police action against
any aggressor anywhere. But, the aggressor was Communist North Korea
backed by the Soviet Union. It becomes necessary therefore to investigate
how intervention in these circumstances looked from the point of view of
American security interests as interpreted in Washington at the time.

Speaking negatively first, the United States was obviously not taking up
arms against a friend or ally. On the contrary, it was setting out to stop
expansion by the Soviet bloc, thus serving what had long been proclaimed to
be the major goal of American foreign policy. It might be argued, however,
that in extending the "containment" policy to Korea, the United States
was diverting military power from Europe, which was considered the chief
danger area. As the war proceeded, and American involvement exceeded
all early expectations, much fear of such diversion was in fact expressed in
Europe. But in this country, the opinion continued to prevail that in terms of
the Cold War it would have been much more dangerous even for Europe if
Communist aggression had gone unpunished in Asia. Moreover, powerful
groups in Congress had long pressed for a stronger stand against Communism in Asia. Thus while the sacrifices in men and resources, borne by the
American people in the course of the Korean War, were far in excess of
even the most pessimistic initial expectations, they did not include the sacrifice or diversion of defensive military power from the tasks of the Cold War.
Instead, the rearmament effort provoked by Communist aggression in
Korea led to a multiplication of this power.

The fact that no sacrifice in terms of national protection against a major
enemy was involved is not enough, however, to explain why this country
should have decided to resort to military force. Except for a radical break with
tradition, nations are not expected to take up arms unless there are interests
which they consider vital at stake. Accordingly, the apparent absence of any
vital American interest in South Korea made it seem as if devotion to collective security alone could have induced the United States to intervene.
It was known that our civilian and military leaders did not consider the
defense of the 38th Parallel or the preservation of a free South Korea a
matter of vital strategic importance to this country, despite the fact that
loss of the area to the Communists would have rendered Japan more vulnerable to attack. The Joint Chiefs of Staff had reached this decision at the time
American troops were withdrawn from the territory of the Republic of Korea,
long before Secretary Acheson made his famous "perimeter" speech. It is
also true that the United States was not bound by any treaty of alliance to
go to the assistance of South Korea. However, this lack of what might be
called a local strategic interest and the absence of any specific commitment to
assist South Korea, other than that implied in the United Nations Charter,
do not suffice to prove that vital interests were not at stake. The fact is that

one can discern a threefold American interest of exactly the kind which, thinking along the lines of traditional power politics, governments would normally consider serious enough to justify military action or even to make it imperative.

In the first place, according to the views prevailing in both political parties at the time of the North Korean attack, any further expansion in any direction on the part of the Soviet bloc constituted a threat to American security. The "containment" policy was under attack not because it went too far in this respect but because it was thought too negative. As a matter of established policy, then, no area adjoining the Soviet Empire was held to be strategically nonvital; any addition to the territory behind the Iron Curtain would threaten to upset an already precarious world balance of power.

In the second place, the United States was vitally interested in proving to its European Allies that they could rely on American military assistance in case of a Soviet attack. NATO, this country's main bulwark against the threat from the East, was weakened by European fears of a resurgence of isolationism in this country. It was strongly felt, therefore, particularly by Secretary Acheson, that if South Korea were left at the mercy of the attacker, all of Russia's weak neighbors—and there were none but weak neighbors—would lose what confidence they had gradually gained that this country meant business when it promised to prevent further Soviet conquest.

As if this were not enough, there was a third reason for this country to be most seriously interested in not allowing a challenge by its number-one enemy to go without military response. The United States was engaged in a vast and strenuous effort to unite the entire free world in a common effort of defense against the Soviet and Communist menace. From most countries, particularly in Asia, it had not succeeded in obtaining commitments of mutual assistance of the kind customarily laid down in treaties of bilateral or multilateral alliance. Therefore, all other non-Communist countries were committed to common defense against Communist aggression only if they could be made to accept the United Nations Charter as such a commitment. Consequently, from the point of view of American security policy, it was of paramount importance that the United Nations be made to serve as a substitute for a formal alliance of the free world. If there was any chance of achieving this result—and subsequent events showed how slim the chance was—it could only be done by demonstrating that under the Charter the United States considered itself committed to take up arms against the North Korean aggressor.

part Two

Cautious Coexistence

INTRODUCTION

THE DEATH OF Stalin in March, 1953, with its world-wide impact and implications, did not necessarily alter the fundamental goals of the Soviet state, but it led to the change of tactics which opened the era of "peaceful coexistence" in the Cold War. The new Kremlin leaders responded favorably to President Eisenhower's call for "the conclusion of an honorable armistice in Korea," which was expeditiously completed in July, 1953.

However, the Korean Armistice did not bring tranquility to the Far East. Communist China, whose "volunteer" troops had been fighting in Korea, could now accelerate moral, material, and military assistance to the Communist-led Viet Minh movement, which was fighting against the French in Indochina under Ho Chi Minh.

With the decisive defeat at Dien Bien Phu and with no hope of securing positive American military aid, the French government decided to salvage the situation by negotiated settlements. At the same time, Ho Chi Minh was persuaded to settle for a limited victory by Moscow and Peking leaders, who were especially anxious to avoid the danger of a direct military nuclear confrontation with the United States. Consequently, delegates from nine nations[1] met in Geneva and worked out armistice settlements for Indochina.

The Geneva Accord provided, among other things, for (1) the division of Vietnam into two zones at the 17th parallel, (2) general elections to be held in Vietnam in July, 1956, and (3) French withdrawal of "its troops from the territory of Cambodia, Laos, and Vietnam at the request of the Governments concerned."

Neither the United States nor South Vietnam gave assent to the final declaration at Geneva. Thus, although it marked temporarily the end of

---

[1]Cambodia, the Democratic Republic of Vietnam, France, Laos, the People's Republic of China, the State of Vietnam (South Vietnam), the USSR., the United Kingdom, and the United States of America.

the fighting phase of the Vietnam conflict, it failed to establish an adequate basis for a permanent settlement.

The Geneva Agreement was generally regarded as a diplomatic victory for the Communists; if so, it was by implication a diplomatic defeat for the West, especially the United States. In an effort to counterbalance the new situation and "to strengthen the fabric of peace and freedom," the United States initiated the formation of the Southeast Asia Treaty Organization (SEATO),[2] which was designed to contain the expansion of Communism as spearheaded by the People's Republic of China.

In contrast to the flexible Soviet approaches to such Cold War issues as the Austrian State Treaty and the convening of the summit conference in 1955, Communist China went on to claim the right to "liberate" Formosa, creating an international crisis over that region.

One of the key provisions of the Shimonoseki Treaty, which terminated the Sino-Japanese War of 1894–1895, stipulated that "China cedes to Japan in perpetuity and full sovereignty . . . the island of Formosa . . . [and] the Pescadores Group." For the following 50 years Formosa (Taiwan) and its adjacent islands were ruled by the Japanese as an integral part of their territories and were subject to their policy of assimilation, which proved only partially successful.

In November, 1943, during World War II, the three Allied leaders— President Roosevelt of the United States, Prime Minister Churchill of Great Britain, and Generalissimo Chiang Kai-shek of China—issued a joint communiqué in Cairo proclaiming that "all the territories Japan has stolen from the Chinese, such as Manchuria, Formosa, and the Pescadores, shall be restored to the Republic of China."[3] This policy declaration un- equivocally laid the foundation for the postwar disposition of Formosa.[4]

After the surrender of Japan in August, 1945, Formosa reverted to China and was ruled by a governor appointed by the Nanking government. Then in December, 1949, in the face of the triumphant rise of the Chinese Com- munists, Chiang Kai-shek retreated to Formosa with the remnants of his government and armies who had survived the Communist onslaught. At this time, Formosa was grossly neglected by United States officials. Secretary of State Dean Acheson stated in the "China White Paper" that the tragic fall of the Nationalists was the product of internal Chinese forces which the United States had tried to influence without success. Therefore, no additional military aid to Chiang Kai-shek was authorized because it would prove futile. President Truman, in January, 1950, declared that the United States had no intention of converting Formosa into an American base of military operations or of pursuing a policy which might result in American entanglement in the Chinese civil war.

[2]Formed in September, 1954, with eight signatories—Australia, France, New Zealand, Pakistan, the Philippines, Thailand, the United Kingdom, and the United States of America.

[3]*Department of State Bulletin*, **9** (December 4, 1943), 393.

[4]Article 2(b) of the 1951 Treaty of Peace with Japan states that "Japan renounces all right, title, and claim to Formosa and the Pescadores."

The outbreak of hostilities in Korea decidedly changed the course of the United States's Formosa policy. President Truman immediately ordered the United States Seventh Fleet to the Taiwan (Formosa) Strait, to protect the Chiang Kai-shek government against any attack by the Chinese Communists but at the same time to prevent Chiang from attempting to carry out his avowed reconquest of the mainland. In addition, the United States resumed active assistance, economic as well as military, to the Nationalist government. Furthermore, the United States sponsored the United Nations resolution branding the Chinese Communist regime as an "aggressor" in Korea, and pursued the dual policy of denying recognition of the Peking regime and opposing its seating in the United Nations. Communist China echoed with the acrimonious charge that the United States, under the dictates of its "imperialist design" in the Far East, was committing an act of aggression in Korea and Formosa.

As the Korean War drew to a close with the negotiated armistice, the Chinese Communists began to demonstrate accelerated belligerency toward the Nationalist-held islands of Formosa and the Pescadores, which they vowed to "liberate" from the "Chiang clique." From the standpoint of Peking, Communist occupation of Formosa with the total elimination of the Chiang regime was a vital necessity for achieving the complete success of the Chinese Communist Revolution. So long as Formosa remained as a bastion of Free China, so long as Chiang Kai-shek stood as the symbol of and the hope for an eventual "return" to the mainland, and so long as the "reactionaries" and the "counterrevolutionaries" within China kept dreaming of a Nationalist recapture of their "lost" territories, the Communist Revolution in China could not be regarded as total, complete, and consummate. The Communist leaders regarded free Formosa, where Chiang's 600,000 troops were training and on constant alert, as "a bone in the throat."

Beginning in September, 1954, the Chinese Communists' determination to "liberate" Formosa took the form of artillery bombardments upon the islands of Quemoy, six miles off the port of Amoy, and Matsu, less than ten miles from the China coast. The shelling appeared to be a prelude to a full-scale assault on Formosa. With a view to thwarting the Communist design and in order to strengthen the American security system in the Pacific, the United States concluded a mutual defense treaty with the Republic of China in December, 1954. The treaty provided:

> Each Party recognizes that an armed attack in the West Pacific area on the territories of either of the Parties would be dangerous to its own peace and safety and declares that it would act to meet the common dangers in accordance with its constitutional process. . . . [T]he terms "territorial" and "territories" shall mean in respect to the Republic of China, Taiwan and Pescadores. . . .[5]

[5]U. S. Department of State, *United States Treaties and Other International Agreements* (Washington, D.C.: U.S. Government Printing Office, 1955), Vol. 6, Part 1, pp. 435–438.

This treaty did not specifically mention Quemoy and Matsu. Hence, it was a moot question whether or not the United States would be obliged to aid Chiang Kai-shek in his defense of these offshore islands in the event of a Communist attack. In clarifying this point, the Congressional joint resolution adopted in January, 1955, stated:

> ... That the President of the United States be and he hereby is authorized to employ the Armed Forces of the United States as he deems necessary for the specific purpose of securing and protecting Formosa and the Pescadores against armed attack, this authority to include the securing and protection of *such related positions and territories* of that area now in friendly hands and the taking of such other measures as he judges to be required or appropriate in assuring the defense of Formosa and the Pescadores.[6]

Thus the United States made it clear that a Communist invasion of these islands could not be a limited operation. Secretary of State John Foster Dulles hinted that the Chinese mainland might be bombed if the Communists launched an attack on Quemoy. United States naval escorts were furnished to Nationalist convoys to Quemoy, and a portion of the Pacific Fleet rushed to the China Sea. There was an anxious moment when an outbreak of hostilities between the United States and the People's Republic of China seemed possible. America's European allies were perplexed and appalled by the United States's attitude, which considered the offshore islands as a test case to demonstrate the free world's courage and determination to use force in deterring Communist aggression, even at the risk of war.

In April, 1955, at the 29-nation Afro-Asian Conference held at Bandung, Indonesia, Premier Chou En-lai of Communist China offered to negotiate with the United States over Formosa to lessen international tensions. For more than three years, negotiations between the two countries were quietly carried out at Warsaw through their respective ambassadors, but no agreement was reached.

Only with the sudden reversal of American policy in the fall of 1958, and the corresponding softening of Communist "hard-line" tactics, was the crisis over the Taiwan Strait and the offshore islands considerably dissipated. Yet it remained as one of the permanent features of the Sino-American antagonism.

While the Formosan crisis remained unsettled in the Far East, the Suez Canal crisis erupted in the Middle East.

The Suez Canal is a 100-mile-long man-made waterway connecting Port Said on the Mediterranean Sea with Suez on the Red Sea. It shortens the shipping distance between Europe and the East by avoiding the long sea passage around the Cape of Good Hope. In 1854, the Viceroy of Egypt, Mohammed Said, granted Ferdinand de Lesseps of France a 99-year concession authorizing the formation of a company to build a navigable channel

---

[6]*Department of State Bulletin,* **32** (February 7, 1955), 213. Italics are mine.

across the isthmus of Suez. Two years later the Second Act of Concession was signed by Said, and in November, 1869, the Canal was opened.

At first Great Britain was opposed to the Canal, both from fear of French penetrations in the Middle East and from uncertainty about the safety of communications with her possessions in India and the Far East. But when Benjamin Disraeli became Prime Minister, he pursued a positive policy on Suez. Realizing the strategic importance and the commercial advantages associated with British control of the Canal, he purchased, in 1875, nearly 50 per cent of the total shares of Suez Canal stock for $4 million from the Egyptian Khedive.[7] This astute move on the part of Disraeli safeguarded Britain's route to India, removed any possible threat to her naval supremacy in the Mediterranean, and at the same time inexorably drew Britain into the domestic and international politics of the Middle Eastern nations.

In 1888, the Constantinople Convention was drawn up and signed by nine European Powers; in subsequent years it was adhered to by most of the nations of the world. This convention established a system of international operation of the Canal whereby it was to be open to all vessels in times of both peace and war.

When Turkey entered World War I on the side of the Central Powers, Egypt became a British protectorate, with British troops stationed on Egyptian soil. This policy continued even after the signing of the Treaty of Versailles. The basic status of the Canal remained unchanged through the years despite the political turbulence in Egypt, World War II, the Arab–Israeli conflict, and the Egyptian Revolution of 1952.

In 1956, Great Britain removed her troops in accordance with the Anglo-Egyptian Suez Canal Base Agreement of October 19, 1954. By this time Egypt had the will, ability, and ambition to change the status of the Suez Canal to its own advantage and interest through nationalization. In the midst of the multiplicity of Middle East tensions, only one incendiary move was needed to precipitate this ambition into action; that move was the United States's withdrawal of its pledge to offer $56 million in economic aid to the Aswan Dam project, a decision based on the report that the Soviet Union was planning to extend loans to help with the dam. Great Britain also cancelled its promise of $14 million financial support, and the International Bank for Reconstruction and Development suspended its $200 million assistance loan. Thus, President Nasser of the United Arab Republic was given "justification" to seize the Suez Canal with the intent of using the revenue from its operation to finance the Aswan Dam project.

In spite of Nasser's pledge to guarantee the right of passage of all ships, except Israel's, through the Canal, Great Britain and France had little trust in his words. They feared that Nasser would use the Canal as an instrument of political blackmail. Moreover, they felt that if Nasser could

[7]Winston S. Churchill, *The Great Democracies* (New York: Dodd, Mead & Co., 1958), pp. 226–227.

challenge the West with impunity, Western influence and prestige would be seriously damaged. Therefore, Britain and France were determined to confront Nasser and to demand that the Canal be placed under international control. Nasser refused. Against this background, Great Britain, France, and Israel invaded Egypt without consulting the United States.

On October 29, 1956, Israeli forces invaded the Sinai Peninsula and drove west toward the Canal. Great Britain and France then demanded that all belligerent troops withdraw to a distance of ten miles from the Canal and asked Egypt to agree to a temporary Anglo-French occupation of the Canal Zone. Nasser once again refused. Two days later British planes began bombing Egyptian bases, followed by the landing of British and French ground forces on Egyptian territory.

Although the United States rejected the Soviet proposal for joint Soviet–American military intervention, Washington threatened to cut off needed petroleum supplies to Britain if the latter continued its attack on Egypt. Faced with the determined opposition of the United States to the Suez adventure, coupled with severe criticism by the United Nations, the Afro-Asian countries, and the Commonwealth, the British Government had little choice but to accept a cease-fire. France and Israel had no alternative but to follow suit. By early November, 1956, most of the fighting had ended.

Meanwhile, the United Nations, through the General Assembly, decided to undertake two specific duties: to police the troubled area with its emergency international forces and to make immediate arrangements to clear the Suez Canal. In an emergency session in November, 1956, the General Assembly passed a resolution calling for a cease-fire and the withdrawal of the invading forces from Egypt. The General Assembly further voted to create International United Nations Command Forces to supervise the withdrawal and to patrol the Israeli–Egyptian frontier. Britain, France, and Israel agreed to evacuate as soon as United Nations forces could occupy the territory adequately and effectively.

The United Nations Emergency Forces arrived on November 15, 1956, and as the troops were augmented, the British, French, and Israeli forces progressively withdrew. The clearance of the Canal began in January, 1957, and three months later the Egyptian government reported to the Secretary-General that the Canal was open for operations.

The following conclusions may be drawn from the Suez crisis: First, the intervention of the United Nations and the United States in a rare collaboration with the Soviet Union shortened the hostilities and contributed materially to a negotiated settlement of the crisis. Second, the Suez crisis resulted in the eclipse of British and French power in the Middle East, the ascendancy of Arab nationalism, the consolidation of Moscow–Cairo cooperation, and the increase of Nasser's prestige and influence in the Arab world. Finally, the Suez invasion overshadowed the importance and seriousness of the 1956 Hungarian Revolt, which was crushed by Soviet armed forces.

The Hungarian Revolt broke out concurrently with the Suez conflict. It constituted one of the serious crises which compelled the Soviet Union to use armed forces to maintain the *status quo* in Eastern Europe.

Following the "de-Stalinization" announcement in 1956, there was a period of controlled relaxation in Soviet domestic and foreign policy known as the "thraw." Internally, it introduced a moderate program of "liberation" in the satellites, and externally, it could be referred to as a *de-icing* of the Cold War.

The thaw released the anti-Soviet, nationalistic sentiments of the East European people and resulted in massive uprisings against Soviet rule. In June, 1956, riots erupted in Poznan, Poland. Realizing the gravity of the situation, the Kremlin made concessions by permitting the ouster of many known Stalinists from the Central Committee of the Polish United Workers' (Communist) Party and the reinstatement on the committee of Wladyslav Gomulka. On October 21, Gomulka, who had been imprisoned for several years during the Stalinist regime as a Titoist, was elected First Secretary of the Party. Soviet leaders agreed not to interfere in Polish internal affairs and to honor Poland's sovereignty and independence.

In Hungary, however, events took a tragic course. On October 23, 1956, peaceful street demonstrations in Budapest, organized by university students in support of the Polish people, turned into a full-scale revolt as the Hungarian security police (AVH) opened fire on the demonstrators. Thousands of workers and citizens instantly joined forces with the student fighters, and a violent revolt of the classic type exploded, spreading rapidly throughout the country.

The following day Soviet armored columns joined the battle on the side of the AVH troops, but the Hungarian army refused to suppress the revolutionists and most of its men supported the rebel cause. The Soviets claimed that their decision to intervene was made on the basis of a request by the Hungarian authorities to help quell the uprising. It was believed that the probable request for Soviet aid was made by either Premier Hegedus, Imre Nagy's predecessor, or Erno Gero, First Secretary of the Hungarian Communist Party. The question of a request was of minor importance. The Soviet Union attempted to justify its unilateral military intervention, but in fact the same decision would have been made in Moscow regardless of what the Hungarian officials might have done.[8]

The Soviet action "restored" order momentarily, but it intensified public hatred not only against the Soviets but also against the AVH and the Hegedus–Gero leadership for their role as "Soviet lackeys." Hegedus was removed from his post, and Imre Nagy became the new Premier. Gero's

[8]United Nations, *Report of the Special Committee on the Problem of Hungary*, General Assembly, Official Records: Eleventh Session, Supplementary No. 18 (A/3592), New York, 1957.

position also became untenable; he was dismissed as First Secretary of the Party and was replaced by Janos Kadar, a supporter of Nagy.

On October 27, Premier Nagy reorganized the government to include some non-Communists and began a number of other reforms. Within a few days Soviet troops withdrew from Budapest. Nagy appeared to be in control of a successful popular revolution which was believed to have culminated in complete national independence. On November 1, Premier Nagy notified U. N. Secretary-General Hammarskjold of Hungary's repudiation of the Warsaw Pact and its intended adherence to neutrality. Nagy requested the Secretary-General to place the Hungarian issue on the U. N. agenda and "to call on the Great Powers to recognize Hungary's neutrality."

The defection of a "fraternal socialist state" to the neutral column was a severe blow to Soviet power and prestige. Suddenly, at dawn on November 4, Soviet tanks and troops roared into Budapest. Premier Nagy addressed the nation over the radio: "Today at daybreak Soviet troops attacked our capital with the obvious intention of overthrowing the legal Hungarian democratic government. Our troops are in combat."[9]

Meanwhile, the Soviets had installed a new Hungarian regime under the leadership of Janos Kadar, who had remained until then in the Nagy Cabinet. Kadar had "requested" the Soviet Army to help "in smashing the sinister forces of reaction and restoring order and calm in the country."

The unequal battle between the Soviet mechanized troops and the Hungarian "freedom fighters"—which included "the whole population of Budapest," as the U. N. report put it—ended in a Soviet "victory." *Pravda* reported: "The government of Imre Nagy, which cleared the road for the reactionary forces of the counterrevolution, has disintegrated and ceased to exist."[10]

In the evening of that fatal day, Imre Nagy and others sought and found asylum in the Yugoslav Embassy. Negotiations were conducted among the parties concerned regarding the fate of the refugees, and on November 22 the group left the Yugoslav Embassy under a safe-conduct from Kadar, only to be seized by Soviet troops. Nagy was later executed by the Soviets.

In the course of the Hungarian revolution, thousands of men, women, and children were killed and tens of thousands fled across the border in a mass exodus. The Hungarians lost their revolution "because of the Soviet armed intervention and because no support was forthcoming for them from abroad."

The only source of any meaningful physical support on which the Hungarian patriots could have counted was the United States. American officials had been talking recklessly about liberating the captive peoples and rolling back the Communists. But the United States was restrained from taking positive action because: (1) it was engrossed in the last days

[9]*Ibid.*, p. 45.
[10]*Pravda,* November 5, 1956.

of the 1956 presidential campaign; (2) the United States, as well as the United Nations, was immersed in the Suez crisis, which was a godsend for the Soviet Union in diverting world attention from Hungary; and (3) most important of all, the United States realized that America's military intervention in Eastern Europe, where vital interests of the Soviet Union were centered, would mean a world war. Hungarian aspirations for liberation and independence had to be sacrificed in the light of the grave consequences of a U. S.–Soviet military confrontation.

In the aftermath of the Suez and Hungarian crises, the political instability and turbulence in the Middle East was further rocked by the unceasing waves of the Cold War.

Besides the Suez Canal crisis and the ever-present Communist threat, other vexing problems in the Middle East prior to 1957 included: (1) the Arab–Israeli feud, (2) the fate of the Arab refugees, (3) the surge of Arab nationalism, (4) the Arab denouncement of the Baghdad Pact,[11] and (5) the Soviet design to expand its influence in the Middle East and Africa.

During and after the Suez crisis, in contrast to the rapid decline of British and French influence in the Middle East, Soviet prestige and dominance rose spectacularly in the Arab world. The Soviets sent military supplies to Egypt to rehabilitate its armed forces which had been badly depleted, and pledged to help build the Aswan Dam. They also shipped both military and industrial equipment to Syria.

Confronted with the accelerated Soviet penetration in the area, the United States, hoping to salvage what was left of Western influence and desiring to maintain a reasonable power equilibrium, decided to clarify its objectives in the Middle East and give a clear warning to the Soviets. In November, 1956, the United States reassured the member nations of the Baghdad Pact that a threat to their political independence and territorial integrity would be viewed with the utmost gravity.

When asked by the "Northern Tier" members to join their military alliance, the United States politely refused the invitation but promised to defend the whole Middle East against Communist attack. On January 5, 1957, President Eisenhower asked Congress for the authority to give assistance to any Middle Eastern state or states requesting such aid, and to employ United States armed forces in the area as he deemed necessary; this later became known as the Eisenhower Doctrine. Congress did not respond as willingly and readily as the President wished. The requested policy declaration was subjected to searching scrutiny. What appeared to be a major flaw in the doctrine was the overemphasis on Soviet "overt

[11]For fear of further alienating Egypt and other Arab nations, the United States did not join the Baghdad Pact, which was signed in 1955 by Great Britain, Turkey, Iraq, Iran, and Pakistan. Just as Turkey was to link NATO with the Baghdad Pact, Pakistan was to link the Baghdad Pact with SEATO; thus, the "wall of containment" of communism was completed all around the globe.

armed aggression," while *covert political subversion* in the area was ignored. Secretary of State Dulles vigorously and successfully defended the doctrine, and in the end Congress approved it in a slightly modified form. Signed into law on March 9, 1957, the joint resolution stated:

> The President is authorized to undertake, in the general area of the Middle East, military assistance programs with any nation or group of nations of that area desiring such assistance. Furthermore, the United States regards as vital to the national interest and world peace the preservation of the independence and integrity of the nations of the Middle East. To this end, if the President determines the necessity thereof, the United States is prepared to use armed forces to assist any such nation or group of such nations requesting assistance against armed aggression from any country controlled by international communism. . . .[12]

The Soviet Union denounced the Eisenhower Doctrine as a threat to the political independence and national sovereignty of the Arab states and accused the United States of imperialistic neo-colonialism in the Middle East. Shortly after the Eisenhower Doctrine came into force, the Kingdom of Jordan became the first storm center of Arab politics and intrigue. The monarchy was threatened by internal disturbances, presumably instigated by Egypt and Syria. Declaring that the independence of Jordan was of vital interest to the United States, President Eisenhower dispatched special units of the Sixth Fleet to the eastern Mediterranean, thus demonstrating America's readiness to render assistance to the Jordanian monarch. The King of Jordan proclaimed martial law, quelled the disturbances, cracked down on the opposition, withdrew from the Egypt–Syria–Jordan alliance, and then turned to the United States for financial assistance. He received $30 million in American aid immediately.

A more serious test of the Eisenhower Doctrine came during the latter half of 1958. In May, Lebanon was threatened by a civil war prompted by the power struggle between Moslems and Christians. The government of Camille Chamoun, a Christian and pro-Western, accused the United Arab Republic of aiding and abetting the rebellion. Chamoun formally requested the U. N. Security Council to take measures against Nasser, who was allegedly endangering the peace of the Middle East. The following month United Nations sent an on-the-spot observation team, which was unable to find evidence to substantiate Chamoun's charge. In July, 1958, a group of army officers in Baghdad staged a coup, overthrew the pro-Western government, murdered the king, the crown prince, and the Prime Minister, and established the Republic of Iraq. The new military regime, headed by General Abdul Karim Kassim, dissolved the union with Jordan and concluded a military alliance with the United Arab Republic.

Meanwhile, the bewildering developments in Iraq frightened Lebanon's President Chamoun, who had sent an urgent plea for help to President

[12] *The New York Times*, March 6, 1957.

Eisenhower. Responding to this plea, Eisenhower rushed Untied States Marines to Lebanon to help defend its independence. Britain likewise sent her troops to Jordan in answer to a similar plea by the King of Jordan.

To Nasser the United States action was "another Suez," and to the Soviet Union it was "an act of aggression in violation of the United Nations Charter." All diplomatic maneuvers in the United Nations to effect a satisfactory solution to the Middle East conflict failed to produce any substantial result. What led to the easing of the tensions in Lebanon was the election to the presidency of Fuad Chehab, an army general acceptable to both sides in the civil strife. Taking office in September, President Chehab quickly won American backing. In the same month the Secretary-General of the United Nations recommended a resolution, which was subsequently adopted by the U. N., that called for observation teams to be stationed in Lebanon and Jordan to prevent unlawful infiltration of subversive elements and illicit introduction of arms into these two countries. As the implementation of these measures became effective, the United States and Great Britain began to withdraw their troops, and by the end of October, 1958, they had completed the evacuation from both nations.

In an age of "revolution for national equality, sovereignty, and independence," the Eisenhower Doctrine was frowned upon by some of the emerging nations in Asia, Africa, and Latin America, because it resulted in United States military intervention in the Middle East. But by demonstrating that the United States would not hesitate to use force in the Middle East, the Eisenhower Doctrine proved to be an effective Cold War weapon to deter potential aggressors in Moscow or Cairo. One of the critics of the Eisenhower Doctrine has observed:

> By attempting in its Eisenhower Doctrine to induce neutral Arab states to become military allies, the United States precipitated events which merged Syria and Egypt into the United Arab Republic, converted Lebanon from an ally into a neutral, transformed Iraq from a Western military ally into a neutral with a distinct anti-Western flavor, immobilized King Saud, and isolated Jordan.[13]

In the wake of the Middle Eastern turmoil, a crisis began to brew in another Asian kingdom—Laos. Laos, with a territory of 89,000 square miles and a population of less than 2 million, is a land-locked country surrounded by Communist China, Burma, Thailand, North Vietnam, South Vietnam, and Cambodia. If Laos should fall into the hands of the Communists, the pressure on Southeast Asia would be unbearably great. Whatever happens to Laos will inevitably affect the course of events not only in its neighboring countries but also in India, Ceylon, Malaysia, Indonesia, the Philippines, and Japan. In Laos, the vital interests of the United States, the Soviet Union, and Communist China menacingly converge together.

[13]William G. Carleton, *The Revolution in American Foreign Policy* (New York: Random House, Inc., 1963), p. 333.

The Geneva Agreement of 1954, which officially ended the war in Vietnam, stipulated that Laos and Cambodia were to be neutral. But its strategic and geographic importance made it difficult for Laos to maintain that status. The Kingdom of Laos is a constitutional monarchy but it is not a functioning democracy. With its independence, it had inherited a formidable group of partisan fighters, called Pathet Lao, who were not represented in the National Assembly, the legislative body. Operating in the northern region near Vietnam during the struggle between the Vietnamese and the French, the Pathet Lao drew both moral and material support from Communist North Vietnam. By 1953 the Pathet Lao had arrogated to themselves a government in the North, and they began to expand their influence and control throughout the countryside, challenging the authority of the central government. Fighting between the Pathet Lao and the government forces led to years of political turmoil and civil chaos until the Geneva Accord provided for the reassembling of Pathet Lao rebel troops in the two northeastern provinces—Phong Saly and Sam Neua—pending final agreement between the warring parties.

During the first four years after the Geneva Agreement, the United States supported the neutral government of Premier Prince Souvanna Phouma, who tried but failed to bring about an agreement with the Pathet Lao. In 1959–1960 the United States backed the right-wing regime led by General Phoumi Nosavan, who had fought the Pathet Lao, and gave him massive military and economic aid. The Soviet Union charged that such aid was a violation of the Geneva Agreements prohibiting the introduction of all kinds of arms. The United States replied that such action was taken upon the request of the lawful Laotian government in its efforts to restore domestic tranquility and, therefore, was not inconsistent with the provisions of the Geneva Accord. The Soviet Union responded in kind: it supplied the Pathet Lao with its own massive aid—guns, ammunition, petroleum, and other military equipment.

This led to a serious confrontation between the anti-Communist government forces and the pro-Communist Pathet Lao, the former trained and equipped by the United States and holding the major cities and towns, and the latter equipped with Soviet arms and controlling the jungles and countryside. The situation appeared to have reached an impasse. Direct military action by the United States on the side of the government forces would most likely cause a counteraction by the Soviet Union, by Communist China, or by both, turning Laos into another Korea, perhaps on a larger scale.

By the time President Kennedy took office in January, 1961, the Soviet Union had established a "beachhead" in Southeast Asia. President Kennedy decided to use diplomacy to solve the problem, which military policy had intensified, and to dislodge the Soviet Union, which had penetrated through the "wall of containment." He clarified America's ultimate objectives and position in Laos—to preserve "a neutral and independent Laos, tied to no outside power."[14] This was in line with the thinking of British and French officials, who had long favored Souvanna Phouma's neutral stance; they were convinced that neither the Soviet Union nor Communist China would intervene against Phouma's moderately pro-Western government. President Kennedy, however, did not rule out military action as an alternative to the establishment of a neutral coalition government in Laos.

The Soviet Union responded favorably to President Kennedy's proposal and suggested a 14-nation conference, which was eventually convened in May, 1961. Unfortunately, the conference soon became deadlocked.

A year later, in May, 1962, the Pathet Lao broke the shaky cease-fire and launched a major offensive against the government forces in the North, forcing them to retreat into Thailand. It appeared that if they were not checked, the Pathet Lao would run over the entire kingdom with ease. President Kennedy responded resolutely to this grave new situation. He ordered the United States Seventh Fleet to proceed to the South China Sea, and dispatched combat troops to Thailand upon the request of the Thai government. These moves were designed to strengthen Thailand's defense along the Laotian border, to honor America's commitment to its allies, to mend the falling "wall of containment" in Southeast Asia, and to apply enough pressure on the Soviet Union, Communist China, and the Pathet Lao through the show of force to make them come to the conference table.

The Kennedy policy achieved its objectives. In June, 1962, the three warring Laotian factions—pro-Western, neutral, and Communist—agreed to a troika government which was to follow a neutral course. The following month the 14-nation commission signed agreements guaranteeing the independence and neutrality of Laos. An International Control Commission composed of representatives from Canada, India, and Poland was formed to supervise Laotian neutrality. Thus another spark of the Cold War was extinguished before it could spread into a world conflagration.

In the summer of 1960, at the peak of the Laotian crisis, a summit conference among the leaders of the four Great Powers—the United States, the Soviet Union, Great Britain, and France—was scheduled to convene in Paris. Undoubtedly the Laotian problem would have been placed on the agenda of their discussion, but the summit meeting itself was torpedoed by Soviet Premier Nikita Khrushchev, who found his "justifiable cause" for action in the so-called "U-2 Incident."

At dawn on May 1, 1960, when Moscow was making ready for its May Day celebration, a Lockheed-built high-altitude plane (U-2) piloted by an American, Francis Gary Powers, took off from Peshawar, Pakistan, and headed toward Bodö, Norway. The flight was to take about nine hours and cover nearly 3800 miles across the heart of the Soviet Union directly over such major cities as Stalingrad, Aral'sk, Chelyabinsk, Sverdlovsk, Kirov, Arkhangel'sk, and Murmansk.

[14]*Department of State Bulletin*, **44** (April 17, 1961), 543.

The daring undertaking was one in a series of reconnaissance flights begun in 1956 under the direction of the United States Central Intelligence Agency (CIA) in cooperation with the National Aeronautics and Space Administration (NASA). The true nature of the U-2 flights over the Soviet Union had been kept in absolute secrecy; it was believed that they were used for weather observation.

Power's "Black Lady" (the U-2 sobriquet) flew over Afghanistan, entered Soviet air space at about 5:30 A.M. (Moscow time), and proceeded to Tyura Tam, the Soviet counterpart of Cape Kennedy, eight miles east of the Aral Sea. Tyura Tam was one of the two intercontinental ballistic missile (ICBM) testing sites (the other was Kapustin Yar) which United States intelligence had uncovered in the Soviet Union.

In early April, 1960, however, a U-2 had spotted traces of unusual excavations along the route Powers was to follow, which had strongly suggested the construction of the first Soviet operational ICBM base. The primary objective of Powers' May Day flight was to photograph the construction of the launching site before the Soviets could camouflage it. The U-2 was equipped with a highly advanced camera capable of taking 4000 paired pictures of a strip of Soviet territory 125 miles wide and 2200 miles long.

The Soviets apparently knew of the overflights prior to Powers' flight; evidences indicated that on several occasions they had made unsuccessful attempts to down the U-2's. Working under top priority, the Soviet Air Defense Command had successfully improved their radar detection system and antiaircraft missiles. The moment Powers' U-2 crossed the border, therefore, it was caught in the web of Soviet radar, and about 9 A.M. (Moscow time) the plane was shot down over Sverdlovsk.

On May 6, 1960, at a meeting of the Supreme Soviet, Premier Khrushchev announced that an American plane had infringed upon Soviet air space and subsequently had been brought down. He then indicated that, in view of the United States's continued and similar provocative activities, the scheduled summit conference in Paris might result in failure.

In response to the Soviet announcement, the United States released a notice saying that a "weather reconnaissance" plane was missing and that it might have been downed by the Soviets after having strayed into Soviet territory. On May 7, 1960, again before the Supreme Soviet, Khurshchev revealed that the U-2 pilot was alive and being held in Soviet custody as a prisoner.

In spite of this disclosure, the United States government at first shirked the responsibility for the flight, although it maintained that such flights could be justified on the grounds that the free world had the right to protect itself from a possible Soviet surprise attack. Then, suddenly, the United States government reversed its earlier position, and in a public announcement, the President assumed full responsibility for the U-2 flights.[15]

When the heads of the Big Four assembled in Paris, Soviet Premier

[15]This was an unprecedented action, since it had been the practice for chiefs of state to hold themselves above and apart from espionage.

Khrushchev laid down two basic conditions for the convening of a summit conference: (1) that the United States pledge the immediate and permanent cessation of flights over Soviet Russia in the future, and (2) that President Eisenhower make a public apology for such flights undertaken in the past. Since the President refused to comply with the latter demand in view of the national and personal prestige involved, Premier Khrushchev resolutely "torpedoed" the intended summit meeting.

It seemed, however, that even before the U-2 incident Premier Khrushchev believed that he could not expect any major concessions from the West and that the summit conference would not bring about any meaningful agreements; therefore, he found in the U-2 episode a ready-made pretext for wrecking the conference before it could really get under way. On the other hand, contrary to Khrushchev's belief, the conference, had it been held, might have produced an East–West *rapprochement*, reducing the tensions in the Cold War. In the final analysis, the U-2 furor had the effect of aggravating, not mitigating, the intensity of the Cold War.

As for the aftermath of this incident, the Security Council of the United Nations debated the U-2 question from May 23 to May 26. The members of the Security Council agreed that the U-2 flight had violated Soviet air space, but except for Poland, they did not believe that it constituted an "aggression" as the Soviet Union charged. On May 26, the Security Council refused to adopt the Soviet resolution condemning the United States for the U-2 flight and calling it an aggressive act. The following day the Security Council adopted, by a vote of 9–0 (with Poland and the USSR abstaining), an alternative resolution expressing their conviction "of the necessity to make every effort to restore and strengthen international good will and confidence, based on the established principles of international law." It also appealed to all members "to respect each other's sovereignty, territorial integrity, and political independence."[16]

Scarcely had the world recovered from the shock of the diplomatic crisis surrounding the collapse of the summit meeting, when another crisis of the first magnitude exploded in the heart of the "Dark Continent" of Africa.

Ideally and theoretically speaking, the independence of the Belgian Congo on June 30, 1960, should have terminated any vestige of ill-feeling between the Congolese and the Belgian colonists. Unfortunately this was not the case. Belgium's "neo-colonialism" lingered on while the Congolese "anticolonialism," tinged with a "get-even" sentiment, emerged. This environment bred inevitable conflict and tensions.

Immediately after independence, three ominous phenomena were crystallized to form the conditions which led to the subsequent instability and chaos in the Congo: (1) the government was split into two factions— one led by President Joseph Kasavubu, who favored a federal system of government, and the other led by leftist Premier Patrice Lumumba, who

[16]See *United Nations Review*, June, 1960, p. 1; July, 1960, pp. 6–7, 38–43.

favored a unitary form of government; (2) a revolt by the military police erupted and the central government was unable to control the situation; and (3) the large, mineral-rich province of Katanga seceded and formed a separate government headed by Moise Tshombe, who was apparently backed by the *Union Minière du Haut Katanga*, the most powerful financial and industrial organization in Belgium.

After the outbreak of the rampageous revolt, which caused indiscriminate destruction of life and property, the Belgian government rushed its military forces back to the Congo to restore order. In July, 1960, Premier Lumumba appealed to the United Nations to deal with the Belgian "aggression," the Katanga secession, and the problem of peace in his country.

The U. N. Security Council passed a resolution authorizing the Secretary-General to provide the Congo with the necessary military aid and called upon Belgium to withdraw its troops. The United States voted for this resolution with a view to preventing any unilateral intervention by the Soviet Union and in order to keep "the Cold War out of Africa." The Communist bloc nations also supported it because they believed that Premier Lumumba's ultimate objectives would coincide with theirs.

The United Nations organized emergency military forces composed of troops from 13 smaller neutral nations. As the United Nations forces arrived and restored order, Tshombe at first refused to allow them in his province of Katanga. In the end, however, he consented when he was given assurance by Secretary-General Hammarskjold that the United Nations forces would only supervise the withdrawal of the Belgian troops and would not interfere with the domestic politics of the Congo. The Secretary-General's assurance of a noninterference policy was assailed by Communist and some anticolonial Powers as a sign of surrender to neo-colonialist pressures. They demanded that the United Nations forces be used to bring Tshombe and Katanga back to Lumumba's fold. The Soviets hinted at unilateral intervention and threatened to dispatch "volunteers" to the Congo to help Patrice Lumumba recover Katanga. In fact, they began to send arms and equipment, accompanied by technicians and advisers, into the Congo. Thus, a big power confrontation seemed to be in the making in the heart of Africa.

At this critical moment the Kasavubu–Lumumba feud came to a head. President Kasavubu dismissed Lumumba as Premier. A civil war between the two factions appeared imminent, but it was averted when Colonel Joseph Mobutu established military rule and adopted moderately anti-Communist policies. Undaunted, the supporters of Lumumba had gathered at Stanleyville to launch a revolt against the Kasavubu–Mobutu government. On his way to Stanleyville to take charge of the development there, Lumumba was arrested by Kasavubu's men and turned over to Tshombe. In February, 1961, Lumumba was killed. The Lumumba followers then organized a government in Stanleyville under the leadership of Antoine Gizenga, claiming that their government was the only legitimate one for the Congolese people.

The killing of Lumumba had further complicated the seemingly insoluble difficulty in the Congo. The Soviets criticized Hammarskjold's handling of the situation and demanded his dismissal as Secretary-General. Again the Soviet Union threatened unilateral intervention. The Communist countries and some nonaligned nations refused to make further monetary contributions to the United Nations operations in the Congo. Nevertheless, the United Nations operations continued, and by early 1961 the primary responsibility of the Secretary-General with respect to the operations in the Congo was to prevent the outbreak of a civil war between the feuding factions. To this end he was authorized to use force if necessary.

After a series of conferences and negotiations, a moderate Premier, Cyrille Adoula, was chosen to form a coalition Cabinet. Gizenga was made First Vice-Premier. Tshombe still remained adamant and retained his foreign mercenaries. In September the United Nations forces in Katanga commenced military actions to force Tshombe to come to terms with the central government. The battle raged between the United Nations troops and Tshombe's armies. At this time, in an effort to negotiate a cease-fire with Tshombe, U. N. Secretary-General Hammarskjold left for Elizabethville in a plane which crashed in the African jungles, killing the Secretary-General.

A cease-fire was later arranged, but bitter fighting broke out again in December. Again, another cease-fire was ordered by U Thant, Acting Secretary-General, on the condition that Tshombe agree to a negotiated settlement with Adoula. Subsequent negotiations lasted throughout 1962 with no substantial results. By the end of the year, with the support of the United States, the United Nations forces in Katanga had completed a considerable arms buildup; now they were ready to execute major military operations designed to destroy Tshombe's mercenaries and to secure the rebellious province. The operation was a resounding success for the United Nations forces. Late in January, 1963, Tshombe admitted defeat and announced the end of the secession.

What was the significance of the Congo crisis? There were a multiplicity of pros and cons with respect to the United Nations operations in the Congo. Strictly in terms of the Cold War context, however, the following conclusions could be drawn. The United Nations operations in the Congo had prevented unilateral intervention by any of the Big Powers, thus preventing a direct, dangerous, East–West confrontation in the center of Africa. The United Nations had proved once again to be a useful instrument in mitigating tensions and in cushioning conflict among nations. Nevertheless, the operations in the Congo had brought the United Nations to near-bankruptcy, revealing one of its basic weaknesses—inadequate source of income. And the financial crisis resulting from these operations aggravated the problems of Cold War diplomacy within the United Nations itself.

VII

Tensions Over the Taiwan Strait

1

United States Foreign Policy and Formosa*

ARTHUR DEAN

Formosa—symbol of the struggle between freedom and Communism in the Orient—poses a test of how far United States foreign policy can combine the ideals of freedom with the flexible realism required by the harsh facts of world politics.

Our friend and long-time ally, Chiang Kai-shek, presently holds Formosa (Taiwan); the Communists hold the mainland. We are unhappy that a great nation with the cultural traditions of China should be under the control of a totalitarian régime which does not share our belief in freedom. But for the present, at least, unless we wish to risk an all-out war, our desire to see the return of freedom to continental China cannot overcome the stark fact of the possession and control of the mainland by the Communists.

United States foreign policy seems to have three major alternative methods of dealing with Formosa. The first is to acquiesce in frightened demands (made, for example, by prominent members of the British Labor Party) that we abandon Formosa to the Communist Chinese. The second is to insist that the Communist rule of the mainland should be formally ignored, regardless of what the alternatives may be or what they hold in prospect for us. The third, an intermediate position, is to accept, albeit unhappily, that at the present time the Peking government controls continental China and that any prospect of stabilizing the Far East may of necessity entail that we negotiate with it. . . .

The juridical status of Formosa and the Pescadores has not been so altered by the Mutual Defense Treaty between the United States and the Republic of China as to preclude a "two China" policy, if it should become in our interest to follow that theory. As Mr. Churchill pointed out in the House of Commons on February 1 of this year, the Cairo Declaration and

*Quoted by special permission from Foreign Affairs, Vol. 33 (April, 1955). Copyright by the Council on Foreign Relations, Inc., New York.

the Japanese Peace Treaty have not operated, in any formal legal sense, to cause Formosa to become a part of China.

The Mutual Defense Treaty, by its terms, does not commit the United States to that position. It is only for the purposes of Articles II and V (providing for joint resistance to an armed attack) that the territories of the Republic of China are defined in Article VI as including Formosa and the Pescadores. And it is rash, in any event, to think that the United States by its unilateral act can alone determine the juridical status of the island.

International law provides two basic ways in which title to a given territory can be acquired. One is formal cession from one sovereign to another; the other is occupation of a *terra nullius*. Japan, in renouncing all right, title and claim to Formosa, did not thereby transfer it to China. Whether a formal cession could now be made by all of the signatories of the Peace Treaty (which does not include the Republic of China or the Democratic Peoples' Republic of China), on the theory that the right to make this cession passed to such signatories, is an open question. But apart from annexation, it would seem, from a legal point of view, that the United States can consummate a cession of Formosa by itself.

Customary international law will allow a country to acquire legal title to territory which is *terra nullius* (unclaimed) by a demonstration of "the intention or will to act as sovereign, and some actual exercise or display of authority." The Chinese Nationalist Government surely has satisfied these requirements. And, if the island of Formosa was not unclaimed territory before the 1951 Japanese Treaty, it probably became so upon the renunciation of Japan's claim.

Even if Formosa were assumed to be a juridical part of the Republic of China, a perfectly good legal means of achieving the political result of two separate Chinese States would be to recognize Communist China as a new State which has broken off from the Republic of China and, at the same time, to acknowledge that the Republic of China has acquired title to Formosa and the Pescadores through occupation, or, if necessary, effect a formal cession of these territories to the Republic of China.

The Republic of China, having a people, a defined territory, and a sovereign government, would continue to satisfy the conditions of statehood stipulated by international law, and have a legal basis for asserting title to assets such as bank accounts and buildings and for undertaking to protect, and for exercising personal jurisdiction over, citizens of China when they are abroad. China's treaty rights, including the seat in the Security Council, would be secured to the Republic of China or appropriate revisions made in the Charter satisfactory to us. Or if the *terra nullius* theory is not accepted, then the Nationalist Government would at least have a juridical status similar to the traditional "government in exile," but even stronger, because it actually holds a portion of its national territory.

The larger aspects of a foreign policy towards Formosa must not be ignored. One danger of devoting so much diplomatic and military energy to this particular problem of Formosa is that of disproportion. American foreign policy in other important areas may well become a mere adjunct to the problems of this small Pacific island if all our political influence must be concentrated on keeping our reluctant allies behind our policy there and if all our military power is to go into maintaining a readiness to rebuff a constantly threatened armed attack there.

The Russians know this. By skillful encouragement of peripheral conflicts, fought by Chinese or satellites, the U. S. S. R. can pin down American troops and matériel, shake the morale of the free nations and divide their unity. An added benefit for the Russians is that such crises absorb the energies of the Chinese Communists and divert their attention from their very real territorial and economic conflicts of interest with the Soviet Union. It is a cheap, useful, yet dangerous ploy for the Russians. The system works well for them as long as no one inadvertently starts a major war.

The Chinese, as the Kremlin surely is aware, are too big to fit easily into the category "satellite." Mao Tse-tung and Chou En-lai are able men and not likely to be unnecessarily subservient when a clear conflict of interest arises between People's China and the U. S. S. R. Significantly, Nikolai Bulganin and Nikita Khrushchev conducted a major part of the negotiations for the Chinese–Soviet agreement of October 1954. The fall of Premier Malenkov, perhaps attributable in some measure at least to the failure of his policy to slow Western defense efforts, has left these two men as the titular and recognized leaders of Russia. The Sino-Soviet partnership is surely a central feature of Communist strength.

Our foreign policy stands to gain if it is free to find sore spots in the relations of the two countries and to add to the frictions by actions like those that the Communists use when they coo and growl, in turn, to divergent opinions in the West. China and Russia have differing interests, even though it is to the Russian interest to keep the issues alive and troublesome, just as it is to ours to smooth out and settle them. The risks of a global atomic war over Formosa surely are not alluring to the U. S. S. R. Russia's historic national interests suffered severely when she was obliged to release Port Arthur and Dairen to maintain the Chinese alliance last fall. And the shipping of economic and military supplies to the Chinese undoubtedly is a potential source of friction—the Red Chinese annoyed by the inadequacy of the shipments, the Russians by the slowing effect on their own industrialization and the inordinate demands involved for their own economy. Moscow can hardly be happy at Peking's decision to go to Bandung, Indonesia, in April for the African–Asian conference, where the "non-white" nations are likely to consider China, not Russia, the apostle of Communist leadership in the East.

Secretary Dulles has already made efforts to emphasize inherent cleavages in the Soviet hierarchy by implying that the United States would be willing to deal with those in the Soviet Union "who are primarily concerned with the welfare, the security and the greatness of the Soviet Union and its people." Nationalism versus internationalism is a good theme to play upon within Russia. We are missing another when we maintain a blanket refusal to consider alternatives to the "outlaw" policy towards the present rulers of mainland China. This precludes both a realistic playing upon the potential split with the Soviet Union and any hope of establishing a staple relationship in the Formosa straits. Our initiative should be along the lines suggested by Secretary of State Dulles when he said:

> It is hardly to be expected, of course, that the Chinese Communists will renounce their ambitions. However, might they not renounce their efforts to realize their goals by force?

If we forswear any possibility of taking such initiative, we may be throwing away the ammunition we need most to combat the dynamic, multi-temperatured offensive with which we are battling. Our policy should certainly not be to "indefinitely pile up one-sided concessions to the Communists." We should be tough realists. If we are, we can exact concessions of equivalent value for each concession we yield—and otherwise simply not make concessions.

This approach may offer some hope of reaching a stable *modus vivendi* in the Far East. It is offered in an effort to show that we need not necessarily resign ourselves to the gradual deterioration of the Far Eastern situation to our detriment, or that the only alternative is war.

2

Basis for Our Defense of Formosa*

G. F. HUDSON

Sir Winston Churchill once said that the rulers of the Soviet Union do not want war, but they want the fruits of war. By this he meant that, without a real intention to risk a mortal clash of arms, they endeavor to gain by bluster, truculence, and threats objectives such as are not normally to be reached by peaceful negotiation, but only by victory on the field of battle. The most striking example of this during the last decade has been the blockade of Berlin, when the Russians used every means short of actual shooting to force the Western Allies out of their legal rights of occupation

From Commentary, Vol. 19 (March, 1955), pp. 236–242. Reprinted from Commentary, by permission; copyright © 1955 by the American Jewish Committee.

in the German capital, but nevertheless refrained from the final step of armed attack on the airlift when they found they could not get their way by intimidation; had there been any flinching on the Western side—and there were frightened souls both in London and Washington who talked about a compromise in order to avert war—Moscow would relentlessly have pressed its advantage and the whole Western position in Germany would rapidly have become untenable. Today an intense and menacing pressure is being applied in another quarter in the hope of adding to the domain of international Communism a piece of territory for which it is virtually certain that the Sino-Soviet bloc is not ready to embark on all-out war. In the present drive to compel the United States to retreat from its commitment in Formosa, as in the drive seven years ago to get the Western Allies out of Berlin, Communism seeks to exploit the Western peoples' horror of war and desire for a quiet life.

But there are significant differences between the current situation with regard to Formosa and that of 1948 in Western Europe—and they cut both ways. On the one hand, the strategic strength of the local defensive position is much greater in the Formosa Strait in 1955 than it was in Berlin or on the Elbe in 1948—and the prospects in an unlimited war probably at least no worse than they were then. On the other hand, the present political situation is undoubtedly more advantageous to the Communist bloc because of the policy rift between the United States and Britain over Formosa in contrast to the unity which they displayed in standing their ground in Germany. . . .

The most dangerous and alarming feature of the present situation, in contrast to the previous crises over Berlin and Korea, is the separation between the United States and Britain. Whereas the Soviet government has publicly pledged support in the most uncompromising fashion for Peking's demands for withdrawal of American forces from the Formosa Strait, the lack of unity between Washington and London is manifest to the world, and British public opinion is, in general, much more adverse to the American policy than the official attitude.

The absence of sympathy in Britain for the American stand on Formosa is not a new development; it goes back to the time of President Truman's original decision to seal off Formosa after the outbreak of war in Korea in the summer of 1950. A divergency of policies at that point was an inevitable sequel to the British recognition of the Chinese Communist regime earlier in the year. In retrospect the act of recognition appears as a decisive parting of the ways between British and American Far Eastern policies, but it should be emphasized that it was not so regarded at the time. The Truman administration, having cleared itself by the famous White Paper, to its own if not to everyone's satisfaction, from all responsibility for the collapse of the Chinese National government on the mainland, was leaving Formosa to its fate. The British Foreign Office understood that the State

Department contemplated recognition of Communist China as soon as the time seemed ripe for it and would not object to Britain making the move first.

Since then the hearings before the McCarran Committee have disclosed the minutes of the conference of experts sponsored by the State Department in October 1949 which indicate that the Department indeed had a more than open mind on the subject. It appears likely that the original intention of President Truman and Mr. Acheson was to transfer diplomatic recognition to Peking after the mid-term Congressional elections of November 1950, delaying the act until then in view of the increasing restiveness of American public opinion on the subject of China.

But what neither the British nor the American government foresaw was the outbreak of war in Korea, which transformed the process of Communist expansion in the Far East from one of domestic subversion into one of direct military assault on a government which had been set up under the auspices of the United Nations. Although the conflict in Korea was held by the Communists and their friends to be, like the civil war in China, a purely domestic matter in which no outside power should interfere, President Truman took the view that a situation of international war had been created and took decisive steps to aid South Korea even before the Security Council (in the absence of the Russian veto) had made South Korea's cause that of the United Nations. . . .

Had the American protection of Formosa remained one of two-way "neutralization," it would have been difficult to represent it to anyone but a Communist or fellow-traveler as a policy of aggression. But during the Korean war American exasperation against Communist China led to "taking the wraps off Formosa," and thus in appearance America assumed responsibility for Nationalist adventures against the mainland. Although Washington in fact obtained assurances from Chiang Kai-shek that no campaign would be launched without consultation, the policy outwardly looked like the underwriting of any action that might be taken by the Nationalists in order to get back to power in China, and British opinion has been very ready to listen to the accusation that America is endangering the peace of the world by supporting the ambitions of a "busted war-lord." The small commando raids carried out by the Nationalists failed to convince anyone of the latters' military capacity, but they were sufficient to create a widespread impression that the Nationalists were the aggressors and provokers in the fighting off the South China coast. . . .

In the Formosa Strait there has so far been no truce, and the Communists, having acquired a fleet of jet aircraft from Russia and having wound up their enterprise in Korea and Indo-China, apparently think that they have prospects of a victorious offensive. If they think so, nobody can stop them from trying; the world can only wait and see how their venture tunrs out. But if they think they can get Formosa merely by making loud noises to

alarm the world with the fear of war and by talking about American interference with their "domestic jurisdiction," then they need to be reminded—
as also do many people not on the Communist side—that the present
situation has arisen out of an international war which the Communists
began, that the state of war continues until ended by a formal cease-fire,
and that the only possible basis for a settlement after a war which has ended
in stalemate is that each side should, as in Korea, keep what it has. . . .

The essential thing in the Formosa crisis is to clarify the issue by stating
it in its proper relation to the war which Communist China waged in
Korea and which automatically internationalized the Chinese civil war,
removing it from the purely "domestic jurisdiction" which Chou En-lai
now claims as if no "People's Volunteers" had ever crossed the Yalu. As a
part of that war the Chinese Nationalist government in Formosa became
within certain limits an ally of the United States, and no apology is needed
for the American government's refusal to abandon that ally now that the
Korean war itself is over. All other arguments in justification of the policy
of protecting Formosa—that it is not yet juridically a part of China or that
it is essential to the strategic security of the United States—merely obscure
the fundamental right of America, as a belligerent in a war in which she
was not the aggressor, to protect an organized government which was
resisting the same enemy in the same region of operations. It only remains
to give this organized government, which was once the government of
China, but now holds only certain islands in the China Sea, the international
status of a separate sovereign state. It is not the first time in history that
war has led to the formation of a new state.

3

On Taiwan Fighting*

CHOU EN-LAI

On September 4, 1958, United States Secretary of State Dulles, under
the authorization of United States President Eisenhower, issued a statement
openly threatening to expand United States aggression against the People's
Republic of China in the Taiwan (Formosa) Strait area and carrying out
war provocation, thereby aggravating the tension in this area created by
the United States and seriously jeopardizing the peace of the Far East and
the world. Regarding this, I have been authorized by the Government of
the People's Republic of China to make the following statement:

*Radio Peking, September 6, 1958.

Taiwan and the Penghu Islands (Pescadoes) have been China's territories from ancient times. Following the Second World War, they were restored to China after being occupied by Japan for a period of time.

The exercise by the Chinese people of their sovereign right to liberate these areas is entirely China's internal affair. This is the Chinese people's sacred and inviolable right. The United States Government itself also declared formally that it would not get involved in China's civil conflict in the Taiwan area.

Were it not for the fact that the United States Government later went back on its own statement and carried out armed intervention, Taiwan and the Penghu Islands would have long been liberated and placed under the administration of the Government of the People's Republic of China. These are undeniable facts recognized by fair-minded world public opinion unanimously.

United States support of the Chiang Kai-shek clique entrenched on Taiwan and the Penghu Islands, which has long been repudiated by all the Chinese people, and its direct occupation of Taiwan and the Penghu Islands by armed force constitute unlawful interference in China's internal affairs and infringement of China's territorial integrity and sovereignty, and are in direct conflict with the United Nations Charter and all codes of international law.

All so-called treaties concluded between the United States and the Chiang Kai-shek clique and all related resolutions adopted by the United States Congress are null and void as far as the Chinese people are concerned. They can never legalize United States aggression.

Even less can they be used as pretexts for the United States to expand its aggression in the Taiwan Strait area.

Supported by the United States, the Chiang Kai-shek clique has for long been using coastal islands such as Quemoy, which is close by Amoy, and Matsu, which is close by Foochow, as advance bases to carry out all sorts of harassing and disruptive activities against the Chinese mainland.

Recently, since the United States launched armed intervention against the Arab states, the harassing and disruptive activities of the Chiang Kai-shek clique against the Chinese mainland have become more unbridled.

The Chinese Government has every right to deal resolute blows on and take necessary military action against Chiang Kai-shek's troops entrenched on the coastal islands.

Any foreign intervention would be a criminal infringement on China's sovereignty, but the United States, in order to divert the attention of the people of the world from continued United States aggression in the Middle East and procrastination of the withdrawal of its troops from Lebanon, attempts to take advantage of this situation and is amassing large numbers of armed forces in the Taiwan Strait area and openly threatening to expand its aggression in the Taiwan Strait area to Quemoy, Matsu, and other coastal islands.

This is a grave war provocation against the 600,000,000 Chinese people and a serious menace to the peace of the Far East and the world.

The Chinese people's determination to liberate their own territory of Taiwan and the Penghu Islands is unshakeable. In particular, the Chinese people cannot tolerate the presence in their inland waters along the mainland of an immediate threat posed by such coastal islands as Quemoy and Matsu.

No war provocations of the United States can cow the Chinese people. On the contrary, they will only arouse even greater indignation of our 600,000,000 people, and their even stronger determination to fight American aggressors to the very end.

The fact that the United States, while not yet withdrawing its forces of aggression from Lebanon, has hastened to create a new danger of war in the Taiwan Strait area has made the peace-loving countries and people of the world see even more clearly the brutish features of the United States aggressors bent on sabotaging peace and that the United States imperialists are the most vicious enemy of all national independence movements in Asia, Africa and Latin America and the world peace movement.

In line with its foreign policy of peace, the Chinese Government has always stood for peaceful coexistence of countries with different social systems in accordance with the five principles and for the settlement of all international disputes by the peaceful means of negotiation.

Despite the fact that the United States has by armed force invaded and occupied China's territory of Taiwan and the Penghu Islands and crudely violated the minimum codes in international relations, the Chinese Government proposed to sit down to negotiate with the United States Government to seek relaxation and elimination of the tension in the Taiwan area.

In the Sino-American ambassadorial talks which started in August, 1955, the Chinese side has time and again proposed that the two parties should, in accordance with the principles of mutual respect of sovereignty and territorial integrity and non-interference in each other's internal affairs, issue a statement declaring their intention to settle the dispute between China and the United States in the Taiwan area through peaceful negotiation and without resorting to the threat or use of force against each other.

But, contrary to Dulles' assertion in his September 4 statement, it is precisely the United States that has refused to issue such a statement and, moreover, has later suspended unilaterally the talks themselves.

After the Chinese Government made in July this year the demand to resume the talks within a set time limit, the United States Government did not make a timely reply, but it has ultimately designated a representative of ambassadorial rank.

Now, the United States Government again indicates its desire to settle the Sino-American dispute in the Taiwan area through peaceful negotiation. To make a further effort to safeguard peace, the Chinese Government is prepared to resume the ambassadorial talks between the two countries.

But the danger of war created by the United States in China's Taiwan area has not been reduced thereby. In view of the fact that the United States Government often acts otherwise than it says and often uses peaceful negotiation as a smokescreen to cover up its actual deed of continuously expanding aggression, the entire Chinese people and the peace-loving people all over the world must not relax in the least their struggle against United States interference in China's internal affairs and against the United States threat to the peace of the Far East and the world.

The Sino-American dispute in the Taiwan Strait area and the Chinese people's internal matter of liberating their own territory are two matters entirely different in nature. The United States has all along tried to confuse these two matters so as to cover up its aggression and intervention in China.

This is absolutely not to be allowed. The Chinese people have every right to liberate their own territory by all suitable means at a suitable time, and will not tolerate any foreign interference.

Should the United States Government, brazenly disregarding the repeated warnings served by the Chinese people and the desire of the people of the world for peace, persist in their aggression and intervention against China and impose war on the Chinese people, it must bear the responsibility for all the serious consequences.

VIII

The Suez Crisis

1

Suez and the Western Powers*

GEORGE LICHTHEIM

When an international crisis bursts upon the world, one of the things it does is to set earlier events in better perspective. Since July this has been true of the East–West struggle for control of Egypt and the Suez Canal. In the light of the long-term issues raised by this conflict, Colonel Nasser's rash defiance of the maritime nations takes on the appearance of a dramatic coup designed to give Egypt the maximum leverage in a situation where East and West alike are bidding for the support of Arab nationalism. Events had been shaping in this way for some time, and we ought not to have been surprised, but it is a rule of experience that the immediate past only begins to be properly understood when a new plateau has been reached whence it can be viewed afresh. . . .

It has been remarked by puzzled observers that of these powers, Russia seems to be the only one that is not afraid of Egypt. But even the Russians must move warily if they are to keep the support of Arab nationalism.

From the viewpoint of the Arab nationalists, this conflict gives the Middle Eastern countries, grouped around Egypt, exactly the kind of central position that Germany for a while was able to exploit. Tactically, Nasser is doing what Hitler did before him, and this (rather than the somewhat farfetched comparisons with the much more potent Axis threat that have suddenly become the fashion in diplomatic quarters and among British and French writers) is the justification for treating his challenge as a sequel to the Euorpean upheaval twenty years ago. It can indeed be demonstrated that the Nasser regime is not fully fascist—if only because Egypt is too backward for a genuinely modern totalitarianism to take root; what cannot be so easily dismissed is the likelihood that the regime will pursue a course calculated to plunge the Middle East into war.

*From Commentary, **22** (October, 1956), 320–325. Reprinted from Commentary, by permission; copyright © 1956 by the American Jewish Committee.

The probability of such an outcome has now at last been realized by the British government, which for years had tried to appease the Egyptian dictator in the hope of confining his ambition to less dangerous projects. Illumination has, however, come under particularly unfavorable circumstances, with France handicapped by the Algerian struggle and the United States plainly inclined to prolong Nasser's stay in power, at the cost to the Egyptian dictator of some not very far-reaching concessions in the domain of international management (or merely supervision) of the Suez Canal. In consequence, there is a danger that Nasser will not merely get away with it, but secure the kind of spectacular triumph that will embolden him to push his campaign a stage further. As the London *Times* correctly observed, "Nasser is poisoning the relations of the West with the Arab world." It might have added that he has successfully done so for years, not least because his outrageous pretense of having to defend the Arab world against Israel was indirectly sanctioned by constant Western babble about the need to "settle" this supposedly all-important obstacle to "better relations."

It is only now, with the facts staring them in the face, that the British government and its supporters have abandoned this nonsense and allowed their true fears to become vocal. In the process they have, however, failed to rally the British public—let alone the Commonwealth—behind them. The switch has been too abrupt, and the brief period of Conservative saber-rattling at the beginning of August (which failed to frighten the Egyptians) thus had a thoroughly unnerving effect on Liberal and Labor circles, to say nothing of public opinion in India, Ceylon, and the uncommitted countries of the Middle East. It is indeed one of the major ironies of the situation that Nasser, having seized the assets of the Suez Canal Company by force and taken illegal possession of an international waterway, has been able to pose as the victim of Anglo-French bellicosity, while the British government has had to apologize to the world, including its own public at home, for daring to take some precautionary military measures.

At the time of writing, no one can say whether and how the Egyptian government will finally be enabled to extend its physical possession of the Suez Canal to effective control of its management, coupled with some financial arrangement giving it the lion's share of all future income from shipping dues. Such an arrangement appeared probable to most observers from the moment it became clear that Britain and France lacked the nerve to impose an alternative solution. With the United States and the USSR looming behind the immediate contestants in the role of watchful guardians of their allies' interests, the role of unofficial mediator was bound to fall to India, which in the circumstances could only mean that Egypt would obtain just enough Asian backing to nullify any serious threat of intervention. In effect, therefore, the conference held in London at the end of August had to settle one point only: the size of the economic bribe that would induce Nasser to consent to some kind of international supervision.

The discrepancy between this outcome and the inordinate hopes, fears, and expectations aroused by the Eden government's brief display of energy in late July and early August has been sufficiently pronounced to drive a good many people—not only Conservatives—to something near despair. But it is the kind of outcome that cooler heads had predicted from the start. Given the state of Asian opinion, which invests any military action against Egypt with the heaviest political risks, it was inevitable that Britain and France should back down—so far as military intervention was concerned. Economic sanctions are another matter.

This, however, is not to say that by backing down they have saved the essentials of the Western position in the Middle East and aligned themselves once more with the main current of public opinion in Asia and Africa. What Britain and France—but above all Britain, which originally took the lead in the drive against Nasser—have done is to react in a manner likely to obtain for him just the degree of African nationalist support that he needs.

It is Egypt which has so far won the war of nerves; and the Egypt we have to deal with is ruled by a dictator who has made it plain what his further aims are. The London *Times* (August 15), which usually tends to wrap political issues in legal cotton-wool, for once refrained from calling a spade an agricultural implement:

> Britain and the West, in taking a stand on the canal issue, have taken a risk. It the situation is mishandled, Arab nationalism may sweep through the oilfields of the Middle East and for some time deprive us of our sources of supply. But the risk, had we stood by idle, would have been greater and might well have become a certainty. The memory of Abadan, the Lebanon's threat to the I. P. C. pipeline, the repudiation of the Indonesian debt, Dr. Azikiwe's remarks on English banking in eastern Nigeria—all these are warnings that the consequences of Nasser's action going unchallenged would be the progressive elimination of European stakes, and European contribution to development, in the emergent countries. . . .
>
> Simple, legitimate interests, and the rule of law, are at stake. They have to be asserted. There is an immense tide of emotional nationalism now in flood. It should be respected, but not feared. The emergent peoples are not fools. . . . They are capable of recognizing when others act of necessity. . . .

This is well enough in its way, but the "tough" line cannot be followed while the U. S. and the USSR cancel each other out, thereby allowing Asian and Arab nationalism to overrun all the old political landmarks. It is this world stalemate that has enabled the Egyptian dictator to blackmail the Western nations. It is the same stalemate that will make it possible for him, with the Suez Canal revenues in his pocket, to turn his attention to Iraq, the only remaining "stable" Arab country and the chief pillar of the Baghdad Pact. One must indeed be blind not to see that the pact is next on his list of victims—there are enough rationalist conspirators in Baghdad to launch the necessary cascade of army coups and assassinations, though whether in the end a country which borders on Turkey can hope to keep the Mosul oil fields if it falls into anarchy is another question. However that may be, this particular avalanche is now well and truly under way, and the only question is whether it can be checked before war has been added to the long list of calamities from which the Middle East is suffering. . . .

Perhaps the only consolation to be derived from the Western diplomacy of the past few months is that it has at least broken up the Bandung camp: instead of standing closer together as a result of the recent upheaval, Russia and India have visibly pulled apart, while on her other flank India has momentarily lost touch with Pakistan, Turkey, and Persia—in short, with the predominantly Moslem countries which are not Arab and have no illusions about Colonel Nasser. This at any rate is something; in the context of Asian and Middle Eastern politics it is quite a substantial achievement, and even in terms of global alignments it is not to be sneezed at. But it does not quite compensate for the impending loss of Western control over Suez, the further undermining of Western influence in the Arab world, and the USSR's growing prestige among the more bellicose and fanatical Arab chauvinists. Mr. Shepilov may not have emerged with brilliant honors from the London conference—seen at close quarters he seems a fairly typical specimen of the Khrushchev era of pompous mediocrity—but though towards the end he had maneuvered himself into something approaching isolation among his colleagues, he managed to retain his hold over the Egyptians. Making Colonel Nasser relinquish the Russian bear's precious support is going to be a difficult operation and, even if successful, may turn out to cost more money than the U. S. originally offered to finance the Aswan dam. The attempt would nonetheless be worth making if Nasser had not already shown himself in his true colors.

It will of course be made anyhow, whatever the reluctance of London and Paris to sanction Mr. Dulles's diplomacy. Britain and France are not in control of the situation; from the outset of the crisis they never were. Their only hope now is that both the United States and the Asian world will become disillusioned with Colonel Nasser before he sets fire to what remains of their earthly possessions. It is a slim hope. The chances are that Nasser will continue to march towards the goal of reviving the "Arab empire" of his schoolboy imagination, with Turkey, Persia, Ethiopia, Pakistan, India, and Indonesia gradually cooling towards him, but not quite fast enough to give him pause. In the interval there is scope enough for the partial fulfilment of his military dreams. Should he come a cropper over Israel or some other obstacle, there are of course rival aspirants for power, able and willing to continue where he left off. At worst, as Mr. Khrushchev pointed out to the British and French ambassadors in Moscow last August, the Arab states, if checked in warfare, can count on Soviet "volunteers" to bail them out. It is not a pretty prospect. . . .

2

U.S., U.S.S.R., and Suez*

VERA M. DEAN

If the distinguished historian, Arnold J. Toynbee, is right in contending that those civilizations have perished in the past which, when challenged, either failed to respond or else made a response that was inadequate, then it may well prove that the Western powers now face at Suez a challenge which could prove the start of their undoing unless they can alter the character of their response. As the second Suez conference summoned by the West in London since Egypt's nationalization of the canal ended on Septemer 21, the sum total of responses made by Britain, France and the United States either separately or together appeared to have weakened the position of the West and strengthened that of the U. S. .S. R., which had emerged as the self-appointed champion of Egypt.

Only a year before, in September 1955, the West had been shocked by the decision of Colonel Gamal Abdel Nasser, then premier, now president, of Egypt to purchase arms from the Soviet bloc in return for long-term exports of Egypt's principal product, cotton, after Cairo had tried in vain to obtain arms from the United States, which was willing to sell only for dollars the Egyptians lacked. This move, which apparently caught Western diplomats by surprise, brought the U. S. S. R. to a strategic position at Suez, and thus at the entrance to the Mediterranean, which the Tsarist Empire had unsuccessfully sought to achieve in the 19th and early 20th centuries. Moscow's new position, moreover, was won without the firing of a shot.

Confronted by Russia's claim to a voice in the Middle East, the United States and Britain sought to checkmate Soviet economic competition by offering to help Egypt build the High Aswan Dam with the aid of the World Bank, only to withdraw this offer in July 1956 when they reached the conclusion that the U. S. S. R., contrary to Cairo's expectations, was not interested in financing this project. This decision not only precipitated Nasser's nationalization of the Suez Canal Company, but left Moscow in the role of the innocent bystander while the Western powers were accused by the Egyptians of undermining their country's economy and blocking its industrialization. Even if Washington and London believed by that time that financing of the dam was genuinely undesirable, Western diplomacy might have avoided this head-on collision with Egypt by either prolonging

*From Foreign Policy Bulletin, **36** (*October 15, 1956*), 23–24. Reprinted by permission.

the negotiations or proposing further technical studies of the project. At the very least, they could have spared Nasser the humiliation of a brusque public rejection accompanied by derogatory comments about his country's economic situation, which even a less fervent nationalist leader would have resented.

Once Nasser had nationalized the canal company, the West could have chosen a number of ways to negotiate with Egypt about guarantees of free navigation through Suez. Without denouncing Nasser personally or revealing a desire to see him overthrown, and without mobilizing their armed forces, Britain and France could have called for orderly review of the Constantinople Convention of 1888, which was signed at a time when modern Egypt was still a part of the Ottoman Empire and not the independent nation it has become since the withdrawal of British forces from the Suez Canal zone, completed only this year. Disturbing as Nasser's unilateral actions have been to the West, as of September 18 he had not violated international law and had carried out his July 26 pledge of maintaining free navigation through the canal for the ships of all nations—with the continued exception of Israel, an exception the Western nations had not previously challenged by force.

Alternatively, the Western nations could have invited UN Secretary General Dag Hammarskjold to study the possibility of reconciling the conflict of interests at Suez through discussions, perhaps of a private character, at the United Nations. It will be recalled that he had shortly before carried out two delicate missions in the Middle East in an effort to ease tensions between the Arab states and Israel, which at one time last spring had threatened to erupt into war. Or the West might have invoked the good offices of some of the Asian and African nations, whose interests are at least as much affected by the Suez crisis as those of Britain and France —such as India, Pakistan, Ceylon and Ethiopia—in an effort to demonstrate that its policy toward Nasser is dictated not only by concern for the living standards of Western nations but by concern for the welfare also of the underdeveloped peoples east of Suez.

Instead, by insisting on a proposal for the establishment of an international authority which would control the canal and not merely advise about its use as proposed by India, the West confronted Nasser with a course of action a nation which had just seen the end of British supervision could not be expected to accept. Then, when the Menzies committee returned from Cairo empty-handed, the West either encouraged, or did not act to prevent, the withdrawal of over 100 Western pilots on the assumption that this might bring traffic through the canal to a standstill, and that Nasser could then be charged with violation of the Constantinople Convention; and, as the threat of war arose again, suggested the formation of a "users' association" whose function would be to challenge Egypt's authority over the canal—a proposal which brought protests from Asian and African countries, even those which regard unhampered use of the canal as essential for their economic survival.

This series of moves, far from strengthening the West in its dealings with Egypt, promptly increased the influence of the U. S. S. R. The world witnessed the spectacle, which would have seemed incredible even a month before, of Russian pilots arriving to help the Egyptians maintain traffic through the canal. Moscow, which in the early summer had taken a dim view of the British Labor party following Mr. Khrushchev's wrangle with leading Laborites during his London visit, applauded Hugh Gaitskell's opposition to the Suez policy of Prime Minister Sir Anthony Eden. And while the West thought it could force Egypt to the wall by economic measures such as the freezing of Egyptian sterling balances in London and Paris and the suspension of all forms of aid to Cairo, the net result may be that not only Egypt but other countries east of Suez will find it a matter of sheer economic necessity to rely increasingly on the Soviet bloc for trade and financing.

The possibility is not excluded that the Suez crisis will actually cut the West off from its traditional economic contacts with Asia and parts of Africa and consolidate the economic penetration of the U. S. S. R. and Eastern Europe, which up to that time had only been in its initial stages. Not only that, but it may prove that West Germany and Japan, both of which have been vigorously cultivating markets in the Middle East and Asia, will decline to be drawn into the West's controversy with Egypt, and find it to their advantage to remain on the sidelines of the economic war which could be the outcome of the Suez crisis. Should this happen, the network of military pacts the United States has been patiently building along the periphery of the U. S. S. R. might be eroded—again without the firing of a shot.

To add to the West's complications, Nasser, who is by no means popular with some of the Arab rulers, notably King Hussein of Jordan and King Saud of Saudi Arabia, becasue of his appeal to the nationalist elements in their countries which might easily favor social revolution, is, by that very token, regarded by these elements as a symbol of Arab resistance to any form of Western "colonialism." In this respect Nasser performs a far more effective role of challenging the West than the U. S. S. R. itself could have done if it were in sole control of Egypt. And the West, by attacking Nasser and clearly indicating its determination to seek his downfall, has actually solidified his position in the Middle East, as indicated by the support Saudi Arabia and Syria now give Egypt.

Thus far the West has failed to meet or turn back his challenge, which Russia, by giving him support that so far costs Moscow next to nothing, is able to utilize against the West in other parts of the world as well. A new phase, however, has been opened by referral of the Suez question to the UN Security Council on September 23.

3

The Suez Canal Issue 1956*

SIEGBERT J. WEINBERGER

When on July 19, 1956 the United States abruptly revoked its offer to help Egypt with the Aswan High Dam project,[1] American policy makers assumed what is termed a "calculated risk." That repercussions were inevitable could not have been doubted, but their scope was certainly not foreseen by Secretary of State John Foster Dulles. Almost within days the issue assumed world-wide proportions and became involved in an intricate mesh of conflicting international policies.

The switch in American policy was motivated by the recognition that President Gamal Abdul Nasser of Egypt had played a successful undercover game involving the East and West in a struggle of competitve bids for Egyptian favor, with the Egyptian ruler acting as sole umpire. What made matters worse from the American point of view was the realization that in contrast with the United States, the Soviet Union had almost nothing to lose in so competing.

The secret game had, on the whole, been played shrewdly, and only when matters began to take on untoward proportions did Western statesmen begin to suspect "blackmail." It was then decided that Colonel Nasser would have to be restrained and brought back to his senses. While a policy directed towards this end involved the dangerous possibility that Cairo might turn entirely to the Soviet Union, it was felt at the time that the Egyptian Government would not be willing to take this extreme gamble.

In its immediate impact the United States' decision manifested a reorientation of American policy in the Middle East, with particular emphasis on the regime of Colonel Nasser, who up to that time had not been unsympathetically regarded in Washington. Only in London and Paris had there been doubts as to his ultimate "reliability." But now the Egyptian ruler had been handed an exceptionally sharp rebuff, and at the instigation of the United States.

Unofficial Egyptian reaction showed that Cairo had been caught off guard. In a series of surprised and angry comments, government circles held that the Anglo-American action constituted a calculated effort to destory Colonel Nasser's prestige. While the manner in which the announce-

*From Middle Eastern Affairs, **8** (February, 1957), 46–50, 56–57. Reprinted by permission.*

[1]The British Government cancelled its offer of aid for the project on July 20.

ment was made to Cairo was admittedly brusque,[2] the Cairo government should not have found the withdrawal of the Western offers peculiarly unmotivated. It had been evident in the preceding months that Nasser's relations with London and Washington were progressively deteriorating. Egypt's increasing trade with the Communist-bloc countries, her recognition of Communist China (May 16, 1956), Nasser's neutralist and often strongly anti-Western statements, Cairo's support of the Cypriot and French North African insurgents, and Egyptian interference in the affairs of Libya, Jordan, Syria and Iraq, all these had aroused apprehensions among the Western powers.[3]

Hand in hand with an increasingly strident propaganda effort, Soviet economic penetration in the Middle East had made particular headway in Syria and Egypt. Moscow's opposition to the Bagdad Pact and its policy vis-à-vis Israel, coupled with its cynical espousal of the anti-imperialist line, found ready support in Cairo. The Communist powers were lauded as the champions of Arab freedom against the intentions of the "imperialists." But if the Egyptian Government had hopes that the Soviet Union would now be ready with assistance to overcome the dilemma created by the withdrawal of the American and British offers, they were soon dispelled. Egypt's policy of pitting the Soviets against the West came to a dead end. Russia, as Western observers had rightly reasoned, was unwilling or unable to underwrite the Aswan project on her own. On July 21, Moscow announced that no consideration was being given to aid Egypt in the construction of the Dam, but that the Soviet Union was prepared to give sympathetic consideration to the development of Egyptian industries. Colonel Nasser's policy had failed.

On July 24, the Egyptian President violently attacked Washington's decision with regard to the Dam. He rejected American insinuations that Egypt would be unable to carry her share of the financial burden for the project. The United States, he declared, had "lied" about Egypt's economic condition. Cairo would go ahead with the project on its own. Washington observers were skeptical.

The safety and maintenance of the Suez Canal as an international waterway open to the trade of all nations had been the principal factor governing big-power diplomacy with respect to Egypt since the Canal's

[2] *New York Herald Tribune*, July 21, 1956, headlined its editorial: "But Is the Kick Necessary?" While admitting the legitimacy of the policy change, the paper asked: "But need the turnabout have been advertised so bluntly and so crushingly as has been done?" In England some organs were similarly critical—*The Observer* (London), July 22, 1956; *The Manchester Guardian*, July 28, 1956.

[3] In the official reasons given by both the U. S. and British Governments for the cancellation of the Aswan High Dam offers, it was inferred that Egypt, having mortgaged much of her national income in the Czech arms deal, would not be financially able to undertake the project. In addition, Egypt had not reached an aggreement with the other interested states (Sudan, Ethiopia, Uganda) on the Nile waters. For full text of the U. S. document, see *Middle Eastern Affairs*, VII, 298–299, Aug.–Sept., 1956.

opening in 1869. The economic and strategic value of the Canal, which is perhaps the most important sea-artery in world commerce, is self-evident. It was therefore not astonishing that Nasser's declaration on July 26 that Egypt had nationalized the Suez Canal Company[4] and taken over the Company's offices in Egypt, and would henceforth operate the waterway herself, created a most serious situation. Colonel Nasser explained that the action was legally proper and that he intended to use the Canal tolls to underwrite the construction of the Aswan High Dam. His unilateral decision was enthusiastically welcomed in Egypt. Western observers were stunned by what had apparently come as a complete surprise.

Hurried initial conferences in London and Paris were indecisive in so far as prompt countermeasures were concerned. The French Foreign Minister commented that the news from Cairo was "of a nature to make one think Colonel Nasser is at bay."[5] It was felt that the Egyptian Government had acted in desperation. London was sharply aroused. Editorial comment suggested that "the Hitler of the Nile" should be stopped, preferably by joint Anglo-American intervention, and that such intervention must not rule out the use of force as a last resort. More moderate opinion held that the principal Western concern in the matter was to assure the continued flow of oil from the Middle East by way of the Suez Canal; at the same time other ways of transporting oil from the Middle East to Europe should be investigated. American condemnation was no less severe. "This plain act of economic aggression" must be strenuously rebuffed; Colonel Nasser's "combination of blackmail, lies and bluff" must be countered. Warning was given, however, that the method would have to be "reason, economics and law."[6]

On July 27 it was reported from Cairo that the Government had decreed general mobilization throughout the country and martial law in the Canal zone. President Nasser declared that Egypt intended to meet "force with force." An official statement emphasized that neither the World Court nor the United Nations Security Council had any jurisdiction in the matter. Egypt considered that she had acted entirely within her sovereign rights.

Official London reacted cautiously. As a first move the British Government sought ways to freeze Egypt's sterling balances and all the assets of the Suez Canal Company in the United Kingdom. Parallel action along similar lines was hoped for from France and interested members of the British Commonwealth. Strong diplomatic protests to the Egyptian Government were immedaitely rejected by Cairo. It became known that Britain and France were moving for Seretary Dulles to come to London on July 30 for urgent consultations. London felt that any action should be closely

---

[4]The official name is *La Compagnie Universelle du Canal Maritime de Suez*. The Company's headquarters are in Paris, but the Company itself is an Egyptian concern.

[5] *The Christian Science Monitor*, July 27, 1956.

[6]Editorials in *The New York Times* and *New York Herald Tribune*, July 28, 1956.

coordinated between Paris, Washington and the Commonwealth nations. In Parliament, Conservatives and Laborites alike were united in condemning the Egyptian act.

The mood in Paris was more militant. It was indicated unofficially that the French Government inclined to favor military occupation of the Canal. On July 27 the French Government declared that Egypt's action was contrary to international law, but a sharply worded protest by M. Pineau to the Egyptian Ambassador in Paris was rejected offhand as "inadmissible and unacceptable." The Suez Canal Company issued a statement in Paris repudiating the Egyptian decree freezing the Company's assets abroad.

The first official American statement on the crisis suggested that the seizure of the Suez Canal Company's installations carried "far-reaching implications" and that the United States Government was "urgently" consulting with the other governments concerned. The crucial question was how best to support Great Britain and France. Meanwhile, the Arab press rejoiced that Washington's decision to withdraw its aid offer had backfired with such vigor and had turned "what should (have been) a defeat into a great victory."

From the beginning Washington undoubtedly regarded the crisis as very serious. On July 28 Acting Secretary of State Herbert Hoover, Jr. protested against Colonel Nasser's statements concerning the United States. It became known that Deputy Under-Secretary of State Robert Murphy had gone to London, at the suggestion of the British and French Governments, for exploratory talks, and it was expected that Secretary Dulles would follow him within a few days.

That same day, the 28th, Colonel Nasser further aggravated the tension by warning the West that to interfere with the Egyptian act of nationalization was to invite "obstruction of navigation" in the Canal. His abusive remarks directed at the three Western powers again drew sharp protests. Only Moscow and Communist China applauded Nasser's policies. The Colombo powers made tentative moves to consult together on the threatening crisis; the Turkish press was unanimous in denouncing the unilateral seizure of the waterway.

With the implications of what had taken place becoming clearer, London's initial hesitancy began to disappear. Anger dispelled the original caution, and public as well as official opinion began to incline increasingly towards the more militant stand advocated by France. As the Egyptian threat to British shipping loomed larger, the use of force to keep the Suez Canal open gained greater consideration in London. While it was still hoped that a joint three-power policy to cope with the situation could be devised, it became clearer that the actual burden of countering Nasser would eventually fall on Britain.

The immediate concern of the French and British Governments was to come to an agreement with the United States on a policy to place the Suez Canal under international supervision. The right to use the waterway would have to be guaranteed by an international body, and the principle of free passage through the Canal laid down in the Convention of 1888 would have to be reaffirmed.

London and Paris were hopeful that the United States would back them should the necessity of sending troops into the Canal zone arise. Furthermore, they hoped that Washington would support economic sanctions if the British and French Governments decided on such action. In a very strong statement before the House of Commons on July 31, Sir Anthony Eden declared that Great Britain would not accept "unfettered control" of the Suez Canal by a single power. He warned Egypt not to hold British employees of the Suez Canal Company at their jobs against their will, and he rejected Colonel Nasser's plan to use Canal tolls for the construction of the Aswan High Dam. However, his statement left unanswered what he intended to do to assure the success of this policy. . . .

The total result of the protracted discussions was negligible. A week of negotiations produced nothing more than a six-point statement of principles which embodied in general terms the views of France and Britain, but made no provision for putting the principles into effect. On October 13, when the two countries moved for a new resolution endorsing the six principles and called on Egypt to propose a system, based on the London recommendations, to implement the principles, the Soviet and Egyptian Foreign Ministers objected. In the subsequent vote the Soviet Union vetoed everything but the six-point statement of principles. London and Paris had gained nothing. They had, in fact, worsened their position since their original intention of obtaining United Nations' approval for the proposed system of international operation of the Suez Canal was completely sidetracked. Nevertheless, Secretary Dulles felt that much had been accomplished and President Eisenhower declared that things were beginning to "look better."

The sanguine American appraisal was not shared by either London or Paris. The British Government made one more effort to persuade Secretary Dulles to join actively in putting the Users Association into effect, and on October 17 Prime Minister Eden and Premier Mollet issued a communiqué in Paris calling on the Egyptian Government to make the next move. They regretted that some quarters in Egypt were already challenging the six-point declaration of principles which had been unanimously approved by the Security Council. In Egypt, expectations were for a new conference to meet in Geneva, probably within the next ten days.

The Egyptian feelers for a new conference, which had been communicated to the British and French Governments through the United Nations, were suddenly rebuffed on October 23. The two Western powers felt that Egypt's proposals were too vague to warrant negotiations, that in fact they could not be "seriously" considered. The crisis seemed to be in a state of complete suspension when the news reached Western capitals that Israel had struck across the Egyptian border into the Sinai Peninsula.

IX

The Hungarian Revolution

1

Eruption in East Europe*

HUGH SETON-WATSON

The Hungarian revolution was precipitated by events in Poland. A demonstration of students laid a wreath on the statue of General Bem, the Pole who had led Hungarian forces in the revolutionary war of 1849. The crowds began to shout for Imre Nagy, whose two years of "new course" had made him popular even among non-Communists, and who was the obvious candidate for the role of Hungarian Gomulka. But Gerö saw fit at this stage to make a broadcast of Stalinian rigidity. Having met both Khrushchev and Tito in the Crimea, and having made the pilgrimage to Belgrade, he no doubt felt strong enough to ignore the popular mood: perhaps he was simply incapable of recognizing it. Nagy himself, who by now had been re-admitted to the party's Central Committee, made a mild speech to a crowd in the square in front of the Parliament which did not satisfy anyone. The crowd then toppled over the giant statue of Stalin, and approached the radio station. It was at this point, on the evening of October 23, that the security police opened fire. The crowd did not disperse, and it was reinforced by armed workers and soldiers.

In the early morning hours of the 24th, Soviet tanks entered Budapest, and it was announced a little later that the government, under the Warsaw Pact, had asked the Soviet army to help restore order. The Warsaw Pact is, of course, a military alliance between states directed against foreign countries (the NATO powers and a re-armed Germany), not against the peoples of the signatory states. It is still not clear who invited the Russians, or indeed whether there was an invitation at all. Imre Nagy some days later denied that he had done so. It was in the late morning of the 24th that the radio referred to Nagy as Prime Minister: when and by whom he was appointed, was not stated. During the 24th the Soviet tanks appear to have taken no

*From Commentary, **22** (December, 1956), 518–524. Reprinted from Commentary, by permission; copyright © 1956 by the American Jewish Committee.

part in the fighting. On the morning of the 25th a large crowd assembled in the Parliament square. It was at this point that Soviet tanks fired into the unarmed mass of workers and students, killing six hundred persons.

Far too little still is known of the confused pattern of events in the whole country. But it would seem that this massacre by Russians was the decisive moment. Thereafter the army, which had hitherto been mainly neutral, though some soldiers had joined the masses, came over to the revolution. The Hungarian nation rose against the Russians, not only in Budapest but in most other large towns. All western Hungary was soon in their hands, but the position east of the Danube has never been made clear.

It might be thought that the Hungarians behaved recklessly, that they were wrong not to follow the example of moderation set by the Poles. But this is a baseless criticism. The decisive difference between events in Hungary and in Poland lies in the different attitudes of the Communist leaderships. Ochab and Cyrankiewicz were wise enough to make way for Gomulka, and Gomulka was strong and clever enough to take and hold power. In Hungary the party was built around the autocracy of Rakosi. In both countries Communism as such was detested by the vast majority of the nation. The Communist parties were small minorities, but while the Polish party was an intelligent minority, the Hungarian was a purely one-man show. Three provocative blunders made an explosion inevitable: Gerö's Stalinist speech of October 23, the invitation to the Russians to intervene, and the massacre in front of the Parliament. After this, what could the Hungarians do but fight or surrender? There was no opening for moderation or maneuver. That they chose to fight is a proof not of recklessness but of courage and national unity.

Dictatorships are as old as the human race, but totalitarianism is a creation of the 20th century made possible by mass means of communication and by the total will to power of secular religions. Totalitarianism, with its all-pervading propaganda, its security police, its invasion of private life and belief, and its systematic atomization of society, has long seemed invincible from within. Only war destroyed Hitler, and Stalin survived even war. But the Hungarians have shown us that a united nation can unseat a totalitarian regime in two days.

The second lesson is that the forces which led the revolution were precisely those on which the regime had counted for support. The intellectual youth were precisely those children of workers and peasants whom for the last eight years the regime had been bringing up, in its indoctrinated schools, colleges, and universities, to be the brains of totalitarianism. It was they who started and led the movement of the nation against the regime. The first mass support of the revolution came from the Budapest working class, in whose name for so many years the Communists have declaimed their stale Leninist rhetoric. Csepel Island, the biggest industrial concentration in Hungary, sent its armed worker guards to join the demonstrators on October 23. As I write, a week after the second Soviet onslaught of November 4, fighting is still going on in two main centers. One is Csepel Island. The other is Dunapentele, until recently known as Sztalinvaros (Stalin City), the new industrial town built round the new steel mill on the Danube near Mohács, where four hundred and thirty years ago Hungary's armies were destroyed by the Turks, invaders humane and honorable when judged by the standards of Khrushchev and Zhukov. The working class, then, provided the core of the nation's resistance. The third factor of course is the Hungarian army. The old army was destroyed in 1944–45; part of it went into exile in Austria and Germany, and what remained in Hungary was purged and disbanded. The new army has been rebuilt since 1947. It is ironical that Moscow, in its desire to train cannon fodder to fight the West, should have allowed Hungary—like Rumania and Bulgaria—to exceed the limits laid down in the peace treaties. Even so, the army was not large or very well equipped. Great care was however lavished by Rakosi's regime on the indoctrination, in Marxist–Leninist fanaticism, of the new army, and especially of its officers. But when the crisis came, the army went with the nation against the regime.

Intellectual youth, workers, and army joined in the Hungarian revolution. The rest of the nation—the peasants and what was left of the old bourgeoisie—were of course behind them. Only the security police were against, and they were quickly overcome. The nation fought the Russian army, and forced it to withdraw. By the middle of the week the revolution had won its first battle, and the adversaries stood facing each other. In Moscow there was irresolution. The Soviet leaders, never united since Stalin died, must have been more uncertain, more fearful of each other and of the world, than they had ever been.

It was at this moment that Israel saw fit to invade Egypt, and that Eden and Mollet saw fit to do likewise.

For Israel's plight I have nothing but sympathy. It has long been clear that Nasser was building his strength up to destroy her. It has also long been clear that Nasser is an implacable enemy of the West, concerned not to obtain satisfaction of legitimate Egyptian claims, but to destroy all European and American interests throughout Africa and Western Asia, to create his own Egyptian empire from the Shatt-el-Arab to the Maghreb, selling himself to Moscow or anyone else for the purpose. All this has long been clear to everyone except the government of the United States. That Israel should resort to desperate action to save herself is humanly understandable. Even so, the moment was terribly chosen. Now for the first time since 1947 a chance appeared of getting the Russians out of Europe, of restoring European peace, and the independence of European nations captive since the 1930's. A change of this immensity would have transformed the whole Middle East as well, would have deflated Nasser and strengthened Israel. It was hardly to be expected of the leaders of Israel, facing a mortal threat, that they should take so wide a view. But of the leaders of Britain and France this must be expected. It was for them to see the meaning of the Hungarian revolution, to advise Israel accordingly, and to bring this to the notice of the government of the United States.

This is precisely what Sir Anthony Eden and M. Mollet did not do. This is the failure for which history will never forgive them. They turned their backs on Europe in Europe's great moment of hope. Then was the chance for Britain to take the initiative, together with the United States, France, and Germany, to approach the Soviet leaders with firmness, tact, and imagination, to begin new negotiations on European security, on the twin problems of German unity and East European independence, to make it clear that the West was willing to offer a price for Soviet concessions, that it was in Moscow's interest to examine this price rather than to destroy Hungary. This was the only way to European peace, which we have not known since 1933 or perhaps since 1914. This was the first moment since 1947 when there was a chance to begin a political action that had a real chance of securing it.

But Sir Anthony's mind was elsewhere. No doubt he would be hurt by the suggestion that he does not care about Europe. But it is true. He believes sincerely in Anglo-French friendship (what civilized Briton does not?) but he conceives it in narrow diplomatic terms, with vague visions of Clémenceau and Cambon and Edward VII. Of the Europe that begins beyond the Rhine he appears to have no notion. Certainly his complaints against Nasser are sound enough. Certainly he has good grounds to be disappointed with the record of the United Nations and of the United States in the Middle East. But even if his action had secured a just and stable peace in the Middle East, it would not have justified the betrayal of Europe. As things are now going, it looks as if in addition to betraying Europe he will have destroyed all European influence from Casablanca to Basra and from Aleppo to Lake Victoria.

Not only did Sir Anthony turn his back on Europe: he did not even act quickly. If ever there was a war which was too serious to be left to the generals, it was this one. While the airmen conscientiously pounded away at Egyptian airfields, and the invasion forces waited day after day in Cyprus, all those whom Britain and France had insulted or ignored had time to work themselves into a frenzy of hate. The Soviet leaders quickly saw that no one was going to pay any attention to Europe, and they gave the word for the butchery. As I write a whole week later, the butchery is still going on, Hungarian children are still dying as they try to destroy Soviet tanks with gasoline bombs, Hungary's workers are still on strike, and the representatives of the "Socialist Sixth of the World" are using starvation to force them back to work. And all the time nobody is considering help to Hungary. The United Nations are fairly fully occupied in saving the human race from the atomic war which Sir Anthony's genius and Khrushchev's blood-lust almost unleashed. And when the United Nations does find time to talk about Hungary, that splendid moralist Nehru instructs his representative to abstain. . . .

And the West? It is still possible to help Hungary, not only with relief to refugees but by massive economic help to the starving nation. If the United States and the West European governments offer such help, unconditionally and on a vast scale, Moscow will have either to agree or to give help herself on the same scale. In either case Western action will have helped Hungary. The West can also give moral help to the Hungarians in their continued and unflinching moral resistance to the Russians. Demonstrations of the unanimity of European opinion, of all classes, all professions, and all political views, are not without their effect on the Russian people. Finally, the West must reopen the whole problem of European security, that is, of the unity of Germany and the independence of Eastern Europe. For this there must be unity of Western Europe and America, a unity transcending the purely military and economic fields. The murder of Hungary was a blow also at Europe. The only way to restore Hungary and to save ourselves from destruction is to create the unity of Europe, which Eisenhower has forgotten, Mollet ignored, and Eden betrayed.

2

Hungary—Were We Helpless?*

RICHARD LOWENTHAL

Twelve years after the Russian armies first established Soviet rule over Eastern Europe, the empire founded by Stalin has been shaken by a revolutionary earthquake of altogether unimagined force and scope. The tragic outcome of the Hungarian revolution must not blind us to the fact that both in Hungary and Poland, essentially revolutionary movements have for the first time not only broken the surface of totalitarian uniformity, but have in their different ways achieved an unprecedented measure of success: moreover, they have done so entirely on the basis of the crises and contradictions which had developed within the Soviet orbit, without the aid of international conflict and indeed despite international diversions favorable to the Soviet rulers. Bloody suppression of the Hungarian movement may restore outward calm for the moment, but the Soviet East European empire will never be the same again.

What was new in the October revolutions of 1956 was not that the national

*From The New Republic, 135 (November 26, 1956), 10–15. Copyright © 1956 by Harrison-Blaine of New Jersey. Reprinted by permission.

and social grievances of two enslaved peoples fused in a powerful outburst of mass revolt; that had happened before, in the whole of Eastern Germany in June, 1953, and in Poznan in June, 1956. What was new and was, indeed, as unexpected as it was unprecedented was that the popular movement for freedom managed to impose a new leadership, committed to national independence and thoroughgoing changes in internal and economic policy of the Communist Party of Poland and through it on the Polish administration and army; and that it succeeded in virtually taking over the army of Communist Hungary, and with its help overthrowing the Communist Party dictatorship—splitting the hitherto ruling party and creating a Democratic national government committed to internal freedom and international neutrality.

The major common factor in the background of both the Polish and Hungarian events was clearly the weakening of Soviet authority both within the international Communist movement in general and within the satellite states in particular. That weakening, which has proceeded slowly and gradually ever since the death of Stalin and the loosening of detailed economic and police controls in the satellites, was greatly accelerated by two major events: the Belgrade declaration of 1955 by which the Soviet rulers recognized Yugoslavia's right to her "own road to Socialism," and the "secret" Khrushchev speech last February about the crimes of Stalin. . . .

The news of the Polish events hit a Hungary already in ferment. When Gero returned to Hungary from Yugoslavia on October 23, he was greeted by the news of a students' demonstration originally arranged without permission of any party organs and banned, and later "legalized" by the leaders of the Petoefi Circle. Originally called for comparatively moderate demands of reform, the demonstration, under Hungarian and Polish national flags, quickly assumed both an unprecedented scale and a marked anti-Soviet note, and by the evening Gero broadcast a warning against "counter-revolutionary nationalism." At that, the demonstrators got embittered, and the secret police lost their nerve and started to fire at them. By nightfall, groups of students and workers had started to fight back—with weapons received from Hungarian Army soldiers and officers who had joined them.

Overnight, the pro-Soviet party leaders realized that a serious rising had started, that the Army was unwilling to fight the people, and the secret police unable to cope with it. By the morning of the 24th, they had called on the Soviet Army for help and at the same time announced the appointment of Imre Nagy as Prime Minister in an effort to calm the population. In fact, the intervention of Soviet troops provoked widespread and desperate resistance, and neither the appeals of Nagy nor the announcement on the following day that Gero had been replaced as First Secretary of the party by Janos Kadar—a former participant in the Rakosi regime but later its victim—made any impact. Army units and officers seem to have joined the insurgents in increasing numbers during the following days, while the government, isolated by the Budapest uprising, lost control of large parts of the country; revolutionary workers and "student councils" were set up in several regions, everywhere putting the withdrawal of Soviet troops at the head of their demands.

By Sunday, October 28, the revolution had won. The Nagy government, now no longer a facade for the pro-Soviet group among the party leaders, proclaimed a cease-fire and called for a withdrawal of Soviet forces from its battered capital. Negotiations for broadening the government by non-Communist elements started in earnest. The Soviet command actually started to extricate its troops from Budapest, and the government promised both to dissolve the secret police and replace it by a newly recruited popular police force and to negotiate with Russia about a general withdrawal of Soviet forces from the country. Gradually, fighting subsided.

The Soviet leaders were now faced with the question whether to accept this second revolutionary *fait accompli*, achieved this time in open conflict with their occupation forces and in circumstances far more damaging to their prestige even than the Polish events. For two more days they seem to have hesitated: reports about the machinations of "counter-revolutionaries" in Hungary ceased, and some publicity was given to Nagy's new version that the victorious popular movement was a natural reaction to the mistakes and crimes of the fomer Hungarian Communist leadership. This policy, motivated apparently by a willingness to cut Soviet losses in order to save what could be saved—*i.e.*, the principle of the Communist regime and Hungary's membership in the Warsaw Pact—found its most far-reaching expression in the Soviet Government declaration broadcast from Moscow on October 30, which generally proclaimed the need for greater independence and equality for the member states of the "Socialist camp," and specifically expressed readiness to discuss the need for further stationing of Soviet forces in Poland, Hungary and Rumania within the framework of the Warsaw Pact. But by the time that declaration was broadcast, the real Soviet policy for Hungary had already turned. For by October 30, the pre-1947 democratic parties of the workers and peasants had already been reconstituted in Hungary, and Nagy had announced the abandonment of the one-party regime, the transformation of his government into a genuine coalition, and his pledge to hold a free election. He had also spoken of Hungary's desire to leave the Warsaw Pact, to become neutral under international guarantee (on the Austrian model), while the command of the Hungarian Army and Air Force had been taken over by "revolutionary council," one of whom threatened the Soviet forces with bombardment in case of refusal to withdraw.

By October 30 at the latest, it was thus clear to the Soviet leaders that nothing whatever would remain of their Hungarian position if they gave in, that the local alternatives were brute force or total defeat. The Hungarian revolution, led not by "counter-revolutionary" emigrés but by workers, students reared under the Communist regime and soldiers of its own army had within a week evolved from a program of "Titoist" independence and reform to one of full democracy combined with both workers' councils and trade union freedom, of an end to both collectivization and forced deliveries in agriculture, of a clean breakaway from the Soviet bloc. If Russia gave in, Hungary would become not a new Poland or a new Yugoslavia, but a new Austria or at best a new Finland.

To tolerate such a development would have started a chain reaction throughout the satellite empire. It would also have inflicted a fatal blow on Communist confidence in the irreversible character of all their conquests, allegedly guaranteed by the laws of history. All considerations of local strategy as well as of ideology thus favored the decision to crush the Hungarian revolution in blood. The only factors that could have prevented such a decision were wider international considerations of overwhelming strength.

It was the task of Western policy in this unique revolutionary crisis to bring these wider international considerations to bear on the decision of the Soviet leaders—a task in which the West failed as utterly as it had failed during the East German crisis of June, 1953.

What could these considerations have been? If we exclude, as we must, the threat of world war, which no Western power will use for offensive purposes, there remain two. The first and most obvious was the effect on the uncommitted countries of Asia. That consideration, implicit in the whole strategy of competitive coexistence, had clearly exercised a restraining effect up to that moment. But as clearly, that effect was bound to reach its limits at some point—once the threat of the loss of the Soviet empire loomed larger than the threat of the loss of sympathies in Asia. The Soviet leaders would rather temporarily accept a setback in the competition for uncommitted countries than put up with the total loss of their own possessions in half a continent. Moreover, the West was at the critical moment prevented from exploiting that restraining factor to the maximum owing to the Anglo-French action against Egypt which made it easy for non-committed Asian opinion to balance Soviet against "Western" inequities.

But there was one other consideration which the West could have brought into play; it could have offered to make the loss of the satellite empire strategically tolerable for Russia by matching a Soviet withdrawal from Eastern Europe with an American withdrawal from Western Europe. The old Soviet proposal for a simultaneous dissolution of the Warsaw and Atlantic Pacts has never been acceptable to the West, basically because the Soviet control of Eastern Europe does not depend on the Warsaw Pact, but on the Communist regimes, and because while Eastern Europe remains under Soviet control, Western Europe cannot defend itself by its own strength. But in a situation where Soviet Communist control of Eastern Europe was actually crumbling, the offer of an American withdrawal on condition of full freedom for Eastern Europe would have transformed the situation; not only would it have given immense encouragement to the freedom movements throughout the satellite states, but it would have added to the calculations of the Soviet leaders the one consideration which might have induced them to give in.

There can, of course, be no certainty that such an offer would have made a decisive difference to the Soviet leaders' choice. What seems clear is that it was the only chance of influencing that choice. During the most profound crisis experienced by the Soviet satellite empire, this chance was missed—just as it was missed in 1953. Now as then, the Western powers faced the Soviet crisis without a prepared policy, even though they had long proclaimed the eventual liberation of the enslaved peoples as one of their long-term objectives. In the hour of need, they had nothing to offer to these peoples but propaganda and charity.

As it was, the Soviet leaders decided to save their empire for the time being by the wholesale butchery of the Hungarian people, even at the price of alienating neutral opinion and endangering the international detente. . . .

3

Soviet Statement*

MOSCOW RADIO

The course of the events has shown that the working people of Hungary, who have achieved great progress on the basis of their people's democratic order, correctly raise the question of the necessity of eliminating serious shortcomings in the field of economic building, the further raising of the material well-being of the population, and the struggle against bureaucratic excesses in the state apparatus.

However, this just and progressive movement of the working people was soon joined by forces of black reaction and counterrevolution, which are trying to take advantage of the discontent of part of the working people to undermine the foundations of the people's democratic order in Hungary and to restore the old landlord and capitalist order.

The Soviet Government and all the Soviet people deeply regret that the development of events in Hungary has led to bloodshed. On the request of the Hungarian People's Government the Soviet Government consented to the entry into Budapest of the Soviet Army units to assist the Hungarian People's Army and the Hungarian authorities to establish order in the town. Believing that the further presence of Soviet Army units in Hungary can

*From Department of State Bulletin, **35** (November 12, 1956), 746.

serve as a cause for even greater deterioration of the situation, the Soviet Government has given instructions to its military command to withdraw the Soviet Army units from Budapest as soon as this is recognized as necessary by the Hungarian Government.

At the same time, the Soviet Government is ready to enter into relevant negotiations with the Government of the Hungarian People's Republic and other participants of the Warsaw Treaty on the question of the presence of Soviet troops on the territory of Hungary.

The defense of socialist achievements by the people's democracy of Hungary is at the present moment the chief and sacred duty of workers, peasants, and intelligentsia, and of all the Hungarian working people.

The Soviet Government expresses confidence that the peoples of the socialist countries will not permit foreign and internal reactionary forces to undermine the basis of the people's democratic regimes, won and consolidated by the heroic struggle and toil of the workers, peasants, and intelligentsia of each country.

They will make all efforts to remove all obstacles that lie in the path of further strengthening the democratic basis of the independence and sovereignty of their countries, to develop further the socialist basis of each country, its economy and culture, for the sake of the constant growth of the material welfare and the cultural level of all the workers. They will consolidate the fraternal unity and mutual assistance of the socialist countries for the strengthening of the great cause of peace and socialism.

X

The Eisenhower Doctrine

1

New Doctrine, Old Realities*

M. PERLMANN

The voting in the UN on Hungary disclosed the pattern of inter-Arab conflict: the Egyptian–Saudi–Syrian bloc holding hands with the "East"; Iraq, with her Bagdad Pact associates, clinging to the "West." Jordan was ready to renounce her treaty with Britain and accept financial support from the Egyptian bloc; her Premier, Suleiman Nabulsi, stated frankly on December 15 that "Jordan cannot live forever as Jordan." Units of Syrians, Iraqis (later withdrawn) and Saudis were stationed in the kingdom, which was increasingly swept by pro-Nasser influence. Lebanon, prudently neutral, was clearly leaning towards the "West," especially with Charles Malik as her Foreign Minister.

The main antagonists, Cairo and Bagdad, exchanged vitriolic verbal attacks. As usual, mutual recriminations about lack of anti-Israel fervor loomed large. The Bagdad Premier related, in a speech in December, how over a year ago the Egyptian President had exchanged messages with him on a possible settlement with Israel. Now Cairo is lumping Iraq with Israel. Bagdad suffered huge financial losses as a result of the Suez conflict and the blowing up of Syrian pipelines ($700,000 daily; oil exports down to one-fifth of normal rate). Parliament was suspended and many politicos were jailed— all to stem the anti-Western trend of the Nasser-oriented forces at home. Nuri Said's government defended the Bagdad Pact, whose continued existence has become the bone of contention between Cairo and Bagdad. Consultations of the Pact countries (minus Britain, in order not to irritate and compromise Iraq) took place.

The clash came to a head in Syria as well, where it was increasingly recognized that the dominant military circles are strongly Soviet-oriented, that information is given a pro-Soviet slant, that siding with the West is considered as subversive pro-Iraqi plotting, and that the "East" is supplying

*From Middle Eastern Affairs, **8** (*March, 1957*), *99–102, 107. Reprinted by permission.*

arms to Damascus. Turkey and Iran were on their guard, the former apprehensive over the prospect of being sandwiched between Soviet Bulgaria to the west and a Soviet-manipulated Syria to the east. While there was no doubt about Soviet arms to and propaganda in Syria, diplomatic statements insisted on Syria's positive neutrality opposed to a policy of blocs and cold war. Syria, it is alleged, fears attack by Israel. Her President "knows" that the old plans of partition by the West ("Sykes-Picot") are being revived and that Israel is to get slices of Syria and Jordan. The Syrian army was doubled in size during the last year or so, and many civilians are equipped with Czech tommyguns. Military expenditures amounted to sixty per cent of the total budget, while the oil revenue (payment for pipeline passage) evaporated. Oil is supplied by the Soviets. The shakiness of the regime and the uncertainty of the situation were thrown into relief when, on December 22, forty-seven prominent political figures (of whom eighteen escaped to Lebanon) were ordered before a court martial on charges of plotting to set up a pro-Iraqi government under Munir Ajlani.

Faced with the rage sweeping through Bagdad–Damascus–Amman–Cairo, it was natural for the Lebanese to be nervous. But Beirut had more concrete reasons to be nervous when a terrorist ring headed by an Egyptian attaché was uncovered in the wake of several bombings. Syria, again in an ugly mood, began moving armed forces to the Lebanese border and demanding access to Lebanese territory. Lebanon did not break off trade and diplomatic relations with France, and on Hungary she voted with the West. For this she was to feel the corrosive ricochet of the virulent strife between the Arab capitals.

Active as ever, Moscow paraded as the champion of Arabs. The West, said Moscow, sought to restore colonialism, and the United States was bent on taking over the positions from which the British and French had been driven. The Bagdad Pact was repeatedly denounced as a machination of the colonialist octopus and its henchmen. But the worst vituperation was reserved, with a fine playing on chords in Arab hearts, for Israel: her leaders ought to be brought to account as war criminals; they were responsible for atrocities in the Gaza strip; they were called on to "stop playing with fire" before it was too late. The very existence of Israel as a state was at stake; Israel was digging her own grave. Syrian fears were played upon and widely broadcast.

In November, the United States declared that if "volunteers" appeared in the Near East "the United Nations would be obligated to take appropriate action" and "the United States would fully support such action." Washington expressed "concern" over "substantial shipments" of Soviet arms to Syria. It stated that a threat to the territorial integrity or political independence of the members of the Bagdad Pact would be viewed by the United States "with the utmost gravity." Despite various attempts to mollify Nasser, there was growing irritation with his acts and propaganda. All the straws in the wind pointed to the molding or recasting of a Middle Eastern policy in opposition to Moscow's machinations. This finally emerged as the "Eisenhower Doctrine," the President's call for wide military and financial powers to act in the oil-rich and trouble-ridden region.

Five days before the delivery of the State of the Union message, Congress listened to a special address on the Middle East by President Eisenhower. The Middle East, said the President, was in a state of disruption and instability, and was endangered by the Soviet Union's power politics and goal of domination. The region's strategic position, vast oil wealth, pipelines, the Suez Canal, and the holy shrines must be preserved for the free world. To avoid the fate of the Baltic states and Hungary, the nations of the Middle East need support in the face of Soviet pressure. Since the United Nations is not a "wholly dependable protector," the United States must take on new responsibility. The nations of the Middle East see the record of the U. S. S. R. in the UN on the Hungarian question, and the record of the United States as the mainstay of UN goals of independence, economic well-being and spiritual growth. The United States must make its willingness to support the independence of the freedom-loving nations of the area ever more evident. Authorization from Congress was sought to enable the President to:

1. Cooperate with and assist any nation or group of nations in the general area of the Middle East in economic development.
2. Cooperate militarily with any nation which desires such aid.
3. Use the armed forces of the United States to secure and protect the territorial integrity and political independence of nations requesting such aid against overt armed aggression from any nation controlled by international communism.

This activity was to be in consonance with treaty obligations and with the United Nations Charter and UN recommendations. The President asked for authorization to spend $200,000,000 in 1958 and 1959. At the same time the Palestine complex (Israel and the Arabs; refugees) and the Suez issue were to be dealt with separately under UN supervision (reference was made to Mr. Dulles' speech of August 26, 1955 outlining U. S. policy on Palestine). "The proposed legislation is primarily designed to deal with the possibility of Communist aggression, direct and indirect." and it was hoped the very act of legislation "will serve to halt any contemplated aggression." A "special mission to the Middle East to explain the cooperation we are prepared to give" was to be sent to the area. James P. Richards (South Carolina Democrat, former Representative and Chairman of the House Foreign Affairs Committee) was appointed head of the mission and the President's "special assistant and adviser on Middle East problems." . . .

Moscow sees the Eisenhower program as a threat to the peace and security of the Middle East, even of the world. A joint communiqué issued by Soviet Premier Nikolai A. Bulganin and Chinese Premier Chou en-Lai declared:

Both sides note that after Britain, France and Israel had suffered defeat in their aggression against Egypt, American imperialism is trying to make use of the situation so as to take the place of the colonialist powers—Britain and France—in the Near and Middle East, to suppress the movement for national independence and enslave the peoples of these countries, and is also striving to step up the policy of aggression and war preparations in this area.

This is precisely the essence of the so-called Eisenhower doctrine. This colonialist policy of the United States in the Near and Middle East creates fresh tensions in this area, recently the arena of hostilities caused by the aggression against Egypt.

The Governments of the Soviet Union and the People's Republic of China resolutely condemn this policy of the United States and are ready to continue rendering the necessary support of the peoples of the Near and Middle East so as to prevent aggression and interference in the affairs of the countries of this area.

Countries accepting American aid were reminded of the horror of atomic bombing and radiation fallout.

Amid pressures at home, in the United Nations, in the world at large, and especially on account of the Egyptian–Israel conflict, Washington's new doctrine may be weighed anew and modified in its relation to other elements of this country's policies. It is doubtful that the doctrine will be able to withstand the force of the realities, of the conflicts in and within the "general area of the Middle East."

2

Eisenhower's Mideast Doctrine*

IZVESTIA

On Jan. 5 U. S. President Eisenhower delivered a special message to Congress on U. S. policy in the countries of the Near and Middle East. In his message, which abounded in anti-Soviet attacks, the President described the present situation in the Near and Middle East as "critical" and called for authority to use U. S. armed forces in the Near and Middle East whenever he deemed this necessary, without asking permission of Congress as the U. S. Constitution stipulates. The U. S. President also asked for authority to extend military and economic "aid" to the countries of this area. The

*From The Current Digest of the Soviet Press, **9** (February 20, 1957), 18–19. Translation from The Current Digest of the Soviet Press, published weekly at Columbia University by the Joint Committee on Slavic Studies, appointed by the American Council of Learned Societies and the Social Science Research Council. Copyright © 1957, by the Joint Committee on Slavic Studies. Reprinted by permission.

message specifically called for the expenditure of $200,000,000 on "economic support" to the countries in that area. . . .

In his message to Congress, the U. S. President spoke of the sympathy and good will which the United States allegedly feels for the Arab countries. Actions show, however, that the American ruling circles are actually pursuing their own selfish aims in this area. . . .

The aggressive tendency of this program and its colonialist nature in regard to the Arab countries is so obvious that it cannot be masked by any nebulous phrases about the love of peace and concern allegedly shown by the United States for the countries of the Near and Middle East.

One may ask: What do the authors of the "Eisenhower doctrine" mean by love of peace when the threat to the security of the Near and Middle Eastern countries emanates from the NATO members themselves, among whom the United States plays first fiddle? What is meant by concern for these countries when the United States and its NATO partners regard these states merely as sources of strategic materials and spheres for the investment of capital so that they can reap maximum profits? Is it not clear that the unwelcome "protectors" of the Near and Middle Eastern countries are actually trying to force the status of a kind of military protectorate on this area and to set these countries back many years in their development?

The American President's statements that the United States will uphold the sovereignty and independence of the Near and Middle Eastern countries are in no way compatible with the adoption of aggressive programs which provide for the use of U. S. armed forces in this area. . . .

U. S. ruling circles consider that the weakened positions of Anglo-French colonialists in the Near and Middle East and the successes of the Arab countries in consolidating their independence have produced a "vacuum" which they would like to fill by military and economic interference in the internal affairs of those countries. But what is this "vacuum"? Since when do countries which have liberated themselves from colonial oppression and are on the road to independent national development constitute a "vacuum"? It is clear that the strengthening of national independence in the Arab countries and the intensification of their struggle against colonial oppression by no means constitute a kind of "vacuum," they mean the restoration of the national rights of the Near and Middle Eastern peoples and are a progressive factor in social development.

The United States is trying to present its policy as anti-colonialist. But it is not difficult to see the falsity of its assertions, which are clearly designed to blunt the vigilance of the peoples in the Near and Middle East. The U. S. program insistently stresses that the Near and Middle East must recognize its "interdependence" with the Western countries, i.e., with the colonialists, particularly in regard to oil, the Suez Canal, etc. In other words, the United States is stubbornly seeking to impose a colonialist "trusteeship" over the peoples of the Near and Middle East. In practice, the "interdependence" of the Near and Middle Eastern countries and the colonial powers means that these countries should place their natural resources and national wealth at the disposal of foreign monopolies. In simple terms, the United States is trying to reinstate the old colonial order in the Near and Middle Eastern countries under a new disguise, capturing dominant positions there.

The authors of the colonialist program are trying to sweeten it by a promise of economic "aid" to the Near and Middle Eastern countries. Every intelligent person understands, however, that in reality the United States is offering as charity to the Arab peoples only a small fraction of what the American monopolies have received and are receiving by plundering and exploiting the natural wealth belonging to these peoples. . . .

President Eisenhower's message contains the assertion that the United States is concerned over the fate of religions in that area, including Islam, which is professed by the majority of the peoples in the Arab East. But this assertion cannot be taken seriously. Islam, as a religion, arose many centuries before America was discovered and has withstood four Crusades. At the present time, the Moslems of the Arab East scarcely need protection for Islam from the United States or anyone else. Assertions that the interests of religion in the Arab East demand the dispatch of American armed forces to that area are utterly untenable. It is not the interests of religion in the Near and Middle East but the interests of the biggest American oil trusts that are prompting the U. S. government to send its troops there. The plans for U. S. interference in the religious affairs of the Moslem countries are rightly regarded as an insult to the religious feelings of the peoples of these countries.

Mention should also be made of the fact that U. S. interference in the internal affairs of the Arab countries and the crude threat to employ force against these countries can only encourage the aggressive tendencies of Israeli ruling circles in regard to the Arab countries. These extremist circles, closely connected with American monopolies and relying on U. S. support, will seek to carry out their predatory plans, which in turn can lead to further aggravation of the situation in the Near and Middle East and greatly increase the threat to peace in that area.

Seeking to conceal their gross interference in the internal affairs of the Near and Middle Eastern countries and their aggressive policy toward these countries, U. S. ruling circles resort to inventions about the existence of a threat to the Arab countries from the Soviet Union. These slanderous assertions will deceive no one. The peoples of the Near and Middle East have not forgotten that the Soviet Union has always defended the self-determination of peoples, the achievement and consolidating of their national independence. They have learned from experience that in relations with all countries the Soviet Union steadfastly follows the policy of equality and noninterference in internal affairs. They also know very well that the Soviet Union actively supports the right of each people to dispose of their own natural wealth and use it at their own discretion. . . .

In the days of hard trials for the Arab peoples only the Soviet Union proved to be their sincere friend and, together with the peace-loving forces of the whole world, took steps to end the aggression against Egypt. All this is well known.

The U. S. President's message demands of the Arab countries that they give up all ties with the Soviet Union and other countries in the socialist camp, which base their relations with the Arab states on the principles of equality and friendship, on the principles of the Bandung Conference. This demand by the U. S. rulers speaks for itself and unwittingly reveals the hidden schemes of those who would like to isolate the newly independent Near and Middle Eastern states so that their resistance to the colonialists could be broken more easily and the predatory plans aimed at establishing the world domination of American capitalism could be carried out.

The policy of setting countries at loggerheads is alien to the Soviet Union, as are aspirations to sow seeds of mistrust between peoples. . . .

It is known that the Soviet Union, unlike the United States, does not have and does not seek to have in the Near and Middle East any military bases or concessions with the object of extracting profits and does not strive to gain any privileges in this area, since all this is incompatible with the principles of Soviet foreign policy.

The Soviet Union is vitally interested in the maintenance of peace in the the Near and Middle East, which is in direct proximity to its borders. It is sincerely interested in the consolidation of the national independence of these countries and their economic prosperity and regards this as a reliable guarantee of peace and security in this area. . . .

The imperialist program of colonialism advanced by the United States shows that American ruling circles have not drawn the necessary conclusions from the failure of the aggression against Egypt. They are clearly trying to return to the bankrupt "position of strength" policy.

All this, far from easing tension in this area, on the contrary aggravates the situation, increases the danger to peace in the Near and Middle East and violates the peaceful principles of the United Nations, by which the General Assembly was guided in condemning the recent aggression against Egypt. The voice of war, not the voice of peace, is heard in Mr. Eisenhower's message.

Authoritative Soviet circles hold that the program on the Near and Middle East outlined by the U. S. government, which foresees the possibility of employing U. S. armed forces in that area, might lead to dangerous consequences for which the U. S. government must bear full responsibility.

3

Truman and Eisenhower Doctrines in the Light of the Doctrine of Non-Intervention*

DORIS A. GRABER

The Eisenhower doctrine was more limited in scope than the Truman doctrine, and more carefully worded to avoid any semblance of unsolicited meddling with the sovereign prerogatives of other nations, which might be excoriated as illegal intervention. The specific purpose of the Eisenhower doctrine was to inform the Soviet Union that the Middle East would be one of the areas where the United States would exercise its right claimed under the Truman doctrine to halt the forcible import of communism. Where Truman had promised aid to stop the subversion of free nations by both "direct and indirect aggression," Eisenhower limited military assistance by American troops to instances involving "overt armed aggression" by "any nation controlled by International Communism." The Truman doctrine, though it was admittedly intended as a blow against communism, had spoken more generally about countering the imposition of "totalitarian regimes." Moreover, the Eisenhower doctrine stressed the need for formal consent by the nation which was to be helped to resist communism. The Truman doctrine did not mention such consent, though it obviously, if not entirely correctly, assumed that peoples who were "resisting attempted subjugation" would welcome assistance in their fight.

The substance of the Truman and Eisenhower doctrines is the assertion that the spread of communism to free countries is a sufficiently grave menace to the safety of the United States to permit it, under international law and in the light of traditional American policy objectives, to intervene on behalf of non-Communist forces contending with Communist forces for the control of a given nation. This claim rests on the assumption that full acceptance of Communist doctrines pledges nations to work diligently for the ultimate violent destruction of non-Communist governments everywhere. Moreover, creation of a Communist government is rarely the result of free popular choice. In most instances, it is brought about as the result of machinations emanating from other Communist countries, primarily the Soviet Union, which by force, intimidation, fraud and deceit secure control of the govern-

Reprinted with permission from the Political Science Quarterly, *LXXIII, No. 3 (September, 1958), 322–323, 332–334. Reprinted by permission of the author and The Academy of Political Science.*

ment, and then proceed to eliminate popular opposition. Hence acceptance of Communist rule is not a purely "domestic" affair which is not properly the concern of other nations. It is not an exercise of the sovereign right of a people to choose any government it likes. Rather, it is a matter closely intertwined with foreign policy and affects the right of third parties who cannot be indifferent to the subversion of national independence of any state by foreign and foreign-dominated agents for the benefit of an aggressive foreign Power. . . .

Returning to the initial question, whether the Truman doctrine and the Eisenhower doctrine can be reconciled with America's traditional non-intervention doctrine and practice, the answer is that their practice has thus far been consistent with American tradition, but that the wording of the doctrines implies in part a wider and in part a narrower use of the right of intervention than ordained by the traditional non-intervention doctrine. Except for a short span at the turn of the twentieth century, the United States has traditionally couched its non-intervention doctrine in cautious, conservative phrases, to the point, at times, of renouncing intervention as a policy alternative at a time when it was being practiced, albeit under a camouflage name. The assertion made in the Truman doctrine that the United States claims the right to intervene wherever free governments are overthrown by totalitarian groups, because the demise of free governments anywhere *ipso facto* menaces the safety of the United States, is too sweeping in the light of past American doctrine and practice. To pick an extreme example: if, in the tribal wars of Central Africa, a democratically ruled tribe is conquered by a totalitarian one, surely this would not be detrimental enough to the United States to warrant it to intervene, even if the intervention could be legally justified on the grounds that a nation has a legal right to intervene when it is adversely affected by illegal intervention conducted against a third state.

It seems ill-advised at the present time to assert an unnecessarily broad right of intervention for several reasons. The justification that it serves as a deterrent to Communist aggression and encourages endangered nations to resist communism has proved false. The Communists are not deterred by what appears to be a bluff, and their prospective victims are little inclined to risk resistance solely on the strength of prospective American aid which they know is not automatically forthcoming. On the other hand, America's friends who fear, probably unduly, that tough language and sabre rattling increase the chance of war with the Soviet Union, in which Western Powers face atomic annihilation, would be much heartened by American verbal restraint. As long as it is obviously impossible to halt all Communist advances, and unwise to broadcast a blueprint of America's exact strategy of resistance, it would be best to reaffirm the traditional rule—which is being applied in practice—that intervention will remain a last resort to be used when the United States considers itself seriously endangered. This more modest claim might to some extent ease the nervous tension in the foreign offices of the free world.

The traditional rule would also serve the United States better than the Eisenhower doctrine which, though more restrictive than the Truman pronouncement, it too broad in claiming unconditionally that the loss of independence and political integrity of any of the Middle Eastern nations would seriously impair the vital interests of the United States, and too narrow in promising to make American interposition dependent on the consent of Middle Eastern sovereigns, in derogation of existing rights to intervene whenever the safety of the United States demands it.

There is historical precedent for expressing the non-intervention doctrine in terms different from its application, if such expression can serve a sound political purpose. The formulation of the doctrine as a political absolute in the early days of the Republic is one example. But just as that formulation changed when it was no longer valuable, so the Eisenhower and Truman doctrines should be clearly brought into conformity with, or rescinded in favor of, the traditional non-intervention doctrine because, as policy expressions, they have failed to deter Soviet aggression, failed to boost the morale of pro-Western Powers, and, in the case of the consent provisions of the Eisenhower doctrine, failed to clear the United States of the charge of imposing its policies on unwilling non-Communist countries. Instead, the excessive claims, even though they have not been put into practice, have been misunderstood and distorted as evidence of bellicose intentions, and the sincerity of the consent provisions of the Eisenhower doctrine has been questioned when it seems obvious that there may be implied reservations.

XI
The Laotian Conflict

1

Laos : Pawn in Power Politics*

THOMAS E. ENNIS

THE SEEDS OF CONFLICT

In the first general elections held in Laos (1957) one-third of the seats in the National Assembly were won by members of the Neo Lao Hak Sat party. Members were unable to take their seats when the Premier, Phoui Sananikone, abruptly suspended the Assembly (December, 1957), disturbed by the growing strength of the Communists. The new National Assembly voted to give the Premier authority to carry out extensive reforms in the rural areas in order to weaken Communist influence (January 14, 1959). The only votes cast against the Premier came from members of the Communist-front parties, the Neo Lao Hak Sat and the Santiphap (Neutrality party).

Prince Souphanou Vong, leader of the Neo Lao Hak Sat, half-brother of the Premier, accused the Assembly of plotting to destroy his party. He threatened to use force in order to survive. Some of the Neo Lao Hak Sats fled to North Vietnam and the prince was arrested for his rebellious conduct.

Tension increased when demonstrations by the Communist troops of North Vietnam (January, 1959), on the eastern borders of Laos proved to the government that every loyal Laotian would be needed to combat those allied in thought and action to the North Vietnamese regime of Ho Chi-minh. The Western world was unaware of any close links to little Laos until September 30, 1959, when Khamphan Panya, Foreign Minister of Laos, reported to the General Assembly of the United Nations.

The minister declared that North Vietnam long had planned to communize his country. He pleaded for United Nations support for his people

*From Current History, **38** (February, 1960), 70–74. Reprinted by permission of the author and Current History.

who were "animated by a sense of humanity and a love of joy and even of the easy life." The hostile groups, he maintained, were mainly Laotian Communists aided by soldiers and arms from North Vietnam. These pro-Communists, the Pathet Lao, were to have been integrated into the Royal Laotian Army, according to the terms of the Geneva accord, but they refused to act because they were to be used to destroy the Laotian government. The Second Pathet Lao Battalion, in May, 1959, refused to be integrated and marched toward the border of North Vietnam. Since then, this group has received arms and rations from North Vietnam and has arranged to have all wounded flown to North Vietnam hospitals.

"For the attack against the posts of Muong Het and Xieng Kho on August 30, 1959," the Foreign Minister charged, "the Democratic Republic of North Vietnam was not satisfied with furnishing assistance and support. It participated in it in broad daylight. Here is the story as given by people who saw it: 'The attack began at dawn in two successive waves, the first made up of Pathet Lao veterans. The second element did not know how to speak Laotian, but Vietnamese.' "

GATHERING THE GRAIN

The conflict broke into the open late in July, 1959, when paratroops were dropped to aid the Laotian Army units in Samneua. At the same time, the British Foreign Office supported the accusation of Laos that the rebels "represented new elements entirely armed, equipped and stiffened by the Democratic (Communist) Republic of North Vietnam." The attacks were intensified after an announcement from Paris that Laos had invited "a certain number" of American civilian technicians to work with French military instructors in training the Laotian Army, armed mainly with light weapons. Radio Hanoi stated "American imperialists" were supporting the new advances. It accused the Laotain Army of "terroristic raids." The Laotian government replied that it had documentary proof of intervention of troops from North Vietnam.

General Ouane Rattikone, Laotian Chief of Staff, declared (August, 15) that about 800 guerrillas, trained by North Vietnam, were spreading out to isolate the provinces of Samneua and Phongsaly from the rest of the kingdom.

General Ankhua Soukhavong, North Laos army commander, who has been fighting the Vietminh since 1945, outlined the tactics of the enemy. They usually attacked between midnight and 5: 00 A.M., then withdrew, to be replaced by Laotian dissidents. "The Vietminh are behind the tribesmen and Pathet Lao groups, pushing them, trying to make it appear as though this is a civil war." The general emphasized the fact that the only way to block the Communist penetration was to induce the local population to ally itself with the government. If not, "all the soldiers in the world will not keep this province (Samneua) for us." The people must be armed, paid and fed.

In the assaults of late August, reports detailed the moves of five mixed battalions of Laotian rebels, Black Thai, North Vietnamese tribesmen and regulars. Vietnamese was used as the command language. Arms included 57-millimeter recoilless guns and 80-millimeter mortars, all captured American weapons. There was also heavy bombardment from 125-millimeter cannon, based on North Vietnamese soil. By September, it was believed that 800 to 1,000 square miles of Samneua Province were either held by the rebels or unable to be occupied by royal troops. The Royal Laotian Army used enemy tactics, casting off uniforms and dressing in peasant garb. Hiding their weapons at daybreak, they struck at nightfall, from hidden jungle posts.

Operations spread to South Laos in October, 1959. Rebel bands raided Pakse (population 30,000), largest town in the region, to menace two battalions of the Royal Army. Western observers considered the many sorties more serious than the three-month-old "war" in the north, because of the appearance of Kha tribesmen against royal soldiery. The Khas are a hardy primitive folk, of Malayan extraction, who inhabited all Laos before being pushed southward by Laotians and Thai clans.

The problems encountered when preparing for extensive military action in Laos are many. There are no railroads, few roads and only grass strip air-fields. The jungle and climate prevent large-scale operations. Hanson W. Baldwin, most astute of military historians, thus views the Laotian skirmishes:

> The Communists probe weak spots. An exploitation of one such area may lead to the weakening of another area, and the dam may eventually burst. Most important: if the United States does not oppose armed Communist aggression everywhere, it will be hard to draw the line anywhere. . . . The statements of Peiping and Moscow indicate clearly that Laos has been selected as a testing ground.
>
> This is the international challenge that has to be met. It is a three-fold challenge: to the United States, which has committed itself morally and tacitly to the maintenance of Laos as an independent state; to the Southeast Asia alliance, which is committed by treaty protocol to the defense of Laos, and to the rest of Southeast Asia, endangered by the tide of Communism.

·   ·   ·

THE WESTERN WORLD

Aid to Laos has cost the United States $225 million since 1955. This aid has been used for the Royal Laotian Army of 25,000 men; jungle highways, a power-station, irrigation dams; health services, sanitation, development of farming, communications, mining; planning for future flood control, power, irrigation projects and training for teachers and technicians.

The United States Department of State clarified (August 12, 1959) the status of American military assistance to Laos. This support began in 1950 under the so-called "pentalateral agreement" among the United States, France, South Vietnam, Cambodia and Laos. In the Geneva accords of 1954, it was agreed that Laos was to continue to accept American succor but Washington was not permitted to create a formal Military Advisory Group in that country. Consequently, the United States has in Laos a Program Evaluation Office, connected with the United States Operations Mission. This office has 71 military aides (1959) who supervise instruction in the use of weapons and logistical support. The United States also has detailed 100 technicians to Laos who instruct in the use and maintenance of weapons and equipment. The Geneva pact gives France alone the right to have a purely military mission which instructs the Royal Laotian Army in tactics.

Moscow accused Laos of violating her neutrality policy by allowing the United States to build a military base on Laotian soil. The United States Department of State replied (August 19) that "contrary to implications in the Soviet statement the Laos Army is controlled exclusively by the sovereign Government of Laos. It is not under the direction of United States military personnel. The few American technicians in Laos are there at the request of the French and Laos governments." The statement also made clear the fact that the United States did not have any heavy or modern armament in Laos nor had it furnished any such matériel. There are no bases or air-strips "as any of the dozen foreign correspondents who are in Laos will attest." United States technicians only train in the use of World War II-type of American equipment.

Washington held that after the integration of the Communist-front Pathet Lao battalions into the army, one of them revolted and some of its roster fled to North Vietnam, "thus providing further evidence of the link between the Pathet Lao and North Vietnam." "These Communist organizations betrayed the trust of the Laotian Government and people. In mid-July they perpetrated insurrection with outside help and direction. It is this Communist-directed action which has broken the peace in Laos." The "dangerous tension" in the kingdom is of "Communist origin."

The first consignment of United States aid during the crisis reached Vientiane on August 31, 1959, in the form of 4,320 pairs of rubber-soled green canvas boots. American arms, munitions and supplies reached South Vietnam from Bangkok early in September, destined for Laos, including six plane-loads of rifles, grenades and helmets. Washington also sent Army Signal Corps troops to Asian areas to aid in air-lifting arms to Laos. General Frank Everest, head of the United States Tactical Air Command, stated (September 5) that his tactical fighters were capable of reaching Laos within 35 hours, after orders had been given.

This activity disturbed Capitol Hill. The most articulate questioning voice was that of Senator Mike Mansfield (D.-Mont.) who cautioned the White House to "go slow on any direct involvement of this nation in Laos." He wanted to know the relationship of the "sprawling growth" of American representation in Laos to "our deepening involvement with that country." The assistant Democratic leader told the Senate that only two members of the State Department were in Laos in 1953, with hundreds of United States officials there by 1959.

> How is it, that after spending hundreds of millions on aid to Laos, after being assured by the Executive Branch . . . that this aid had built stability and kept out the Communists, the defense of the entire country can be so rapidly undermined by a battalion or two of Viet Minh forces?

The Washington Post (October 25, 1959) summed up the thinking of realists:

> No sensible person can envisage Laos as a military ally or as an extension of Western power. The Geneva armistice contemplated a neutral status for Laos, and that is all that can reasonably be expected in fulfillment of the country's independence. But neutrality also ought to encompass the right of the legal government in Vientiane to exercise control over the entire country, or else the independence of Laos will be spurious.

The French Embassy of Laos, in September, claimed there was no active fighting and all reports of skirmishes were based on Laotian and American propaganda. The Laotian government resented the French attitude, asserting that the French were undermining civilian and military morale. The French also were criticized for making no effort to train Laotian troops and for interfering with American attempts to aid the menaced kingdom without going through French military channels. Some Laotians believed that relations with France would be severed if Washington aid continued.

Premier Sananikone sought to scotch anti-French sentiments. He stated (September 26) there had been some concern in government circles over French policy and future relations with Paris. The Premier, speaking in French, declared that as far as he was concerned, "French-Laotian friendship was too old . . . to change. The Laos are not superficial people. They think things over deeply."

The frankest expressions of English feelings regarding Laos are found in the influential monthly, *Eastern World* of London, for September, 1959. The "proper view of Laos" should recognize the fact that

> the danger that exists in Laos . . . is less from the fighting . . . than from what action the United States might initiate in the event of a collapse of the Sananikone Government. This possibility is not at all remote. Certain elements of a neutralist, non-Communist, complexion, but who would not be averse to forming some kind of coalition with the Pathet Lao, are becoming increas-

ingly restive at the Government's almost sychophantic attachment to the United States. The fantastic extent of bribery and corruption by the ruling circles in Laos could not have gone unnoticed by the moderate groups, especially since the Americans themselves, through a Congressional inquiry in the United States, have revealed how appallingly aid funds to Laos were misused.

LAOS—WHAT NOW?

The future of all Southeast Asia depends upon happenings in Laos. Dire destruction surrounds these peoples, hemmed in by valley and moun- tain. And yet thousands of Laotians, especially women, go about the daily work, planting rice, picking poppies, weaving garments, standing before gods within temples, preparing for the almost weekly festival in honor of a local deity, unknown to dwellers on the other side of the densely wooded hills. Some are caught to die between the fire of royal troops and rebel fighters, without having lived long enough to distinguish between freeman and slave.

The history of Laos is found in an ancient Laotian adage:
> "The water drops, the ants eat the fish.
> The water rises, the fish eat the ants.
> So it is better to love than to hate."

2

Laos: Civil War or Aggression ?*

MARIO ROSSI

In mid-September a United Nations fact-finding subcommittee went to Laos to investigate Laotian charges that Communist North Vietnam was guilty of "flagrant aggression." The fact-finding mission is strictly circum- scribed by this definition of Communist intervention. In its assignment there is no question of ascertaining whether the Pathet Lao (Communists) in the northern part of the country has rebelled against the government of anti- Communist Premier Phoui Sananikone. No one denies this rebellion, and this would in any case be an internal matter outisde the competence of the UN.

Nor is the UN subcommittee supposed to investigate whether rebel Pathet Lao activities have been directed and supported from Hanoi, capital

*From Foreign Policy Bulletin, **39** (November 1, 1959), 25–26. Reprinted by permission.*

of North Vietnam. Such aid, if proved, would constitute indirect aggression such as the UN found was committed against Lebanon in 1958, but not a "flagrant aggression, for which the Democratic Republic of Vietnam must bear the entire responsibility," as stated by Laos.

Will the Sananikone government be able to substantiate charges of Vietminh armed intervention? Many observers familiar with the area doubt it. The Laotian military commanders have often shown ignorance of what was going on along the country's northeastern border. All means of communications in the area are most arduous due to a combination of high mountains, difficult to traverse, with small enclosed valleys, where roads are hardly passable. The task of fact-finding is made even more difficult by racial and linguistic affinities between the peoples on both sides of the border. Under the circumstances, North Vietnam might have intervened militarily and then withdrawn its forces without leaving a trace.

The subcommittee was set up after Mr. Hammarskjold, on September 4, had received a note from Vientiane charging North Vietnam with "flagrant aggression" and requesting UN assistance, in particular "the prompt dispatch of an emergency force to halt aggression and to prevent its spreading." The note left it up to the secretary-general to apply the appropriate procedural action. The next day Mr. Hammarskjold requested the president of the Security Council, Ambassador Egidio Ortona of Italy, to convene the council "urgently." The council met on September 7 to consider the note from Vientiane and a note from Hanoi stating that the government of the Democratic Republic of Vietnam was "highly indignant" at the "fabricated complaints" put forward by Vientiane, and that "the civil war now in progress in Laos was started by the Americans and the Phoui Sananikone government." The United States representative introduced a resolution cosponsored by Britain and France under which the council would appoint a subcommittee composed of Argentina, Italy, Japan and Tunisia "to examine the statements made before the Security Council concerning Laos, to receive further statements and documents and to conduct such inquiries as it may deem necessary and to report to the Security Council as soon as possible." The word "inquiries" rather than "investigation" was used to support the contention that the decision was procedural under Article 29 of the Charter, and therefore not subject to the veto. The Soviet delegate protested that the resolution had "no binding force on anyone" as it had been adopted by "an illegal procedure."

The fact-finding mission might fail to find in Laos convincing proof of "flagrant aggression"; it will find, however, a civil war with one side being supported by the Communist bloc, the other by the Western powers. The issue can be solved either militarily or politically. Military intervention would involve the United States in another Korea, which at present no one appears willing to consider. Thus there seems to be no alternative to a political solution and this, in turn, implies the search for a compromise formula.

TWO BASIC POINTS

In this connection two points are basic: (1) Laos is bound by the 1954 Geneva agreements, which ended the war in Indochina and recognized the independence of Laos, Cambodia and Vietnam; (2) since signing the agreements, Laos has become a member of the UN, thus acquiring new rights and obligations. At Geneva the powers offered the three countries, previously under French control, a sort of "package deal." The underlying philosophy was that while Vietnam was recognized as one country, it was in fact divided into two parts, one Communist and the other anti-Communist, with two separate governments. Laos and Cambodia were to do nothing that might upset the *status quo* until a "political solution" had been reached in Vietnam—in other words until the reunification of that country. Laos undertook to follow a neutral policy, not to join military pacts and not to establish new military bases.

Control over the execution of the agreement was entrusted to an international commission composed of India, Canada and Poland. In 1957 the commission negotiated the so-called Vientiane agreement which ended the rebellion of the Pathet Lao against the royal government of Laos. The compromise collapsed when Phoui Sananikone took power in 1958. He caused the withdrawal of the international commission (which legally cannot be dissolved until the agreement on Vietnam is implemented), and with United States moral and material support undertook an increasingly anti-Communist policy. According to Joseph Alsop the Laotian government had foreseen a Pathet Lao countermove to its new policy with North Vietnamese backing. The Soviet Union, as cochairman with Britain of the Geneva Conference, had proposed first the reconvening of the international commission and later, on September 14, a new conference of the nations present at Geneva. Laos' right to appeal to the UN and to refuse the international commission cannot be denied, while the conference proposed by Moscow would, as the State Department has pointed out, ignore the authority of the UN.

The immediate problem is how to reconcile the Geneva agreements, whose continued validity no one has contested, with the rights Laos has acquired since becoming a UN member. Whatever the new formula, it is generally agreed that the balance in Indochina cannot be upset without serious consequences in the whole area of South Asia. Laos' interest can best be served by insisting that the country keep out of the cold war. Its neutrality is not only prescribed by international agreements, but would also reflect political and geographical realities in a vulnerable strategic sector of the world.

3

Laos in Geopolitics*

JOSEPH S. ROUCEK

A small country, of no industrial importance and with no irreplaceable resources, Laos became the Number 1 item in international headlines in March, 1961, when a small Communist-led opposition, which for six years had kept the country in varying degrees of turmoil, was just about ready to conquer the established Government—with the help of the USSR and her satellites. The situation was so serious that the United States sent 16 more troop-carrying helicopters to Laos, thus enlarging the present force of four helicopters within the framework of US military movements in the Asian area, and President Kennedy proclaimed his Government's determination to support the Government and the people of Laos in the maintenance of their independence and neutrality.

The international interest in the control of this landlocked South-East Asian country is purely geopolitical. Should the Communists grab Laos, the rest of South-East Asia would be in grave danger of a similar takeover, and the American position—and thus the position of the Western Allies—in the Pacific would be much less secure than it is now.

For Laos pushes finger-like south from Communist China, past Red North Viet Nam and non-Communist South Viet Nam, to Thailand and Cambodia. Should Laos fall to the Communists, it would leave these three non-Communist countries exposed to Red attack; Malaya, Singapore and Burma would similarly be threatened.

Furthermore, Laos is placed in South-East Asia, whose lands and island areas control water passage between the Indian and Pacific Oceans. Since this area controls these crossroads, historically, the region has been continuously attacked from outside; its history has been a story of successive waves of cultural and commercial influences, each doing away with the old to some extent and each fusing with the old to produce a richer cultural hybrid. Thus South-East Asia has been a melting pot of Asian cultures, civilizations and ethnic groups, with some veneer of Western European influences. This, in turn, has forced the peoples here to adjust continuously to new rules and governments.

The same process is going on there today, because most of the independent nations and peoples here (with the exception of Thailand) have

*From Contemporary Review, *Vol. 199–200 (May, 1961), pp. 242–245. Reprinted by permission of the Contemporary Co., Ltd., London.*

emerged as free states only since the end of World War II, from former colonial powers in the area: France, Great Britain and the Netherlands. Colonialism is gone from South-East Asia, replaced with new nations, but none much more than a decade old. None of these new states had been adequately prepared for independence and responsibility. Added to the havoc of revolutions and the remnants of colonialism, illiteracy, poverty, sub-standard health conditions and economic unbalance make the workings of the newly established system quite difficult. Communism, sponsored from the Communist bloc, has been feeding here upon general discontent. And, above all, the area is dangerously close to Communist China, which has been persistently growing more and more aggressive politically and economically.

Laos used to be part of French Indo-China, and has been independent only since 1949; it joined the United Nations in 1955, and has had several hundred million dollars' worth of aid from the United States. Its people are mainly Buddhists, who hate to kill people. On the whole, this Land of the Million Elephants (as Laos is historically known) is an antique, sleepy country whose people want little more than to be left alone in their paradise of poppy fields and gilded temples.

This little land, 8,560 miles from New York, 5,840 miles from London, 5,830 miles from Paris—and 4,200 miles from Moscow—is mostly a set of deeply dissected plateaux, 3-6,000 feet high. There are plains bordering the Mekong along the south and south-western edges of the country. The rivers drain to the Mekong, which forms the western boundary between Laos and Thailand for hundreds of miles. Most of the country is covered with tropical monsoon forest and there are extensive stands of teak. The native animals include elephant, tiger and gaur (wild oxen). The easy-going people of Laos, some 1,500,000, in this little land of 91,500 square miles of bamboo forests, rice paddies, and palm and banana groves, raise rice and fruit, catch fish and carry on some lumbering in the dense teakwood forests. The country was formed out of several states some 600 years ago. But for most of their history the Lao people were dominated by neighbouring peoples—the Khmers (Cambodians) and the Thai. Laos was never a strong power; when not invaded by their neighbours, the Laotians wrangled among themselves. A great hero, Fa Ngoun, united Laos in the fourteenth century under the name of the Land of the Million Elphants and the White Parasol. But when France made it a Protectorate in 1893, Laos was again a patchwork of small states.

Fifty years of uneventful French rule were followed by Japanese occupation during World War II and a brief resistance to the French return. During the seven year Indo-Chinese war between the French and the Communist Viet Minh, most Laotian rebels stayed prudently in exile, returning only to take over the Government when Laos was granted autonomy in 1949. Under the terms of the 1954 Geneva agreement, France was allowed to maintain 5,000 troops in Laos, and was entrusted with the training of the Royal Laotian Army, but did such a miserable job that many of the Laotian's army of 25,000 men are still incompetent to handle anything heavier than a submachine gun.

Strangely enough, scarcely any country on earth is less fitted to serve as a pivotal point in the struggle against Communism than Laos. Shaped like a pistol with the butt pressing against Red China and the barrel aimed at Cambodia, Laos has no railroads, but two capital cities, Luangprabang for the royal family, Vientiane for the civil government. Except for jungle paths, navigable rivers like the 1,200 mile long Mekong, and barely 500 miles of all-weather roads, all travel is by plane from rutted airstrips surrounded by tree-clad hills and swamps.

Soviet Russia and Red China had long had designs on Laos. In the latest attempt to communise the country, Khrushchev has been calling the play and furnishing the war supplies. He operates through the Pathet Lao, a bunch of Communists based in the northern provinces and numbering some 8,000 against about 25,000 soldiers fielded by the pro-West Government of Prince Boun Oum. These latter troops have no great fondness for Boun Oum, whereas the Pathet Lao followers are convinced Reds.

Why is it that the royal régime is hardly able to survive, in spite of some $310 millions poured into Laos by Washington between 1954 and 1960? The Laos army is equipped, trained, paid and even fed by the United States. Uncle Sam covers 85 per cent of the costs of the police force and contributes $5 millions annually to the support of the civil budget.

The United States entered Laos militarily on the shirt-tails of France, and from the very beginning of US responsibility in Laos (January, 1955) there was a spirit of urgency. Americans still remembered Korea; the French had just lost Indo-China. The cocky Chinese and Vietnamese Communists, fresh from the unhappy Geneva Conference, seemed poised to move again. To the Secretary of State—the late John Foster Dulles— Laos was a crucial link in a chain of defences the US was trying to forge for South-East Asia. But the troubles began nearly immediately. Feeding, equipping and paying the army at one of the highest pay scales in Asia, the US flooded the country with dollars, making Laos too rich for a simple economy to absorb. And, above all, the Washington-sponsored military command wanted a large army "to assure internal security" and to "provide initial resistance in case of invasion," instead of adopting the tactics to Communist-style guerrilla type of warfare. The Laos army also got US equipment—most of it unsuited for Laos: armoured cars, jeeps and trucks which rusted in parking lots for lack of roads; artillery designed to cannonade fixed targets but which are no answer to flushing out small, mobile, elusive Pathet Lao guerrillas in the jungle. (Virtually the only effective combat units are the two battalions of paratroopers—now opposing each other.) When the "Operation Booster Shot" was started in 1957 to benefit the countryside, it was rather late to get much benefit out of it. The jungles make air reconnaissance difficult and virtually stop the use of tanks and other heavy equipment. There are only five important airfields, but none can take jet traffic. (Only the base of Seno, built and operated by the French near Vientiane, offers enough landing space for four-engine troop carriers.) And, ironically, a lot of US military equipment had fallen into the hands of the rebels, captured by pro-Communist forces in the neighbouring North Viet Nam during the Indo-China war.

The Soviet Union started the airlifting of artillery and other arms and ammunition in mid-December, 1960; these weapons bore Soviet, Chinese Communist and American markings, and apparently included American weapons captured in North Viet Nam; the rebel forces also cleaned out the arsenal in Vientiane before they were driven out of this capital at the end of 1960. And it was the Soviet airlift of arms and other supplies from North Viet Nam that turned the Pathet Lao's forces of jungle-wise guerrillas into a competent, hard-hitting army; supplementing the airlift are convoys of Soviet trucks that rumble from North Viet Nam's big military-supply base down Queen Astrid Highway to rebel supply centres in Xiengkhouang Province. In addition, the Pathet Lao army has something the Royal Army lacks—tough, disciplined cadres from outside the country. Each Pathet Lao company has a "seasoning" of at least seven Communists, who train and also fight. The Royal Army has American and Filipino technicians in the field; but their job is primarily advisory—and they do not fight.

The Kennedy Administration has been trying to persuade Khrushchev to encourage Laos to become a genuinely neutral state. Khrushchev has shown few signs of "buying that" up to now (March 30), apparently afraid to lose face with Red China. But whenever the Western Allies have called his bluff, notably in Lebanon and West Berlin, he has crawfished. It looks as if only a strong stand on America's part can cool-off his ambition to make a great leap forward in South-East Asia.

XII
The U-2 Incident

1

Downing of U-2*

NIKITA S. KHRUSHCHEV

On instructions of the Soviet Government, I am duty bound to report to you on aggressive acts directed in the last few weeks by the United States of America against the Soviet Union.

What form did these aggressive acts take? The United States sent its planes, which violated our state frontier and intruded into the airspace of the Soviet Union.

Its last but one aggressive act was perpetrated by the United States of America on April 9, 1960.

A United States plane intruded into the airspace of our country from the Afghanistan side. Of course, no man in his right senses can think and assume that this violation was done by Afghanistan, a country which is friendly with us.

We are convinced that this plane belonged to the United States of America and obviously was based somewhere on the territory of Turkey, Iran or Pakistan, which are linked with the U. S. A. by obligations under the aggressive CENTO bloc.

American military men apparently liked this impunity as it happened on April 9, and they decided to repeat the aggressive act.

Selected for this was the most festive day for our people and the workers of the world—the day of May the First—the international holiday of fraternal solidarity of the working class.

That day, early in the morning, at 0536 hours, Moscow time, an American plane flew over our frontier and continued its flight into the interior of the Soviet land. A report on this aggressive act was immediately given to the Government by the Minister of Defense.

The Government had stated this: Since he realizes what he comes up

*Address to the Supreme Soviet, May 5, 1960. Excerpts.

against when intruding into a foreign territory, if he gets away with it he will attempt fresh provocations. Therefore, the plane must be shot down.

This task was fulfilled and the plane was shot down.

According to first information, it has transpired that the plane belongs to the United States of America although it bears no identification signs.

Now an expert commission is studying data that fell in our hands. It has been established that this plane that crossed the state frontier of the Soviet Union was coming either from Turkey, Iran or Pakistan.

After the study of all materials that are now at our disposal, the Soviet Government will lodge with the United States of America a strong protest and will warn it that if similar aggressive acts against our country continue, we reserve the right to respond to them with measures we shall find necessary in order to insure the safety of our country.

We shall also give the most serious warning to those countries that put their territories at the disposal of the United States of America for aggressive acts directed against our country.

The following conclusion comes to mind: Aggressive imperialist forces in the United States in recent times have been taking the most active measures to undermine the summit or at least to hinder any agreement that might be reached.

The question then arises: Who sent this aircraft across the Soviet frontier? Was it the man who is Commander in Chief of the American armed forces who, as everyone knows, is the President? Or was this aggressive act carried out by Pentagon militarists? If such actions are taken by American military men on their own account, it must be of especial concern to world opinion.

Perhaps it was a result of the friendship that is now forming between the United States and Franco that the American militarists decided to act independently, as did the Spanish military junta, which rose up against the legal Spanish Government.

Thus, in the so-called free world, military dictators not seldom set up their regimes using the methods of Franco. But the peoples are beginning to understand where true freedom is and where there is tyranny.

Take, for instance, the events in South Korea. The head of the puppet Syngman Rhee regime, the best friend of the United States and the father of his country as someone or other called him in America, has now been overthrown by the people and is now a political corpse. And it was not the Communists who were behind these events; even American political leaders have had to admit.

The sufferings of the Korean people led them to rise up against the bestial yoke, and the peoples understand that it was not only a question of Syngman Rhee himself who was to blame but all those who supported him and hung him round the necks of the South Koreans.

It is no coincidence that the free world sees so many popular demonstrations demanding freedom.

Comrade Deputies, the impression is being formed that the aggressive actions newly undertaken by the United States against the Soviet Union are a foretaste of the summit meeting.

Are they taken in order to exert pressure on us and to attempt to frighten us with their military superiority in order to undermine our determination to work for easing tension, to eliminate the cold war and to put an end to the arms race?

All these missions are sent in order to prevent any agreement on vexing questions, for we cannot say that this aircraft was a harbinger of peace, that it was on a goodwill mission. No, it was a real bandit flight with aggressive intentions.

We can say to those gentlemen who sent the aircraft that if they think they can bend our knees and our backs by means of such pressure, this will have no effect on us. The Soviet Union has every means to give a rebuff to those who want to exert pressure in order to achieve a solution convenient to aggressors.

In the name of the Soviet Government let me express thanks to the men of the military units who carried out with honor the task laid on them in defending the frontiers of our motherland.

Comrades, the Soviet people and Government have always expressed their peaceful intentions and friendly feelings toward the United States, but in answer to this we have black ingratitude.

It is understood that this has aroused feelings of indignation against the activities of the American military men. But we must control this feeling and must be ruled not by our emotions, but by reason.

Government leaders interested in preserving peace must soberly consider the consequences of such actions and think what they might lead to.

Hitler's aircraft before the war used to intrude into our airspace. The Soviet Government would protest, but Hitler refused to pay attention and then attacked us. And where did that all end?

How do we assess the incursion of American aircraft—as a precursor of war or a foreshadow of attack, of the repetition of what Hitler did? The Soviet Government thinks that all the same there is no reason to draw such conclusions.

There is another relationship of power in the world, and in this the people's will to peace plays a great part and this is why we do not conclude that this is a prewar trial of strength or a reconnaissance made to try our nerves, preserve the atmosphere of the cold war so that the imperialists can continue to bind their peoples with taxation, to carry on the arms race, and to keep their people in a state of fear of war and to continue to impose their will.

The Soviet Union has no aggressive intentions, we do not want the cold war, we want disarmament and our proposals made to the United Nations on this subject remain in force still. Once again, we repeat that disarmament is the right way to preserve peace and in such conditions no country would be able unilaterally to arm and attack another. The Soviet Government once again calls on the Government of the United States to end the cold war. All states must act peaceably so that calm, peace and happiness can prevail.

2

Long Range Lessons of the U-2 Affair*

TELFORD TAYLOR

The handling and consequences of the U-2 affair are still being debated, and their importance has been underlined by the recent episode of the RB-47 reconnaissance aircraft. So far, most of the discussion has centered on the timing of the May Day flight that failed, and on the content of the official explanations that ensued. Overemphasis on these transient aspects has obscured the enduring significance of an episode that signalized revolutionary developments in peacetime intelligence methods. In its military and political implications, Francis Gary Powers' falling plane was a comet with a very long tail.

The unprecedented and largely unforeseen results of this event stem from the peacetime use, for intelligence-gathering purposes over foreign soil, of an aircraft—usually regarded as a major weapon of warfare, like a tank or warship—which can be combated only by other large weapons, such as anti-aircraft projectiles and interceptor planes. As a result of this circumstance, and of the route of this particular mission and the great altitude at which the U-2 flies and "sees"—

1. It was difficult, and was officially determined to be inexpedient, for the United States Government to follow the tradition of conventional espionage by "disowning" the pilot and denying responsibility for the flight.

2. Allied nations were involved (apparently without their knowledge), since their air bases had to be used to launch and recover the U-2.

3. Extensive, though incomplete, information concerning the history and fruits of the U-2 reconnaissance program was made public, and has had a profound impact on current appraisals of Soviet and American comparative military strength.

4. The U-2 must be regarded as a harbinger of future means of aerial

reconnaissance, such as observation satellites. It appears probable that outer space and perhaps the upper atmosphere will become a common international highway, like the high seas—but a highway from which it will be possible to see into everybody's backyard.

The U-2 episode must be viewed with an understanding of the nature of *intelligence* and *espionage*, and their traditional employment in peace and war. Espionage is a means of intelligence, but not all intelligence is espionage. Espionage is the quest for closely guarded official information by undercover agents, who customarily employ bribery, impersonation, theft, or other deceptive and clandestine means.

In recent weeks it has been said time and time again that espionage is a "dirty business," but that it is necessary for national security. This popular attitude is strangely illogical. If espionage is really necessary to a nation's military security, why should it be regarded as "dirty," or its practitioners as subject to condemnation? In fact, we do not scorn the memory of our most famous spy, Nathan Hale; rather, we place a memorial to him in the Yale quadrangle and teach his last words to our children. Only when espionage is coupled with treason does it become a disgraceful pursuit.

Espionage is but one of a number of branches of intelligence. In wartime the others include the capture and interrogation of prisoners of war, study of captured documents and weapons, monitoring of radio communications and reconnaissance—in the old days by cavalry and in modern times chiefly by aircraft.

Intelligence is unique among military activities in that it is "operational" in peace as well as in war. This is a lesson that the United States took a long time to learn. American intelligence withered away to almost nothing after World War I, but World War II brought the realization that our intelligence agencies should never sleep.

However, intelligence methods are not all the same in peace as in war. There are combatant and noncombatant forms. Combatant forms, such as the interrogation of enemy prisoners, are possible only in wartime. Some noncombatant sources—information from military missions and diplomats and the observations of travelers—are generally available only in peacetime. Other methods, including espionage and radio monitoring, are carried on in both peace and war.

The reason the U-2 episode was so bewildering to many people was that it involved a form of intelligence-gathering—aerial reconnaissance—which has hitherto been regarded as a wartime method, basically combatant in nature. President Eisenhower, for obvious reasons, sought to obscure this aspect when he described the U-2 as a nonmilitary, unarmed aircraft. But the distinction is an empty one. In wartime, reconnaissance aircraft are lightly armed, and rely on speed and altitude, rather than on armor or guns, for their safety.

In no essential respect was the Powers flight different from a military reconnaissance mission. Espionage agents can be coped with by counter-intelligence methods, and spies can generally be apprehended with weapons no larger than a revolver. But aerial reconnaissance can be countered only by anti-aircraft artillery, rockets and interceptor planes. The U-2 flights, in short, were not espionage in the conventional sense.

This does not establish that the U-2 flights should not have been undertaken. But it does indicate that the decision involved factors very different from and much graver than those involved in conventional cases of peace-time espionage. The hazards of failure—both political and military—were far more serious.

The public has not been told how many overflights like the Powers mission had previously been successfully undertaken, nor how many U-2's had been lost. Secretary of State Herter testified that none had been lost over the Soviet Union, and the implication that there have been losses elsewhere is supported by published reports (based on anonymous "background" sources) that about half a dozen U-2's have disappeared or crashed; on July 14 the Air Force announced the explosion of a U-2 high over Texas. The obvious inference is that the U-2 had not been frequently used for deep penetrations of Soviet air space.

Thus, while the prospects that the Powers flight would succeed might prudently have been assayed as favorable, the risk of a loss deep in Russia was not negligible in the sense that it could be disregarded. This being so, careful preparations should have been made to minimize the adverse consequences of failure. In the event, these preparations proved woefully inadequate, and it is in this respect that the "handling" of the Powers mission appears to be most subject to criticism.

In the light of what has since been disclosed, the main purposes of the advance preparations for failure should have been:

(1) Salvage of all or some of the aerial reconnaissance program for the future, since it has proved a valuable source of vital intelligence.

(2) Mitigation of the adverse political consequences, at home and abroad.

Neither of these purposes was achieved. The initial cover story was a misfit because, as Secretary Herter put it, "the actual circumstances turned out to be rather different from anything that had been anticipated in the preparatory work that had been done." Thus it was worse than useless, since the explosion of a cover story may reduce official credibility to the point where nothing but avowal can survive ridicule. In any event, no other cover had been prepared to conceal, or at least obscure, the identity and status of the pilot, or the flight's origin and destination.

In consequence, President Eisenhower soon found himself in such a position that, in order to avoid condemnation by the Security Council or other dangerous diplomatic repercussions, he felt compelled to promise that the flights would be discontinued. Under present circumstances, resumption of the reconnaissance program would involve the grave risk of compromising the President's personal integrity.

In addition to disclosing many details of the Powers flight, our Government also chose to reveal—by way of both official statement and "background" leakage—much information concerning the U-2 program as a whole, including its remarkable fruits. Why? One can only speculate, but it appears that at least one reason was to allay domestic criticism. Nothing succeeds like success, and those who might question the wisdom or morality of peacetime aerial reconnaissance over foreign soil could thus be buried under a tide of optimistic descriptions of the valuable military results.

In recent times the halls of Congress resounded and the public prints were filled with serious and often gloomy descriptions of the approaching "missile gap," which would put us at a dangerous disadvantage in military competition with the Soviet Union. Russian superiority in the exploitation of outer space was widely acknowledged and almost universally lamented. Russian technology and educational methods were acclaimed, often with an overtone of fear.

Now it is being given out, not so much by official statements as by anonymous "background" informants, that the U-2 photographs show Soviet missile emplacements to be far less formidable than had been previously supposed. The U-2 overflights are described as a "milk run," and their success is taken to prove that Soviet aircraft and anti-aircraft rocket defenses are far inferior to our own, and quite incapable of defending Soviet territory against attack by the Strategic Air Command. Soviet rocketry is said to be superior only in the field of propellants, and to lag badly in electronic controls. Commentators and cartoonists suggest that our military posture is far superior to that of the Soviet Union.

Perhaps some or much of this is true. But the few facts definitely known to the public about the U-2's achievements afford no basis for such sweeping conclusions. No doubt the Central Intelligence Agency has evaluated the military significance of the U-2 flights more soberly. But in order to justify the aerial reconnaissance program, and to silence criticism of the Powers fiasco, such extensive and rosy-hued claims have been poured out that popular concern for defense, and for the development of our national resources, may have been given a sleeping pill.

This is a dangerous trend, for it may be very difficult to reawaken the public. The basic factors of Soviet strength and growth have not been changed by the U-2, and there is no more reason for complacency today than there was before May Day. Indeed there is less, for the exposure of the U-2 program portends new developments, both military and political, for which we should be better prepared than we were for Powers' failure to reach his goal.

Despite this misadventure, the U-2 has proved that peacetime aerial reconnaissance is feasible and valuable. What we have done, others will attempt and we ourselves will undertake again, when the prospects of success appear to outweigh the risks.

It has been suggested that President Eisenhower's renunciation of future U-2 flights has cost us little, because the same information will soon be obtainable from observer satellites. No responsible public official has made any such claim and, despite the wonders of modern long-range photography, there is no immediate prospect that satellites at an altitude of 100 miles or more can approach the accomplishments of the U-2 at 70,000 feet. If we must await the sufficient development of satellite photography, there will be a costly gap in the continuity of our intelligence coverage.

The prospect of observation satellites lends practical importance to the question of how far up a nation's sovereignty extends. Under the old common-law rule, a property owner's rights ascend to the heavens—*usque ad coelum*. For individuals, this principle has had to give way to the necessities of aerial navigation. But for nations the doctrine has been carried into international law. Under the Chicago Convention of 1944, national sovereignty includes airspace without limitation. Now this rule is being eroded by the orbits of satellites, which pass overhead without protest from the countries beneath.

Just as the airplane of conventional type spelled the death of old-fashioned concepts of private property above the earth's surface, so the U-2 symbolizes the decay of current concepts of sovereignty in the space overhead. The high seas have long been regarded as an open thoroughfare, but to this day the nations are plagued with arguments about three-mile, twenty-mile and even 200-mile limits. In any event, analogies from the sea to airspace are dangerous. The oceans are finite and, of course, do not offer the opportunity for observation of a nation's interior that overflights afford.

Under the growing pressure of missiles and satellites, all sorts of suggestions have been advanced as the basis for new limits of sovereignty in space. Should it be restricted to the range of the earth's atmospheric envelope? No one yet knows that range with sufficient certainty. Should it be as high as the air offers support for winged flight? This will vary with the progress of design, as the U-2 itself demonstrates, although, of course, there is an ultimate limit, which some have estimated at about twenty-five miles.

It has also been suggested that the test should be the range of effective control, but this would simply mean that a nation's military capacity for defense against high-altitude incursions would be the governing factor—i. e., high might makes high right, a principle hardly designed for harmonious and peaceful application.

It may safely be predicted that, in the long run, the practicalities will be determinitive, rather than scientific estimates of the reach of atmospheric gases. The two basic problems are traffic control and, in the present state of international relations, observation of areas which a nation wishes to hide from view.

If the upper atmosphere and space become dangerously congested, traffic controls will have to be provided through conventional agreement rather than by unilateral, sovereign edict. As for observation, as the arts of high altitude photography and "space vision" progress, aerial "curtains" will become increasingly futile.

All this indicates the necessity of steps, by international convention or otherwise, to clarify the dangerous confusion generated by the friction between traditional concepts of spatial sovereignty and the realities of the space age. As things now stand, the resumption of aerial reconnaissance at U-2 levels would be likely to precipitate the very perils that we seek to avoid.

The U-2 affair has shown that we are in a period of transition. New problems are bound to arise, and novel, unexpected events to occur, that will require the imagination, alertness and coordinated decision-making that were so sadly lacking at the time of the Powers mission.

If the transitional phase can be survived, the U-2 may appear in retrospect as an omen of peace. In the nature of things, the trend of the future is toward "open skies." If close observations can some day be made from 300 miles up, there will be much less sensitivity about flights at lower levels. No doubt, other means of concealment will be used, but routine aerial observation is bound to depreciate the secrecy and security values that the "closed countries" now gain from their Iron Curtains. In the long run, this should diminish tensions and be conducive to peaceful intercourse among the nations.

3

Legal Aspects of the U-2 Incident*

QUINCY WRIGHT

The Senate Foreign Relations Committee agreed with Secretary Herter's testimony that the U-2 incident and the United States' handling of it were contributing factors to the breakup of the Summit Conference. It concluded that "in spite of political opposition to it in some communist quarters, and to doubts as to its success, it would probably have been held had it not been for these circumstances."

*From The American Journal of International Law, 54 (October, 1960), 840–842. Reprinted by permission of the American Society of International Law.

In any case the Summit Conference was not held and President Eisenhower's scheduled visits to Russia and Japan were canceled. On May 18, the Soviet Union requested that the United Nations Security Council be convened to consider "Aggressive action by the Air Force of the United States of America against the Soviet Union." The Council considered the question from May 23 to 26.

Soviet Foreign Minister Andrei Gromyko opened the debate by charging that the U-2 flight was an "aggressive action unheard of in peace time . . . deliberately prepared and carried out with knowledge and on the instructions of the United States government." Since one plane can carry an atomic weapon, such an act, he declared, justifies military retaliation. The U-2 flight was only one of a number of violations of Soviet territory by United States planes, to all of which the Soviet Government had protested, and to some of which it had drawn the attention of the Security Council in 1956 and 1958. After its first "lying version," the United States had confirmed its responsibility and "proclaimed systematic espionage and sabotage incursions inside another state as an integral element of its state policy." President Eisenhower's rejection of Khrushchev's demands at the Paris Conference gave further evidence of that policy. Gromyko also charged the United States with "perfidy" in talking with Khrushchev "of the necessity to strengthen mutual confidence" at Camp David and in preparation of the Summit Conference while directing "a program of aggressive acts" against the Soviet Union. "The integrity of the territory of all states has always been and remains," he said, "a major and generally recognized principle of international law," observance of which is "the backbone of peaceable relations between states." The American effort to justify its action by referring to the secrecy of Soviet defense measures was "absurd." That the Soviet Government was not overemphasizing the incident becomes evident, he said, if one considers "the legitimate indignation which would spread over the United States" if a Soviet plane were shot down over Chicago, Detroit or San Francisco and the Soviet Government sought to justify its action by the need to collect military information. "It is well known," said Gromyko, "that the Soviet Union does not intend to attack any one but even if there are people in America who, because of misunderstanding or ignorance, fear the Soviet Union, this does not justify such provocation."

> If the concept: "If I am apprehensive and do what I want myself and nobody else is the judge of my action" were to prevail in relations among states, it would be the aggressor and only the aggressor who would stand to gain. On the contrary states for whom aggressive intentions are alien would always be subject to the danger of military attack.

Gromyko also characterized the states which had permitted the use of their territory for the U-2 and other flights as "accomplices and parties" to aggression, opening themselves to bombardment of the bases. At the end of his remarks, he presented a draft resolution in the following terms:

The Security Council

Having examined the question of "Aggressive acts by the Air Force of the United States of America against the Soviet Union, creating a threat to universal peace,"

Noting that violations of the sovereignty of the state are incompatible with the principles and purposes of the Charter of the United Nations,

Considering that such actions create a threat to universal peace,

1. *Condemns* the incursions by the United States aircraft into other states and regards them as aggressive acts;

2. *Requests* the Government of the United States of America to adopt immediate measures to halt such actions and to prevent their recurrence.

In defense, United States Ambassador Henry Cabot Lodge denied that the United States had committed any aggressive action against the Soviet Union. President Eisenhower had said in Paris that the flights

had no aggressive intent but rather were to assure the safety of the United States and the free world against surprise attack by a power which boasts of its ability to devastate the United States and other countries by missiles armed with atomic war heads.

Ambassador Lodge insisted that the United States had not threatened to continue such flights, but on the contrary the flights had been suspended and would not be resumed. This was a permanent policy, not a mere temporary suspension. He referred to the extensive use of espionage by the Soviet Union, by sea, on land and by hiring American aviators to take pictures of American strategic places. He also referred to several aggressions and threats by the Soviet Union, saying:

Here is a government well known for its expansionist activities and armed to the teeth, which has repeatedly, in contravention of article 2(4) of the Charter . . . used force and threats of force in its relations with other sovereign states. . . . When such a government insists on secrecy it is in effect also insisting on preserving its ability to make surprise attacks on humanity. If the free world failed to protect itself against such a danger, it would be inviting destruction. . . . This afternoon the Soviet representative has had something to say about international law. One may ask where the Soviet Union's concern for international law was when communist armed forces invaded the Republic of Korea in 1950, or where that concern was when the Soviet Union forcibly and brutally snuffed out the independence of Hungary in 1956.

The "heart of the matter," he said, was the general apprehension of further Communist assaults and the finding of means to relieve that apprehension.

The other members of the Security Council made comments, all agreeing that the U-2 flight had violated Soviet territory, although the representatives of the Republic of China and Italy noted that in view of the flights of man-made satellites and their potentialities for observation, air sovereignty had become more or less a myth. All but the Polish representative, however, refused to agree with the Soviet contention that the U-2 flight constituted "aggression," and thought the central problem was to restore confidence, to which the proposed Soviet resolution would not contribute.

The representatives of France, Great Britain, Italy, the Republic of China, Argentina and Ecuador agreed with the United States that the Soviet Union had exaggerated the seriousness of the incident, that the United States' declaration that flights over the Soviet Union would not be resumed should have ended the controversy, and that the Soviet Government's own behavior was a major cause of anxiety. . . .

XIII
The Congo Crisis

1

The Urgent Need for Congo Reconstruction*

G. MENNEN WILLIAMS

Disorder in the Congo very nearly led to an East–West confrontation in central Africa in the early days of Congolese independence, and continued disorder keeps alive the threat of such a confrontation. It was only through the medium of the United Nations that such a showdown was averted in 1960. The speed and skill with which the U. N. moved into the Congo situation as a stabilizing force—with no comparable experience to draw upon, I might add—makes that operation a major contribution toward the maintenance of world peace and security. . . .

During those early grim days of Congolese independence the situation was blurred and confused by Congolese appeals for aid to the United States and the Soviet Union in addition to the United Nations. The rapid Communist response gave the United States three policy alternatives to consider.

First, we could have done nothing and abandoned the Congo as an unwanted problem. Unquestionably, this would have led to continued chaos and the strong likelihood that a Communist foothold would have been established in the middle of Africa.

Second, we could have intervened directly with sizable numbers of American troops, leading to a direct confrontation between U. S. and Soviet power in central Africa.

The third alternative was to throw our total support behind a coordinated U. N. military and economic effort—an effort which would unite the world community in the common task of preserving world peace and security. We chose this course as the best way to deter unilateral actions by external powers. In retrospect this course seems to have been the best possible choice for our country.

Since the U. N. responded to the Congolese request for assistance, there

*Address delivered before the Jefferson Society of the University of Virginia at Charlottesville, Va., on November 9, 1962. Excerpts.

has been visible evidence of progress in the Congo. Stability and order have been largely restored to the country. Farming and business have resumed but are still below normal because of secession. A moderate parliamentary central government under Prime Minister Cyrille Adoula has been formed, and it is operating effectively and supported broadly everywhere except in Katanga. The pretensions of the opposition Orientale Province government have been ended, and [Antoine] Gizenga has been effectively neutralized. The Communists have been barred from continuing their direct support of left-wing elements in the Congo. The United Nations presence has deterred precipitous action by those who favor a violent solution to Congolese problems. And, perhaps most importantly, the U. N. has served as a point of contact between the Central Government and the Katanga secessionists. Without the United Nations on the scene, there would be complete chaos, as President Kennedy has pointed out. . . .

Ever since Katanga's secession, the Congolese Central Government, the United Nations, the United States, and other friendly nations have encouraged the reintegration of the Congo. These efforts have not met with more than mild success in the nearly $2\frac{1}{2}$ years since Katanga proclaimed its independence.

On August 20 of this year, however, a most important new step toward finding a basis for agreement among Congolese leaders was taken by U. N. Acting Secretary-General U Thant. On that date he announced the United Nations plan for Congo reconciliation.

This plan is based upon proposals from many different quarters, including the Congolese Central Government and Katanga Province, and was developed by the Secretary-General following consultations with Belgium, the United Kingdom, and the United States.

The U. N. plan calls for:

1. A federal constitution to establish a federal system of government for the Congo.
2. A new law for division of revenues, and regulations and procedures for the use of foreign exchange.
3. A plan for national currency unification.
4. Integration and unification of all Congolese military units.
5. The nationalization of foreign affairs.
6. A general amnesty.
7. Full cooperation with the United Nations by all Congolese authorities.
8. Reconstitution of the national government to provide equitable representation for all political and provincial groups.

Following its announcement by the Secretary-General, the plan was widely approved by the nations of Africa, as well as those of Asia and Europe. The United States fully supports the plan and believes it is a reasonable and necessary step to get the Congo on the road to unity and progress. Prime Minister Adoula unequivocally accepted the plan, and Mr. Tshombe has given it his general approval.

The next step was and is implementation of the plan in good faith. It is of the highest importance that urgent priority be given to such implementation by all of the parties involved.

The United States last month reaffirmed its support of the U. N. plan and its implementation of the plan when Under Secretary of State George McGhee visited the Congo to see what progress had been made. His presence there stimulated considerable activity. However, as of this date, only very modest progress has been made by the Central Government and Katanga Province toward implementation of the plan. Within the context of specific U. N. proposals, three steps have been taken:

The Central Government has presented a draft constitution to the provincial presidents for study. This plan was prepared by experts provided by the United Nations.

Central Government and Katangan officials have met in committees on finance and military affairs in Elisabethville to work out details of integrating these critical fields. They have achieved no final conclusions, but they have produced some information and cleared away some preliminary obstacles. . . .

2

Moscow and the Congo*

ALEXANDER DALLIN

Khrushchev had made the Soviet bloc the self-appointed champion of the emerging nations. Blaming all their ills on the colonial and "neocolonial" powers, Moscow strove to work with the nationalist leadership of these countries, realizing the weakness of Communism in most of them. Africa in particular raised a host of problems, ranging from the near-absence of Communist parties to the inapplicability of many concepts of Soviet "class analysis." Moreover, Moscow had not foreseen the rapid and wholesale achievement of independence in 1960, which brought the Black Continent into the United Nations in considerable numerical force.

*From The Soviet Union at the United Nations, by Alexander Dallin, published by Frederick A. Praeger, Inc., Publishers, New York, 1962 (pp. 140–146). Reprinted by permission.

But Soviet promises were on record. Mikoyan had told a Baghdad audience on April 15, 1960, that "all the peoples of Asia, Africa, and Latin America can be fully confident that the Soviet Union will protect their interests everywhere and at all times," and Khrushchev emphasized that "the Soviet Union will be their most loyal and unselfish friend and ally." In mid-July, Moscow pledged 2.5 million rubles for economic aid to Africa through the U. N. and embarked on one of its most intensive propaganda campaigns under the banner of anticolonialism.

Moscow had nothing to lose and everything to gain from these efforts, which embarrassed and tended to divide the West. Khrushchev's assertion that "the Soviet Government is prepared to do everything for the collapse of colonial slavery" no doubt endeared it to some of the new nations during "Africa year." Yet for many of them, the Soviet image changed perceptibly as the Congo crisis unfolded.

Within a fortnight after the proclamation of independence on June 30, 1960, the Republic of the Congo was in the throes of chaos and terror. Fighting among warring tribes, and between Africans and Europeans, and the nearly total absence of governmental authority set the stage for the reintervention of Belgium, which in turn led the young republic's President, Joseph Kasavubu, and Premier Patrice Lumumba to appeal for help to the United Nations. Within a day, the Secretary-General had convened the Security Council, which on his recommendation unanimously called on Belgium to withdraw its troops from the Congo and authorized the Secretary-General to provide military assistance. As Dag Hammarskjold formulated its ground rules (later endorsed by the Security Council) the U. N. force (known by its French initials, ONUC) was to be recruited primarily from other African states and was to exclude nationals of the Great Powers; it was not to intervene in the internal strife of the Congo Republic.

Here was an international armed force precisely of the sort that the U. S. .S. R. had heretofore opposed. The Soviet vote in favor of its establishment was above all an extension of its policy to befriend the African states, for the Congo crisis looked like an ideal case in which the Communist states could "protect" the new nations against the West. It could not very well fail to support this first showdown on colonialism in Black Africa. Indeed, the initial Soviet statement on the Congolese request for aid accused the United States, Britain, and France of violating international law and the U. N. Charter by "unleashing armed aggression" and warned NATO against being the "international gendarme in the colonial subjugation of the peoples of Africa."

In this, the first and "hopeful" stage of the Congo operation, Moscow claimed that "the firm stand of the U. S. .S. R. in defense of the Congolese people's lawful rights undoubtedly had an exceptionally important role in the adoption of the [Security Council] decision." Later, Moscow looked back wistfully on the initial prospects: The U. N. "could have emerged from the Congo tangle with flying colors. . . . At first it seemed that that would be the outcome."

The Soviet Union even suppressed its customary concern with national sovereignty once it became apparent that the United Nations Force could not restrict itself to token operations. When in early August, 1960, the ONUC command had to choose between failure (because of its commitment not to "interfere" in internal Congolese strife and because of its inability to do its job without the use of force) and shooting its way into Katanga, whose independence had been declared by the pro-Belgian Moise Tshombe, Soviet representative Vasili Kuznetsov urged the U. N. to enter the area by force, arrest the Tshombe regime, and use arms to suppress all resistance. The awkwardness of the Soviet position was apparent when Kuznetsov, isolated among his colleagues, wound up voting for the milder resolution (introduced by Tunisia and Ceylon), which called for an immediate Belgian withdrawal from Katanga and instructed the Secretary-General to help carry out the move. The Soviet Union, Kuznetsov explained, was still pursuing the primary goal of getting the "imperialists" out; nor was it prepared, he might have added, to publicize a split with the unaligned states, which were advocating a more moderate policy.

By early September, the U. N. operation looked like a near-total success. The Belgians had completed the withdrawal of their combat troops (though assuredly not of various military and civilian "advisers"), and the U. N. contingents had taken up positions in Katanga. But all this Moscow chose to ignore. Instead, it charged that Secretary-General Hammarskjold had not even tried to get the Belgians out.

The special position adopted by the U. S. S. R. had its roots in the first days of the Congo crisis. Unable to regard ONUC as a "neutral" force, Moscow was bound to look for evidence of an "imperialist" (and above all an American) plot. As early as July 13, it charged that United Nations Under-Secretary Ralph J. Bunche—an American citizen—was being used in Léopoldville to promote plans for the intervention of the Western powers. When, on request from the U. N., the United States Army provided communications personnnel and aviation technicians to help ONUC in Léopoldville, Arkadi Sobolev on July 19 demanded the "immediate withdrawal" of American troops, whatever the "pretext" for their aggressive presence in the Congo.

Hand in hand with its efforts to keep the United States out, Moscow began to develop a conspiracy theory whose full fruition was not to come for another six months. In essence, Belgian "aggression" was blamed on its stronger partners in NATO. How indeed would little Belgium dare act on its own? Too weak to satiate their colonialist appetites singly, the imperialists in the era of their decline had embarked on "collective colonialism"; "the bayonet was Belgian, but the bosses were the United States, Belgian, British, and West German big monopolies."

The logical corollary of these allegations was the Soviet offer to support the Congo Republic outside the framework of the United Nations. In an increasingly vituperative campaign, Khrushchev promised the Congo "the necessary help that may be required for the victory of your just cause" —if need be, by unilateral action defying the West. The political support pledged by Moscow was supplemented by Soviet promises of economic and technical aid and, beginning in late July, the dispatch of transport planes, trucks, and other equipment from the U. S. S. R., without any reference to the United Nations. In the following weeks, a variety of (partly unverified) reports spoke of other, unpublicized forms of Soviet and Czechoslovak aid to the Stanleyville regime, including food and medical supplies and, apparently, also small arms.

This was the occasion of the first serious clash between the Secretary-General and the Soviet Union over the Congo. According to the Secretariat's rules (approved by the Security Council, including the Soviet Union) the Great Powers were not to intervene with troops or matériel, directly or indirectly. When reminded of these terms, Moscow remained silent. On September 5, Hammarskjold reiterated his demand that Soviet shipments to the Congo cease. By then, Lumumba (backed by the U. S. S. R.) and Kasavubu (backed by the United States) had "dismissed each other" from office. Moscow saw the Congo situation finally polarized into friends and foes, and Hammarskjold had lined up with the foes.

As a matter of principle, Moscow asserted, the Soviet Union was free to enter into such agreements as it desired. The United Nations resolution, it argued,

> does not restrict and, of course, cannot restrict the right of the government of the sovereign Republic of the Congo to request assistance from the governments of other countries besides the United Nations and to receive such assistance.

The Secretary-General's note was therefore labeled

> an attempt at taking control over the relations between the Congo Republic and other states, especially the Soviet Union . . . [whereas] not a single United Nations administrative official has the right to intervene in the relations between sovereign states if these states do not request it.

But there was more involved than principle. Hammarskjold had been the one to challenge Moscow's right to act unilaterally after voting not to do so. Even earlier, Hammarskjold had been publicly identified by Moscow as "scandalously" partisan and as "playing a very unseemly part in this NATO plot against Africa." Now the Soviet Union charged the senior representatives in the Congo (above all, Ralph Bunche, who was replaced by Rajeshwar Dayal of India in September) with "outrageous colonialist behavior" and protested the Secretariat's "functioning most unashamedly on the side of the colonialists."

Moscow was witnessing the failure of its hopes that the Congo operation would open new opportunities for Soviet influence, via ONUC. The U. N. administration was unwilling to leave an ambiguous and hazardous vacuum in the Congo. Whether or not it could in fact fill it remained to be seen, but it would not tolerate Soviet efforts to short-circuit the attempt. This was the essence of the Secretary-General's response to Soviet charges that he had violated the Security Council's instructions. Moscow was once again stymied by the Secretary-General, who was beyond the reach of its veto. But so also was the General Assembly: Gathered in special session when a Soviet veto forestalled Security Council action, the Assembly, on September 20, passed an Afro-Asian resolution (by a vote of 70: 0, with the Communist bloc abstaining) explicitly calling upon all states to refrain from direct or indirect military assistance in the Congo "except upon the request of the United Nations through the Secretary-General."

What could Moscow do? Behind the scenes, Soviet advisers were active with Lumumba's staff, and help appears to have come to his forces from other Communist states. Moscow supported him against his domestic rivals —Kasavubu and Colonel Mobutu in Léopoldville, Tshombe in Elisabeth-ville—and against the United Nations force. But Khrushchev had clearly decided to avoid a total break with the U. N. Confronted with the choice between risking conflict—with the West as well as with many Afro-Asian states—by giving Lumumba outright support, including arms, and having its policy exposed as a bluff, Moscow in obvious frustration opted for the safer though more distasteful course. (Moreover, while it might have produced a mobile force to serve abroad, Moscow and its allies had no overseas bases—and ONUC had taken control of airports in the Congo Republic.) The broad needs of "peaceful coexistence" had to come before victory in the Congo.

This was a bitter pill. How had the runaway Congo operation resulted in such a failure for the U. S. .S. R.? How could Moscow make sure that such a sequence of events would never recur? What moves could it take to restore its position? The Congo experience prompted top-level Soviet rethinking in the first half of September, 1960. By the time Khrushchev addressed the General Assembly on September 23, the new strategy had been set.

3

Plans to "Balkanize" the Congo*

E. PRIMAKOV

The situation in the Congo has deteriorated again. Tshombe planes have dropped bombs on Central Government troops in North Katanga.

*From New Times, *November 28, 1962, pp. 8–10.*

The Central Government, for its part, threatens to retaliate if the U. N. troops do not moderate the Katanga puppet.

Uninformed people may think this turn of events surprising. Three months ago Western propaganda maintained that rapid and full reconciliation between the Katanga separatists and the Central Government was a foregone conclusion and that the "Congo tragedy" was over and done with. Western observers gave big play to a so-called national reconciliation plan, which was at the time being foisted on the Congo by U. N. officials. Yet, objectively, the plan itself, and the events that accompanied attempts to put it through, gave little hope of an accommodation of the Congo crisis. On the contrary, there was evidence that the manoeuvres of the imperialist powers would, far from adjusting, deepen the crisis in the Congo.

To begin with, the plan with the U. N. label on it was not a U. N. plan at all. It was never discussed in the Security Council or the General Assembly, or in any of its committees. It had not been worked out within the U. N. framework. It was devised in Washington, jointly with London and Brussels representatives. In other words, it was the upshot of collusion between the imperialist powers, whose monopolists have interests in the Congo and are jockeying for priority influence in that country.

* * *

The keynote of the "U. N. plan" was concessions to the Katanga separatists. Since it was Tshombe's prime purpose to maintain Katanga's independence from Leopoldville (but by no means from the Anglo-Belgian Union Minière), the Central Government was asked to work out a new constitution and to convert the Congo Republic from a unitary into a federal state.

What imperialists mean by "federation" always depends on the circumstances. They have a big range of interpretations for the term. In this particular case their objective was to preclude Central Government control over the Katanga clique, and especially over its economic policy. Leopoldville's authority over the member-states of the projected federation would, in fact, have been a mere fiction.

The Congo's biggest political parties, the Congolese National Movement, the Party of African Solidarity, the Balubakat Party and the National Unity Party, described the plan in a joint statement as "the first stage in a simple and undisguised effort to Balkanize the Congo, paving the way to its final disappearance, in the interests of a handful of individuals in the service of foreign quarters."

In compensation for its consent to partition the republic, the Central Government was promised a fifty–fifty share of the revenue Katanga received from Union Minière, the restoration of a single currency, and even the incorporation of Tshombe's armed gangs in the national army.

Tshombe's forces had been somewhat weakened at the time by a spanking they received from the U. N. troops in September 1961. Furthermore, it was a time when, for tactical reasons, Tshombe had dismissed some of his white mercenaries. In those circumstances, Tshombe thought it prudent to let his spokesmen assist in working out a constitution based on the "U. N. plan." It is all too clear today, however, that this was no more than a dodge on Tshombe's part, advised by well-wishers in high places, in whose game Tshombe is a mere pawn.

In the negotiations Tshombe and his accomplices evaded any and all clear-cut decisions by making all sorts of reservations and excuses. Tshombe's main concern lay in the financial area, which the Information Bureau of the Congo Republic described as "the most important area in the problem of Katanga." Tshombe refused to live up to his promise concerning the fifty–fifty share of Katanga revenue. He also scuttled all attempts to unify the armed forces. Katanga retains its own currency, distinct from that of the Congo Republic, issues its own visas, etc.

Tshombe was playing for time, to reinforce his armies. Reuters reported on November 11 that "there are now 1,500 trained white soldiers in the Katanga army." The London Observer reported on the same day that British rocket-carrying Vampire jets had arrived in Katanga. "Airstrips have been built in the bush," the paper wrote, "to make up for the airports seized by the U. N., and rocket-proof underground hangars are envisaged."

* * *

Tshombe would never have been so defiant if he had lacked support from the U. N. representatives in the Congo. The Paris Le Monde, of August 22, reported that arrivals landing at the Elisabethville airport were at once assailed by the "blue helmets" (meaning U. N. troops), who interrogated them, searched them and rummaged in their personal effects, searching for "hidden arms or compromising documents" which would lead to their exposure as camouflaged "mercenaries." The real mercenaries, in the meantime, the paper wrote, "prefer to enter Mr. Tshombe's realm by a highway exclusively controlled by the Katangans, which connects Katanga with Northern Rhodesia." Tshombe's position was further strengthened when the U. N. representatives decided on evicting 70,000 Africans of the Baluba tribe, who opposed separatism, from South Katanga to its northern section. Le Monde notes that the Balubas, who are "under close surveillance of the U. N. forces, have no chance to arm themselves, and the guerilla warfare they waged last year has therefore been virtually snuffed out."

Under the pretext of concern for peace in the Congo, U. N. representatives obstruct operations by Central Government troops against the Katanga separatists. In any case, the recent Katanga air raid on Central Government troop positions has gone unpunished.

Having thus again bared their fangs, the Katanga separatists followed up with a nonchalant statement that they really had no objections to negotiating a federal constitution, but that they insisted on the acceptance of the demands which Tshombe formulated as follows:

"The new constitution should guarantee non-interference by Leopold-ville in our internal affairs. Alongside the federal forces, which are to defend the frontiers of the federation, we must dispose of our own troops. . . . Katanga's economy and finances will be in our charge. . . . We shall retain our own currency, but it should be negotiable in the rest of the country, just as the Congolese franc will be negotiable in Katanga."

Once Katanga obtained these privileges, they would automatically spread to the other territories claiming the status of member-states of the projected federation.

What would then be left of the Congo Republic? It would become a fiction and would soon, beyond doubt, break up into some two dozen puppet states. That is just what the imperialists want. The federation plan has the ultimate purpose of eliminating the Congo as a united state.

* * *

It is a widespread notion that puppet Tshombe is controlled by Union Minière alone, in which British and Belgian capital predominates. The section of the American press close to the State Department has gone out of its way to promote this belief. Tshombe has indeed come into prominence through the efforts of Union Minière, and depends on its support to this day. But he would have gone down hook, line and sinker long ago if the United States had wished to put him out of the way as an obstruction to Katanga's reunification with the republic. Washington would not even have needed to intervene directly, for the U. N. forces would have coped with the task if the U. S. .A. had not hindered them from implementing the well-known Security Council decisions.

But that is just the point. The United States considers Tshombe a trump card in its efforts to break up the Congo Republic, in which federation is no more than a means to that end. Twice did the U. N. soldiers begin armed operations in Katanga, and twice did Tshombe receive a reprieve by orders from across the Atlantic. And when he embarked on dilatory tactics in his negotiations with the Central Government concerning a federal consti-tution, the American press advanced a thousand excuses for his intransigence.

The New York Herald Tribune, of August 27, for example, said "the revenues from Union Minière . . . would help the Central treasury—but not much." The paper went on to say that "if Katanga's army and currency are integrated with those of the Central Government, as the U. N. insists, the problems of military indiscipline and monetary instability will persist."

The New York Times, of September 10, recalled that Tshombe "has his own flag, his postage stamps, his army, which started from scratch and is now jealous of its power. He has a government of well-paid ministers and civil servants and generals." It ended up by saying that Katanga would not be easily induced to give up all this.

How neatly this clicks with Tshombe's demands of the Central Govern-ment! One might almost think the Katanga ruler formulated his demands after reading the American paper.

But, to be sure, Tshombe does not get his directives from the New York papers alone. In the last three months he was twice visited by George McGhee, U. S. Under-Secretary of State. Tshombe has also played host to Ralph Johnson Bunche, an American closely connected with the State Department and now special political advisor to the U. N. Secretary-General. The hours these highly-placed gentlemen spent with Tshombe were reminiscent of meetings of a mutual admiration society. McGhee was so captivated by the Katanga warlord that he helped the Kennedy Administration to form "a higher opinion of the man." That, at least, was what the U. S. press reported.

According to the American papers, Washington feels that the breakdown of the negotiations between Katanga and the Central Government concerning the "U. N. plan" is not to be blamed on Tshombe, but rather on Cyrille Adoula's administration. "The Administration in Washington," said the New York Herald Tribune on October 20, "according to good authority there wants communication reopened with Tshombe." It was Adoula's "intransigence," the paper went on to say, that had created the "crisis."

Unquestionably, Tshombe's air raid on Central Government troop positions, which has again whipped up tension in the Congo, had Washington's approval. Its purpose was to exert pressure on Leopoldville and make it meet Tshombe's demands half-way, though that would mean the beginning of the end for the Congo Republic.

*   *   *

There are deep-going contradictions between the imperialist powers that stand behind Tshombe. But they have apparently receded into the background in face of the common imperialist objective gradually to break up the Congo Republic. The matter that divides the imperialists—the sharing of the loot—is apparently to be thrashed out after this common goal is attained.

One cannot help coming to the conclusion that the Congo Republic, its territorial integrity and its independence, have never been in greater danger than they are today. Public attention has been glued to the crisis in the Caribbean, created by U. S. aggressive moves against Cuba. The imperialist governments and the monopolies behind them have taken advantage of this. They seem to reckon that the propitious moment has come to strike at the national-liberation movement in Africa, and in the Congo first of all.

part Three

Balance of Sanity

INTRODUCTION

WHEN JOHN F. KENNEDY became President, he sincerely hoped to lessen the tensions in the Cold War. This, he believed, could be done through negotiations conducted at the appropriate time with the appropriate method. In his inaugural address, he had said: "Let us never negotiate out of fear. But let us never fear to negotiate." In this spirit, President Kennedy met Soviet Premier Khrushchev at Vienna in June, 1961, in an effort to find common grounds for a relaxation of the Cold War. But little was gained from the meeting; Kennedy rightly predicted "a long cold winter" in the international climate. His prediction was substantiated. The Soviets erected the Berlin Wall, the Americans increased their Polaris deterrent power, and they both resumed nuclear-weapons testing. The world steadily drifted toward a dangerous nuclear confrontation, culminating in the Cuban missile crisis.

The "Bay of Pigs" fiasco[1] in April, 1961, momentously accelerated the steady deterioration of American–Cuban relations, which had been worsening since Fidel Castro's rise to power in January, 1959. United States hostility toward the Castro regime was based on the conviction that Cuba had become, for all intents and purposes, a Communist state closely allied with the Soviet Union and international communism. As such, Cuba had switched sides in the Cold War, and the world Communist movement had established in the Western Hemisphere a beachhead of enormous political as well as psychological potency. Castro's Cuba was regarded as the harbinger of

---

[1]This was the abortive invasion attempt by the Cuban Brigade, consisting of 1400 Cuban refugees. The Brigade had been trained, equipped, and directed by the Central Intelligence Agency (CIA) and the United States military. The CIA drew up the invasion plan and the Pentagon approved it. The invasion itself began at midnight on Sunday, April 16, 1961, with a landing in the town of Playa Giron in the Bay of Pigs. The Brigade had hoped that the United States would supply the support necessary to secure its hold for 72 hours, during which time a government would be established; however, the United States did not intervene, although U. S. naval units were in the waters nearby. The invasion ended on April 19, with the total defeat of the Brigade.

Communist penetration and expansion into Latin America, which historically had been considered to be solely in the United States's sphere of influence and interest. This unforeseen development disturbed the collective security system of the Organization of American States (OAS) and disrupted hemispheric solidarity under the leadership of the United States.

Capitalizing on this situation, the Soviet Union—seemingly by gross miscalculation of America's firmness and with a casual disregard of the consequences—voluntarily undertook the risky venture of introducing offensive missiles into Cuba during the late summer and fall of 1962. Seeking to radically alter the strategic and diplomatic balance of power to its favor, the Soviet Union had installed, on a permanent basis, a number of missile sites within the Western Hemisphere in close proximity to the United States.

If launched, these short-range and intermediate-range missiles could reach any point of the United States or Latin America. Concurrently, the Soviets undertook the construction of air bases in Cuba capable of accommodating jet bombers carrying nuclear warheads. By mid-October, United States aerial photographs positively established proof that these missiles and air bases had become operational. The imminent menace to the security of the United States and Latin America demanded prompt and decisive action.

On October 22, 1962, President Kennedy, in an address to the nation, proclaimed the United States decision of a "strict quarantine" of Cuba to prevent the further introduction of offensive military equipment into that island country. Moreover, President Kennedy firmly demanded the immediate "withdrawal and elimination" of the missiles and other offensive military equipment from Cuba. He unequivocally warned the Soviet Union that any missile assault from Cuba against a nation of the Western Hemisphere would be regarded "as an attack by the Soviet Union on the United States, requiring a full retaliatory response upon the Soviet Union."

At first the Soviet Union reacted to the maritime quarantine by accusing the United States of "a naval blockade" in peacetime and "piracy" on the high seas. The Soviets concluded that the United States had engaged in "unprecedented aggressive actions by alleging that a threat to the national security of the United States emanates from Cuba."

America's allies supported President Kennedy's resolute stand. The NATO members gave full sympathy and support to the United States actions: Prime Minister Harold MacMillan told the House of Commons that the Soviet activity in Cuba was a "new threat to security" and that President Kennedy's quarantine measures were designed to meet an unprecedented situation; President Charles de Gaulle pledged French support and understanding of the United States policy toward Cuba. The Organization of American States unanimously endorsed the American policy and remained firm in its intent to enforce the quarantine. It adopted a resolution expressing its determination to take all measures deemed necessary to safeguard the hemispheric peace and security which was threatened by the offensive weapons in Cuba.

The Soviet leaders came to understand the gravity of the problem they had initiated. Confronted with President Kennedy's stern ultimatum and realizing that to resist it by force would most likely precipitate a thermonuclear holocaust of mutual annihilation, they chose to make a tactical retreat. On October 25, Soviet Premier Khrushchev announced in a letter to Lord Bertrand Russell that he would "do everything to eliminate the situation fraught with irreparable consequence which had arisen in connection with the aggressive actions of the United States Government."[2] Three days later Khrushchev informed President Kennedy that "the Soviet Government, in addition to earlier instructions on the discontinuation of further work on weapons construction sites, has given a new order to dismantle the arms which you described as offensive, and to crate and return them to the Soviet Union."[3]

Thus, the missile threat was removed and the naval quarantine was lifted in late November, but the vexing problem of Castro's Communist regime remained unchanged. The United States government has since intensified its endeavor to isolate Cuba economically and has rendered support to Cuban exiles in their bid to reconquer their homeland and overthrow the Castro dictatorship.

The missile crisis ended in an American "victory" in the Cold War; as such, it had far-reaching implications and enduring effects. By demonstrating the will to use force in defense of vital national interests, the United States cast off the image of "a paper tiger," a label the militant Chinese Communists had used to describe America's "timidity." Moreover, through proper and astute use of power, the Kennedy foreign policy came to assume more confidence and dependability.

Having been forced to retreat from a military confrontation, the Soviet Union came to adhere more faithfully to its policy of "competitive coexistence." Khrushchev's "ignominious retreat" from Cuba infuriated the bellicose Chinese Communists, widened the Sino-Soviet rift, and was believed to have contributed partly to Khrushchev's eventual ousting in 1964.

Indeed, the Cold War had been subjected to its most crucial test to determine which alternative would be followed: competitive coexistence or catastrophic co-annihilation. The sanity of man prevailed.

The Cuban missile crisis marked the maximum danger point for a possible armed conflict between the United States and the Soviet Union; at the same time it heralded the birth of "a new Cold War" between the Soviet Union and Communist China.

The reasons for Communists China's belligerent attitudes toward the

[2] *The New York Times*, October 25, 1962, p. 22.
[3] *Department of State Bulletin*, **47** (November 12, 1962), 743.

United States were varying and numerous; one was the conviction that the United States stood athwart its goal—the attainment of the status of a great world power. Therefore, by challenging the United States's leadership in world affairs and by belittling America's power position in the international arena, Communist China hoped to elevate its own status to stand in parity with that of the United States. In this struggle the Peking leaders had expected all-out support and assistance from their "comrades" in Moscow. Later, when it became evident that the Soviet Communist policies and principles were not in line with what the Chinese had expected and that Moscow's response to their advocacy of an aggressive international strategy was less than positive, they began to pick a quarrel with their "fraternal colleagues" in the Kremlin.

Although at first the "family quarrel," as the Soviet leaders called it, was hardly apparent, it had been brewing for a number of years. The Chinese Communist leaders had never been entirely satisfied with Khrushchev's de-Stalinization policy of 1956, which opened a Pandora's box of dissent and disunity within the Communist world. Peking regarded the Poznan revolt in Poland and the Hungarian uprising in 1956 as the direct consequences of the Soviet "bankrupt" policy of denunciation of Stalin. The Soviet leaders, on the other hand, were not totally pleased with the "Chinese way to socialism," the "Great Leap Forward," or the Chinese communes, all of which they described as "old-fashioned" and "reactionary."

In 1961, Khrushchev had chastised Albania's "dogmatism" as a front for an attack on the Chinese Communists, who, in turn, assailed Yugoslavia's "revisionism" as a veil for an attack on Khrushchev. Soviet economic and technical assistance programs to Peking had come to a halt with the withdrawal of Soviet technicians and experts from China. The volume of Sino-Soviet trade dwindled conspicuously. The undercurrents of Sino-Soviet tensions gradually came to the surface to form "a new Cold War."

Then came the Cuban affair. From the standpoint of Communist China, Khrushchev's "ignominious retreat" in the face of "Kennedy's intimidation" was another Munich. The Chinese Communists accused Khrushchev of cowardice, and ridiculed his claim to have saved humanity from a world holocaust. On the contrary, they maintained, the Soviet backdown from the Cuban missile confrontation would prove more conducive to war because the imperialists' aggressiveness and belligerence would increase. They argued that "the revolutionary people" should never bow before the imperialists or even compromise with them. The Peking leaders concluded that Khrushchev and his comrades in the Kremlin were not fit for the world Communist movement.

By the summer of 1963, the Sino-Soviet rift had become an open fact. The range of their disputes, as manifested in their polemics, covered a variety of issues: war and peace, disarmament and nuclear weapons, revolution and world communism, revisionism and dogmatism, economic relations and

Soviet development, the cult of personality and the Communist Party, and racism.[4]

The Soviet position on these issues was, briefly, as follows. First, wars are no longer inevitable. What is inevitable is the triumph of socialism without war. The destruction in a thermonuclear war would be so great that Communists must make every effort to avoid the outbreak of such a catastrophe. The Chinese Communists erroncously encourage illusions that mankind could build a bright future upon the ashes and ruins of what would remain of world civilizations after nuclear devastation. Second, part of the traditional Communist doctrine on war has been made obsolete by the reality of nuclear weapons; general and total disarmament could be realized even while capitalism exists and Communists should fight for it and its benefits. Third, armed revolution should be waged only when proper revolutionary situations exist, but Communists should try first to take power in different countries by peaceful means, using democratic and parliamentary processes. Fourth, Yugoslavia is a socialist state and its leaders are true Marxists who do, however, have some incorrect ideas. The Chinese encourage the Albanians to adopt an incorrect "dogmatism," and use them as "mouthpieces" against the Soviet Union. Fifth, the Soviet Union is now rapidly moving toward Communist affluence, which will be achieved within a few decades. The Communist states should strive for maximum economic integration to achieve the maximum efficiency through international division of labor and specialization. Sixth, the Soviet Union and world communism have become stronger because of the exposure of Stalin's crimes, but the Chinese leaders have betrayed Leninism by supporting the "cult of personality" of Stalin. The Chinese are deliberately trying to split the world Communist movement by encouraging pro-Chinese and anti-Soviet groups in many parts of the world. And finally, the Chinese Communists are actually pursuing a racist, anti-white policy which has nothing in common with Marxism–Leninism; they are damaging the national liberation movement by seeking to divorce it from the working-class revolutionary movement.

Against these Soviet views, the following *résumé* summarizes the Chinese Communist contentions on the same issues. First, wars are inevitable as long as capitalism exists, but Communists should avoid being paralyzed by the fear that any clash might spark a thermonuclear war. Taking a bourgeois pacifist attitude, the Soviet leaders exaggerate the impact of nuclear weapons in an attempt to justify revisionist retreats from revolutionary Marxism–Leninism. Second, no general or total disarmament could be possible; such slogans should be used as propaganda to expose the capitalist warmongers. Nuclear weapons add nothing fundamental to the international situation and have not changed the Marxist–Leninist doctrine about the course of

[4]See *A proposal Concerning the General Line of the International Communist Movement* (Peking: Foreign Language Press, 1963), and "Open Letter to the Central Committee of the Soviet Communist Party, July 15, 1963," *The New York Times*, July 16, 1963, pp. 4, 7.

world history. Third, there is no historical precedent of a Communist seizure of power by peaceful means. The Communists should resort to armed revolution to take power; they should encourage and support the oppressed peoples of Asia, Africa, and Latin America in their liberation struggles. The Soviet leaders are seeking to weaken the world revolutionary movement by over-emphasizing legal and parliamentary means of overthrowing capitalism. Fourth, Yugoslavia has returned to capitalism and its leaders are traitors to the world Communist movement and agents of bourgeois capitalism. The Soviet leaders are solely responsible for the break with Albania and for the crime of exposing the dispute to the world. Fifth, the Soviet leaders have deceived their people with groundless illusions that Communist abundance can be achieved in this generation. They are trying to discard the dictatorship of the proletariat and to help restore capitalism. Sixth, the Soviet leaders have caused grave damage to the world Communist movement by their reckless and senseless attacks on Stalin. Moreover, they are trying to force all Communist parties to accept the Kremlin's unilateral decisions as binding doctrines, imposing their will especially on the Chinese. And finally, the Soviet leaders give credence to the principle of colonialism and the rule of "superior" nations over "inferior" ones, while denying top priority to the national liberation movement of the oppressed peoples of the world.

After the ouster of Khrushchev from power in October, 1964, the new Brezhnev–Kosygin collective leadership in the Kremlin made several attempts to adjust Sino-Soviet differences, but their fundamental positions remained unchanged. There was no sign of any amelioration in their disputes. It could be assumed that these "ideological" controversies are in reality only the manifestations of the deep-rooted, traditional, historic power rivalry between China and Russia. Their strong feelings of national pride, their urge for expansion, and their desire for undisputed leadership seem to transcend the tenets of Marxism–Leninism.

Thus, the Sino-Soviet split, coupled with the rapid rise of Chinese power, has somewhat eased the U. S.–USSR Cold War and at the same time created a variable which prevents a return to bipolarity. The Soviet Union has long been viewed as the center of international communism and the major problem for American foreign policy. This view is now being changed; Communist China looms large on the landscape of American foreign affairs and in the course of the Cold War.

The new Moscow–Peking Cold War, brewed in the historic power rivalry, fostered in ideological controversy, and accentuated in the Cuban crisis, had another cause for its intensification—the Chinese invasion of India.

Communist China's attack against India was one of the major international crises in the 1960's. The sudden deterioration of Sino-Indian relations—from cordial friendship to coarse friction—was attributed partly to China's changing attitude toward neutralism and partly to its increasing tendency toward imperialistic expansionism.

The Sino-Indian frontier, where actual hostilities took place, had aroused little interest between the two countries until the withdrawal of the British from India in 1947 and the Communist ascendancy to power in China in 1949. The area through which the boundaries run covers rugged mountainous terrain and is so sparsely populated that neither nation attached much importance to it.

A number of agreements designed to define sections of the frontier were signed from time to time by various authorities on both sides. The most ambitious attempt at determining the boundary was made as early as 1914 by the Simla Convention, attended by officials from China, India, and Tibet. No definite agreement was reached at this convention, but China raised no objection to the demarcation of the boundaries between India and Tibet, later known as the McMahon Line.

On October 25, 1950, the same day Communist China intervened in the Korean War, the Peking government issued a brief communiqué stating: "People's army units have been ordered to advance into Tibet to free 3 million Tibetans from imperialistic oppression and to consolidate national defenses on the western borders of China." This was the first indication of Communist China's design for westward expansion toward the Indian border.

In 1954, India and China entered into a treaty which regulated their relations in this area: India recognized China's claim to Tibet, withdrew its right to station a garrison in Tibet for the protection of Indian trade with Lhasa, and transferred its control over posts and telegraphs in Tibet to the Communist authorities. At this time, the Peking government neither questioned the validity of the McMahon Line, nor gave any indication of challenging the arrangements.

Sino-Tibetan relations became openly strained in March, 1959, when an armed revolt broke out in Lhasa against the Chinese rule. The insurrection was suppressed by the Chinese army, and the Dalai Lama (the spiritual and temporal leader of Tibet) took refuge in India, where he was granted political asylum over the protest of the Peking government.

This incident placed greater strain on the already deteriorating relations between Peking and New Delhi. In August, 1959, Chinese Communist troops invaded Indian territories on both flanks of Tibet and captured frontier posts. India charged Communist China with aggression, while China countercharged India with interference in China's Tibetan affairs. The following month the Peking government laid claim to 12,000 square miles in the western sector of the Indian–Chinese border (the Ladakh region) and 30,000 square miles in the eastern region (McMahon Line). Chinese authorities maintained that the Sino-Indian boundary had never been delimited, and they refused to accept the McMahon Line, which they described as the "product of British aggression."[5]

[5]*Peking Review*, No. 37 (September 15, 1959), p. 7.

The Soviet Union became extremely disturbed by the Sino-Indian dispute and was anxious to see it settled amicably. The Soviets had maintained their neutrality in the dispute and reiterated not only their fraternal ties with Communist China but also their friendly relations with India. The Chinese were disgusted with the Soviet attitude but were not yet in a position to defy the Soviet Union openly. In any case, it appears that Soviet Premier Khrushchev, during his visit to India in March, 1960, prevailed upon Indian Prime Minister Jawaharlal Nehru to confer with Chinese Premier Chou En-lai. The following month a meeting between Nehru and Chou took place in Delhi. They discussed the border controversy for nearly a week but failed to reach any agreement.

The boundary dispute, to be sure, was a symptom and not a cause of the broad political and ideological differences between China and India. From the standpoint of Communist China, India was pursuing an "antirevolutionary, reactionary" course which the Peking government could neither endorse nor tolerate. India had established a system of mixed economy within the framework of democratic parliamentarianism; India was "shamelessly" receiving economic aid from both the "archcapitalist" United States and the "revisionist" Soviet Union; India claimed to be *the* leader of the neutralist emerging nations of the world, especially coveting the hegemony of Asia; India welcomed the Soviet–American *détente* in all areas of international affairs; India was in collusion with forces of neo-colonialism—in short, India had gone over to the enemy. Therefore, India's image, if not the country itself, should be destroyed. To whip India directly was to slap both the Soviet Union and the United States indirectly.

In October, 1962, Communist China launched a massive attack against India. India, which was totally unprepared for major military operations in terms of trained men and adequate equipment, appealed immediately to the Western Powers, especially the United States, for arms. The arrival of military supplies in quantity from the United States coincided with Peking's announcement of a unilateral cease-fire and the withdrawal of its troops behind the McMahon Line in the eastern sector and the Aksai Chin road in Ladakh in the western theater.

The decision by the Chinese to cease fire while at the height of their military victory was motivated by numerous reasons, one of which was the Chinese Communists' fear of a direct confrontation with the United States. It must have become obvious to the Chinese that even if this could be avoided, it would be futile to wage a war with India—a country, not unlike China, with enormous sources of manpower, augmented by ample war supplies from the United States. The Peking leaders were convinced that this kind of "proxy" war with the United States through India, in which they were not assisted by the Soviet Union, would only spell irreparable disaster for them. The Chinese authorities appear to have concluded that, since they had achieved most of their political and strategic objectives, they should demonstrate magnanimity and reasonableness by offering India the opportunity to negotiate as a "defeated party." India refused to accept the terms laid down by Communist China but at the same time did not attempt to reoccupy the entire area the Chinese had taken and now vacated.

The Sino-Indian hostilities ended, but hostile relations between the two countries lingered on.

President Truman once said that it was no longer practical or realistic to draw a neat distinction between domestic and foreign policies because they were invariably intertwined. Likewise, in an age of "revolution in science, technology, and communication," which has telescoped the nations of the world into next-door neighbors, it has become increasingly impossible to confine a nation's domestic crises within its national boundaries. Such an internal crisis invariably comes to affect the *international* community. The Sino-Indian conflict, to be sure, was *international* in nature from the beginning. The Cyprus issue was initially a *domestic* crisis, which developed into an *international* issue.

The island of Cyprus, located at the northeast end of the Mediterranean Sea, has been for centuries a land of historic contest and conflict. Heavily influenced by Greek civilization, it is inhabited by a Greek majority and a Turkish minority, the latter constituting about 20 per cent of the population.

During the period of British rule, which began in 1878, the Greek Cypriots frequently argued, petitioned, and demonstrated for their independence to no avail. Finally, the violence and turmoil on the island throughout the latter half of the 1950's culminated in the Zurich and London Agreements of 1959, which granted limited independence.

When Cyprus was given an independent status within the British Commonwealth in 1960, its Constitution guaranteed minority rights to the Turks in a proportion that was considered to be far in excess of that justified by their numbers. The Turkish Cypriots were to hold the vice-presidency and to maintain control over their own education, religion, and cultural affairs through separate legislative chambers. By 1963, the demand for a revision of the Constitution had become almost unanimous on the part of the Greek Cypriots.

Meanwhile, for a few years after independence, Greek and Turkish Cypriots maintained a precarious coexistence, which was marked by frequent clashes between the two communities. On December 21, 1963, the long-simmering conflict culminated in full-scale civil strife, with bitter fighting between Greek and Turkish soldiers in Nicosia, the capital of Cyprus.

Among the multiplicity of causes for the new flare-up were: (1) racial and religious issues, (2) extremists' designs to further their political aims, (3) the problems of adjustment to independence, and (4) conflicts of interest among foreign powers. At the heart of the dispute, however, lay the Turkish Cypriot policy of division as opposed to the Greek Cypriot policy of *enosis* (union with Greece): the former demanded partition in order to secure total protection from Greek Cypriot "tyranny," and the latter insisted on a close alignment with Greece.

When President Makarios proposed constitutional amendments designed to ensure more expeditious functioning of the government, the Turkish Cypriots revolted for fear of losing their minority rights guaranteed by the Constitution, including the veto power, which had been exercised over such critical areas of national policy as taxation, foreign affairs, domestic security, and national defense.

The fighting in Cyprus reached international dimensions with the formation of joint peace-keeping forces by Greece, Turkey, and the United Kingdom under the Treaty of Guarantee, and with the threat of unilateral Turkish intervention under the provisions of the same Treaty. Consequently, Greece and Turkey were catapulted to the brink of war.

While the fighting between the two hostile communities declined somewhat in January, 1964, the threat of war between Greece and Turkey persisted. The United States Sixth Fleet, a self-contained unit which usually patrolled in the Mediterranean area, appeared in the Cyprus waters with a view to dampening the war talks and forcing a new awareness of the extensive United States power in that area. The United States was deeply concerned about a possible Communist foothold in the Mediterranean. To involve Greece and Turkey—both NATO Powers—in a war would open the eastern Mediterranean sector to Soviet penetration. Although it was primarily a conflict between the two allies and not against communism (despite strong Communist influence and agitation), the situation was ripe for Communist intervention. Western disunity would only add to the Soviet power potentiality.

At this juncture the issue was brought to the attention of the United Nations Security Council, which in March, 1964, adopted unanimously a resolution calling for the creation of a United Nations peace-keeping force in Cyprus (UNICYP).[6] UNICYP became operational late that month. Its principal objectives and responsibilities were: (1) to safeguard against a recurrence of fighting, (2) to facilitate the resumption of normal life in Cyprus, (3) to insure security and freedom of movement for the ordinary man, and (4) to prevent a direct clash between Turkey and Greece and, more important, between the United States and the Soviet Union.

When the Soviet Union learned of the United Nations mediator's plan[7] for *enosis*, Premier Khrushchev decided to offer assistance to Cypriot nationalists in case of invasion. *Enosis* would certainly weaken the Soviet position in the Mediterranean. Khrushchev suggested that Cyprus should forget *enosis*, refuse all foreign bases, and remain neutral. Furthermore, he accused the United States of "unwarranted interference in Cypriot internal affairs."

[6]UNICYP was composed of approximately 5000 troops from Austria, Canada, Finland, Ireland, and Sweden.
[7]Sakari S. Tuomioja of Finland was then the official U. N. mediator in Cyprus.

Makarios' pro-Moscow inclination led to speculation that Greece and Turkey would jointly invade Cyprus to prevent that island country from becoming a Mediterranean Cuba.

In the summer of 1966, Carlos Bernades, a special envoy sent to Cyprus by Secretary-General U Thant, proposed to the authorities of both Greece and Turkey the following formula:[8]

1. Cyprus would have an independent regime, no longer guaranteed by the 1959 Zurich and London Agreements, but by the United States, the Soviet Union, Britain, and France; that is, by the permanent members of the Security Council with the exception of Nationalist China.
2. The 1959 treaties would be suspended for three to five years, after which negotiations would begin for a final solution.
3. The rights and well-being of the Turkish minority in Cyprus would be guaranteed by the Security Council; in addition, a United Nations observer would reside in Nicosia to report to the Council periodically on the situation.
4. Greek and Turkish troops now stationed on the island would be evacuated.

Nevertheless, there was no significant progress in settling the fundamental problems. The shaky truce was marked by the familiar pattern of numerous incidents and provocative acts, including deliberate breaches of the cease-fire, bomb explosions, terrorist activities, and reinforcement of fortifications.

In view of these circumstances, on December 15, 1966, the United Nations Security Council unanimously adopted a resolution to maintain the U. N. peace-keeping force in Cyprus for a further period of six months, ending June 26, 1967. The Security Council hopefully stated its "expectation that sufficient progress toward a solution by then will make possible a withdrawal or substantial reduction of the force."

The expenditure for the United Nations peace-keeping force in Cyprus has been financed entirely by voluntary contributions. The crucial problem which plagues the United Nations' fiscal integrity stems primarily from the two other peace-keeping operations: the United Nations Emergency Force (UNEF) in Egypt, and the United Nations Operation in the Congo (UNOC).

There were four categories of United Nations operational budgets: (1) the regular budget of about $90 million a year, (2) the budgets of the specialized agencies at approximately the same amount, (3) an annual expenditure of about $200 million for the voluntary economic and social programs, and (4) the peace-keeping operations in the Middle East and the Congo. It was this fourth category which brought the United Nations to the verge of bankruptcy, incurring a debt in excess of $150 million by 1965.

[8] *The New York Times*, May 15, 1966, p. 30.

A significant portion of this deficit resulted from the manifest inability of several member nations to sustain the United Nations forces in the Middle East and Africa. The greater portion of the deficit was the product of the politically motivated refusal of some member states to pay their assessments. The Soviet bloc, for example, strongly urged the General Assembly to force Great Britain, France, and Israel—the "aggressors"—to pay the costs for the United Nations force in Egypt, and it refused to honor its assessments.

With respect to the Congo operation, the Communist bloc, led by the Soviet Union, had supported the United Nations resolution calling for the dispatch of U. N. forces into the Congo to restore order and preserve peace. By the time of pro-Communist Patrice Lumumba's death, however, the Soviets had become extremely disenchanted with the operation of the United Nations forces in the Congo and had withdrawn all support. Earlier, they had attempted to deal directly with Lumumba by circumventing the United Nations and providing his forces with logistic support. When Secretary-General Hammarskjold, who was enforcing the measures set forth by the United Nations, protested this action, the Soviets labeled him a "stooge" of the imperialist powers.

France, on the other hand, because of its apprehensions about the apparent political "immaturity" of emerging African nations and because of its appreciation for Belgian anxiety, abstained from voting in the Security Council and later refused to pay its assessments for the maintenance of the forces in the Congo.

It should be pointed out that the United Nations operation in the Congo was initiated by the Security Council, and the United Nations Emergency Force in the Middle East had been sponsored by the General Assembly. Both actions received wholehearted approval with no dissenting votes. In spite of this overwhelming support, a question arose concerning the legality of the assessments. A clear establishment of the constitutionality of such actions was required before member nations would consider paying their respective shares.

On December 20, 1961, the General Assembly asked the International Court of Justice for an advisory opinion: Did UNOC and UNEF constitute "expenses of the Organization" within the meaning of Article 17, paragraph 2, of the Charter of the United Nations?[9] On June 20, 1962, the Court rendered its opinion that the United Nations had, from the beginning, included "operational items in the regular budget, such as the annual appropriations for 'special missions and related activities,' 'unforeseen and extraordinary expenses' relating to the maintenance of peace and security, as well as a variety of expenses for technical assistance, programs of economic

[9]This paragraph states: "The expenses of the Organization shall be borne by the Members as apportioned by the General Assembly."

and social development." The majority of the members of the Court upheld further the right of the General Assembly to make these special assessments, reaffirming the "Uniting for Peace" Resolution.[10]

Within three months after the decision, 37 nations had paid over $6 million—a sizable amount but a far cry from the total arrears due from the Soviet Union and France. The unwillingness of these two permanent members of the Security Council to acknowledge collective financial responsibility forced the United Nations to take an emergency measure; it authorized a $200 million bond issue. The response was favorable and immediate; 60 governments absorbed approximately $150 million worth of bonds, half of which were purchased by the United States.

By mid-1963, however, the bond money was exhausted; by the end of the year, only 25 per cent of the 1963 budget appropriation was available for the combined forces of UNEF and UNOC. By the summer of 1964, when the United Nations forces withdrew from the Congo, the financial problem had reached such a critical point that the UNICYP expenditure had to be met through voluntary contributions every three months.

The financial crisis metamorphosed into a constitutional issue, touching upon Article 19 of the Charter: "A Member of the United Nations which is in arrears in the payment of its financial contributions to the Organization shall have no vote in the General Assembly if the amount of its arrears equals or exceeds the amount of the contributions due from its for the preceding two full years."

As the United States at first appeared to press for the enforcement of this provision against the delinquent members, especially the Soviet Union, the issue became dangerously engulfed in the Cold War. It was interpreted widely as a "confrontation" between Major Powers. However, the United States did not pursue the strict application of Article 19. On August 16, 1965, Arthur Goldberg, United States Permanent Representative to the United Nations, stated: "Without prejudice to the position that Article 19 is applicable, the United States recognizes, as it simply must, that the General Assembly is not prepared to apply Article 19 in the present situation and that the consensus of the membership is that the Assembly should proceed normally."[11] The United States policy was designed, he declared, "to strengthen, not weaken, the United Nations by adhering to rather than departing from basic, sound principles."

[10]Adopted in November, 1950, this resolution empowered the General Assembly to employ collective measures. In the event that the Security Council fails to act on a threat to and breach of the peace, or an act of aggression, because of a lack of unanimity among its permanent members, the General Assembly "shall consider the matter immediately with a view to making appropriate recommendations to Members for collective measures," including the use of armed forces.

[11]Statement made in the U. N. Special Committee on Peace-keeping Operations on August 16, 1965 (U. S./U. N. press release 4615).

A Major Power confrontation surrounding the financial crisis was thus avoided, but the financial difficulties of the United Nations continued to prevent its effective operation.[12]

Early in October, 1964, at a time when the financial crisis in the United Nations threatened the very existence of that organization as an effective instrument for the maintenance of international peace and security, Secretary of State Dean Rusk forewarned the nation and the world of another source of imminent "danger"—a Chinese Communist atomic explosion. His warning was substantiated a few days later by the Peking announcement: "China exploded an atomic bomb at 1500 hours on October 16, 1964, and thereby conducted successfully its first nuclear test." The detonation took place near Lake Lop Nor in the Takla Makan desert in the province of Sinkiang, China. It was reported to be a low-yield device—equivalent to 20,000 tons of TNT—about the size of the bomb dropped on Hiroshima toward the end of World War II.

In their relentless pursuit of Great Power status since the establishment of the Communist regime in China, the leaders of the Peking government had literally blasted into the exclusive "atomic club." They held that their country had all the essentials for a Major Power—the largest population in the world (over 750 million), huge territories stretching from Siberia to the South China Sea, a brilliant history spanning several millenia, and an "effective" government based on the principles of "New Democracy." What they needed was the indispensable symbol of national power and modern technology—the atomic bomb!

Communist China's research into nuclear physics was first made at the end of the Korean War. In January, 1955, the Soviets pledged scientific and technological aid to China for the peaceful use of atomic energy, and enabled the Chinese to complete their first atomic reactor by March, 1958. Furthermore, the Soviets invited Chinese scientists to work at the Joint Institute for Nuclear Research at Dubna in the Soviet Union. However, in June, 1959, with the growing deterioration of Sino-Soviet relations, the Soviet Union withdrew its commitment to aid the Chinese nuclear program. The Soviet decision, undoubtedly a severe blow to China, could only hinder, not halt, China's development of a nuclear technology. Western experts had long agreed that Chinese scientists had the technological knowhow to detonate an atomic explosion.

The 1964 explosion meant little in terms of the immediate balance of military power because it was estimated that it would be another decade before Communist China would have both a sufficient stockpile of nuclear weapons and enough intercontinental missiles to deliver them. President

---

[12]Secretary-General U Thant's report showed that net expenditures for 1966—the funds contributed by member states—were estimated at $101,776,720, or 2.44 times what was spent in 1954, when the amount was $41,645,791.

Johnson shared this view when he said: "It is a long, hard road from a first nuclear device to an effective weapons system."[13]

Politically, Peking's nuclear status made it more difficult for the Soviet Union to substantiate its claim to the undisputed leadership of the world Communist movement. China—long regarded as a model of backwardness—had successfully challenged the West and the Soviet Union on their own ground of modern technology, in spite of the latter's "betrayal."

Ideologically repudiating the predominant role of the Soviet Union in the Communist bloc, the Chinese Communist leaders began aggressively to foster Peking-oriented factions in many of the Asian, African, and Latin American countries, and laid the foundation for a separate Communist movement under their leadership. China's prestige in the underdeveloped areas of the world was momentously enhanced by the atomic mushroom in Sinkiang, which served as a tangible symbol of achievement in constructing a modern industrial state from an agrarian society.

With nuclear capacity, the Peking regime moved into position to erect a token nuclear deterrent against the United States, the Soviet Union, or any potential adversaries, and to project itself into the world arena as a power to be reckoned with. Moreover, Communist China could use its nuclear status to intimidate its neighbors, to blackmail America's Asian allies into severing their military ties, or to create a militarily impregnable position in combination with its almost unlimited conventional forces. China's new status represented a new factor in the balance of power in the world as a whole, and in Asia in particular, which neither the United States nor the Soviet Union could ignore.

In addition, China's bomb had a specific psychological impact on its neighboring Asian nations. Japan and other smaller countries, which might be within striking distance of a delivery system, showed grave concern and apprehension about their national security. In Southeast Asia, where Chinese penetration had been strongest, local Communist movements were reinforced by the presence of the "invincible" nuclear fraternal Power in the heart of the Asian Continent. India, involved in a border war with China, accused the Peking regime of building up offensive weapons of mass destruction and of creating "a danger and a menace to mankind."

While Communist China was improving its nuclear technology through successive testings, it did not cease to demonstrate its antagonism and bellicosity toward the United States as well as toward its former ally, the Soviet Union. The Chinese Communist leaders argued that the United States was the "enemy" of all the peoples in the world, whereas the Soviet Union was the "traitor" of all the Communists. They feared that there was a conspiratory collusion between the United States and the Soviet Union to

[13]Address to the Nation, October 18, 1964.

keep China in a position of permanent subordination and perpetual inferiority. Communist China's Premier Chou En-lai declared: "Khrushchev allied himself with United States imperialism but the [present] leaders of the Soviet Union have gone a step further and extended their alliance to include some of the main hatchetmen of United States imperialism."[14] In the same vein, Foreign Minister Chen Yi echoed: "Soviet leaders, both Khrushchev and the present ones, have betrayed us many times. The nuclear test-ban treaty was such a betrayal. They did not ask us, either, when they shipped missiles to Cuba. This was a dangerous step, but they did not ask China or any other socialist state in advance. They cannot be trusted. In 1960 they withdrew their technical experts from China to strangle our economy. Their propaganda is not aimed against the United States but mostly against China."

From the standpoint of Communist China, and probably with some justification, one end of the Cold War has been shifting from Moscow to Peking. Or perhaps the Cold War has now come to rest in a Washington–Moscow–Peking tripolarization.

The greatest danger at the present time of upsetting this tripolarization and of involving the Big Powers in an armed conflict lies in the war in Vietnam.

The conflict in Vietnam is a sad story of continuous struggles which span both World War II and the Cold War. A few months before Pearl Harbor, Japan landed its troops in French Indochina[15] to secure a staging area for subsequent military operations in Southeast Asia. During the war years, the Japanese allowed the French to continue to administer the colonies in much the same way as in the preceding decades. At the same time the Japanese imbued the Vietnamese with the idea of "Asia for Asians" and, to a lesser degree, with the idea of "national independence." Some Vietnamese nationalists welcomed and cooperated with the Japanese, but others such as the Vietminh[16] were opposed to both the continued presence of the French and the new occupation by the Japanese.

In March, 1945, the Japanese ousted the French authorities and allowed Vietnam, Laos, and Cambodia each to declare its independence. Thus, the three "independent" states were born out of the French colony of Indochina. Vietnam was headed by Emperor Bao Dai of Annam. Denouncing the Bao Dai regime as "illegitimate" and "puppet," the Vietminh organized their own provisional government for Vietnam. Upon the surrender of Japan to the Allies, Bao Dai abdicated his nominal throne. Ho Chi Minh's provisional

---

[14] *The New York Times*, May 8, 1966.

[15] Indochina was formed from the combined territories of Laos, Cambodia, and Vietnam, and was under French colonial rule from 1861 to 1954.

[16] The League for the Independence of Vietnam, formed in 1941 in South China under the leadership of Ho Chi Minh.

government took over control of the state, moved into Hanoi, and declared independence for Vietnam.

After a brief period of occupation of Indochina by the Allied Powers— North by the Chinese and South by the British—in March, 1946, the French government and Ho Chi Minh negotiated an agreement whereby France would formally recognize Vietnam as a *free*, but not *independent*, state within the French Union and the Indochinese Federation. The French, however, were determined to re-establish their undisputed control over all of Indochina and to wrest Vietnam from Ho's control. In December, 1946, as French troops began to return to the North, hostilities broke out between Vietminh and French forces.

As the war dragged on with no satisfactory solution in sight, the French decided to ignore the Ho regime and to create in its stead a new government with Bao Dai as head. On July 1, 1949, Bao Dai formally established the State of Vietnam within the French Union and provided "a basis for its organization on a constitutional framework." In February, 1950, the United States and Great Britain extended *de jure* recognition to Vietnam, and in December, when the war in Korea was only six months old, the United States signed a Mutual Defense Assistance Agreement with France, Cambodia, Laos, and Vietnam to supply them with indirect American military aid.

By this time the Vietminh held the countryside and enjoyed the loyalty of a large segment of the rural population. Ho organized the Working Peoples Party as the political arm of his policy, and the United National Front as the military arm of his strategy. He declared that his war was an anti-colonial, anti-imperialistic national liberation war, which constituted an integral part of the world revolution. His fighting forces showed kindness, generosity, and thoughtfulness when they were able to marshal widespread public support for their cause, but they ruthlessly employed violence, cruelty, savagery, and terrorism when they were unable to muster wholehearted cooperation in achieving their objectives.

The war in Vietnam was bitter in nature, severe in character; the destruction of lives and property was wanton. As the Chinese Communists, relieved of their fighting in Korea following the armistice, stepped up their assistance to the Vietminh, the war became even more intensified. The prospect of an inevitable defeat, as evidenced by the fall of Dien Bien Phu on May 7, 1954, pressed France into seeking a negotiated peace. The Geneva Conference, to which the nine interested parties were invited, was convened in the summer of 1954.

By the final agreement reached on July 20, 1954, Laos and Cambodia were permitted to "play their part, in full independence and sovereignty, in the peaceful community of nations." They were not allowed to join a regional alliance, to have foreign bases on their territories, or to seek foreign military assistance. Vietnam was divided into the northern Democratic Republic of Vietnam and the southern Republic of Vietnam at the 17th parallel "with a view to ending hostilities," and the stipulation was made that the military demarcation line was "provisional" and "should not in any way be interpreted as constituting a political or territorial boundary." General elections were to be held in 1956 throughout Vietnam to unify the country. An International Supervisory Commission was established to oversee the truce agreements. All participants, with the exception of the United States and South Vietnam,[17] signed the final declaration pledging themselves to respect the independence, sovereignty, and territorial integrity of these three nations.[18]

The destiny of post-Geneva South Vietnam depended upon the political ability and personal integrity of a new leader—Ngo Dinh Diem—a Roman Catholic, who became Premier on July 7, 1954, just two weeks before the signing of the Geneva Agreement. The task confronting him was staggering. He had inherited a feeble political system, a disorganized administration, a bankrupt economy, a corrupt social order, chronic factional strife, and swarming refugees.

During his first year in office, encouraged and assisted by the United States, Ngo Dinh Diem managed to assume effective control of his government and the military, and brought about a degree of internal stability and security. In a national referendum held in October, 1955, Bao Dai was deposed, and a Republic was proclaimed by Ngo Dinh Diem, who became the first President of South Vietnam.

From 1955 to 1960, a considerable amount of constructive work was accomplished. Internal security and land reform provided the impetus for increased agricultural production. Industrialization made a modest beginning. Education and other social services were expanded. The authority of the Saigon government reached other major cities as well as rural areas as communications were restored and enlarged. During the same period, on the other hand, Communist guerrilla warfare was waged in the South on a major scale, directed against both the Diem government and United States support forces. In October, 1957, Communist guerrillas bombed the United States Information Service (USIS) and Military Assistance Advisory

[17]Both the United States and South Vietnam rejected, and refused to sign, the Geneva Agreement and the final declaration. The United States reiterated that any nation divided against its will should be allowed "to achieve unity through free elections supervised by the United Nations," and that it would not join in any arrangement contrary to the principle of national self-determination. The Government of South Vietnam was opposed especially to: (1) the partition of the country, (2) "the hasty conclusion of the armistice agreement by the French and Viet Minh High Commands alone," and (3) compromise clauses dealing with the political future of the Vietnamese people, such as fixing the date of elections.

[18]For the complete text of the agreement and the final declaration, see *Further Documents Relating to the Discussion of Indochina at the Geneva Conference* (Miscellaneous no. 20, Command Paper, 9239), XXXI (London: Great Britain Parliamentary Sessional Papers, 1953–1954), pp. 9–11, 27–38.

Group (MAAG) installations; in July, 1958, they attacked the Vietnam military base at Bien Hoa, killing and wounding several U. S. MAAG personnel. Radio Hanoi praised the establishment of the "National Front for Liberation of South Vietnam," allegedly founded in October, 1960, and went on to broadcast that the "sacred historic task" of the National Liberation Front was "to overthrow the U. S.–Diem clique" and "to liberate the South."

The subsequent three years from 1961 to 1963 covered a period most critical to the Diem regime and to South Vietnam. As the Communist guerrillas expanded their control and influence, while the Diem government apparently was unable to cope with the situation, President Diem began to lose the confidence of the people. He was frequently accused of political and administrative inefficiency because of his reluctance to delegate authority to his subordinates. He was criticized for his undue reliance on his family for advice and guidance in state affairs. His regime was described at home and abroad as autocratic, authoritarian, antidemocratic, and dictatorial. In contrast with Diem's deteriorating position, the numerical strength of the Vietcong (Vietnamese Communist) guerrillas increased steadily. At the time of the cease-fire in 1954, about 10,000 Vietcong had infiltrated into the peasant population.

> These men became the nucleus of the new force which the Communists have built. The number has expanded by local recruitment as well as by infiltration from the North until it has reached an estimated 22,000 to 24,000 regulars with a supplement of local irregulars of over 100,000. The force is equipped largely with primitive, antiquated, and captured weapons. In recent months, some sophisticated equipment has been employed in battle against the government forces.[19]

This state of affairs prompted Secretary of State Rusk to call the situation in Vietnam "difficult and dangerous," and to warn that a quick victory over the Vietcong could not be expected. He added that the United States role would continue to be "limited and supporting."

At this juncture, the Buddhist affair erupted in the summer of 1963, plunging the nation into unprecedented internal political turmoil. Through political ineptitude, religious intolerance, and repressive measures, the Diem government failed to mollify the inflamed feelings of the Buddhists. Instead, it aggravated their grievances and roused the people to anti-Diem sentiment. On September 2, 1963, in a television interview with a CBS correspondent, President Kennedy declared that the United States was prepared to continue to assist South Vietnam, then added, "but I don't think that the war can be won unless the people support the effort and, in my opinion, in the last two months, the [Diem] government has gotten out of touch with the people." A week later in another televised interview President Kennedy stated that

---

[19]*Vietnam and Southeast Asia*, Report of Senator Mike Mansfield [and others] to the Committee on Foreign Relations, United States Senate, 88th Congress, 1st Session, 1963, p. 5.

he would not reduce United States aid to South Vietnam, because that might bring about a collapse similar to that of the Chiang Kai-shek government in China after World War II. He then ordered Secretary of Defense Robert S. McNamara and General Maxwell D. Taylor, then Chairman of the Joint Chiefs of Staff, to go to South Vietnam to review the military efforts against the Vietcong. After a ten-day visit to South Vietnam, they made a report to the President and the National Security Council on their mission. Their statement said that the United States would continue its "policy of working with the people and Government of South Vietnam to deny this country to Communism and to suppress the externally stimulated and supported insurgency of the Vietcong as promptly as possible." By this time the number of United States military personnel sent to South Vietnam exceeded 16,000.

America's accelerated efforts to help fight the Vietcong failed to produce the expected results because of internal political crises in South Vietnam. On November 1, 1963, a military coup, organized by the key generals in the armed forces, overthrew the Diem regime. Rebellious troops laid seige to the Presidential Palace in Saigon, which was captured by the following morning. President Diem and his brother–advisor, Ngo Dinh Nhu, escaped from the Palace but were taken by the rebels a few hours later. They reportedly were killed by an "accidental suicide" on the way to rebel headquarters in an armored carrier. The military junta, headed by General Duong Van Minh, declared that it had "no political ambition" and that the fight against the Vietcong would be carried on to a successful conclusion. This coup heralded the beginning of added turbulence in Vietnamese politics; it was the forerunner of a series of subsequent coups. In an 18-month period, from November, 1963, to June, 1965, there were no less than ten government changes by coups.

In the meantime, the war kept escalating in terms of intensity, scale, and scope. In August, 1964, when the United States destroyers *Maddox* and *C. Turner Joy* were attacked in international waters off the coast of Tonkin by North Vietnamese torpedo boats, President Johnson "directed air action against gunboats and supporting facilities used in these hostile operations." Furthermore, the President asked Congress for a resolution "expressing the unity and determination of the United States in supporting freedom and in protecting peace in Southeast Asia." In response, Congress approved and supported the determination of the President "to take all necessary measures to repel any armed attack against the forces of the United States and to prevent further aggression." Then in February, 1965, Vietcong guerrillas attacked a United States compound at Pleiku, and United States forces retaliated by bombing military targets in North Vietnam. This was the beginning of America's air assaults on Ho Chi Minh's territories. By this time the United States forces in South Vietnam totaled 23,000.

The escalation of the war was often marked by an escalated desire for peace. On April 7, 1965, in a speech at Johns Hopkins University, President

Johnson offered "unconditional" negotiations for peace and suggested that once the Communists agreed to a settlement in which the independence of South Vietnam was guaranteed, the United States would be prepared to provide a $1 billion aid program for Southeast Asia, including North Vietnam. This offer was rejected by the Hanoi regime as a "dollar bait" to camouflage "United States imperialism."

Throughout the year 1965, with changes in the composition of the opposing forces, the character of the war changed sharply. By the end of that year, there were approximately 170,000 United States troops in South Vietnam; these troops were directly involved in battle against the Communists, in contrast to earlier years, when they had only served the role of "advisers" and "supporting units." The Vietcong strength in South Vietnam at that time was estimated at 230,000 men. This number was twice as large as that of three years earlier. The total Vietcong strength had been steadily increasing despite the heavy casualties which these forces had suffered during the preceding months. The Vietcong, through local recruitment in the South and infiltration from the North, could substantially increase their numbers at any given moment.

Despite unceasing aspirations, at home and abroad, for a negotiated settlement of the tragedy in Vietnam, the war never ceased to escalate. A steady increase in casualties on both sides, Ho's general mobilization for the war effort, and the continued United States bombing of North Vietnam, including the Hanoi–Haiphong areas, were but a few indisputable testimonies to this fact. The Communist regular forces were not destroyed or forced to withdraw to North Vietnam. They often shifted their tactics toward small-scale guerrilla actions which were difficult to counter. Many United States authorities came to hold the view that the military outcome of the war would be determined by the guerrilla struggle, which was closely related to the important task of pacification. With a military build-up over half a million troops by mid-1967, the United States was apparently determined to achieve a dual task: to find and defeat the Vietcong guerrillas and political agents embedded in the rural population on the one hand, and to build and maintain stable political and economic structures in South Vietnam on the other.

XIV
The Cuban Missile Crisis

1

Missiles in Cuba*

JOHN F. KENNEDY

Good evening, my fellow citizens:

This Government, as promised, has maintained the closest surveillance of the Soviet military build-up on the island of Cuba.

Within the past week, unmistakable evidence has established the fact that a series of offensive missile sites is now in preparation on that imprisoned island.

The purpose of these bases can be none other than to provide a nuclear strike capability against the Western Hemisphere.

Upon receiving the first preliminary hard information of this nature last Tuesday morning at 9 A.M., I directed that our surveillance be stepped up. And having now confirmed and completed our evaluation of the evidence and our decision on a course of action, this Government feels obliged to report this new crisis to you in full detail.

The characteristics of these new missile sites indicate two distinct types of installations. Several of them include medium range ballistic missiles, capable of carrying a nuclear warhead for a distance of more than 1,000 nautical miles. Each of these missiles, in short, is capable of striking Washington, D.C., the Panama Canal, Cape Canaveral, Mexico City, or any other city in the southeastern part of the United States, in Central America or in the Caribbean area.

Additional sites not yet completed appear to be designed for intermediate range ballistic missiles—capable of traveling more than twice as far—and thus capable of striking most of the major cities in the Western Hemisphere, ranging as far north as Hudson's Bay, Canada, and as far south as Lima, Peru. In addition, jet bombers, capable of carrying nuclear weapons, are now being uncrated and assembled on Cuba, while the necessary air bases are being prepared.

* Televised address to the nation, October 22, 1962.

This urgent transformation of Cuba into an important strategic base—by the presence of these large, long-range and clearly offensive weapons of sudden mass destruction—constitutes an explicit threat to the peace and security of all the Americas, in flagrant and deliberate defiance of the Rio pact of 1947, the traditions of this nation and hemisphere, the joint resolution of the 87th Congress, the Charter of the United Nations, and my own public warnings to the Soviets on Sept. 4 and 13.

This action also contradicts the repeated assurances of Soviet spokesmen, both publicly and privately delivered, that the arms build-up in Cuba would retain its original defensive character, and that the Soviet Union had no need or desire to station strategic missiles on the territory of any other nation.

The size of this undertaking makes clear that it had been planned some months ago. Yet only last month, after I had made clear the distinction between any introduction of ground-to-ground missiles and the existence of defensive antiaircraft missiles, the Soviet Government publicly stated on Sept. 11 that "the armaments and military equipment sent to Cuba are designed exclusively for defensive purposes," that "there is no need for the Soviet Union to shift its weapons . . . for a retaliatory blow to any other country, for instance Cuba," and that "the Soviet Union has so powerful rockets to carry these nuclear warheads that there is no need to search for sites for them beyond the boundaries of the Soviet Union."

That statement was false.

Only last Thursday, as evidence of this rapid offensive build-up was already in my hand, Soviet Foreign Minister Gromyko told me in my office that he was instructed to make it clear once again, as he said his Government had already done, the Soviet assistance to Cuba "pursued solely the purpose of contributing to the defense capabilities of Cuba," that "training by Soviet specialists of Cuban nationals in handling defensive armaments was by no means offensive," and that "if it were otherwise, the Soviet Government would never become involved in rendering such assistance."

That statement also was false.

Neither the United States of America nor the world Community of nations can tolerate deliberate deception and offensive threats on the part of any nation, large or small.

We no longer live in a world where only the actual firing of weapons represents a sufficient challenge to a nation's security to constitute a maximum peril.

Nuclear weapons are so destructive, and ballistic missiles are so swift, that any substantially increased possibility of their use or any sudden change in their development may well be regarded as a definite threat to the peace.

For many years, both the Soviet Union and the United States—recognizing this fact—have deployed strategic nuclear weapons with great care, never upsetting the precarious status quo which ensured that these weapons would not be used in the absence of some vital challenge.

Our own strategic missiles have never been transferred to the territory of any other nation under a cloak of secrecy and deception; and our history—unlike that of the Soviets since World War II—demonstrates that we have no desire to dominate or conquer any other nation or impose our system upon its people.

Nevertheless, American citizens have become adjusted to living daily on the bull's eye of Soviet missiles located inside the U. S. S. R. or in submarines.

In that sense, missiles in Cuba add to an already clear and present danger—although, it should be noted, the nations of Latin America have never previously been subjected to a potential nuclear threat.

But this secret, swift and extraordinary build-up of Communist missiles—in an area well-known to have a special and historical relationship to the United States and the nations of the Western Hemisphere, in violation of Soviet assurances, and in defiance of American and hemispheric policy—this sudden, clandestine decision to station strategic weapons for the first time outside of Soviet soil—is a deliberately provocative and unjustified change in the status quo which cannot be accepted by this country, if our courage and our commitments are ever to be trusted again by either friend or foe.

The 1930's taught us a clear lesson: Aggressive conduct, if allowed to grow unchecked and unchallenged, ultimately leads to war. This nation is opposed to war. We are also true to our word.

Our unswerving objective, therefore, must be to prevent the use of these missiles against this or any other country, and to secure their withdrawal or elimination from the Western Hemisphere.

Our policy has been one of patience and restraint, as befits a peaceful and powerful nation, which leads a world-wide alliance. We have been determined not to be diverted from our central concerns by mere irritants and fanatics.

But now further action is required—and it is under way; and these actions may only be the beginning. We will not prematurely or unnecessarily risk the costs of world-wide nuclear war in which even the fruits of victory would be ashes in our mouth—but neither will we shrink from that risk at any time it must be faced.

Acting, therefore, in the defense of our own security and that of the entire Western Hemisphere, and under the authority entrusted to me by the Constitution as endorsed by the resolution of the Congress, I have directed that the following initial steps be taken immediately:

First: To halt this offensive build-up, a strict quarantine on all offensive military equipment under shipment to Cuba is being initiated. All ships of any kind bound for Cuba, from whatever nation or port, will, if found to contain cargoes of offensive weapons, be turned back. This quarantine will be extended, if needed, to other types of cargo and carriers. We are not at this time, however, denying the necessities of life as the Soviet attempted to do in their Berlin blockade of 1948.

Second: I have directed the continued and increased surveillance of Cuba and its military build-up. The Foreign Ministers of the OAS in their communiqué of Oct. 6 rejected secrecy on such matters in this hemisphere. Should these offensive military preparations continue, thus increasing the threat to the hemisphere, further action will be justified. I have directed the armed forces to prepare for any eventualities; and I trust that, in the interest of both the Cuban people and the Soviet technicians at these sites, the hazards to all concerned of continuing this threat will be recognized.

Third: It shall be the policy of this nation to regard any nuclear missile launched from Cuba against any nation in the Western Hemisphere as an attack by the Soviet Union on the United States requiring a full retaliatory response upon the Soviet Union.

Fourth: As a necessary military precaution, I have reinforced our base at Guantanamo, evacuated today the dependents of our personnel there and ordered additional military units to stand by on an alert basis.

Fifth: We are calling tonight for an immediate meeting of the organ of consultation under the Organization of American States, to consider this threat to hemispheric security and to invoke Articles 6 and 8 of the Rio treaty in support of all necessary action. The United Nations Charter allows for regional security arrangements—and the nations of this hemisphere decided long ago against the military presence of outside powers. Our other allies around the world have also been alerted.

Sixth: Under the Charter of the United Nations, we are asking tonight that an emergency meeting of the Security Council be convoked without delay to take action against this latest Soviet threat to world peace. Our resolution will call for the prompt dismantling and withdrawal of all offensive weapons in Cuba, under the supervision of UN observers, before the quarantine can be lifted.

Seventh and finally: I call upon Chairman Khrushchev to halt and eliminate this clandestine, reckless and provocative threat to world peace and to stable relations between our two nations. I call upon him further to abandon this course of world domination, and to join in an historic effort to end the perilous arms race and transform the history of man.

He has an opportunity now to move the world back from the abyss of destruction—by returning to his Government's own words that it had no need to station missiles outside its own territory, and withdrawing these weapons from Cuba—by refraining from any action which will widen or deepen the present crisis—and then by participating in a search for peaceful and permanent solutions.

This nation is prepared to present its case against this Soviet threat to peace, and our own proposals for a peaceful world, at any time and in any forum—in the OAS, in the United Nations, or in any other meeting that could be useful—without limiting our freedom of action.

We have in the past made strenuous efforts to limit the spread of nuclear weapons. We have proposed the elimination of all arms and military bases in a fair and effective disarmament treaty. We are prepared to discuss new proposals for the removal of tensions on both sides—including the possibilities of a genuinely independent Cuba, free to determine its own destiny. We have no wish to war with the Soviet Union—for we are a peaceful people who desire to live in peace with all other peoples.

But it is difficult to settle or even discuss these problems in an atmosphere of intimidation. That is why this latest Soviet threat—or any other threat which is made either independently or in response to our actions this week—must and will be met with determination. Any hostile move anywhere in the world against the safety of freedom of peoples to whom we are committed—including in particular the brave people of West Berlin—will be met by whatever action is needed.

Finally, I want to say a few words to the captive people of Cuba, to whom this speech is being directly carried by special radio facilities.

I speak to you as a friend, as one who knows of your deep attachment to your fatherland, as one who shares your aspirations for liberty and justice for all. And I have watched with sorrow how your nationalist revolution was betrayed—and how your fatherland fell under foreign domination.

Now your leaders are no longer Cuban leaders inspired by Cuban ideals. They are puppets and agents of an international conspiracy which has turned Cuba against your friends and neighbors in the Americas—and turned it into the first Latin-American country to become a target for nuclear war—the first Latin-American country to have these weapons on its soil.

These new weapons are not in your interest. They can only undermine it. But this country has no wish to cause you to suffer or to impose any system upon you. We know your lives and land are being used as pawns by those who deny you freedom.

Many times in the past, the Cuban people have risen to throw out tyrants who destroyed their liberty, and I have no doubt that most Cubans today look forward to the time when they will be truly free—free from foreign domination. Free to choose their own leaders. Free to select their own system. Free to own their own land. Free to speak and write and worship without fear or degradation. And then shall Cuba be welcomed back to the society of free nations and to the associations of this hemisphere.

My fellow citizens: Let no one doubt that this is a difficult and dangerous effort on which we have set out. No one can foresee precisely what course it will take or what costs or casualties will be incurred. Many months of sacrifice and self-discipline lie ahead—months in which both our will and our patience will be tested—months in which many threats and denunciations will keep us aware of our danger. But the greatest danger of all would be to do nothing.

The path we have chosen for the present is full of hazards, as all paths are—but it is the one most consistent with our character and courage as a nation and our commitments around the world. The cost of freedom is always high—but Americans have always paid it. And one path we shall never choose is the path of surrender or submission.

Our goal is not the victory of might but the vindication of right—not peace at the expense of freedom, but both peace and freedom, here in this hemisphere, and, we hope, around the world. God willing, that goal will be achieved.

2

Enemies of Peace*

PRAVDA

Alarming news has spread throughout the world: The American imperialists have adopted unprecedented aggressive measures, confronting the world with the threat of a global thermonuclear war. Having concentrated its Atlantic fleet in the Caribbean area, the American government has with unparalleled effrontery announced, in the person of President Kennedy, its intention to impose a naval blockade against the Republic of Cuba and has placed its armed forces in a state of combat readiness.

American imperialism, assuming the role of international gendarme, has for some time now been weaving provocative nets around the Cuban Republic. The events of Playa Giron are still fresh in our minds. The attacks of the American mercenaries, who committed arbitrary acts on the high seas and carried out bandit raids on peaceful towns and villages in Cuba, aroused the indignation of the whole world. The American ruling circles tried at that time to shield themselves behind false statements that they were not implicated in these matters. But now the cards have been placed on the table once and for all. The whole world can see that what is going on now is the logical outcome of the criminal plan inherited by the Kennedy administration from the Eisenhower administration and carried out on orders of the Pentagon.

The actions undertaken by American ruling circles constitute a scandalous violation

From "Foil the Criminal Schemes of the Enemies of Peace," in The Current Digest of the Soviet Press, **14** (*November 21, 1962*), 4, 6. Translation from The Current Digest of the Soviet Press, *published weekly at Columbia University by the Joint Committee on Slavic Studies, appointed by the American Council of Learned Societies and the Social Science Research Council. Copyright © 1962, the Joint Committee on Slavic Studies. Reprinted by permission.*

of the elementary norms of international law and of all international customs. They are incompatible with the principles of the U. N. Charter. They represent a challenge to all peace-loving nations. Such actions constitute a direct revival of piracy and international lawlessness, which mankind hoped had been ended forever with the conviction in Nuremberg and Tokyo of the leading war criminals responsible for unleashing World War II, for crimes against peace and against humanity.

In embarking upon the new venture, the American ruling circles are behaving like cowardly predators. They know that the peace-loving nations will brand them with infamy, and therefore they lie and squirm. President Kennedy's radio and television address was filled with falsehoods and dissimulation from beginning to end. It could be likened to the highwayman's prayer before he takes to the road.

President Kennedy could devise nothing better than to direct against Cuba long-refuted accusations to the effect that it supposedly constitutes a threat to U. S. security. But the whole world knows that revolutionary Cuba—a nation that has chosen the path of freedom, the path toward the building of a new society—does not, and by virtue of the nature of its new social order cannot, represent a threat to anyone. All the Cuban people want is to secure their nation against the threat of the U. S. imperialists. The Cuban government is calling upon Washington to establish normal relations and to settle controversial issues through negotiation.

The American ruling circles can see that the ideas of national independence and social justice kindled by the Cuban revolution in the Western Hemisphere are finding understanding and support in the hearts of the Latin American peoples. They are afraid of the inexorable march of history. They are becoming convinced that even in their own country they cannot cope with the social problems born of the internal contradictions of capitalism. The position taken by the U. S. A. is evidence not of the power but rather of the historical doom of the regime of capitalistic exploitation.

The actions of the American militarists represent a crude form of blackmail that is capable of bringing down catastrophic results upon all mankind. The American ruling circles are playing with fire when they threaten war against the Soviet Union. They cynically declare themselves ready to rain down atomic and hydrogen bombs on the heads of hundreds of millions of people, to destroy what it has taken human civilization centuries to build.

However, the time when pirates could act with impunity is past. *"If the aggressors unleash a war,"* the statement of the Soviet government published today says, *"the Soviet Union will strike a mighty retaliatory blow."* The Soviet government's statement is a stern warning to those who are losing their reason. The Soviet Union, the countries of socialism and the peace-loving nations have enough strength and means *to put a strait-jacket on the aggressors.*

Thousands-strong meetings are being held all over the Soviet land. The working people of the Soviet Union are indignantly protesting against the reckless actions of the American maniacs. *The Soviet people are united in* their support for the peace-loving policy of the Communist Party and of their government. *They are also unanimous in their readiness to increase still further their labor efforts in behalf of the economic and defense might of their homeland.*

The Soviet Union and the countries of socialism have firmly stood and now stand on positions of peace in all their activities in the international arena. The countries of socialism are for solving all disputed questions not through military means but at the negotiation table, on a mutually acceptable basis.

But our people have good memories. We remember the perfidious intrigues of the aggressors who unleashed the second world war, and we shall not be taken by surprise. We are building the bright edifice of communism for ourselves and for our children, and we shall permit no one to violate the peace. The Soviet Armed Forces, equipped with the best and most modern combat equipment in the world, stand guard over peaceful labor.

A wave of furious protests against the monstrous actions of the American military is rolling over the whole world. The mighty socialist camp and all peace-loving nations of the globe are with revolutionary Cuba. Let the authors of the criminal plans make no mistake. The countries of socialism are one in their desire to halt any aggression at its very outset. We have powerful forces and an unbending will to protect peace.

An appeal for the defense of Cuba against aggression is resounding on all continents, in hundreds of languages. In a short time revolutionary Cuba has won the sympathy, respect and love of millions of the laboring masses who are fighting for democracy and progress. The peoples of other countries see in the aggression against Cuba an attempt on their own rights and freedoms, on peace and security all over the world. The peoples cannot remain indifferent to the events in the Caribbean area. *Energetic actions, united efforts and a common will can stay the hand of the American aggressors raised against peace. In the face of the reckless venture by the U. S. government, the peoples demand: Stop this dangerous playing with fire, bring the American aggressors to their senses! The imperialist aggressors must remember that if they try to spark the conflagration of a world war, they will inevitably burn in its fire!*

In the situation that has arisen a special responsibility falls on the United Nations. It was set up after World War II to stand guard over peace. The peoples have placed in it their hopes, which unfortunately have not always been fulfilled. At the present decisive moment the United Nations has been confronted with a new and extremely serious test. The question is whether it fulfills the mission with which it has been charged by the peoples, and thereby justifies its true purpose, or whether there lie in store for it the fate of the League of Nations and the general contempt of the peoples. There is no third way.

Dark storm clouds have gathered over the world. In these terrible days one must look reality soberly in the face. The atomic maniacs want to play with the destiny of human civilization. The peoples warn them: It will not work! The criminal designs of the enemies of peace must be thwarted. The will of the peoples is one—to defend and strengthen peace on earth!

3

Lesson of the Cuban Crisis*

H. C. ALLEN

The acute crisis of Cuba may perhaps have passed, but the chronic condition persists. Nothing else was to be expected, for it is just the sort of condition which the Communist architects of the Cold War desire; and their zealous and unremitting siege of the free world has certainly not come to an end. Russia has drawn back from the brink of nuclear war, but is very unlikely to surrender the lesser leverage which her satellite government in Cuba gives her. This is especially so because of the continual possibility that the disease of Castroism may infect other areas of the Western Hemisphere, all too often so weak economically as to be able to offer little effective resistance to the virus.

It is true that there are three possibilities of change which might be hopeful to the West. One is the long-term hope on which our whole policy of vigilant and constantly resolute resistance to Communist aggression and infiltration must be based—that with the passage of time, under the influence of such forces as increasing popular prosperity and education in the Soviet Union, the iron and doctrinaire policies of the Kremlin may weaken further. But it would be the height of folly to assume that a drastic change of this kind will be rapid, let alone that it is imminent. We may now be more confident that Mr. Khrushchev really does believe that co-existence should be peaceful in the sense that it eschews nuclear war: we dare not suppose that the competitive struggle will be other than bitter, prolonged and fierce in every sphere besides this.

Marxist-Leninst policies, however, have always drawn an important distinction between strategic ends and tactical means. (This is one of the reasons why the Soviet Government could about-face so suddenly at the height of the crisis without any embarrassment. Another is, of course, their control over their own Press. The West is usually, in fact, overconcerned about the results of Russian loss of face.) Tactical shifts in Moscow's attitude

*From Contemporary Review, *Vol. 203 *(January, 1963), pp. 9–12. Reprinted by permission of the Contemporary Co., Ltd., London.*

to the United States and other powers are always possible, and at this time the enigma of Chinese policy makes conceivable a tactical change of unusual, indeed profound, importance.

Many Europeans, inured to *realpolitik*, have long nourished the hope of a serious Sino-Soviet breach. (It should be chastening to Britons to remember how many of them expected, only ten years ago, to wean the "agrarian reformers" of China away from Russia!) It has been clear for some time that the Russians are apprehensive of Chinese extremism and the Chinese contemptuous of Russian caution. Behind this increasingly overt struggle for the leadership of the world-revolutionary movement lies a deep Russian fear of what President de Gaulle has, with his accustomed clarity, called the "masses of China, numberless and impoverished, indestructible and ambitious, building through trial and hardship a power which cannot be measured and casting her eyes about her on the open spaces over which she must one day spread." At last perhaps China has the makings of a great modern state, and the Soviets cannot feel easy at the prospect of these Chinese neighbours—inventors, after all, of the kowtow—obtaining, before too long, control of nuclear weapons. Though it would be most rash to count on it, there does now seem a real possibility that Chinese militancy may push the Soviet Union into a *détente* with America.

None of the four nuclear powers desires to see the further spread of these weapons with whose fearful destructive potentialities they are thoroughly familiar. (Russia is said to have no missile bases at all, except the Cuban ones, outside her own territory.) Having, perhaps for the first time, been fully convinced during the recent crisis of the readiness of the United States to accept, if need really be, not merely the risk but also the reality of nuclear war, it is just possible that the Soviet Government may be willing seriously to consider some limited forms of nuclear disarmament. Perhaps a test ban treaty might prove a first step. Perhaps some form of agreement to alleviate the fear of surprise attack. (Both Russia and America have suffered sudden and treacherous blows of this kind at the hands of the Japanese, and fears of such action run deep, especially in the United States since Pearl Harbour.) Even initial moves towards the distant vision of controlled nuclear disarmament may have come within the bounds of possibility; physical, on-the-ground inspection is not quite so essential technically as it once was, and, though agreed inspection of Russian missile-carrying ships by American forces off Cuba is a far cry from foreign armament inspectors on Russian soil, it is something.

Even setting aside the nightmare of the "mad General" who presses the button, it may be that President Kennedy was right when he wrote to Mr. Khrushchev that "you and I . . . were aware that developments were approaching a point where events could have become unmanageable." It is possible that these circumstances may have gone some way towards persuading the Soviet Government of the need to negotiate seriously about disarmament: it is even just conceivable that the fact that the two leaders had no alternative at the height of the tension but to trust each other's word (at least for a time) might be a small beginning to an improvement in the atmosphere in which the negotiations would be conducted.

But it is only just conceivable. These can be no more than hopes. We may have no sober expectation beyond the removal of Russian missile bases in Cuba, and the lifting of the immediate threat of nuclear war. On the contrary, we must expect the continuation of the obduracy and fanaticism of a Castro receiving every other form of support from the Communist world, and a corresponding continuation of determined American counter-action.

Have we, then, gained nothing else from this alleviation of the continuing Cuban crisis? In my view we should have gained some valuable lessons from it.

The first is that "the young man in the White House" has mastered not only the machinery for governing his own country but also the technique for dealing with a Soviet Government actively, indeed recklessly, stoking the fires of the Cold War. The Government of the United States showed itself swift and resolute in action, not sudden and quick in quarrel; and in success it displayed commendable moderation and restraint. In future it will not merely be presumptuous in us to think that we can teach the Americans anything much about international diplomacy: it is to be hoped that it will be seen by us to be presumptuous.

The second, which has been even less recognized in Britain, is how well our own Government came out of the affair. So firmly did they reject what might have been a human tendency to give the Americans just a tiny little drop of their own Suez medicine, that the idea became a current joke. They took no action to increase the tension, but they supported, clearly and firmly, our best, our one indispensable, ally. Lord Home directed attention to the heart of the matter in the most critical period by reminding the country forcefully that lies and deception have been the persistent means of Soviet policy. Mr. Macmillan's letter to Mr. Khrushchev, though it arrived after the swift Russian decision to retreat had been taken, made it unequivocally clear that the British Government stood "squarely and publicly with the President." We do not know what, if anything, passed privately between Mr. Macmillan and Mr. Kennedy, and this is as it should be; in future crises let us always remember that privately we may warn if we wish, but that publicly we must never waver in our support.

But if the Government commendably kept its head, many about it were certainly losing theirs, and blaming it on all and sundry. The Prime Minister was justified in his characteristically phrased jibe that "a febrile, excited nervosity which expresses itself in frantic demands that somebody ought to do something or other is not always the most helpful contribution."

Lord Home's incisiveness compared extremely well with the woolliness of the blanket with which his opposite number, Mr. Wilson, in a TV interview at the critical moment, contrived to blur all the vital issues. It was to be expected that some elements on the extreme Left would follow the "party line" by attacking the United States, and that the heterogeneous, wholly misguided and partly idealistic, mass of aged and youthful nuclear disarmers would shout loudly and sit down bravely outside the wrong embassy.

Neither was it surprising that some lofty-minded intellectuals turned instinctively on the Americans when the chips were down, and were unable to see any difference between American bases in Turkey and Soviet bases in Cuba. (Quite apart from the fact that one is friendly and the other hostile, these critics also seemed oblivious that the former were the logical and open outcome of the NATO alliance, formed more than a decade ago to prevent Europe from falling into the hands of Communism, and the latter of a novel, sudden and deceitful Russian attempt to upset, in one rash throw, the whole delicate balance of international military power.) What was a little disquieting, however, was the impression of hesitancy, even vacillation, created by some people, and some organs of opinion, on the Right itself; not all of them were prepared to stand straight up and be counted.

This is understandable enough. No man but a fool could have failed to feel some measure of fear in his heart at an hour as grave as this: the alternative to a settlement could have been the holocaust, even conceivably the beginning of the end of the human race. But it is also folly to allow oneself to believe that one can judge more wisely in the grip of fear than one could in calmer mood.

For more than ten years now we have, in cool blood, made the nuclear deterrent and our alliance with the United States the fundamental basis of our policy; we have thought our freedom more important than the threat of nuclear annihilation. We are always free to change that policy; any intelligent man must keep his mind open to conviction that the point has really come when the only alternatives are the triumph of Communist tyranny or the end of the species, if not of life on this planet. No sane man, once convinced, could hesitate as to his answer.

But the height of a desperate crisis is not the moment to change; the mind alarmed is no fit instrument for rational decision. Policies deliberately made dependent on cool nerves in the crunch cannot safely be jettisoned when the crunch comes.

And for my part, I believe it to be as true now as it was in the relative calm of 1946 when Sir Winston Churchill said it: "I do not believe that Soviet Russia desires war. What they desire is the fruits of war and the indefinite expansion of their power and doctrines. . . . I am convinced that there is nothing they admire so much as strength, and that there is nothing for which they have less respect than weakness, especially military weakness." Everything that has happened in the last two weeks appears to me to bear out this wise judgement. Let us, in case Cuba flares up again, or in any other crisis, not forget the fact. In the words of President Kennedy nearly two years ago, let us never fear to negotiate, but let us never negotiate from fear.

XV

A New Cold War—Sino-Soviet Rift

1

The Conflict—A Survey*

HARRY GELMAN

At the end of the summer of 1962, the Chinese fired the opening salvos in a renewed anti-Soviet campaign which has gone on continuously ever since. On three separate occasions, at the Rumanian (August 23), Vietnamese (September 1), and Bulgarian (September 8) national anniversary receptions held in Peking, Foreign Minister Chen Yi alluded to socialist countries which attempted to forcibly impose . . . [their] views on others" and "replaced comradelike discussions . . . with interference in [others'] internal affairs." Soon afterwards, in mid-September, the Chinese and Albanian press launched an obviously coordinated and violent assault on "modern revisionism," timed to coincide with the visit of Leonid Brezhnev, Chairman of the Presidium of the USSR Supreme Soviet, to Yugoslavia.

Curiously, Soviet propaganda displayed remarkable restraint as the Chinese attacks continued, and there was even an attempt to appease Peking. In meetings with the departing Chinese Ambassador Liu Hsiao on October 13 and 14, Khrushchev, according to Soviet statements last year, asked that Mao forget the past and "start our relations with a clear page." Moreover, according to the Chinese, the Soviet leader expressed complete sympathy for Peking's stand on the border conflict with India, implicitly endorsed the Chinese intention to use force in that conflict, and promised to stand by Peking if hostilities again arose. These private statements by Khrushchev were followed on October 25 by an equally remarkable editorial in *Pravda* which, for the first and last time in the three years of the Sino-Indian border controversy, sided with Peking. One can only speculate that the adoption by Moscow of a conciliatory posture was motivated by the approach of the Cuban crisis, which erupted into the open on October 22—that is, by Soviet desire to assure bloc solidarity at a time

*From Problems of Communism, **13** (*March–April, 1964*), *13–15. Reprinted by permission of the United States Information Agency.*

of military crisis and also, perhaps, to buy Chinese forbearance if it should become necessary to back down over the issue of Cuba.

As it turned out, the Soviets did have to back down, but the Chinese did not forbear and instead proceeded to belabor Khrushchev unmercifully for his "betrayal" of Castro. Placed on the defensive, Moscow edged back toward its previous neutral position vis-à-vis the Sino-Indian border conflict and then organized a thoroughgoing counterattack against the Chinese party.

The counterattack was pressed with mounting intensity throughout November and the first week of December at the successive congresses of the Bulgarian, Hungarian, Czechoslovakian and Italian Communist parties, each of these meetings witnessing the dragooning of a still larger number of the CPSU's foreign adherents into joining a chorus of denunciation first against the Albanians and later against the Chinese as well. The climax was reached in early December with the extremely violent anti-Albanian-and-Chinese speeches delivered by the Czechoslovak and Italian party secretaries, Koucky and Pajetta. There followed the elaborate state visit of Tito to the Soviet Union, where on December 12 the Yugoslav leader heard Khrushchev deliver an angry speech before the Supreme Soviet impugning Chinese motives and policies.

Mao's response was to open the sluice gates. In a succession of articles published between mid-December 1962 and March 1963, the CCP completed the process it had begun in 1956, gradually making explicit its past grievances and present ambitions. The Chinese party called on the Communists of the world to revolt against the "baton" of the CPSU; it derided the Soviet "temporary majority"; and it challenged Moscow to convene a meeting of the world movement, thus repeating publicly the demand made privately early in 1962. At last, Peking attacked, by name, the CPSU and its leading adherents in the West as betrayers of the revolution, simultaneously elaborating its 1960 thesis that the real focus of revolutionary struggle against "imperialism" was now in the underdeveloped areas of the world and that the real leader of this struggle was the Chinese Communist Party.

In response, Moscow began in February 1963 to intimate that its adversary was seeking to divide the revolutionary movement along geographical and racial lines—a complaint which was eventually expanded into thunderous denunciations of Chinese "racism," coupled with charges that Peking was attempting to isolate the European "socialist" states from the "national liberation movement" and to distort reality by claiming that imperialism's main conflict was now with the underdeveloped world (led by Peking's rhetoric) rather than with the bloc (led by Soviet military might).

In the meantime, however, it became clear early in 1963 that the Chinese public demand for a world Communist meeting had embarrassed the CPSU. In his January address to the East German party congress, Khrushchev not only proposed—as if it were his own idea—a suspension of polemics between the two factions, but also acknowledged the existence of pressure on him from "some comrades" to convene a world conference. He insisted, however, that the time was not ripe for such a meeting. The Soviet leader then went on to declare that he had no desire to excommunicate the Albanians from the bloc and challenged the Chinese to treat the Yugoslavs similarly. But even while extending this olive branch to Mao, Khrushchev could not forbear striking him with it: the East German congress was made the occasion for new attacks on the Albanians and the Chinese, and the CCP delegate was interrupted and subjected to apparently well-organized booing and hissing, an unprecedented insult to the Chinese party. Nevertheless, in February, the CPSU retreated a step further and sent Peking a fairly mild letter agreeing in principle to a world meeting and proposing bilateral talks to prepare for it.

The Chinese, however, were in no conciliatory mood and—as the Soviets later said—took Moscow's offer as a sign of weakness. They were by then in the midst of a vast new offensive against the CPSU and were vigorously proselytizing in every part of the world. To this end, the various CCP statements and editorials were being assembled in brochures and distributed in many languages. In February, the Chinese openly attacked Soviet influence at a Tanganyika meeting of the Afro-Asian Solidarity Organization (using racial arguments, the Soviets said), and at the same time they began setting up counterparts to the existing world front organizations, excluding the Soviets from participation in the new bodies.

After receiving the CPSU letter of late February, the Chinese party responded with new public attacks of still greater violence. It was at this time that the CCP initiated the practice of publishing its current communications to the CPSU (forcing the Soviet party to do likewise), so that even the exchanges between the two Central Committees, hitherto kept in the form of confidential letters, now became a part of the open polemic. Thus, in spite of a promise given on March 9 that it would desist from further public attacks, Peking clearly had no intention of doing so.

This was dramatically demonstrated on the eve of a CPSU Central Committee plenum and three weeks before the scheduled opening of bilateral Sino-Soviet talks in Moscow, when the Chinese distributed in the Soviet capital—and subsequently throughout the rest of the world—the CCP letter of June 14, 1963, explicitly indicting Soviet domestic policies for the first time and announcing Peking's intention to split every Communist party whose leadership continued to support Moscow. In this proclamation of Peking's "general line" for the Communists of the world, the Chinese also promised to anoint as honorary Marxists–Leninists all revolutionaries now *outside* the Communist movement who would carry their banner.

The Soviet leadership now reacted forcefully. The Chinese officials who had distributed the CCP letter in the Soviet Union were formally expelled, and after the Central Committee had pondered its course at the mid-June plenum, the Soviet case against the CCP was placed before the world in the form of a CPSU "Open Letter" released on July 13. A highly emotional speech delivered by Khrushchev six days later, on July 19, made it clear that he regarded the Chinese action as nothing less than an attempt to subvert his position at home and abroad.

Meanwhile, CPSU and CCP representatives opened their scheduled bilateral talks in Moscow, but even as the talks ground on toward eventual fruitless suspension, the Soviet government concluded a partial nuclear test-ban agreement with the United States on terms which it had previously rejected. Throughout the summer and autumn Soviet propaganda heavily exploited this agreement in an effort to isolate the Chinese, who were placed in the vulnerable position of having to defend before world opinion their determination to acquire nuclear weapons and their refusal to adhere to the test-ban treaty.

Sino-Soviet relations had now reached a point where both sides were caricaturing and attacking each other's leaders by name, and where both proceeded to publish statements revealing hitherto secret aspects of their dealings with each other since the beginning of the dispute. The Soviets spoke of Mao as a senile "Trotskyite" tyrant and racist who sought world war, who had made monumental blunders in domestic policy, and whose government maintained "concentration camps" and massacred minority peoples, forcing them to seek haven in the USSR. The Chinese, in turn, characterized Khrushchev as a cowardly traitor allied with "imperialism" who was striving to restore capitalism in the Soviet Union and to undermine Marxism–Leninism throughout the world.

In September–October 1963 there were reports in the Western press, supported circumstantially by hints in Soviet propaganda, which suggested that the CPSU was almost reconciled to the consequences of a schism and was now considering the convocation of a world Communist meeting at which the Chinese and their supporters would be called upon to recant their factional activity or depart. In late October, however, the CPSU— apparently again under pressure from members of its own camp—temporarily abandoned this intention and instead began calling once again for an end to public polemics.

The CCP, however, would not relent, and by late January 1964 Peking had begun to announce formal recognition of pro-Chinese factions which had rebelled and seceded from the established Communist parties of such countries as Ceylon, Peru, Belgium, and Switzerland as *the* official Communist parties in those countries. These ominous organizational measures were followed in early February by a new Chinese pronouncement—the most outspoken to date—which proclaimed Peking's intention to recognize and support such "revolutionary" Communist parties everywhere.

The formalization of the worldwide Communist schism had now begun.

2

Sino-Soviet Split in Perspective*

ROBERT A. SCALAPINO

The conflict between Russia and China, now burning at white-heat intensity, will almost certainly be recorded as one of the most significant events of the twentieth century. Less than a decade ago, the Eurasian continent seemed destined to be dominated by the Sino-Soviet alliance. That alliance, formally consummated in 1950, united nearly a billion people, with additional millions in East Europe, North Korea, and North Vietnam directly affected. Intimate political, military, and economic ties were fashioned among governments sharing a common ideology and common global objectives. The power potential of this union was truly awesome. To many observers, the critical question of the future was whether a revitalized, unified West Europe in concert with the United States could withstand the inevitable pressures from the East.

Seldom in history has a major alliance collapsed so quickly. Today, the Sino-Soviet alliance is an empty shell, and there is little likelihood that it can be reconstructed in the near future. It is conceivable that, if Khrushchev and Mao were to pass from the scene, a fresh start could be attempted, but, in view of the issues that have now been raised and the tactics that have been employed, the removal of personal antagonisms alone would scarcely suffice to mend the breach. At this point, the struggle has reached an unprecedented level of bitterness and intensity. Communism has been turned inward against itself. The tactics so long employed against democratic opponents are now being used against "comrades" with the same deadly passion. . . .

In tactical terms, the Sino-Soviet dispute has thus far involved five stages, each marked by special characteristics. The first stage was characterized by primary reliance upon private bilateral discussions in which Russian and Chinese authorities in the 1956–1957 period sought to persuade each other of the merits of their respective positions. These discussions and the communications involved appear to have been shared with a relatively small number of comrades from other parties. At this point, the controversy was on a strictly party-to-party basis and did not even involve the whole of the international Communist movement.

The second stage, dating from the fall of 1957, represented the beginning of formal disputation, and quickly the debate was carried into the main

*From The Annals of The American Academy of Political and Social Science, *Vol.* 351 (January, 1964), p. 2, pp. 11–14. Reprinted by permission of the author and the American Academy of Political and Social Science.

stream of the international movement. This stage culminated with the truly fierce interparty and interpersonal attacks that took place at Bucharest and Moscow in 1960. Already, the dispute had produced some factionalism both among and within parties. Moreover, the Soviet Union had commenced punitive actions against Albania and China in a desperate effort to stop the dangerous trend toward an open defiance of Soviet leadership. Attempts were being made on both sides to support "antiparty" elements within the opposing camp. Thus, state-to-state relations were now deeply involved.

The public attack by Khrushchev on Albania in October 1961 inaugurated the third stage, marking the official entry of the controversy into the public arena. In this period, also, Albania and Yugoslavia were used to symbolize China and Russia respectively, and thus the full range of the dispute—and the bitterness attending it—were progressively explored and revealed to the world. Now Communist parties everywhere were forced to take positions on many of the burning issues. Some parties, notably in Asia, sought to establish a neutralist position. Most parties elsewhere ultimately lined up behind Moscow on the critical points. A noticeable weakening of discipline occurred, however; Moscow was now paying a heavy price for the dispute. Meanwhile, Peking began an intensive propaganda campaign directed toward every revolutionary center in the world but especially toward the non-Western areas. State-to-state relations between the Soviet Union and China now deteriorated sharply, with each side accusing the other of subversive activities and interference in internal affairs.

A fourth stage developed in the fall of 1962, in the midst of the crises over India, Cuba, and Yugoslavia. The use of Albania and Yugoslavia as stalking horses gradually ceased, and the main targets—still garbed in anonymity—were brought forward. The Chinese tactic was to use terms like "some people" and "some parties." The Communist party of the Soviet Union, furious at Chinese criticism of Soviet policy in Cuba, retaliated by using various party congresses in East Europe for the open criticism of the Chinese Communist party. Chinese spokesmen quickly responded by issuing a running series of pamphlets surveying in comprehensive fashion their position and excoriating their opponents. Meanwhile, China was gathering support from most Asian parties and building factions throughout the world as Moscow held firmly to most of the official party organizations outside the Far East.

The famous June 14 letter from Peking and the abortive Moscow meeting of July 1963 which followed shortly opened the fifth and present stage. For the first time, the Chinese openly and vehemently attacked Khrushchev by name, demanding nothing less than his total repudiation by true Communists as a revisionist and traitor to the movement. Russian sources answered with direct and vigorous attacks upon the Chinese Communist party, although no Chinese leaders were mentioned by name. State-to-state relations continued to be very bad. Economic intercourse was only a fraction of the 1959 figures, and China appeared to be turning increasingly to the non-Communist world for her needs. Cultural exchange was minimal and political relations cool. The reverberations of the split within the international Communist movement continued to be very serious. Some parties uncovered pro-Peking factions significant enough to be troublesome, but, outside of East Asia and the Pacific, the Soviet Union held its earlier wide support. However, a new note of independence was sounded with increasing frequency by certain parties basically supporting Moscow. Could the Soviet Union ever regain its old hold on the international Communist movement?

A careful analysis of the tactics employed thus far in the Sino-Soviet dispute suggests three significant points. First, despite some impromptu and impetuous words and actions, this dispute, from the beginning, has been taken very seriously by the two major parties and every effort has been made to contain it. The escalation of the dispute in tactical terms has only occurred after a series of failures at resolution. The tactics of each successive stage, moreover, give evidence of the most careful planning and thought and represent controlled accelerations. It is true, however, that, in the initial stages of the dispute, it was generally the Soviet Union that took the harder tactical line whereas, more recently, it has been China.

If proof were ever needed that, in a Communist society, party and state are inextricably connected, the Sino-Soviet dispute gives the needed evidence. From a very early stage, it became impossible to separate party and state relations, despite strenuous efforts so to do.

One is prompted, finally, to note the telling impact upon this dispute of the absence of a tolerant tradition within the Communist world. On both sides, the ferocity of words, the starkness of actions, and the flat finality of pronouncements are shocking to one who has been schooled in the democratic way. Perhaps, in this respect, the Chinese have more basis for complaint—at least in terms of the early stages—than the Russians, and clearly they were outraged by many events. But they, too, came into the conflict as prophets armed, armed with all of the self-righteousness that a combination of Chinese tradition and Marxian ideology could produce.

In any intense and bitter conflict, personal rivalries and animosities play some role. It is clear, for example, that, to the Chinese Communist party leaders today, Khrushchev personifies evil and error. They regard the Soviet premier as an impetuous, vulgar, unpredictable bureaucrat who consistently reveals his peasant background. They see him as a man uninterested in theory and incapable of leading the great movement which he inherited. They identify him with narrow nationalism and big-power chauvinism. Some of them at least believe that, if a man like Molotov could have been placed at the head of the Soviet government, the history of the last eight years would have been vastly different. It is only partially a tactical maneuver, therefore, that causes them to try to separate "the Khrushchev group" from the Soviet people.

For their part, the Soviet leaders have also developed some personal antagonisms, no doubt. They see in men like Mao and Liu leaders devoid of practical judgment and a capacity to encompass the world in which they live. These self-proclaimed intellectuals are fanatics who devote themselves to theoretical "purity" even when it spells disaster to the Chinese people and Communists everywhere, in Khrushchev's mind. And, he might well add, one only has to be confronted with their rigidity and hauteur to dislike them thoroughly.

In a very important sense, however, one cannot separate these personal considerations from broader, impersonal ones. The Soviet Union and Communist China are, at present, in two very different stages of their respective revolutions. In Russia, the revolution is nearly a half-century old, and a second-generation functionaire leadership has emerged, dedicated to the businesslike job of consolidating and advancing the gains made, defending the very substantial stake which the Soviet people now have in the *status quo*, and learning how to act as a major world power. In China, a first-generation intellectual, revolutionary elite still holds power, and the revolution remains in its opening phases. Incredible sacrifices have to be made. The primary task is to keep the revolutionary fervor high and, by using this fervor, to change conditions as quickly and drastically as possible. Is it surprising that communication between the Soviet and Chinese elites should be difficult?

One is forced to conclude that nationalism has not only survived communism, it has in certain very real senses triumphed over it. The very fact that the words being stressed in Communist polemics today are words like independence, equality, and sovereignty is eloquent testimony to the trends. For the Communist world as for the non-Communist world, the nation-state remains the most dynamic and powerful form of political organization, despite its various deficiencies and notwithstanding Marxian theory. Indeed, paradoxically, the nation-state at this point may be more significant to the Communists than to others, both because they have come to it so recently in many cases and are still seeking to consolidate it and because they have had less success than the West in operating effectively international organizations.

Nationalism in its broadest meaning symbolizes the existing pluralism of the Communist world: states—or parties within states—having different cultural heritages, different environmental conditions, different timings of revolution, and different levels of power. Yet Marxism–Leninism, despite certain attempts at modification, continues to insist upon a modification, continues to insist upon a monolithic truth—a single, fundamental, finite doctrine to which all shall adhere. This great paradox between the pluralist realities of the Communist world and the monolithic proclivities of Communist ideology represents the underlying motive force behind the Sino-Soviet dispute.

3

China Is Waging " Expansionist " " Cold War "*

PRAVDA

As is evident from the interview of the C. P. C. Chairman, the Chinese leaders now do not even try to disguise their expansionist aspirations. According to the Japanese press, Mao Tse-tung did not even mention ideological questions. His talk does not contain a word about Marxism–Leninism, about socialism, about the unity of the working class, about the struggle for the interests of the international workers' and national-liberation movement. His talk bears not a trace of class analysis of the present-day world, of a class approach to the choice of friends and allies in the struggle against imperialism. The main thing with which Mao Tse-tung is concerned is to whip up anti-Soviet feeling, to play on the nationalist sentiments of the most reactionary forces. . . .

How far the Chinese leaders have gone in the "cold war" against the Soviet Union is graphically clear from Mao Tse-tung's pronouncements on the territorial question. He does not simply claim this or that Soviet territory, but portrays his claims part of some "general territorial question."

We are faced with an openly expansionist program with farreaching claims.

This program did not appear today or yesterday. In 1954 a textbook on modern history was published in the Chinese People's Republic, with a map of China showing that country as it was, in the opinion of the authors, before the first opium war. Included as part of China on this map were Burma, Vietnam, Korea, Thailand, Malaya, Nepal, Butan, Sikkim; in the north, the border ran along the Stanovoi mountain range, cutting the Far Eastern Territory off from the U. S. S. R.; in the West, a part of Kirgizia, of Tadzhikistan and of Kazakhstan (up to Lake Balkhash) was also included in China. Sakhalin also was shown as Chinese territory. If one were to believe the textbook, all these lands and countries comprised "state territory of China" and had been taken away from her.

*From The Current Digest of the Soviet Press, **16** (September 16, 1964), 3–7. Translation from The Current Digest of the Soviet Press, published weekly at Columbia University by the Joint Committee on Slavic Studies, appointed by the American Council of Learned Societies and the Social Science Research Council. Copyright © 1964, the Joint Committee on Slavic Studies. Reprinted by permission.*

At the time, it seemed that the publication of such a textbook was the result of an oversight or of provocational activities of nationalistic elements. But subsequent events refuted this conjecture. Maps showing now these, now those parts of the Soviet Union and other countries neighboring on China as Chinese territory continued to be published in the C. P. R.

Chinese representatives lately have begun to refer with increasing frequency to hundreds of thousands of square kilometers of Soviet territory allegedly belonging "by right" to China.

A recent issue of the Peking magazine Lishi Yanchu (No. 4, 1964) asserts that "Russia seized vast lands to the north of the Heilungkiang (Chinese name for the Amur.—Ed.) River and to the east of the Ussuri River," . . . "at various times Russia annexed vast lands in Sinkiang and in the northeastern area."

Now Mao Tse-tung declares in his talk: "The region east of Baikal became the territory of Russia approximately 100 years ago, and since then Vladivostok, Khabarovsk, Kamchatka and other points have been the territory of the Soviet Union. We have not yet presented the bill for this roll call."

But by what right do the Chinese leaders lay claim to lands that did not belong to China? They cite the fact that many hundreds of years ago Chinese troops came to these parts and that the Chinese emperor once used to collect tribute from the local inhabitants. Indeed, were the question involved not so serious, such "historical arguments" could be called nothing but childish.

The history of mankind is full of examples of the emergence and fall of states and the resettlement of peoples, in the course of which the boundaries between states changed more than once. By resorting to the method of "citing history," on the question of boundaries one could prove anything. One could, for instance, prove that England is French territory, because she was once the domain of a Duke of Normandy. One could demonstrate, on the contrary, that France is an English possession, since at one time, during the Hundred Years' War, she was almost completely conquered by the English. With the help of such arguments one could also prove that the boundary of the C. P. R. passes only along the line of the Great Wall of China, less than 100 kilometers away from Peking. Indeed, the boundary of China did once pass there, the evidence of which is the wall itself.

But even if one took the references to "historical rights" seriously, it would turn out that in this case they do not correspond to the facts at all. It is known that in the middle of the 17th century China's possessions reached only to the Hingan mountain range, i.e., considerably south of the Amur. The territories north of the Hingan were populated by indigenous local tribes (Evenki, Dauri, et al.) who from time to time were raided by the Manchurians and paid tribute to them. There was no indigenous Manchurian and Chinese population in the Amur area. The process of the definition of actual borders took place as Russia took possession of the northern half of the Amur basin and China took possession of the southern part. This condition of the boundary was fixed more than 100 years ago in the Aigun and Peking treaties. . . .

In his talk Mao Tse-tung bemoans the fate of Mongolia, which, in his words, the Soviet Union "placed . . . under its domination." This can evoke nothing but indignation. Everybody knows that for more than 40 years the Mongolian People's Republic has been a sovereign socialist state and enjoys all the rights of an independent country. Why did Mao Tse-tung have to make such obviously wild statements? The whole point is that the existence of an independent Mongolian state which maintains friendly relations with the U. S. S. R. and other countries of socialism does not suit the Chinese leaders. They would like to deprive the Mongolian People's Republic of independence, to make it a Chinese province. The C. P. R. leaders proposed to N. S. Khrushchev and other Soviet comrades, during the latter's visit to Peking in 1954, that they "reach agreement" on just this.

Naturally, N. S. Khrushchev refused to discuss this question and told the Chinese leaders that the destiny of the Mongolian people is determined not in Peking and not in Moscow, but in Ulan-Bator, that only the country's working people themselves and no one else could decide the question of Mongolia's statehood.

As has already been noted, the Chinese leaders are trying to elevate territorial claims to the level of some general principle. But this involves the fundamentals of international relations. What would happen if all states were to follow the Peking recipe and start presenting mutual claims to one another for revision of historically formed boundaries? The answer to this question is simple. This path would mean inevitable aggravation of international tension, it would be fraught with military conflicts, with all the consequences that follow from this.

The question of territorial disputes and boundaries is extraordinarily complicated. One must distinguish the nature of the territorial issues. It is one thing when the matter is a question of the just striving of peoples to eliminate the survivals of the shameful colonial system, to get back old territories populated by the nation concerned and held by imperialists. For instance, the right of the Indian people to bring Goa back into the motherland was indisputable. Indonesia's right to bring West Irian back into the republic is just as indisputable. We have declared and declare that People's China has every right to bring about the liberation and reunification of Taiwan and Hong Kong, which are part of the country and in which Chinese constitute the majority of the population. One could mention many more such examples.

Territorial claims stemming from attempts to revise historically formed boundaries between states, to force in any form a revision of the treaties and agreements concluded after World War II as a result of the rout of

Hilter's fascism and Japanese militarism, are quite another matter. The peoples who won victory at the cost of millions upon millions of lives will never agree to such strivings.

In his talk with the Japanese Socialists, Mao Tse-tung crossed out with amazing ease the entire system of international agreements concluded after World War II and meeting the interests of strengthening peace and the security of peoples. He declared: "The places occupied by the Soviet Union are too numerous"—and he even named some areas with the obvious purpose of pouring on fuel to inflame nationalistic passions. It is hard to believe that the Chinese leader does not understand the reasons for and the historical circumstances of the formation of the present boundaries between states in Europe and Asia. It is hard to believe another thing, too—that he is unware of the very dangerous consequences that could arise from any attempt to recarve the map of the world in the present conditions. Mao Tse-tung pretends to be threatening the interests of only our country, but it is obvious to everybody that such a provocational appeal to revise borders (if it is taken seriously) would inevitably generate a whole series of mutual demands, claims and insoluble conflicts among countries of Europe and Asia. That all this is self-evident is beyond doubt and gives grounds for declaring that only those who find it advantageous for some reasons to sow mistrust and animosity among peoples of the countries of socialism can act in such a manner.

It is with precisely this aim that Mao Tse-tung is trying to fabricate so-called territorial issues between a number of socialist countries. But these attempts are doomed to failure in advance. No one will succeed in undermining the friendship and cooperation of the peoples of the countries of socialism.

The rulers of the capitalist world have been watching the Chinese leaders' nationalism, their great-power manner, for a long time. It was no accident, therefore, that the representatives of the right wing of the Japanese Socialists put the question of the Kurile Islands precisely to Mao Tse-tung; and they got from the Chairman of the C. P. C. precisely the answer they needed.

It is known that the transition of these islands into the full possession of the Soviet Union was not at all the result of Soviet expansion, as Mao Tse-tung tries to assert. This act was dictated by the need to stop the aggressive policy of Japanese imperialism, which since 1918 harbored plans of seizing Soviet territory in the Far East and repeatedly tried to carry them out in actuality. The Kuriles were given a special role in the Japanese militarists' aggressive plans—the role of an important beachhead for attacking the Soviet Far East. It is understandable that the Japanese military had to be deprived of this possibility. This was done, and in the past the Chinese representatives more than once approved this security measure. On Aug. 15, 1951, statement of the C. P. R. government pointed out that

" . . . the Kuriles must be handed over and the southern part of Sakhalin and all the islands adjacent to it returned to the Soviet Union."

Can one say that the situation in this area has essentially changed since then and that the menace of aggression against the U. S. S. R. and other countries of socialism has completely disappeared? Not at all. Militarist forces that would like to lead the country along the old road of military ventures are becoming active in Japan, contrary to the will of her people. There are U. S. military bases in Japan that are maintained by the Pentagon, not for nothing, near the Soviet Union and other socialist countries of Asia. Only a few days ago the Japanese government, yielding to U. S. pressure, granted the U. S. A. the right to bring nuclear submarines into Japanese ports, that is, it allowed the U. S. A. to use these ports as U. S. military bases. In these circumstances the statement that the U. S. S. R. should give up the Kuriles to Japan plays into the hands not only of Japanese but of American militarists.

If one accepts Mao Tse-tung's so-called historical principle, then all rights to this territory belong to the Soviet Union. But Chairman Mao treats quite arbitrarily the principles he himself advances. He cites them when he finds it advantageous and flouts them if his political designs require this.

There are not and cannot be any grounds, either legal or moral, for claims to the Kurile Islands. This, however, does not mean that in changed circumstances searches for solutions that would not infringe upon the interests of the U. S. S. R. and would meet the needs of the Japanese people would be excluded.

Mao Tse-tung cannot but realize that the Chinese leadership's position on the territorial question is far from internationalism. To smooth over this impression, he appeals not only to history but to "justice." His thesis essentially boils down to the fact that the population of the globe is unevenly distributed and hence, if you please, justice demands a redistribution of territory.

The demagoguery of this thesis is evident to everyone. The distribution of people in the world is the result of a long and complicated development, by virtue of which different peoples live in different conditions. Communists fight precisely for ensuring all peoples a better life. When socialism triumphs throughout the world and the productive forces attain a high level everywhere, the process of the rapprochement of nations will result in the gradual disappearance of the differences in the living conditions of peoples of different countries, and state boundaries will lose their significance. In these conditions it will become possible to solve the problem of more even distribution of people in the world.

But this is a matter for the future. To raise this question today, when opposing social systems exist, when the objective process of the strengthening of statehood and sovereignty is going on, is extremely harmful.

It should not be forgotten, incidentally, that history knows many instances in which the most reactionary wars were undertaken for the purpose of enlarging "Lebensraum." So Mao Tse-tung's pronouncements about "unfair distribution of territory" are not so very new. He has predecessors of whom he can hardly be proud.

Also, one cannot overlook Mao Tse-tung's statement, quite surprisingly coming from a Communist, about "the greatness of Japan." The great-power views of the C. P. C. leaders, their admiration of the factor of brute force in international relations, show clearly in these statements.

Where does Mao Tse-tung see the greatness of the Japanese people? In their industriousness? In the fact that they succeeded in a short space of time in bringing their country into the ranks of the leading powers of the world and in creating a wonderful material and spiritual culture? No, it is not this that attracts his attention. He speaks with extraordinary enthusiasm of the crimes of the Japanese military who occupied tremendous expanses in Southeast Asia and Oceania at the start of the 1940s. In short, Chairman Mao declares the aggressive actions of the Japanese samurai to be Japan's national greatness—that is, actions the Japanese people themselves regard as a national disgrace.

History teaches that no country has ever achieved greatness on the path of military ventures and aggressions. True greatness of peoples is achieved by the paths of social progress, friendship and cooperation. We are convinced that the vital interests of the Chinese people lie on these same paths.

All who cherish the interests of socialism, the interests of preserving peace and the security of peoples cannot but denounce most emphatically the expansionist views of the C. P. R. leaders, their attempt to start playing with questions that affect the destiny of the peoples.

The true designs of the Chinese leaders are becoming obvious. These designs have nothing in common with the interests of the struggle for the victory of the cause of peace and socialism; they are permeated through and through with great-power chauvinism and hegemonism. Mao Tse-tung's talk with the Japanese Socialists is the most eloquent and graphic evidence of this.

XVI

Communist China's Attack on India

1

China's Himalayan Frontiers*

K. S. SHELVANKAR

The 'boundary dispute' between India and China stems from the Chinese demand for over 50,000 square miles of territory adjoining the frontier, territory which is, and has always been, a part of India. China has already occupied by force some 12,000 square miles in north-eastern Kashmir. Tension is at present most acute in this area; it could die down—or flare-up in some other sector of the 2,500-mile frontier. No one can chart this crisis in advance. But it is clear that if the Chinese demand were conceded, the Himalayas and its ancillary ranges would cease to be the frontier between the two great civilizations, as they have been for ages past, and Chinese power would reach down to the edge of the Indian plains.

This state of affairs is in sad contrast to the good relations which pre-vailed at first between the newly-independent India and the People's Republic of China. Looking back, the manner in which China abused India's confidence and eventually brought this claim into the open is tiself significant—and disturbing. . . .

In general, the Chinese allege that the Indian frontiers were fixed arbi-trarily by the British, as far north as they could reach in the days of their maximum power, and that India is seeking to hold on to the ill-gotten gains of British imperialism. The implication is that these areas were stolen from China by guile or force. Whatever one may think of British policies, this particular charge does not bear examination. No doubt, India as a unified modern State took shape under British rule; it is also undeniable that Central Asia in the last century was the scene of rivalries and intrigues involving the three big Empires: Britain, Russia, and China. It is one thing to recognise these facts; quite another to assert that the *raison d'être* of India's present frontier is that it happens to mark the line at which British expansion, at the cost of China, suddenly came to a halt.

On the contrary, the extension of British power in these regions was

*From International Affairs, **38** (October, 1962), 472–477. Reprinted by permission of the author and The Royal Institute of International Affairs, London.

part of the process of completing and consolidating the conquest of India. The Karakoram and Kuen Lun mountains formed the traditional boundary of Sinkiang—even Chinese documents testify to this—and the territory to the south of these ranges, including Aksai Chin, belonged to Kashmir and Ladakh, sovereign principalities, linked to India, but with a long history of their own. Ladakh was briefly and loosely associated with Tibet, but broke away nearly a thousand years ago, and, after a period of independence, it was absorbed into the Mughal Empire. Following the downfall of the Mughals, it was united with Kashmir in the new State which was founded about the middle of the nineteenth century. As a province of Kashmir, it subsequently came into India and has been under Indian (Kashmir) administration since then.

The history of the Eastern Sector is likewise far from being a blank, nor had it much in common with that of China. The region is inhabited mostly by people ethnically akin to the hill tribes in the interior of India, and owing no allegiance to Buddhism, or the Lamaist faith. For centuries it was under the sway of the Hindu dynasties of Eastern India. In the thirteenth century it passed to the Ahom rajas (who came from the Burmese hills, but were soon Hinduised), and later on from them to the British, who annexed the entire province (Assam) in 1842.

India's northern frontier is thus much older than the British raj, and was determined by geographical factors and a historical process which did no violence to Chinese rights. Besides, it was not an abstract or theoretical line, but one which marked the limits up to which India exercised effective jurisdiction—and still does, except where the Chinese have intruded. For obvious reasons, the administrative system could not be of the same type as in the plains. Ladakh is a desolate region, sparsely populated, if at all; and in the North-east, it was at one time thought best to leave the tribal organizations more or less intact, so far as their internal affairs were concerned.

Subject to these conditions, the Government of India discharged all the usual administrative functions, including the basic ones of tax collection and the maintenance of law and order. There are stacks of official records relating to the now disputed regions which provide ample proof of this. They contain a regular sequence of reports, stretching over decades, on such varied matters as revenue assessments and police activities, public works projects and the control of trade routes, as well as periodical census returns and detailed reports of survey and mapping operations. There is nothing comparable to this wealth of documented evidence to support the Chinese pretension to have administered these areas until recent times; indeed, there cannot be, for two different administrations could not have been functioning for long over the same territory.*

*During the joint meetings of Indian and Chinese officials in 1960, India proposed that the evidence submitted by each country on these and other points in dispute should be presented in a form which would enable a reader to view the two sets of submissions side by side and draw his own conclusions. The Chinese objected to the suggestion and it had to be abandoned.

India's stand is further vindicated by several inter-governmental agreements, of different dates, and relating to different parts of the frontier. One of them, the tripartite Simla Agreement of 1914 between India, Tibet, and China has acquired special prominence in this controversy. Its effect was to formalize the traditional alignment in the Eastern Sector under the name of the McMahon Line. The Chinese now refuse to recognize the legality of this Line, not only because the Chinese Government of the time did not ratify the agreement, but on the grounds that Tibet was not competent to conclude treaties.

It would take us too far afield to pursue the ramifications of this question, but it should be said that here again we have one of those curious contradictions which make the Chinese case puzzling, if not incomprehensible. Much of the material that China herself relies upon to support her claims in the Middle and Western Sectors comes from the Tibetan archives, and carries the implication that that Government was entitled to negotiate with foreign powers. What is more, China has herself been ready, in other contexts to recognize the validity of treaties signed by Tibet. Her 1956 Treaty with Nepal, for example, expressly abrogated the 1856 Treaty between Nepal and Tibet; and in 1947 she took the initiative in asking India whether, on attaining independence, she assumed the treaty rights and obligations existing till then between India and Tibet. Such moves would surely have been superfluous if Tibet had been considered to have had no treaty-making powers.

It is true that this long frontier is not everywhere demarcated on the ground—the nature of the terrain precludes it. But it has solid support in history and tradition as well as in a series of inter-State transactions, and, above all, in India's unbroken record of continuous administrative control. Moreover, it conforms for the most part with the generally accepted principle that where a mountain range forms the boundary the watershed constitutes the natural frontier.

Allowing for some sporadic minor troubles and disagreements, this has been on the whole a remarkably peaceful frontier. There was never any secret about its location; it was defined from point to point, and publicly and authoritatively affirmed in different forms and on different occasions by the Government of India. It was also specifically referred to, at various dates, before and after independence, in communications between India and China, or India and Tibet. No government in Peking, or Lhasa, ever challenged it wholesale, or made even a perfunctory protest, or asked for clarification, or raised any serious complaint or objection. And it is only eight years since China signed a treaty with India, containing promises of mutual non-aggression and respect for territorial integrity. She was fully aware at the time of the extent of India's territory; but she did not reveal, and India was not to know, until five years later that she had her own plans for redrawing the map.

China's pretext for tearing up this treaty—and denying all the history it embodied, and the hopes it epitomized—is that there is no formal boundary agreement between the two Governments. This is true enough, but not in itself unusual, or an occasion for a dispute. Even today there are a large number of international boundaries which have not been defined in a boundary agreement; nor does a long-established frontier necessarily require treaty sanction to make it legally valid. Secondly, the Chinese argue that it has become necessary to delimit the India–China frontier through 'joint surveys' and 'consultations'. This seems an innocuous proposal; but a procedure which may be excellent for negotiating minor adjustments of a recognized frontier is hardly relevant when what is at stake is the cession, under duress, of territory about the size of England.

Failing to secure India's compliance, China is endeavouring to seize what she can by force. At the same time, and contrary to her earlier attitude, she has begun to take a hand in the Kashmir dispute by siding with Pakistan, and is apparently preparing for a move into Skkim and Bhutan by questioning India's responsibility for their defence and territorial integrity. This whole policy of violence and intimidation, with its ill-defined objectives, is buttressed by a ramshackle structure of highly questionable arguments, replete with contradictions, disdainful of facts and indifferent to the pledged word.

It is hard to believe that it is only territorial ambition which is driving China on this course. Other explanations are, however, equally unsatisfactory. Retaliation for the hospitality extended by India to the Dalai Lama and other Tibetan refugees? Fear that some day India may allow these mountains to serve as a springboard for an attack on China? Some esoteric calculation deriving from the ideological divisions in the Communist world? Whatever the answer, and whatever the vicissitudes of the totally unnecessary conflict that has been thrust upon India, one thing is already patent and is bound to have a long-term effect: it has spread disillusionment and revulsion amongst a people who would have willingly lived in peace and friendship with their neighbour.

2

Communist Comment on the India–China Dispute*

NOTE OF THE MONTH

The reactions of Communist Parties and allied organizations to the fighting on the Indian–Chinese frontier have been far from monolithic. They range

*Reprinted from The World Today, the monthly journal published by the Royal Institute of International Affairs, London, **18** (December, 1962), 495–497. Reprinted by permission.

from open disapproval of China's policy, emanating, perhaps reluctantly, from the Indian Communist Party, to fervent support from Albania, North Vietnam, and North Korea. Although the Chinese, in their press and speeches, claim that 'all honest and progressive people' in Asia, Africa, and Latin America understand and approve Peking's actions, they bring little supporting evidence.

One Somali weekly, published in Arabic, is quoted as condeming India for 'taking arms from the imperialists', and applauding China's 'reasonable' proposals. But if, as is widely believed, the Chinese have invested substantial sums in certain African newspapers, they do not appear to have yielded high dividends so far. Two Iraqi papers (*Sawt Ahrar* and *Fourteenth July*) have condemned India's refusal to negotiate, while the Iraqi branch of the Afro-Asian solidarity committee went no farther than urging a peaceful settlement.

In Latin America, Ecuadorean Communists have been most outspoken in support for Peking. Their central committee denounced 'Indian aggression'; the U. S. monopolies were working hand in glove with Indian reactionaries to launch an attack on China; the 'submissive attitude' of the Ecuadorean Foreign Ministry in siding with India would 'please the provokers of war and the enemies of freedom'. A spokesman for the 'Association of Democratic Journalists' described Mr Nehru's policy as 'provocative'; U. S. imperialism was 'working through reactionary Indian groups' to split the Asian peoples. The chairman of the Ecuadorean 'writers for peace' association echoed these words, and the chairman of the 'Union of revolutionary youth' announced that body's 'full support' for China.

The Chilean *El Siglo* (a Communist paper) explained that India had rejected the Chinese proposals because, 'in collusion with foreign capital', she aimed to provoke conflict and hatred among the Asian Powers. The 'U. S. extremists' were trying to open a new war front. In Brazil *Liga* deplored Mr Nehru's 'strange type of neutralism'; his rejection of the Chinese proposals was 'shameless', his provocation 'vicious'. This, judging from the Chinese press, appears to be all the comfort that Peking has found in Latin America.

It is in two of China's Communist neighbours that support has been most vocal and the attacks on India most vituperative. India, say the North Vietnamese, is looking for dollars, and Washington wants to stir up strife. The shipment of U. S. arms to India from Thailand showed how necessary it was for the cause of peace to force the United States to withdraw her troops from South-East Asia. 'The Afro-Asian peoples who are united as one in their opposition to imperialist aggression could not but oppose the Indian warlike expansionists.' The Indian authorities were moving from the policy of non-alignment and becoming a tool of U. S. imperialism, out to undermine Asian solidarity. These sentiments are exactly paralleled in statements from North Korea.

The Japanese Communist Party has also come down to China's side,

and has urged India to agree to negotiate on the basis of the Chinese proposals. After a three-day conference it called on the Indian Government
'to abandon its unilateral claims and settle the issue through negotiation'.
India had encroached on Chinese territory and the Chinese counterattack was 'proper and timely'. India, violating the five principles of peaceful
coexistence, was using the border trouble to get more dollars.

The Communists of Ceylon appealed for renewed efforts to settle the
dispute; their party secretary described the Chinese proposals as 'constructive'. The Burmese Communist Party published its approval of 'the consistently peaceful and good-neighbourly policy' pursued by China, whereas
the Indian ruling classes 'oppress the people of their country and collaborate
with the imperialists'. In Singapore the newspaper *Barisan* attributed the
conflict to 'imperialism' in an effort to 'split the Asian peoples'. *Harian
Rakjat*, the Indonesian Communist paper, was 'disappointed with India's
attitude', which was incompatible with the five principles.

The North Vietnamese were the most explicit in linking the present
Communist dilemma to the older dispute represented on the one side by
Albania, China's European ally, and on the other by Yugoslavia, standing
in for Moscow. 'The Indian expansionist group', stated an editorial in the
leading Hanoi paper, was backed by American and British imperialism,
'as well as by all imperialist lackeys, including the Yugoslav revisionists'.
The Albanians themselves write of India's 'criminal acts of provocation',
her 'premeditated, planned, and systematic' aggression. 'The modern
revisionists, renegades to communism' had joined the imperialist chorus.
'The Yugoslav revisionists have degenerated into fawning henchmen and
brokers of the reactionaries throughout the world and of U. S. imperialism.'

In fact, the Yugoslavs have, like the Soviet Communists, handled the
dispute very cautiously. If anything, they implicitly condemned India's
refusal to negotiate, on the ground that hostilities were bound to make the
situation worse; on the other hand, their press has suggested that the Mac-
Mahon line, hitherto respected by both sides, must be the starting-point
of negotiations.

The Chinese press also claims that Peking has the support of the Communist Parties of Canada and Sweden. In London the *Daily Worker* is uneasily
trying to sit on the fence, though leaning very markedly towards Peking.
Two great peoples, anxious for peace, were being pushed by Washington
into war; 'the spirit of John Foster Dulles stalks the passes of the Himalayas.'
China could not renounce territory, nor could India accept encroachments.
The reason why China had not been able to reach agreement with India,
as she had elsewhere, lay in Washington. India was very anxious for U. S.
credits, and between them Washington and Indian big business were out
to 'misrepresent and blacken China' in the eyes of the Indian masses. One
reader suggested that it might be the Chinese who had 'driven the Indians
into the arms of America', and another deplored China's failure to play

the game. If they wanted to regain territory they claimed as their own, why didn't they try someone their own size? What about Hong Kong and Formosa?

Peking does not claim support from any other European Communist Party. It does not mention the Soviet Union in this context. Incidentally, none of those who condemn India for accepting arms from 'imperialism' refer to her willingness to accept arms from the U. S. S. R. as well.

It is interesting to compare the present Communist line-up with the positions taken after the attack on Albania just over a year ago. The change is most marked in Latin America, where previously the Communist Parties had always fallen into line with Moscow. The attitude of the British Communists has also changed, though less decisively; here personal dislikes may well have played their part. For the rest, the alignment appears to have remained steady; most Communist Parties have refrained from expressing an opinion.

3

Testing of Non-alignment*

CECIL V. CRABB, JR.

Prevailing American and neutralist interpretations of the diplomatic consequences of the Himalayan fighting were thus largely antithetical. Whatever else the Sino-Indian crisis has achieved, it had focused attention sharply upon an increasingly grave and recurrent problem in American relations with governments espousing non-alignment, currently representing one-third of the human race. For the predominant response in the United States to the Himalayan conflict demonstrated incontestably that Americans had a most imperfect understanding of the neutralist mentality, of the major connotations of non-alignment as a foreign policy credo, of the forces attracting and holding countries to this doctrine, and—above all—of the extent to which the doctrine accorded both with the achievement of neutralist policy goals and with the objectives of the United States in global affairs. In their crudest, least sophisticated manifestations, American appraisals equated non-alignment variously with deliberate or indeliberate appeasement of communism, diplomatic myopia, or sheer opportunism in foreign relations. Even among more knowledgeable American observers, non-alignment was frequently held to derive chiefly from a persistent lack of

*From The Western Political Quarterly, **17** (September, 1964), 519–522. Reprinted by permission of the University of Utah, copyright owners.

realism in neutralist capitals in assessing the Communist danger, to the operation of a double standard when neutralists assessed Western and Communist diplomatic behavior, or to a Machiavellian indifference in neutralist circles to crucial global issues, manifested by the tendency of non-aligned states to seek the best of both worlds in the acquisition of Western or Communist economic and military assistance. Secretary of State John Foster Dulles' characterization of neutralism as "an obsolete conception, and, except under very exceptional circumstances . . . an immoral and shortsighted conception" had earlier expressed what was to become a dominant national sentiment.

In addition to a deeply ingrained American predisposition against the idea of non-alignment, three other factors prompted Americans to anticipate sweeping changes in Indian, and more broadly, neutralist policies in the wake of Red China's Himalayan expansionism. Long before the Himalayan imbroglio, American skepticism about non-alignment generally had tended to focus upon the government of India, fountainhead of the postwar neutralist movement. Nehru's India (sometimes in company with Tito's regime in Yugoslavia) had displayed a unique capacity for irritating American sensibilities and arousing American ire. On a succession of incidents and issues—ranging from the Kashmir dispute, to the Korean War, to the creation of an Asian defense system (SEATO), to the Tibetan crisis, to the Goa incident—American opinion was, in greater or lesser degree, unfavorable to India. American reaction to the Belgrade Conference of Non-Aligned States in September 1961 provides a case in point. Official and unofficial sources in the United States did not conceal their chagrin over the Belgrade proceedings—for which they tended to allocate major responsibility to Nehru of India. The prevailing American verdict was that this conclave was a psychological victory for the Communist bloc. Following neutralist failure at Belgrade to condemn Moscow's resumption of nuclear testing or to castigate Soviet "colonialism" as forcefully as Western varieties, reports circulated openly that the Kennedy Administration proposed to re-examine the provision of foreign aid to neutralist states. A few weeks later, President Kennedy referred publicly and disparagingly to "so-called neutralists," leaving the unmistakable impression that at least certain (unspecified) varieties of neutralist thought and diplomatic behavior were prejudicial to American diplomatic interests. In the light of such reactions in the United States, an Indian observer reluctantly concluded that (despite some indication to the contrary) in its relations with neutralist countries, the Kennedy Administration sought essentially the same goal as Eisenhower and Dulles: "a closer identification with the West to the point where New Delhi would not be able to escape the entanglements of the cold war." Developments in the interim between the Belgrade Conference and the outbreak of Himalayan fighting late in 1962 indicated clearly that the American attitude toward non-alignment ranged between two predominant reactions: outright hostility and reluctant toleration of the viewpoints and activities of neutralist states in the global arena.

If Americans anticipated sweeping modifications in Indian foreign policy after the Himalayan crisis in part because of their unconcealed desire for such changes, a second influence re-enforced this expectation. This was the initial Indian reaction to Chinese aggression which, along with the responses in other centers of neutralist thought, sustained American hopes. News media in the United States, for example, gave prominent attention to Nehru's confession that India had been "living in an artificial atmosphere of our own creation and we have been shocked out of it. . . ." From the Indian Ambassador in the United States came the opinion that "the effect of the invasion on our external political policies is likely to be . . . profound. The shock of war and the feeling of betrayal . . . has been a traumatic experience which has caused a turmoil in Indian political thought."

Comparable assessments came from other neutralist circles where expressions of shock and outrage at Peking's perfidy alternated with candid expressions of apprehension about the future of non-alignment in the post-Himalayan crisis period. Prominent neutralist figures like the former President of the UN General Assembly, Mongri Slim of Tunisia, sharply castigated Red China and stated that its conduct had given non-aligned countries reason to re-examine their neutralist status. Summarizing reactions on the African scene, one observer believed that proponents of neutralism interpreted the Himalayan affair as a "serious, if not fatal, setback to the whole conception of a neutralist attitude in the Asian–African world." The dominant theme in such reactions was perhaps most poignantly expressed by the Lebanese journal *Al Kifab* which commented editorially: "The policy of non-alignment and peaceful coexistence . . . is facing bitter trial. . . ." Neutralist sources outside India thus tended to admit freely that the concept of non-alignment hung precariously in the balance or, by applying terms like "aggression" and "treachery" to Chinese conduct, seemed implicitly to have accepted estimates long identified with the Western bloc in describing Communist motivations in world affairs. Either way, Americans who followed these developments might have concluded, the concept of neutralism had suffered a blow from which it was not likely to recover.

A third factor explaining the dichotomy between American and neutralist viewpoints with which we are concerned lay in the failure of American observers to realize that the outbreak of Himalayan warfare late in 1962 did not actually pose a *new* problem to Indian policy-makers. The border crisis with Red China had been accelerating for at least five years; and the relationship between India's policy of non-alignment and rising Sino-Indian tension had been under continual evaluation and re-evaluation for many months. On several occasions in this period, Indian officials had reiterated that mounting difficulties with Red China required no fundamental readjustment in the policy of non-alignment. As a critical "time of testing" for

India's policies approached, Nehru asked rhetorically: "Are we to say that when we were safe we waved our flags bravely, but when danger comes our hands shiver, our feet become cold and we want to shelter under somebody's umbrella? Is that how a proud nation behaves? I am surprised at this kind of argument."

To critics who blamed mounting tensions with China upon the policy of non-alignment, Nehru replied late in 1961 that if India had *not* sought peaceful relations with Peking—if instead it had aligned itself diplomatically and militarily with the West—then the anticipated showdown with Peking "would have come in any case, and perhaps sooner and in a worse form." We must reserve fuller appraisal of Nehru's meaning for a later stage. Meanwhile, it is sufficient to emphasize that the continued viability of New Delhi's non-alignment policy had been under continuing study throughout the months preceding the Sino-Indian crisis and that Indian officials had discovered no compelling arguments for rejecting that policy as the guiding principle in its approach to problems of the cold war.

XVII

The Cyprus Issue

1

The Cyprus Dispute*

HARRY J. PSOMIADES

The potentially pernicious character of the Cyprus dispute raises for the United States a dilemma of major proportions. If we side with the Greek Cypriots in their struggle for majority rule on Cyprus, we weaken our alliance with Turkey; if we oppose the Greek Cypriot majority, we impair our ties with Greece and run the risk of turning Cyprus into a Mediterranean Cuba. If we straddle the fence on the Cyprus issue, we incur the enmity of both Greece and Turkey, and open new opportunities for Russian diplomacy in its historical quest for power and influence in the Mediterranean world and beyond.

From the days of the Truman Doctrine, it was clearly understood that Greece and Turkey should be bound together in the same defense establishment, essentially within the larger context of the Atlantic Community, and that they should not allow their differences to obscure the larger issue of Western unity and security. But it is precisely because the mutual interests which bind Greece and Turkey are presently limited to a commitment to common action in the very unlikely event of Soviet aggression that the maintenance of Greek–Turkish solidarity has become increasingly difficult. Another element which critically complicates our security arrangements in the eastern Mediterranean arises from the fact that whereas prior to 1959 there were only three parties to the Cyprus dispute—Britain, Greece, and Turkey—all members of the NATO alliance, after 1959 there have been four parties to the dispute—Britain, Greece, and Turkey, and a non-NATO member, the sovereign Republic of Cyprus. . . .

The clashes that began on December 21, 1963, and culminated in full-scale civil strife, caught the leadership of the two communities completely unprepared. It was popular knowledge that both communities had built

*From Current History, **48** (*May*, *1965*), *269, 275, 305–306. Reprinted by permission of the author and* Current History.

up supplies of arms and had planned for a show of force, but there was no indication that the incidents which sparked the outbreak of violence had official sanction. Indeed, chaos and confusion reigned in Cyprus during the first week of the fighting and Makarios and Küçük tried to stop the clashes by issuing several common appeals for order and reason.

The deteriorating situation in Cyprus also caught the United States and the protecting powers completely unprepared. On December 23, in an effort to avert the impending explosion, the acting British high commissioner and the United States ambassador called on President Makarios and expressed the grave concern of their governments at the turn of events in Cyprus. They appealed for moderation from both communities. The Greek government also urged Makarios to use his influence to end the inter-communal bloodshed, and the Turkish government appealed to the Turkish Cypriots to assist responsible administrators with calm and dignity.

It was too late. Relations between the two communities had been allowed to decline to a point of no return. Makarios would not alter his intention to have the constitution amended and Küçük would not agree to a compromise formula. Moreover, the fighting had created further hatred and suspicion and revealed the clandestine military and political preparations of the two communities. Control over the impatient extremist elements and the irregular armed bands within the communities was also completely lacking.

The renewal of the Cyprus conflict brought Greece and Turkey once again to the brink of war. The joint plea for peace issued by the protecting powers on December 23 was followed the next day by rumors of a Turkish invasion.

On March 4, the Security Council unanimously recommended the establishment of a United Nations peace-keeping force and the appointment of a mediator "for the purpose of promoting a peaceful solution and an agreed settlement of the problem confronting Cyprus, in accordance with the Charter of the United Nations, bearing in mind the well-being of the people of Cyprus as a whole and the preservation of international peace and security." The Force was to be stationed in Cyprus for three months, and all costs were to be met by the states providing contingents and by the government of Cyprus and by voluntary contributions.

On March 13, after another Greek Cypriot complaint of Turkish preparations to invade Cyprus, the Security Council adopted a resolution calling upon all members to comply with its resolution of March 4 and to refrain from any action which might worsen the situation. The Security Council subsequently extended the term of the peace-keeping force.

The most dangerous point in the Cyprus dispute came in early August, 1964. As Greek Cypriots pressed their attacks on Turkish Cypriot positions in northwest Cyprus, jet planes from Turkey retaliated by strafing Greek Cypriot forces.

The Turkish government maintained that the air strikes were provoked by Greek Cypriot attacks, and that the Greek Cypriot military buildup on Cyprus was the real cause of tension. The Greek Cypriots maintained that a military buildup was necessary to counter the real possibility of a Turkish invasion. The representative of Greece declared that unless the Turkish attacks ended immediately, Greece would assist Cyprus "by all the military means available to it." On August 11, the Security Council adopted a resolution sponsored by Britain and the United States calling for an immediate cease-fire and for full cooperation of all concerned in the restoration of peace.

All parties agree that the present constitutional framework is no longer viable. Greece and the Greek Cypriots, with the exception of the Greek Cypriot Communists, favor the right of self-determination for a unified Cyprus, which is another way of saying that they favor the union of the island with Greece. Nonetheless, they are apparently willing to give up the idea of *Enosis* and would be content with the existence of two Hellenic states —Greece and Cyprus.

Turkey and the Turkish Cypriots favor partition, with the right of self-determination for each community. They are willing, however, to support the idea of a federal state provided that the Turkish Cypriots are moved into cantons of their own.

Britain, it appears, would favor a solution agreeable to Greece and Turkey which would allow her to maintain her bases on the island. However, Britain would probably not insist on holding her bases if relinquishing her sovereignty over them would lead to a permanent Greek–Turkish settlement. Britain and the United States would go along with almost any plan agreeable to Greece and Turkey.

The main concern of the United States is to prevent war between her two NATO allies. To this end we have on several occasions held the Turks back from invading Cyprus and have pressured the Greek government to exert its influence on Makarios. We recognize the Zurich and London agreements as valid but agree that they should be renegotiated.

The United States has suggested a compromise solution (the Acheson Plan), based on *Enosis* and compensation to Turkey. Under the plan, a military base on Cyprus would be ceded to Turkey along with one of the smaller Greek islands, and the Turkish community would be given two cantons under its own administration. But the Greek Cypriots have rejected this plan, as well as any other solution that would call for the mass exchange of Greeks and Turks on Cyprus and allow for a Turkish military presence on the island.

The Soviet Union began by favoring the right of self-determination for a unified Cyprus but since December, 1964, has changed her position in favor of an independent Federal Republic of Cyprus. Russia is, in fact, determined to play it both ways with the Greeks and Turks. But in the last resort the Russians are bound to support the side that opposes *Enosis*. The union of the island with Greece or even a portion of the island with Greece would drive AKEL, or the Communist party of Cyprus, underground. The Communist party is outlawed in Greece and in Turkey.

The Arabs favor a Greek Cyprus with the elimination of the British bases and the absence of NATO bases on the island. These bases, the Arabs fear, would be used by the West in the event of an Arab–Israeli war or as a means to intimidate the Arab world. They have not forgotten the Suez invasion of 1956 which was launched from Cyprus.

In spite of all his efforts, the United Nations mediator, Galo Plaza, on his way through London on March 2, 1964, said that an "agreed solution" was impossible at the moment. The opposing sides will have to consider discussing ideas they have automatically rejected in the past if Cyprus is to return to a state of peace and security. A new and critical phase of the Cyprus question is probably about to begin.

2

The Cyprus Conflict*

T. W. ADAMS AND A. J. COTTRELL

On the present role of Cyprus, one commentator on military strategy has observed: "Malta is no longer officially regarded as a suitable point of departure for mobile operations by the [British] Army and Air Force and from that standpoint the chief United Kingdom base in the Mediterranean is now Cyprus." In truth, the Cyprus base serves primarily to protect the Middle Eastern oil supplies which are so vital to Britain's industry and financial solvency.

Gradual attrition of other British bases in the Middle East has given Cyprus its vital position. The strong base of Aden at the tip of the Arabian Peninsula, which Britain has held since 1839, is too remote to be considered the key strategic nexus of the Middle East. If anything, Aden serves to emphasize that Britain's primary interest is still centered in the protection of the Persian Gulf. Libya at one time could have provided a possible staging area, but the Libyan government has declared that it will not renew the present U. S. lease after 1971, nor the British base agreement scheduled to expire in 1973. When Great Britain was virtually forced by Egypt to withdraw from the Suez Canal Zone in 1954, the military establish-

*From Orbis, **8** (September, 1964), 77–79, 81–83. Reprinted by permission of the Foreign Policy Research Institute, University of Pennsylvania.

ment for the defense of Suez had to be shifted elsewhere. The loss of Suez, coupled with the surrender of Palestine in 1948, has therefore made Cyprus the primary point of British power in the Mediterranean.

Even the presence of NATO bases in Turkey cannot minimize the crucial location of Cyprus. Perennial concern for adequate defense measures against her traditional Russian enemy inspired Turkey to depart from her World War II neutrality and join NATO. This paved the way for the construction of a number of important Western bases on the Soviet periphery. However, the Turks, possibly responding to Soviet admonitions, have thought it unwise to give complete control of the bases to the United States or other NATO members. This again emphasizes the necessity of having sovereign British bases in Cyprus. Although these areas on Cyprus do not fill the logistical needs of an ideal defense base, largely because of a shortage of fresh water and the lack of a good harbor, there is seemingly no substitute for Cyprus within the geographical boundaries of the Middle East.

For the West in general, the unique location of Cyprus vis-à-vis Europe, the USSR, the Levant and Africa makes it a topic of renewed salience in present international relations. In 1964 the Soviet Union opened up a Moscow–Nicosia air route which is only 1,500 miles in length and provides ready access to a number of potential targets within a 1,000-mile radius of the island. The vital importance of Cyprus is also based on its geographical proximity to the Dardanelles and to Turkey's main southern port of Iskenderum, terminal of the oil pipeline from Iraq. Beyond its military significance, it is of considerable psychological value as a symbol of the West's power and concern in the eastern Mediterranean. After the evacuation of Suez, Britain cannot afford to beat another hasty retreat in the Middle East from Cyprus; nor would such an act serve to bolster the prestige of the West. Indeed today the British bases on Cyprus fulfill the purpose for which they were originally intended when Britain occupied the island in 1878, namely, protecting Turkey against Russia. . . .

The British declaration of intent that the Sovereign Base Areas would be used for no other than military purposes was possibly the key element which caused Archbishop Makarios to drop his demand for civil administration of the areas in 1959. His fears that the gestation of colonialism would always be represented in the bases were not eliminated by virtue of the declaration, but they were sufficiently allayed for as long as it took to sign the final treaties. Makarios explained his rationale for the retreat from his original stand in this way:

> We had to accept the offers made to us and to sacrifice some of our rights *temporarily* [italics supplied] instead of sticking to all our demands and obtaining nothing. That was because we wanted to get rid of the colonial shackles. I am happy that we have gained our freedom . . . we oppose colonialism and support freedom everywhere.

The allusion which the President of the Republic of Cyprus made to the temporary sacrifice of rights has disturbed many Western statesmen. It appears that Makarios looks upon the intricate Cyprus solution more as a *modus vivendi* than a finality, and such an attitude in a person of his stature is indeed a threat to the future of the British bases. An Egyptian journalist managed to draw this statement from the Archbishop during an interview in Cairo:

> We have made it clear to Britain that if the bases were ever used in a manner that prejudiced our relations with other countries or were equipped with atomic weapons, we would rise in revolt once more. Personally, I believe that all bases, particularly atomic bases, should be put under the supervision of the United Nations. The world seeks peace and does not want to live in the shadow of fear. At any rate, it was not Cyprus that gave the bases to the British. Those bases must return to Cyprus one day.

Perhaps it is not surprising that the opinion of Makarios is close to that of the Kremlin. The Soviets feel that the bases "constitute a continuation of British imperialism in the Eastern Mediterranean, which can transform Cyprus into a nuclear base for NATO."

The viewpoints expressed above hardly augur well for the perpetuation of the status quo in Cyprus. The statements seem consistent with the attitudes of neutrals as well as the Soviets toward Western bases in general. Makarios, however, is too shrewd a politician and diplomat to attack the Cyprus treaties blatantly. While he would like to place restrictions on the uses the British make of their sovereign base areas, he knows full well that there is no legal or economic way by which he can justify such action. Yet even the spoken desire of the Archbishop–President to place the British bases "one day" under Cypriot sovereignty creates a disruptive potential. Makarios represents, or better yet embodies, the two most powerful institutions in the Republic: the Presidency, the repository of the political power of the Cypriot nation, and the Church (Ethnarchy), the repository of the national conscience of the majority of the Cypriot people. Together these two institutions constitute a force that could be suppressed only by military power—an alternative the British would rather not face, either now or at some future date.

The British base issue was temporarily overshadowed by the rampant communal violence of early 1964. However, the presence of British troops trying to keep the peace outside the sovereign enclaves has indeed suited the communist propaganda line against the bases. *The Economist* recently speculated on what the present state of affairs in Cyprus could portend:

> In this atmosphere, two nightmarish possibilities will have to be faced by the British. The first is that the next target for Greek Cypriot wrath will be the British bases, which hitherto have not been a factor in the dispute. . . . The second possibility, hideous to contemplate, is that Greek security forces, now being trained to fight against the Turks, will be used against the British. . . . One incident could spark off an inferno and put the clock back ten years.

Cyprus is a critical issue for NATO and the entire Free World. Hatred and bloodshed between the Greek and Turkish Cypriots probably has passed the point of no return. Hence, there can hardly be a political settlement patterned after the terms of the Zurich–London Agreements.

Current proposals for resolving the Cyprus conflict have bypassed the terms of the Republic's Constitution and treaties. Whether it be *enosis*, partition, plebiscite, resettlement, unitary state, federation or confederation, the Zurich–London Agreements are not applicable. The requisite tolerance, good will and common sense have already vanished.

The overriding criterion for any permanent solution in Cyprus should be its effect on the Western alliance. In the interests of NATO and world peace, Greece and Turkey again must abandon their extreme views on Cyprus, as they did in 1959, and cooperate to bring about a new, workable *détente*. The present conditions only enhance the influence of the indigenous communists and the Soviet Union in this eastern Mediterranean trouble spot. How to prevent large-scale communist intervention, while simultaneously negotiating a peaceful Cyprus settlement and avoiding the mistakes and emotions of the past, is the challenge which still confronts Western statecraft.

3

Who Is Stirring Up Trouble Over Cyprus ?*

V. KONDRATYEV

. . . The Cyprus crisis, as is known, arose and is developing in a dangerous direction entirely as a result of the policy of the North Atlantic bloc, the leaders of which imposed the enslaving Zurich–London agreements on the Cypriote people in 1959. Two big British military bases have been maintained on the territory of Cyprus, constituting a source of alarm not only for the Cypriotes but also for other peoples, especially the peoples of the Arab East.

As a result of unceasing NATO interference in the domestic affairs of Cyprus and of repeated threats of intervention, the Cyprus question became a subject of discussion in the U. N. Security Council. On March 4 and 13 the Security Council unanimously adopted decisions confirming the sover-

*From The Current Digest of the Soviet Press, **16** (August 5, 1964), 17–18. Translation from The Current Digest of the Soviet Press, published weekly at Columbia University by the Joint Committee on Slavic Studies, appointed by the American Council of Learned Societies and the Social Science Research Council. Copyright © 1964, the Joint Committee on Slavic Studies. Reprinted by permission.*

eignty and territorial integrity of the Republic of Cyprus. On June 20 the Security Council again called on members of NATO to refrain from any aggressive actions against Cyprus and to respect the latter's sovereignty.

In the spirit of the U. N. resolutions, the government of Cyprus, headed by President Makarios, took several measures to normalize the situation in the country, create an atmosphere of mutual understanding between the communities and strengthen security and defense capacity. Some representatives of NATO apparently did not like the fact that the Cyprus conflict had begun to dissolve. While voting publicly for the Security Council resolutions, they are trying secretly to thwart their fulfillment and to impose, by crude pressure, a settlement of the Cyprus question that would be in the interests of the aggressive bloc. Violations of the territorial waters and of the air space of Cyprus, encouragement of the subversive activity of the extremist elements in the country, methods of political blackmail—these are the means. The NATO military pressure on Cyprus in early July was a diversion aimed at thwarting the Security Council resolutions on peaceful settlement of the Cyprus crisis. . . .

Revealing the intentions of the enemies of Cyprus, the British newspaper Daily Telegraph recently declared without embarrassment that, as a result of a "wholesale" deal between NATO, Greece and Turkey, Cyprus would "voluntarily" surrender its sovereignty to others and become a NATO base, while dissatisfied Cypriotes could leave their homeland for a "financial compensation." There is no need to say that the authors of this plan, which arose within NATO, count on simpletons. It is clear to everybody that the basis of this plan is an imperialist plot to strangle the Republic of Cyprus and make the entire island a nuclear and missile base of the North Atlantic bloc against the peoples of Africa and the Near and Middle East. To all these imperialist intrigues, the Cypriote people reply with a resolute "No!" . . .

The Soviet government has repeatedly emphasized that in our epoch nobody can ignore the rights of a sovereign state that is an equal member of the U. N. merely because this state is small and because its armed forces are not strong. The West cannot disregard this obvious truth, because this truth is now being defended by ever broader strata of the world public and by more and more peace-loving states and peoples.

That is why Washington politicians had to give up a frontal attack on the independence and sovereignty of Cyprus. The government of Greece announced its refusal to follow the path onto which it is being zealously pushed by American diplomacy. Greek Prime Minister Papandreou declared on June 30 that Cyprus is a sovereign state and that Greece and Turkey have no right to decide its fate. These are just words, and one cannot but agree with them. "There is only one way to seek a settlement," he declared, "and this is the Security Council, the U. N. mediator and the United Nations."

It is impossible not to note, however, that NATO circles have not abandoned searches for new variants of a "private" solution of the Cyprus problem.

Judging from press reports, ideas are being hatched about a tripartite conference of the "guarantor" countries (again behind the back of the Republic of Cyprus!) and broadening the powers of the U. N. troops on Cyprus with a view to their assuming the functions of the legitimate government of Cyprus. Finally, it is impossible to ignore the fact that the U. S. A. is trying, with the help of NATO emissaries, to push aside U. N. mediator Tuomioja, who was appointed in accordance with the Security Council decisions, and that the persons proposed for this role of "pacifier" are such zealous drummers of the "cold war" as former Secretary of State Acheson, one of the founders of NATO, and the not unknown Gen. Norstad. The Cypriotes indignantly reject the attempts of the U. S. A. and Britain to assume control over the activity of the U. N. mediator and to bind Cyprus to NATO through bilateral or trilateral negotiations in Geneva.

It is impossible not to be alarmed also by the statements heard in Ankara concerning a "military solution" of the Cyprus question. Such statements are increasing tension on Cyprus and in the Eastern Mediterranean and helping to fan nationalist passions, and consequently they play into the hands of the NATO "strategists" who, as N. S. Khrushchev, the head of the Soviet government, emphasized, have only one aim, to make Cyprus their "unsinkable aircraft carrier."

NATO circles continue to hope for a split in the unity of the Cypriote people and for a weakening of their struggle for their rights. In this connection it is impossible to ignore the press reports about the appearance on Cyprus of General Grivas, with whom reactionary circles link their designs that are far from the true interests of the republic. . . .

XVIII

The United Nations Financial Crisis

1

The U.N. Charter, the Purse, and the Peace*

ABRAM CHAYES

The central fact of that plight is that the United Nations is burdened with a deficit of $125 million, mainly representing expenses incurred in earlier peacekeeping operations. But bankruptcy is not the problem, at least not yet. Most of these obligations run to member states in the form of accounts payable by the United Nations. These states thus far have not pressed their claims to the point of precipitating an immediate cash crisis.

The problem centers on the U. N. effort to collect its accounts receivable —primarily the assessments for peacekeeping in the Congo and the Middle East that have been levied on members in accordance with the regular fiscal procedures of the United Nations. A number of members still fail or refuse to pay these assessments, some of them, including the Soviet bloc and France, on grounds of principle.

The chief formal sanction for enforcing payment of financial obligations is article 19 of the United Nations Charter. It provides that a member more than 2 years in arrears in its contributions to the organization "shall have no vote in the General Assembly." Eighteen members, including the Soviet Union and several Communist countries, have overpassed the limit. Unless they make payments against their arrearages to bring them under that ceiling before the next General Assembly session, the charter sanction will apply.

Thus far the Soviet Union has maintained that it will not pay. So a constitutional battle of major dimensions may erupt in the next meeting of the Assembly. The shadow of that coming battle is what "sicklied o'er" the action of the Security Council on Cyprus. And as the Cyprus case foreshadows, what is ultimately at stake is not the U. N.'s ability to pay its bills but its ability to do its job. . . .

*Address delivered before the International Law Association at Montreal, Que., Canada, on May 15, 1964 (Press release 233). Excerpts.

244

There was an obvious way to resolve these issues. The charter provides in article 96:

> The General Assembly or the Security Council may request the International Court of Justice to give an advisory opinion on any legal question.

Pursuant to this article, the General Assembly put to the Court the question whether the expenses authorized in the assessment resolutions covering the U. N. operations in the Congo and Middle East were "expenses of the Organization" within the meaning of article 17 of the charter so that, by virtue of article 17, they "shall be borne by the members as apportioned by the General Assembly."

Twenty countries made written submissions in the case—more than in any other World Court proceeding. They represented many parts of the globe and all major legal systems. Nine pleaded orally before the Court. The United Kingdom and Ireland were represented by their Attorneys General; Australia by its Solicitor General; Canada, the Netherlands, Italy, Norway, and the United States sent the Legal Advisers of their respective Foreign Offices. The U. S. S. R. appeared in the Court for oral argument for the first time in history, represented by the distinguished lawyer, Mr. Grigory Tunkin, former Chairman of the International Law Commission and Director of the Juridical-Treaty Department of the Soviet Ministry of Foreign Affairs.

On July 20, 1962, the Court, by a vote of 9 to 5, gave an affirmative answer to the question presented. It held that the expenditures authorized in the financing resolutions were indeed "expenses of the Organization" within the meaning of article 17, with the consequence that assessment of those expenses by the General Assembly was binding on the members.

The opinion of the Court in a case like *Certain Expenses of the United Nations* is characterized as "advisory." It cannot be "binding" in a juridical sense because there are no parties before the Court upon whom a judgment could operate. But for all other purposes, I would suppose that the opinion of the Court in an advisory case properly before it is an authoritative statement of the law. In the *U. N. Expenses* case all the conditions were met. The case was before the Court at the request of the General Assembly under article 96 of the charter. The issue was a narrowly defined question of legal liability, fully matured and ripe for adjudication on concrete facts comprehensively developed before the tribunal.

But whether or not the opinion by its own force establishes the law, the General Assembly has removed any possible question about the status of the Court's pronouncement. The opinion was transmitted to the General Assembly at its 17th session. After consideration and debate, both in appropriate committee and on the floor, the Assembly, by a vote of 76 to 17, with 8 abstentions, declared that it "*Accepts* the opinion of the International Court of Justice on the question submitted to it." Thus this phase of the case came to a close. . . .

What then is the Soviet position? The U. S. S. R. has argued that the

General Assembly must decide by vote to apply the article 19 sanction and that the decision must be taken by a two-thirds majority. This is said to follow from paragraph 2 of article 18, which provides that among the "important questions" requiring a two-thirds majority of the Assembly are "the suspension of the rights and privileges of membership" and the "expulsion of Members." But this passage refers to articles 5 and 6, not to article 19. Indeed it tracks the language of the former articles, specifying the circumstances under which a member "may be suspended from the exercise of the rights and privileges of membership" (article 5) or "may be expelled from the Organization" (article 6), in each case "by the General Assembly upon the recommendation of the Security Council." In contrast to these articles, with their use of the permissive "may" and their express requirement of action, the self-executing statement of article 19—that a member in the requisite arrears "shall have no vote in the General Assembly"—leaves no room for the operation of article 18. There is no decision to be taken, whether by a vote of two-thirds or by simple majority.

A second contention is that a General Assembly decision is required before the sanction of article 19 can be applied in order to confirm the existence of the required 2 years' arrearages. The arrearages, however, are calculated arithmetically. The process is governed by accounting procedures laid down in the organization's Financial Regulations and Rules, already unanimously approved by the Assembly. Their execution is no more than a ministerial act to be performed by the Secretariat. And so it has uniformly been regarded in the practice not only of the U. N. itself but of the specialized agencies as well. The General Assembly cannot by its vote alter the rules of addition and subtraction. And it does not take a two-thirds majority of the nations of the world to check the Secretary-General's arithmetic.

Of course, if a member believes that a mistake has been made on the U. N.'s books, it may seek an Assembly decision on the matter. A member may assert, for example, that it is entitled to a setoff of its unpaid claims against the organization for goods or services, and the Assembly might have to decide this question. What the General Assembly may *not* lawfully decide is whether a member 2 years in arrears shall, absent conditions beyond its control, have a vote in the Assembly. That question was decided by the charter.

The U. S. S. R. also argues that arrears on assessments for the peacekeeping operations in the Congo and the Middle East should not be included in calculating article 19 arrears. These operations, it says, were illegally authorized; peace and security, including the financial aspects, are the sole province of the Security Council. The Congo and UNEF operations, involving General Assembly action, were thus *ultra vires*, and the Assembly was without power to make assessments binding on the members to defray those costs.

The argument has a number of lacunae.

First, the Congo force, accounting for much the greater part of the outstanding arrearages, *was* initiated by Security Council resolution. And the Soviet Union, which now complains that the operation was a camouflage for a colonialist adventure, was recorded as voting in favor not only on the first Security Council resolution of July 14, 1960, but, except for one abstention, on each of the subsequent Council actions dealing with the operation from 1960 to date.

Second, the Soviet argument overlooks express charter language. Article 11 authorizes the Assembly to "discuss any questions relating to the maintenance of international peace and security brought before it by any Member . . . and . . . make recommendations with regard to any such questions. . . ." And article 17 has been held more than once by the International Court to vest plenary authority in the Assembly to assess members for the payment of any and all expenses lawfully incurred by the organization.

Third, and perhaps most important in an assemblage of lawyers, this very contention was made to the International Court of Justice in the *U. N. Expenses* case and was explicitly rejected by it. After fully considering the contention, ably and forcefully argued to the Court by Mr. Tunkin, the Court held that article 11, paragraph 2, "in its first sentence empowers the General Assembly, by means of recommendations to States or to the Security Council, or to both, to organize peacekeeping operations, at the request, or with the consent, of the States concerned." As I said a moment ago, this decision was overwhelmingly accepted by the General Assembly.

States may, of course, continue to persist in their refusal to pay. But they cannot ask us to accept that their refusal is based on legal grounds. When they argue for a result different from that pronounced by the Court, they assert the right to be judges in their own case. . . .

2

Dangerous Venture*

N. KURDYUMOV

It is not the first that enemies of the Soviet Union have undertaken a provocational racket, trying to cast a shadow on the prestige of the Soviet state, the friend and defender of oppressed peoples, the standard-bearer

*From The Current Digest of the Soviet Press, **16** (September 23, 1964), 24–25. Translation from The Current Digest of the Soviet Press, published weekly at Columbia University by the Joint Committee on Slavic Studies, appointed by the American Council of Learned Societies and the Social Science Research Council. Copyright © 1964, the Joint Committee on Slavic Studies. Reprinted by permission.*

of the struggle for peace, progress and friendship among peoples. But it is the first time that such provocations toward the Soviet Union have been encountered on the East River, in the United Nations. It is no secret, after all, that the policy of the U. S. S. R., which from the high rostrum of the U. N. constantly unmasks the aggressive designs and unseemly actions of colonialists of all stripes, sticks in the imperialists' throats. We would like to dwell on one such provocational operation of American diplomacy in the United Nations.

The U. S. State Department raised a fuss as early as this spring about the "financial bankruptcy" of the U. N. and, under cover of this uproar, dragged out the so-called question of the financial "arrears" of the Soviet Union to the United Nations. In doing so, United States officials, from the State Department head, Dean Rusk, to Adlai Stevenson, the U. S. representative in the U. N., have gone so far in their speeches as to allow themselves to voice thinly veiled threats against the Soviet Union, one of the founders of the United Nations. Rusk and Stevenson alike, for instance, have publicly declared that if the U. S. S. R. does not pay its "accumulated arrears," sanctions should be applied against it, including depriving it of voting rights in the General Assembly on the basis of Art. 19 of the Charter of the international organization.

What can be said about this unseemly fuss? Facts demonstrate the absurdity of the assertions about the Soviet Union's "arrears" to the U. N. As is well known, the U. S. S. R. has invariably fulfilled and is fulfilling the financial obligations imposed upon it by the U. N. Charter. Moreover, the Soviet Union makes the second largest contribution to the regular budget of the United Nations. Consequently, there can be no question of any "financial arrears" of the Soviet Union.

As for the hopes of State Department officials of compelling the Soviet Union to participate in defraying the expenses of the colonialists' adventures in the Middle East and the Congo, first of all, they have clearly lost all sense of reality, and secondly, this has nothing whatsoever to do with Art. 19 of the Charter, which concerns U. N. members' liabilities for the regular U. N. budget, not for special expenses.

Responsibility for the consequences of aggression, including financial consequences—and this is the principled position of the Soviet Union—must be borne by those, and only those, who committed the aggressive acts. As for the Congo, for example, where the imperialist powers used the name and the banner of the U. N. as a cover for their colonialist policy, the perpetrators of the venture, i.e., the actual debtors, are well known.

Any other approach would be an obvious mockery of common sense, tantamount to patting the aggressors on the head and encouraging them to new adventures.

In connection with the provocational maneuvers of the United States in the U. N., another subject must be mentioned. Washington officials should have understood long ago that it is not recommended that anyone, including the U. S. A., speak to the Soviet Union in the language of open or veiled threats. Threats will bring nothing but disappointment to the authors of a "tough" approach to the U. S. S. R.

In this connection, it is necessary to recall the statement of the Soviet government, which as early as March of this year issued a warning to those who had undertaken an unfriendly campaign against the U. S. S. R. "If anyone," this statement pointed out, "has any illusions that the Soviet Union might reconsider its refusal to pay the expenses of U. N. operations in the Middle East and in the Congo and that it can be forced to do so through pressure, the Soviet government can only warn that not only are such suppositions completely groundless but any attempt to act upon them may compel us to reconsider anew our attitude toward the activity of the United Nations."

The initiators of the maneuver against the Soviet Union in the U. N. well know, of course, how absurd and provocational the campaign they have undertaken is. They have nothing with which to oppose the principled position of the U. S. S. R. regarding the actions of the colonialists and the consequences of these actions. Nevertheless, they deliberately continue to whip up tensions over the United Nations. The American Congress too has been enlisted in the fanning of the provocational racket.

The other day the House of Representatives appealed to President Johnson to instruct the American delegation to the U. N. "to exert every effort" toward depriving the Soviet Union of voting rights in the General Assembly. Reporting on the special resolution in this score passed by the House of Representatives, the Washington Star emphasized that is was passed "with the active support of the White House and the State Department." On Aug. 20 a similar resolution was adopted by the American Senate.

The Congressional resolution means nothing other than Washington's intention to continue deliberately whipping up tensions. Of course, such a policy, especially in an election year, may appeal to all kinds of American "madmen," but as far as the U. N. is concerned, it may cause severe damage to the international organization and the cause of international cooperation, not to mention the fact that it would destroy the first shoots of trust between countries, which have appeared in connection with the signing of the Moscow treaty partially banning nuclear tests.

It must be said that the world public correctly perceives a dangerous game in the actions of the United States. Thus, the British newspaper Guardian believes that the provocation being undertaken in essence poses the question of whether the U. N. is to be or not to be. The Swedish newspaper Stockholms-Tidningen takes a similar position. This newspaper notes in an editorial that the move planned by Washington would have "serious consequences for the further activity of the U. N. and for the international situation as whole. No one can be unconcerned with the Soviet Union's leaving the U. N."

This is a sober judgment. At any rate, one thing is clear: The realization of the plans of American diplomacy for the U. N. would be a blow, first of all, at the states of Asia, Africa and Latin America. They would find themselves in the international organization face to face with the imperialists, who have long been striving for a free hand.

The peoples of Asia, Africa and Latin America well know and remember that the Soviet Union, as a genuine friend and loyal defender of small nations, has always barred the way to the aggressive designs of today's colonialists. The whole history of the United Nations from the day of its founding is moving testimony to the indefatigable struggle of the U. S. S. R. for the independent national emergence of the peoples of Asia, Africa and Latin America, as well as to its unfailing help and support to them when in trouble. That is why the colonialists gnash their teeth when they recall the resolute support the U. S. S. R. rendered to Egypt at the time of the tripartite aggression of 1956, to the people of Indonesia in the liberation of West Irian, to the people of Lebanon at the time of the American intervention, etc.

The U. S. S. R. is not only the initiator of the historic General Assembly declaration on granting independence to colonial countries and peoples. It is an active fighter for its realization, supporting the long-suffering people of Angola and all African peoples who are against the racist regime in the South African Republic. The Soviet Union is a true friend of the heroic people of Cyprus and South Vietnam, it is on the side of all peoples who are for freedom, independence and progress. Therefore, one can understand the profound concern of the small countries for the fate of the U. N. in connection with the unworthy campaign launched by the United States in the United Nations against the Soviet Union.

In the light of this incessant malicious campaign in the United Nations, the question legitimately arises: What do the leaders of the United States actually want to accomplish? Do they want to preserve the U. N., or are their assurances about a desire for international cooperation empty phrases? If, however, anyone in the American capital still has any illusions that the Soviet Union can be intimidated, that one can "exert pressure" on the Soviet Union, only one thing can be said to them: You are mistaken, gentlemen!

3

Crisis at the UN*

PHILIP GEYELIN

"We will begin with a minute of prayer or meditation," replied a veteran United Nations diplomat the other day, when asked what to expect from the

*From The Wall Street Journal, *LXXI* (*November 25, 1964*), *1* ff. Reprinted by permission.

annual UN General Assembly scheduled to get under way here next Tuesday. And then what?

"And then," he continued, "anybody who claims to know what's going to happen is talking through his hat."

It's not a joke to grim-faced UN delegates. Before this year's Assembly can even begin to tackle disarmament or Communist Chinese membership or racial discrimination or any of the scores of new or old issues overloading its agenda, it must first deal with the annual election of an Assembly president. And barring a break in what appears to be a tight deadlock over UN finances and voting rights, the first call of the roll will plunge the world organization into a conflict so bitter and profound and complex that there could quite conceivably be no real Assembly session at all. Ultimately the upshot might be no real UN, at least in anything like its present form.

BIG AS CUBAN CRISIS?

"This is going to be the biggest Cold War confrontation since the Cuban missile crisis," says one U. S. mission member, who fears the coming clash could well "chill East–West relations all across the board." At the very least, it promises to confound U. S. dealings, not only with Red nations, but with France and a host of African and Asian countries, to an extent all out of proportion to the relatively minor, mundane controversy over money that's causing all the fuss.

The immediate issue is whether Russia should be deprived of Assembly voting privileges for failure to pay its share of special assessments levied to finance UN "peace-keeping" missions in the Congo and the Middle East. UN rules specify that any member in arrears by more than its total assessments during the most recent two-year stretch must lose its vote; by the U. S. reading of the rules, the Russians will be nearly $6 million beyond this limit when the Assembly convenes.

But Russia argues the Congo and Mideast operations were illegal, either in the way they were launched or conducted, and that, besides, the UN voter-eligibility rule applies only to delinquency on regular budget assessments not special "peace-keeping" costs. The U. S. hotly disagrees and has an International Court opinion to reinforce its arguments—an opinion which the Assembly itself endorsed earlier this year.

Moreover, the U. S. contends that freedom for members to "pick and choose" which UN expenses they will pay would make a fiscal shambles of the organization. So this country is all ready to challenge the first attempted Russian vote, and is equally ready to do the same to France and perhaps some other members whose arrearages will creep past the two-year limit at the beginning of next year.

CONCILIATION EFFORTS

The U. S. has hoped the threat of a bruising showdown would induce the Soviets to soften their stand, rather than risk being blamed for forcing the

the issue to the breaking point—and even at this late date the chance for a last-minute, face-saving compromise cannot be ruled out. Frantic conciliation efforts are under way, sparked by Afro-Asian members who fear their favorite forum might be shattered by a big power clash. Some have suggested, with scant success so far, that a special "rescue" fund be established; the Russians and other delinquents would "voluntarily" contribute to it, and UN bookkeepers, as one official puts it, would "quietly transfer the proceeds to the account of the Congo and Mideast operations in the dead of night."

Another formula, perhaps illustrating the air of desperation hereabouts, would have the new Assembly president elected by acclamation, obviating the need for a vote. Since the next order of business would be general debate, which could drag on for several weeks, this would merely postpone a showdown to give more time for the conciliators to work.

Potentially far more significant is a U. S. proposal which points up a larger, longer-range aspect of the whole affair. If those in arrears will simply settle up old debts, American representatives are now arguing, the U. S. will be ready to consider some quite radical new formulas for future financing of United Nations activities; these formulas would move significantly toward the Russian–French position that the great powers ought not to be obliged, by a majority vote of far lesser nations, to pay for UN activities of which they do not approve.

TEMPERS ARE SHORT

The trouble is that time is short, and so are tempers. The Afro-Asians are riled by thinly veiled U. S. suggestions that America's hefty financial support for the world organization may shrink drastically unless the Soviets pay up. U. S. diplomats, in turn, deplore the double standard of the "nonaligned" countries which accuse this country of "blackmail," while taking a much milder view of the Soviets' threats to boycott UN activities unless they get their way.

More important, perhaps, the issue of past arrearages has been built into a matter of such high principle and reduced to such stark either-or terms that the chief antagonists have left themselves little room for maneuver. "Normally you can at least conceive the rough outlines of acceptable compromise," says one long-time veteran of UN diplomacy. "This time you just can't put a finger on the elements that could give everybody a graceful way out."

The UN, of course, has proved itself a master at postponing or papering over seemingly hopeless internal conflicts. "Without a near-miracle, we will open in crisis," says one top assistant to UN Secretary General U Thant, "but we subsist on near-miracles." Almost all that authorities are asking for at this point, however, is that a showdown can somehow be postponed. For if there is no compromise in sight by the time of Tuesday's opening prayer, the UN will almost immediately be careening out of control toward the worst internal conflict in its turbulent 19-year history. Where it would then end up is anybody's guess; almost none of the alternatives gives much cause for U. S. cheer.

"We can't even win by winning if this thing does come down to a vote," groans one top U. S. diplomat, who feels confident the U. S. could attract enough Assembly support, despite an anticipated wave of abstentions, to strip the Russians of their Assembly voting rights. The question troubling him and others, however, is just what this would do for the UN as a peace-keeping instrument.

Nobody is quite sure what the Russians would do. But the guessing is that they might well stay in the Assembly, as a vocal, if nonvoting, source of disruption, and would almost certainly remain in their seat in the power-ful, policy-making 11-nation Security Council, where their "permanent member" status (together with the U. S., Britain, France and Nationalist China) entitles them to a veto as well as a vote. The Security Council is not touched by the argument over arrearages. "The Soviets can't have forgotten that the last time they left the Security Council it enabled us to approve the UN role in the Korean War," says one Western diplomat.

However the Russians played it, maximum obstruction would still almost surely be their aim. Moreover, to the extent that the loss of their Assembly vote diminished Soviet participation, it would rob the UN of much of its appeal to the smaller nations, whose weight in the world body derives at least in part from the opportunity it affords them to play the two great powers off against each other. With a semiactive and embittered Russia, the UN would seem more of a Western-dominated club and less of a repre-sentative world forum.

Finally, U. S. officials reason, a Russia blackballed from Assembly voting at U. S. demand would hardly be in a mood to pursue further disarmament measures or expand accommodation with the West, both of which are well-established U. S. policy aims.

Should Russia win a showdown on voting rights, the U. S. might be in an even more awkward spot. Even if U. S. diplomats found a way to swallow the question of high principle, the U. S. Congress, which must appropriate the American contribution to the world organization, might not. Just a few months ago the House and the Senate unanimously voted a resolution exhorting the Administration to make "every effort" to strip the Soviets of their vote should they refuse to pay their UN debts.

Already, pending settlement of the arrearages fight, the U. S. has pointedly declined to come forth with the annual pledges it usually makes to cover 40% of voluntary economic aid and technical assistance schemes operated by the UN at a total cost of more than $150 million annually. The U. S. contributes even more lavishly to peace-keeping operations, which can be costly indeed; in four years the Congo bill topped $400 million, with the

U. S. paying the bulk of it, and the Soviet share, as yet unpaid, a mere $40 million.

Any Congressional heel-dragging on UN appropriations could cripple the organization's activities. Yet if the U. S. did not register its disapproval in this way, a General Assembly decision upholding the Russian side of the argument might well encourage other delinquents, leaving the U. S. to bear an even larger proportion of UN costs. "If the Assembly doesn't use the voting privilege, which is the only weapon it has to enforce its power to assess its members, it's an invitation to financial anarchy," says one U. S. official.

XIX

China's Atomic Bomb

1

On Red China's Nuclear Testing*

DEAN RUSK

Mr. Herman: Mr. Secretary, you have said that you expected this development in Red China. The President today said that it was cranked into their plans and expectations ahead of time. How did you expect it? What plans were made? How did you figure it in?

Secretary Rusk: Well, we have known for some years that the Chinese were working on a nuclear weapons system and that there would come a point when they would detonate their first device. More recently we have had very clear indication and evidence that this could come at any time. On September 29 I announced that we expected it at any time.

But for the past several years we have assumed that they would be going down this trail. They made it very clear that they were not going to sign a nuclear test ban treaty but they would try to equip themselves with nuclear weapons. And so we have taken this fully into account in our own defense plans with respect to nuclear weapons, both in production and in such things as deployment, so that there is no possibility whatever that there is any lack of security for the free world in the Pacific Ocean area as a result of the detonation of this first device by Peiping.

Q. The President said today that he thought that this was not an incident leading immediately or in the foreseeable future to war. Do you think, however, that it might lead to increased militancy by the Chinese Communists? Might they be tougher now?

A. Well, Peiping has been preaching the doctrine of militancy and has been pressing in action—for example, their pressures in Southeast Asia. They have pressed it to a point where their attitude has created very serious differences, even within the Communist world, and of course it has created opposition and resistance on the part of the free world. I think we will just

On October 16, 1964, Secretary of State Dean Rusk was interviewed by George Herman on a CBS television program, "The Communist Explosion." This is the transcript of the interview.

have to wait and see what effect this will have on their attitude. If they continue their course of pressure and militancy, then of course some very serious events are ahead.

On the other hand, when they see one of these things go off, even the most primitive type of device, and realize the scale on which nuclear war can occur if they invite such a war, this may also inject into their own thinking some caution that might not otherwise have been there.

Q. You think that they were not fully aware before of the consequences of nuclear war?

A. Well, I think they have undoubtedly, as an intellectual matter, known—recognized what this destructive power can be. But I think also that those who see it firsthand might have a little different appreciation of what it might mean, particularly when what they have seen can be multiplied by the thousands and thousands of times if they invite the results of their aggression.

Q. How about those who see it at first hand across the border—China's neighbors? Do you think that this might weaken their determination to resist Communist expansion?

A. No, I don't think so. I think that these developing, sophisticated neighbors in that part of the world have a full understanding of the gap in power that exists in the world today. They have shown their determination to take care of their own independence and freedom, and I don't believe that this is going to have any influence in undermining their determination to be independent. This is not something that will change that fundamental attitude.

Q. Might there be some pressures from our allies in the Far East for accommodation of the Chinese Communists' call for a summit meeting?

A. Well, this call for a summit meeting is a smokerscreen. They used that at the time that they refused to sign the nuclear test ban treaty. But we know from many signs that they are not seriously interested in disarmament. They have made it very clear, for example, if I can quote them, that disarmament can be realized only after imperialism and capitalism and all systems of exploitation have been eliminated.

Now, we have had some exchanges of words in the Warsaw talks that have been going on over the last 8 years on the subject of disarmament. No interest. No interest. This is an attempt on their part to pretend to be interested in the serious measures of disarmament in order to meet the concerns of almost the entire rest of the world, particularly the Afro-Asian world, about their coming into the nuclear testing program and contaminating the atmosphere.

I don't attach any serious significance to this call for a summit meeting for such a purpose. If they are interested in disarmament, then the first step from their point of view is to stop this course of aggression and pressure and militancy. And if they would make it quite clear that they are prepared to leave their neighbors alone, then maybe steps in the reduction of the arms race can be seriously taken up.

Q. Do you have any particular steps as sort of prerequisite steps?

A. No. These equestions of disarmament have been explored in great detail in Geneva, and they will be explored there further. But as far as China is concerned, we see no indication that they are seriously interested.

Q. I just wanted to ask you, if I could, sir, in light of the last 24 hours, do you see any connection in the headlines between—in the 24 hours—the fall of Khrushchev and the Chinese explosion?

A. No. I don't think so. I think some of the stresses and strains within the Communist world, including the Moscow–Peiping dispute, might have had something to do with the situation in Moscow. But I don't think that it has had, on its side, anything to do with the explosion of the device in Peiping.

Q. Thank you.

2

China's " Manhattan Project "*

CHALMERS JOHNSON

Fifteen years ago China had no more than ten nuclear physicists, all of them educated abroad, and it had not a single acceleration device for atomic experiments. China was the very model of a "backward nation," having, in addition, been ravaged by continuous warfare since 1937. Now China has paid her initiation fee into the world's most exclusive club. The explosion on Oct. 16 of her first atomic device will have a great psychological impact on the other underdeveloped nations of the world, and this in turn will help China to break out of her American-and-Russian-imposed isolation. It will also do much to bolster the national pride of the Chinese people, who have sacrificed so much to building their nation.

Although it is unquestionably true that China will not have an intercontinental delivery system for several years and that one explosion does not indicate a stockpile of bombs, the Chinese test is not without military

*From The New York Times Magazine, *October 25, 1964, pp. 23* ff. Copyright © 1964 by the New York Times Company. Reprinted by permission.

significance. To date, the American presence in East Asia has rested on a base of expedient policies and historical accidents largely constructed by John Foster Dulles. This base has its weak places, one of the chief being Taiwan. While the Chinese are not likely to initiate an atomic attack on Taiwan, there is little doubt they would use their bomb if they were attacked by Chiang Kai-shek's forces. Thus, Chinese possession of an A-bomb points up the futility of the Nationalists' policy of a "mainland counterattack," which in turn is the *raison d'etre* for Chiang's enormous army.

The Chinese bomb also poses new problems for Japan. The Japanese Government may decide to revise its views on rearming (at present forbiddent by Article 9 of the Constitution), while at the same time it may want to curtail the role played by the United States in its security system.

Finally, Chinese possession of an A-bomb makes even more unrealistic a United Nations and an international disarmament organization without China as a member.

These and similar considerations ought to persuade Americans to think again about the meaning of the Chinese revolution and the tempo of change in the Orient. It is easy to say, as every American political and military figure does when talking about China's atomic progress, that a Chinese bomb means nothing in terms of the present balance of power. It probably doesn't. The Chinese have shown time and time again that they appreciate the fact that the American "paper tiger" has nuclear teeth. The Chinese are therefore not likely to risk atomic war with the United States unless they are pushed to an extreme. What is harder for American leaders to admit is that China is succeeding in its drive to become, not just another "transitional society," but a Great Power.

Today not only is industrialization the *sine qua non* of a truly "sovereign" state, but a new and unmistakable mark of greatness has been added: possession of the atomic bomb. As long as the Chinese leaders believed that they could not build a bomb and were depending on the Soviet Union's nuclear capacity, they denigrated the bomb as a "paper tiger"—something with which the imperialists tried to frighten the world. Then the Soviet Union proved to be a weak reed, a nation both proud and jealous of its own Great Power status, and it refused to supply China with nuclear weapons technology and a sample bomb. This refusal became one of the basic issues in the Sino-Soviet dispute, further exacerbated by Russia's accession to the nuclear test-ban treaty. It was as much to challenge Russia as to be secure against the West that China launched its own bomb project.

In China today we can distinguish two kinds of science: developmental science and political science—and the latter is not a branch of what Americans call the social sciences. Developmental science is concerned with geology, chemical engineering, agronomy, water conservancy, hydro- and thermal-electric power development and all the other branches of technical knowledge useful for turning a preindustrial agricultural region into an economically viable nation-state. Political science is concerned with atomic energy, rocketry and all the other items of national jewelry.

In neither field have the Communist Chinese made important contributions to theoretical or basic scientific knowledge. However, they have been relatively successful in applying the general fund of scientific knowledge to concrete Chinese problems, and both types of science are considered indispensable to China's "national" development.

There have been three distinct phases to China's nuclear research effort. The first, from 1949 to 1954, was a period of educational and scientific reorganization at home and of negotiation abroad with the U. S. S. R. for technical assistance. The second period, 1955-59, saw the high tide of Sino-Soviet atomic cooperation; the main accomplishments were the training of experts and the peaceful application of atomic energy. Only during the third phase, from 1960 to the present, did China actually launch her bomb program.

Two Chinese have emerged as the leaders of the bomb project. One of these is Chien San-chiang, a former researcher in nuclear physics at the Curie Institute in France and now director of the Institute of Atomic Energy of the Chinese Academy of Sciences.

The other man is Wang Kan-chang, a nuclear physicist of the highest qualifications and reputation. Born in 1907 in Kiangsu Province, Wang, the son of a famous physician, graduated first in his class from Tsinghua University in 1929. In 1934, he received his Ph.D. from the University of Berlin where he studied nuclear physics with the renowned Dr. Lise Meitner. Wang taught physics in China at National Chekiang University throughout the nineteen-forties, retreating to the southwest after the Japanese invasion and carrying on his research with limited equipment and under primitive conditions.

After the war, his colleagues voted to send him to the University of California at Berkeley, where he was a research associate in physics in 1947-48. Under the Communists, Wang became one of China's privileged scientific researchers, and during the late fifties, he worked in Russia with the Italian–British nuclear scientist Bruno Pontecorvo, who had defected from the West in 1950.

According to Hong Kong reports, Wang is the man actually in charge of the Chinese bomb project. Chien and Wang together lead an élite force of about 1,000 qualified scientists and technicians—approximately the same number required to build the first United States atomic bomb.

The earliest information available on Chinese atomic research dates from 1949. After the Communist victory the new Government established the Chinese Academy of Sciences under the Cabinet. This academy brought together all of China's scientific personnel and organized them into insti-

tutes of chemistry, geology, metallurgy, physics and so forth. In February
and March, 1953, just before the death of Stalin, Chien San-chiang, then
head of the new Physics Research Institute, led an Academy of Sciences
mission to the U. S. S. R. He and 25 colleagues visited the Russian atomic
center near Lake Baikal and undoubtedy lobbied for a Chinese role in the
Communist bloc's nuclear-energy research activities.

Meanwhile, Russian bomb production had already involved China if
not yet China's scientists. Contrary to estimates by certain Western analysts,
scattered deposits of uranium and thorium have been discovered in China,
particularly in Sinkiang, Inner-Mongolia and Heilungkiang. On March
27, 1950, supplementary to the Sino-Soviet treaty of alliance, Russia and
China set up a "Joint Non-Ferrous and Rare Metals Corporation" near
Urumchi, the capital of the Chinese province that is officially known as
the Sinkiang–Uighur Autonomous Region.

The U. S. S. R. constructed a mill near Urumchi for processing uranium
ore, which was then sent to Russia for refining; it also began an extremely
extensive geological survey of Sinkiang to search for uranium deposits. The
Chinese probably participated in these activities, but the Soviet Union
appears to have dominated them.

One man who was reported in 1951 to be working first in Urumchi and
then at an atomic energy center at Ining in western Sinkiang, was the former
nuclear physicist at the British Harwell experimental atomic laboratory,
Pontecorvo. His name will appear again in the record of Chinese atomic
development.

During 1954, China negotiated strenuously with the new Soviet leader-
ship in order to revise certain of the harsh terms Stalin had imposed on
China in the basic treaties of 1950. One of the changes included in the
Sino-Soviet treaty of October, 1954, was the return to China of the joint
Russian–Chinese companies, including the Sinkiang uranium works.
The Chinese and the Russians also signed their first scientific and technical
cooperation agreement. After Jan. 1, 1955, China continued to supply
Russia with uranium, but she now received something in return.

On Jan. 17, 1955, the Soviet Council of Ministers announced that it was
providing experimental reactors and cyclotrons for China, Poland, Czechoslovakia, Rumania and East Germany; and on April 29, China and Russia
signed the actual agreement whereby Russia gave China a reactor, a
cyclotron, fissionable materials and technical experts. On Feb. 15, 1956,
the Chinese announced that they had begun to erect the experimental
machines at the Atomic Energy Research Institute on the outskirts of Peking.

Two years later, in June, 1958, a Soviet-supplied heavy-water type
nuclear reactor—the largest in Asia—went into operation. It has an efficiency of 7,000 to 10,000 kilowatts and was originally utilized for research
and for the production of isotopes needed in medical science. Today it is
undoubtedly producing plutonium-239.

At about the same time, the Russians and the Chinese completed their first cyclotron, capable of accelerating atomic particles up to 25,000,000 electron volts. In the presence of Dmitri V. Yefremov, deputy director of the Soviet Bureau for the Utilization of Atomic Energy, Marshal Nieh Jung-chen dedicated the new equipment with these words: "We are going to build more atomic piles and cyclotrons. I want to warn the United States that atomic weapons cannot be monopolized by it alone."

By this time the Soviet Union had already decided not to supply China with atomic *weapons* technology, but there is no indication that the Chinese immediately converted their Russian gifts to military operations.

The Chinese did indeed build more atomic equipment. In November, 1960, at the Moscow conference of Communist parties, Chairman Liu Shao-chi said, "Communist China has four atomic reactors in operation. These reactors can be used for war as well as for peaceful purposes."

The figure of four reactors has been corroborated by Chinese Nationalist intelligence, which further indicates that a fifth reactor probably has been constructed since 1960. One experimental reactor is located in the Physics Department of Nankai University in Tientsin, but it does not appear to figure in the bomb project. Another is certainly at Urumchi, and the others are probably at Wuhan, Changchun and Sian. The original Soviet reactor in Peking remains the largest.

In addition to reactors and cyclotrons, however, China needed more scientists. The Soviet Union's contribution to this phase of China's atomic development was ultimately more important than its providing of equipment. On March 26, 1956, Communist China, Russia, Albania, Bulgaria, Hungary, East Germany, North Korea, Poland, Rumania and Czechoslovakia signed an agreement "to establish a joint nuclear research institute." On July 1 of that same year the institute opened its doors at Dubna, north of Moscow. The Dubna Institute has played a key role in training Chinese nuclear manpower.

The shares of expenses at Dubna borne by the various Communist states reveal their respective influence there. Russia pays 47.25 per cent of the costs, China 20 per cent, East Germany and Poland 6.75 per cent each, and Rumania and Czechoslovakia 5.75 per cent each. Eleven Chinese scientists began work at Dubna at its inception, including Wang Kan-chang and Chao Chung-yao—the latter a nuclear physicist at the California Institute of Technology until he returned to China in 1951. Many more Chinese were trained there between 1956 and 1960.

The names of two Dubna scientists stand out—Bruno Pontecorvo and Wang Kan-chang. In December, 1957, Dr. Pontecorvo was named director of the nuclear problems laboratory. In January, 1959, Dr. Wang became deputy director of the entire Dubna Institute. During 1958, Pontecorvo and Wang also headed a team of scientists that discovered certain new atomic particles using a powerful synchrotron at the Institute. In 1963, Pontecorvo received the Lenin Prize for his part in this research.

At the same time that China was acquiring Russian atomic equipment and sending its top scientists to Dubna, it reorganized its own nuclear research administration. In May, 1957, the old Physics Institute was replaced by a new and streamlined Institute of Atomic Energy. Chien San-chiang remained in charge of this new I. A. E., and the following nuclear physicists were named vice directors: Peng Huan-wu, Wang Kan-chang, Chao Chung-yao, Cheng Lin and Chang Ching-hua. The institute has control over all aspects of nuclear physics, radiological chemistry, radiobiology, cosmic ray experiments, reactors and accelerators in Communist China.

The only major flaw in this smoothly running operation was that the Soviet Union didn't like it. The growing difference of opinion between Khrushchev and Mao inevitably affected their nuclear relations.

Sobered by the Taiwan Straits crisis of 1958, the Soviet Union—in the words of the Chinese—"unilaterally tore up the 'Agreement on New Technology for National Defense'—concluded between China and the Soviet Union on Oct. 15, 1957—and refused to provide China with a sample of an atomic bomb and technical data concerning its manufacture."

This "tearing up" took place on June 20, 1959, and it provoked a furious debate within the Chinese Politburo. A number of Chinese generals, who were afraid to cut China's ties with Russia, finally lost out to the party leaders, who decided to go it alone. As Chinese Foreign Minister Chen Yi told a group of Japanese newsmen last October, China intended to acquire nuclear power "because without it China would remain a second- or third-class country."

In July and August, 1960, Russia abruptly withdrew all its technicians from China, throwing much of the Chinese economy into chaos. The Sino-Soviet dispute developed at an accelerating pace. At the November, 1960, Moscow meeting of the world's Communist parties, China circulated a paper saying that China's reactors had been built for peaceful purposes but that they would have to be turned to weapons development if China's security needs could not be met otherwise.

Also, at the same time that Soviet scientists were returning home, a less heralded reverse exodus was occurring. According to a Hong Kong report of November, 1960, Dr. Wang Kan-chang had arrived in Peking in February of that year. Simultaneously, rumors spread that the regime was beginning to construct atomic bombs at 20 different locations in Sinkiang. The man in charge was said to be the same Dr. Wang Kan-chang.

Japanese Government specialists estimate that the Peking reactor has a production capacity of from 2.5 to 3 kilograms of plutonium-239 per year. More than ten kilograms are required to trigger a nuclear device. Therefore, given China's four or five reactors, her plutonium requirements should have been met in 1963 or early 1964.

Another major ingredient of one of the various kinds of atomic bombs is uranium-235, which must be removed from uranium ore by a very expensive process known as "gaseous diffusion." In 1960, the Germans discovered an easy gaseous centrifuge method for separating U-235, but at the request of the United States they kept the technique classified. Gaseous diffusion also requires large amounts of electric power and precision equipment, such as that used by the United States at Oak Ridge, Tenn.

Most observers had concluded that internal production of U-235 was as yet beyond Chinese capabilities. However, in 1963 or earlier, U. S. intelligence derived from satellites and Nationalist-flown U-2's seems to have located a gaseous diffusion plant near Lanchow in Sinkiang's neighboring province, Kansu. This plant, powered from the Liu Chia Hsia dam across the gorges of the Yellow River, about 60 kilometers from Lanchow, began supplying hydro-electric power in 1960. Undoubtedly it was detailed information concerning these and other projects that lay behind Secretary of State Dean Rusk's prediction, on Sept. 29, of Red China's imminent entry into the Nuclear Club.

Whatever else this first atomic test signifies, it constitutes a major historical landmark in the course of events that began a century ago when China was defeated by Britain in the Opium War. The Chinese dragon indeed has awakened. If we in America are to perpetuate the test-ban treaty, which many people hold to be a living memorial to President John F. Kennedy, we must find some way to bring China under its provisions.

In so doing, we shall have to bear in mind the fact that the French are also scheduled to detonate a thermonuclear device in the Pacific during 1965. Nationalism and nuclear weapons appear to be umbilically connected, and attempts to limit the spread of such weapons must not become a devotion to treating the symptoms rather than the disease.

3

Political Effect of the Chinese Bomb*

ARTHUR S. LALL

The explosion of the Chinese atomic bomb is the most significant military event in Asia since 1904, when Japan defeated imperial Russia. This statement is made with full consideration of other climacteric events such as the defeat of the French in Southeast Asia, or the near military retreat of the Netherlands from West Irian. The Chinese test on October 15, 1964, already has produced more political reverberations than any of these events

*"Political Effect of the Chinese Bomb," by Arthur S. Lall, is reprinted with permission from the February, 1965, issue of the Bulletin of the Atomic Scientists (**21**, 21–24). Copyright © 1965 by the Educational Foundation for Nuclear Science.

including that of 1904. It has given notice to the world that the successors
of the Middle Kingdom are in a position to exercise their hegemony in
Southeast Asia.

Of course, the world has greatly changed since the time of the dynastic
hegemonies of China. Most Asian countries are "equal" members of a
world body—the United Nations—and some have significant ideas concerning their own influence in parts of Southeast Asia. The officials of the
"new" Middle Kingdom cannot call the representatives of distant lands
barbarians. Although China is proud and imbued with a sense of her own
destiny, she is the first major Asian country to adopt a totally foreign
ideology as the basis of her own political, economic, social, and international
postures. Finally, and no less important, there are other countries today
considerably more powerful than China. Indeed, even in Asia, if Japan
were to defy the constitutional interdiction she herself has placed upon
the development of nuclear weapons, she could outstrip China in their
development. Some of these facts must be known to thoughtful Chinese,
and indeed, all of these facts and others which would caution prudence
must be quite apparent to the leaders of China.

But China does not have to be very overt in order to assert a degree of
hegemony in Southeast Asia. Let us consider some of the developments
which have taken place since the Chinese explosion. Cambodia congratu-
lated China, as did North Vietnam. Laos expressed concern—not condemnation. And what of the countries with western orientation? The most
significant response came from Bangkok, where the prime minister, General
Thanom Kittikachorn, preferred to "wait and see" before commenting.
Malaysian Deputy Prime Minister Abdul Razak said that the Chinese
nuclear test had "strengthened the Communist position" in Southeast Asia.
Premier Lee Kuan Yew said in Singapore that "this is the first time that
an Asian power has emerged as a member of the nuclear club. We do not
know whether it will be a force of peace or of world war. We will have
to wait and see."

These six countries expressed sentiments ranging from admiration and
respect to concern. We must remember that they are all China's neighbors
and are bound to feel that they must live in peace with her. How will these
neighbors—relatively small countries—come to terms with a nuclear China?
I suggest that the most likely course is the adoption of some form of neutralism. In the past, before the United Nations and before the rapid means
of communication with other power centers in the world, I would have
anticipated that these countries would have fallen more directly under
Chinese hegemony. However, in the present world, it is more likely that
developments in Southeast Asia will be toward nonalignment. In such a
situation China will not be able to describe her neighbors as running dogs
of imperialism and reactionary capitalism.

While China has not always treated nonaligned countries exactly gently, it is a mistake to place too much emphasis on China's relations with India. India, and more importantly India under Nehru, was a rival. There is reason to believe that Nehru thought India a military match for China, and in other areas—such as the pace and general direction of economic development—he believed that India was superior to China. There is evidence that many countries in Asia, as well as outside Asia, thought that Nehru was perhaps right. Furthermore, Nehru was not in a negotiating mood with China over the border dispute for several years before the Chinese took military action in the autumn of 1962. To the Chinese, Nehru appeared downright truculent. I know this is so because of what Marshal Chen-yi, China's vice prime minister and foreign minister, said to me during the negotiations at the Conference on the Question of Laos (1961-62). For these reasons, the case of India must be set apart. A more typical case, or so it must seem to the neighboring small countries, is the treatment accorded to nonaligned Burma by China. This treatment might be described as generally benign and could serve as a pattern for other states of Southeast Asia in their relations with a nuclear China.

I would suggest that such a development need not be regarded as a retrograde step in the peaceful evolution of an independent Southeast Asia. To begin with, we should consider the historic past which, by and large, has been one of greater acceptance of Chinese primacy than would be compatible with a nonaligned or even a neutralist status—the latter is regarded by the nonaligned world as a more supine position and one which most reject for themselves. Second, I would draw attention to the fact that the only country of Southeast Asia, except South Vietnam, which has been critical of the Chinese nuclear explosion is the relatively well-established non-aligned country, Indonesia. On October 21, 1964, Dr. Subandrio, deputy prime minister, foreign minister, and (at the time he made the statement) acting president of the Indonesian Republic, stated: "Nuclear detonations are unwelcome because they pollute water and air." Subandrio also cold-shouldered the Chinese proposal for a world conference on nuclear disarmament—in doing so exhibited a degree of sophistication which has distinguished the nonaligned more than the aligned in recent years. Would one expect the United Arab Republic, for example, to favor the obviously stacked Chinese proposal? The answer is flatly negative. This feel for the realities results from the need of the nonaligned to assess the factors of a given situation and come to a position. This, it must be remembered, is not an imperative for the aligned countries—they can paraphrase the position of the side in the tepid war to which they adhere. The point is that the nonaligned are more likely to exercise a robust judgment in international affairs than those of the less developed countries which have lined themselves up one way or the other. This is a fundamental point which even so able a man as John Foster Dulles missed.

Third, what development is likely to be the least divisive in Southeast

Asia, and threrefore the most likely to result in unified and strong positions? The answer, on any reasonable reckoning, is nonalignment. It would be artificial in the extreme to expect the whole of Southeast Asia to espouse the Western cause (in the international political sense) and likewise to expect them to adopt the Chinese brand of Marxism or whatever it is that the Chinese imagine they are adopting. The remaining course is that of some brand of nonalignment—and I use the words "some brand of" deliberately. The strength of nonalignment is that unlike other contemporary postures it does not require of its adherents (in itself perhaps too strong a word to describe the very loose relationship between the countries of nonaligned persuasion) a rigid uniformity of position. These countries will stand together mainly in any situation that evokes the memory of colonialism—in the context of Southeast Asia, in any situation that creates the apprehension of hegemony, overlordship, or any of the forms of international influence which are loosely called neocolonialism. I would suggest that the Chinese bomb encourages such a development, and it is not one which any one should regret. The West should indeed regard such a development as one to which it had contributed, because it is largely the Western world which has developed the present world idiom, its main manifestation being the United Nations and its agencies. In a world of equal sovereign states the old ideas of hegemony, though they die hard, are much more difficult to realize than they were in the past when they were more successfully nurtured. . . .

In reality this attitude highlights one of the fundamental difficulties in the way of implementing proposals to prohibit the dissemination of nuclear weapons. What the Asian and African countries are saying, among other things, is that it is a good thing that they, too, now have the bomb in a world where others have it. Is this not basically de Gaulle's attitude, and is it not an attitude which is spreading in Western Europe and results in calls for an independent deterrent and an end to dependence on other nuclear powers? In short, in a nuclear age there are two courses which make sense to most people, including, it seems, most statesmen. These two courses are either equal (in kind but not necessarily in quantity) armament or equal (and preferably total) disarmament. If this basic truth were really accepted by the two nuclear giants, they would realize that their nibbling proposals to prevent the proliferation of nuclear weapons are impotent palliatives; that the only way to handle the enormous problem of the arms race is to get on with the job of disarmament itself. Dr. Subandrio was right when he added—to those same remarks to which we have referred—that one advantage of the Chinese bomb may be that it could make the nuclear club speed up the process of disarmament.

What is more likely is that the nuclear club will do no such thing because the Chinese explosion is not in fact the beginning of a nuclear weapons race among another group of powers. The present members of the nuclear club will be mildly annoyed at the Chinese developments but will become relaxed when, in another year or so, it seems that other countries are not following the example of China. The nuclear powers probably will eventually deal with China in an appropriate disarmament forum. But in a few years there will be another crop of nuclear powers appearing, and then perhaps the original members of the club will get down to the business of disarmament. Till then it looks as if, the Chinese explosion notwithstanding, we are in for a period of flirting with ideas on the periphery of disarmament —and hoping for the best. In short, I do not see the Chinese bomb having any great effect on the handling of the question of disarmament. I have implied in the above remarks that India, Japan, Sweden, and other countries are not going to denounce the partial test ban on the plea that the Chinese explosion has materially changed the circumstances of their security. This, I believe, will be the case unless the Chinese, carried away by their new achievement, do something spectacular, such as another attack on India, or explosion of such a comprehensive series of tests that it is clear that they mean to develop a first-class nuclear arsenal. Since the Chinese have already once attacked India they might do so again, though I would tend to believe that their new bomb is not by itself going to be the cause of such an attack. If an attack comes, it will be the result of the touchiness of two "great" and sensitive countries again building up to a border situation which becomes so precarious that it only resettles after a few local conflicts. Unfortunately, both sides are still capable of contributing to such steps, though India is more cautious today than she was in 1960-62. To conclude this particular point, I would judge that if the Chinese were to launch another armed attack against India, internal developments in India would result almost certainly in a new group coming into power, which would probably go ahead with the development of nuclear weapons.

The present government of India will almost certainly not develop nuclear weapons, even though the interesting person who is now prime minister has said that he is not as innocent as he looks. Indeed, on November 24, 1964, after having given the impression that India would definitely keep to the road of strictly peaceful development of the atom, Shastri told the Indian Parliament that all the implications of the manufacture of the bomb must be carefully weighed. He added that it is necessary that the country know the technique of the manufacture of the bomb. Two days later the executive committee of the Congress Parliamentary Party endorsed these views. There the matter is likely to rest unless some startling international development of direct concern to India occurs. These remarks must not be taken to mean that there is not a considerable body of opinion in India which is strongly in favor of going ahead with the manufacture of the bomb. Of course there is. Indeed, there are those who feel very sore that India did not get the jump on China, and who are convinced that India could by now have had a nice little cluster of bombs. But these people as yet are not in control of the situation.

So far as Japan is concerned, I think there is little doubt that in various

ways the country must be making sure, here and now, that it is in a position
to manufacture nuclear weapons with all speed. For Japan the decisive
factor will probably be the rate at which China develops her own arsenal.
The faster and the more comprehensive China's development, the surer
it is that Japan will find a way around her present interdiction and plunge
into the nuclear bomb business. So far as Sweden and Switzerland are
concerned, their future course will be more affected by European developments than those in Sinkiang. I would say that the Chinese bomb is not
relevant to them. But it is difficult to imagine the Australian government
not taking stock of its capacities in the nuclear field with a view to manufacture if the situation becomes increasingly menacing. In the Middle East
the Chinese bomb will have some effect—if only that it will give certain
countries another excuse to accelerate their plans and redouble their
efforts. But, for various reasons, these developments will remain highly
secret—so much so that we will not know when at least two countries in
that area actually have started building up their nuclear arsenals. Perhaps
they already have; after all, test explosions are not absolutely necessary
any longer.

In conclusion, as a result of the bomb it is going to be much more
difficult to keep China out of the United Nations. But the way things are
going, a vote in the General Assembly in favor of the Peking government
will be a Pyrrhic victory. The Peking government is not going to come to
New York, it seems, unless the Taiwanese can be extracted from the Security
Council. This is going to be more difficult to achieve. Similarly, though
there might be a vote in favor of China being brought into the Eighteen
Nation Disarmament Conference, she will not participate until the Taiwanese quit the Security Council. Finally, the Chinese bomb will increase
pressures for negotiations on the issues in Southeast Asia which plague the
world. If we do get such negotiations, rather than an intensification of the
military conflict, this could be the most constructive effect of the Chinese
bomb.

XX
The War in Vietnam

1

Aggression from the North*

U. S. DEPARTMENT OF STATE

The Third Lao Dong Party Congress in Hanoi in September 1960 set forth two tasks for its members: "to carry out the socialist revolution in North Vietnam" and "to liberate South Vietnam."

The resolutions of the congress described the effort to destroy the legal Government in South Vietnam as follows: "The revolution in the South is a protracted, hard, and complex process of struggle, combining many forms of struggle of great activity and flexibility, ranging from lower to higher, and taking as its basis the building, consolidation, and development of the revolutionary power of the masses."

At the September meeting the Communist leaders in the North called for formation of "a broad national united front." Three months later Hanoi announced creation of the "Front for Liberation of the South." This is the organization that Communist propaganda now credits with guiding the forces of subversion in the South; it is pictured as an organization established and run by the people in the South themselves. At the 1960 Lao Dong Party Congress the tone was different. Then, even before the front existed, the Communist leaders were issuing orders for the group that was being organized behind the scenes in Hanoi. "This front must carry out . . ."— this is the way Hanoi and the Communist Party addressed the "Liberation Front" even before its founding.

The Liberation Front is Hanoi's creation; it is neither independent nor Southern, and what it seeks is not liberation but subjugation of the South.

In his address to the Third Lao Dong Party Congress, party and government leader Ho Chi Minh spoke of the necessity "to step up the Socialist

<hr/>

*From Aggression from the North—The Record of North Vietnam's Campaign to Conquer South Vietnam [*U. S. White Paper*], *February 28, 1965. Excerpts. See also* The New York Times, *February 28, 1965, pp. 30* ff.

revolution in the North and, at the same time, to step up the national democratic people's revolution in the South."

The year before, writing for *Red Flag*, the Communist Party newspaper of Belgium, Ho had said much the same thing:

> We are building socialism in Vietnam, but we are building it in only one part of the country, while in the other part we still have to *direct and bring to a close* the middle-class democratic and anti-imperialist *revolution*.

In the same vein, the commander-in-chief of the North Vietnamese armed forces, Vo Nguyen Giap, spoke at the 1960 Party Congress of the need to "*step up* the national democratic people's *revolution in the South*." Earlier in the year, writing for the Communist Party journal *Hoc Tap* in Hanoi, General Giap described the North as "*The revolutionary base for the whole country*."

Le Duan, a member of the Politburo and first secretary of the Lao Dong Party, was even more explicit when he talked at the Party Congress about the struggle in the South and the party's role. After noting the difficulties involved in overthrowing the existing order in South Vietnam, Le Duan said:

> Hence the Southern people's revolutionary struggle will be long, drawn out, and arduous. It is not a simple process but a complicated one, combining many varied forms of struggle—from elementary to advanced, *legal and illegal* —and based on the building, consolidation, and development of the revolutionary force of the masses. In this process, *we must constantly intensify our solidarity and the organization* and education *of the people of the South.* . . .

Another high official of the Hanoi regime, Truong Chinh, writing in the party organ *Hoc Tap* in April 1961, expressed confidence in the success of the struggle to remove the legal Government in South Vietnam because: "North Vietnam is being rapidly consolidated and strengthened, is *providing good support to the South Vietnamese revolution, and is serving as a strong base for the struggle for national reunification*."

He outlined the steps by which the Communists expect to achieve control over all Vietnam as follows: The "Liberation Front" would destroy the present Government in the South; a "Coalition Government" would be established; this Government would agree with the North Vietnamese Government in Hanoi regarding national reunification "under one form or another." It takes little imagination to understand the form that is intended.

"Thus," wrote Truong Chinh, "though *South Vietnam will be liberated by nonpeaceful means*, the party policy of achieving peaceful national reunification is still correct."

The official government radio in Hanoi is used both overtly and covertly to support the Vietcong effort in South Vietnam. Captured agents have testified that the broadcasts are used sometimes to send instructions in veiled code to Vietcong representatives in the South.

Hoc Tap stated frankly in March 1963: "They [the authorities in South Vietnam] are well aware that *North Vietnam is the firm base for the Southern revolution* and the point on which it leans, and that *our party* is the steady and experienced vanguard unit of the working class and people and *is the brain and factor that decides all victories of the revolution.*"

In April 1964 the Central Committee of the Lao Dong Party issued a directive to all party echelons. It stated:

> When the forces of the enemy and the plots of the enemy are considered, it is realized that *the cadres, party members, and people in North Vietnam must . . . increase their sense of responsibility in regard to the South Vietnam revolution by giving positive and practical support to South Vietnam in every field.*

Nguyen Chi Thanh, writing in a Hanoi newspaper in May 1963, underlined the importance of the role of the North Vietnamese army in Hanoi's plans to unify Vietnam under Communist rule:

> Our party set forth two strategic tasks to be carried out at the same time: to transform and build socialism in the North and to struggle to unify the country. *Our army is an instrument of the class struggle in carrying out these two strategic tasks.*

The VC military and political apparatus in South Vietnam is an extension of an elaborate military and political structure in North Vietnam which directs and supplies it with the tools for conquest. The Ho Chi Minh regime has shown that it is ready to allocate every resource that can be spared— whether it be personnel, funds, or equipment—to the cause of overthrowing the legitimate Government in South Vietnam and of bringing all Vietnam under Communist rule.

Political direction and control of the Vietcong is supplied by the Lao Dong Party, i.e. the Communist Party, led by Ho Chi Minh. Party agents are responsible for indoctrination, recruitment, political training, propaganda, anti-Government demonstrations, and other activities of a political nature. The considerable intelligence-gathering facilities of the party are also at the disposal of the Vietcong.

Overall direction of the VC movement is the responsibility of the Central Committee of the Lao Dong Party. Within the Central Committee a special Reunification Department has been established. This has replaced the "Committee for Supervision of the South" mentioned in intelligence reports two years ago. It lays down broad strategy for the movement to conquer South Vietnam. . . .

The National Front for the Liberation of South Vietnam is the screen behind which the Communists carry out their program of conquest. It is the creature of the Communist Government in Hanoi. As noted above, the Communist Party in the North demanded establishment of such a "front" three months before its formation was actually announced in December 1960. It was designed to create the illusion that the Vietcong campaign of subversion was truly indigenous to South Vietnam rather than an externally directed Communist plan.

The front has won support primarily from the Communist world. Its radio faithfully repeats the propaganda themes of Hanoi and Peking. When its representatives travel abroad, they do so with North Vietnamese passports and sponsorship. The front's program copies that of the Lao Dong Party in North Vietnam.

Military affairs of the Vietcong are the responsiblity of High Command of the People's Army of North Vietnam and the Ministry of Defense, under close supervision from the Lao Dong Party. These responsibilities include operational plans, assignments of individuals and regular units, training programs, infiltration of military personnel and supplies, military communications, tactical intelligence, supplies, and the like. The six military regions are the same as those of the VC political organization.

The military structure of the Vietcong is an integral part of the political machinery that controls every facet of VC activity in South Vietnam under Hanoi's overall direction. . . .

The evidence presented in this report could be multiplied many times with similar examples of the drive of the Hanoi regime to extend its rule over South Vietnam.

The record is conclusive. It establishes beyond question that North Vietnam is carrying out a carefully conceived plan of aggression against the South. It shows that North Vietnam has intensified its efforts in the years since it was condemned by the International Control Commission. It proves that Hanoi continues to press its systematic program of armed aggression into South Vietnam. This aggression violates the United Nations Charter. It is directly contrary to the Geneva Accords of 1954 and of 1962 to which North Vietnam is a party. It shatters the peace of Southeast Asia. It is a fundamental threat to the freedom and security of South Vietnam.

The people of South Vietnam have chosen to resist this threat. At their request, the United States has taken its place beside them in their defensive struggle.

The United States seeks no territory, no military bases, no favored position. But we have learned the meaning of aggression elsewhere in the postwar world, and we have met it.

If peace can be restored in South Vietnam, the United States will be ready at once to reduce its military involvement. But it will not abandon friends who want to remain free. It will do what must be done to help them. The choice now between peace and continued and increasingly destructive conflict is one for the authorities in Hanoi to make.

2

The Rusk–McNamara Containment Policy*

WALTER LIPPMANN

There has recently been a report from Peking that the Chinese Government has decided to prevent the Soviet Union from supplying North Vietnam by air and railroad across Chinese territory. The official reason given is said to be that the Chinese railroads and Chinese air space are overcrowded. But surely the real purpose would be to force Moscow to choose between abandoning North Vietnam or sending many more ships to the port of Haiphong and challenging American sea power. Of course, we must bear in mind that the report may be an exaggeration or that it may be a neat Machiavellian invention.

The report has reached Washington from several sources, and while I have no way of knowing what there is in it, I had it first from a wholly reputable European source. In any case, the incident brings out into high relief the most important, indeed the crucial, equation of power politics in the world as it is today.

It is that the containment of China depends upon whether the Soviet Union on the one hand, the Western Alliance and the United States on the other, can move on parallel lines rather than divergent lines. For when the lines are parallel, as for example quite notably in respect to India and Pakistan, the opportunity exists to bring about a certain tranquillity.

When the lines of policy in Moscow and Washington diverge, as they do because of the war in South Vietnam, the prospects of international order around the globe become very much dimmer. For while it is dangerous and arrogant nonsense to think the United States can alone bring order into the world, it is the part of wisdom to regard parallelism and agreement among the great powers as the way to order in the world.

For world order depends in the last analysis upon the chance of agreement among the great powers. This is not easy, for there are many rivalries among the great powers. But it is not impossible, because their vital interests in survival outweigh their conflicts. The game of power politics is a complex game. But no statesman is worth his salt if relations with the other great powers are not his primary and paramount concern. It is a sure sign of immaturity and inexperience to put abstractions and generalities based on obscure and deliberately opaque documents above actual relationships with the great powers concerned.

From The Washington Post, March 8, 1966. Reprinted by permission of the author and The Washington Post Company.

Mr. Rusk and Mr. McNamara believe that what they are doing in Vietnam is the highest kind of great power politics. They actually believe that they are containing China, and they persist in their belief despite the fact that they have alienated the Soviet Union, spread doubt and division in Japan, have no support in Pakistan and India. In the realm of great power politics in Asia the United States is playing a lone hand. So the question is: How have the earnest and serious men come to believe that they are containing China?

Their belief rests on the idea that the Vietnamese war is a crucial test of whether revolutionary wars encouraged by the Chinese Communists will be stopped or will continue. This, they tell us, is it. This is where the future is being decided. Believing this, they are engaged in containing China not by dealing with the Chinese, but by fighting the Vietcong and the North Vietnamese Army south of the 17th parallel.

For anyone who thinks that great power politics have not been abolished, the notion that China can be contained in South Vietnam south of the 17th parallel is sheer mythology. It is a pernicious mythology in that it has diverted the President and his advisers from the true containment of China, which is possible only as and if her great Asian neighbors, the Soviet Union, Japan, India, and Pakistan, are alined together or are at least acting on parallel lines.

It does not make the matter easier or clearer for Mr. McNamara to say with increasing fervor that we are not preparing to attack China. The critical question is whether in the pursuit of the victory that eludes us, we are not only escalating the war in South Vietnam but are expanding it to a big war on the periphery of China. Mr. McNamara takes great comfort in a new calculation that while North Vietnam can enlarge its forces very considerably, there is nevertheless a "ceiling" above which it cannot increase its forces (in South Vietnam). Whether or not this is another of Mr. McNamara's unfortunate hopeful predictions, it leaves out of account the fact that Asia is much bigger than South Vietnam and that the war can be expanded not only in southeast Asia but in northeast Asia as well.

3

A Middle Way out of Vietnam*

ARTHUR SCHLESINGER, JR.

Why we are in Vietnam is today a question of only historical interest. We are there, for better or for worse, and we must deal with the situation

*From The New York Times Magazine, September 18, 1966, pp. 47 ff. Copyright © 1966 by The New York Times Company. Reprinted by permission.

that exists. Our national security may not have compelled us to draw a line across Southeast Asia where we did, but, having drawn it, we cannot lightly abandon it. Our stake in South Vietnam may have been self-created, but it has nonetheless become real. Our precipitate withdrawal now would have ominous reverberations throughout Asia. Our commitment of over 300,000 American troops, young men of exceptional skill and gallantry engaged in cruel and difficult warfare, measures the magnitude of our national concern.

We have achieved this entanglement, not after due and deliberate consideration, but through a series of small decisions. It is not only idle but unfair to seek out guilty men. President Eisenhower, after rejecting American military intervention in 1954, set in motion the policy of support for Saigon which resulted, two Presidents later, in American military intervention in 1965. Each step in the deepening of the American commitment was reasonably regarded at the time as the last that would be necessary; yet, in retrospect, each step led only to the next, until we find ourselves entrapped today in that nightmare of American strategists, a land war in Asia—a war which no President, including President Johnson, desired or intended. The Vietnam story is a tragedy without villains. No thoughtful American can withhold sympathy as President Johnson ponders the gloomy choices which lie ahead.

Yet each President, as he makes his choices, must expect to be accountable for them. Everything in recent weeks—the actions of the Administration, the intimations of actions to come, even a certain harshness in the Presidential rhetoric—suggests that President Johnson has made his choice, and that his choice is the careful enlargement of the war. New experiments in escalation are first denied, then disowned, then discounted and finally undertaken. As past medicine fails, all we can apparently think to do is to increase the dose. In May the Secretary of the Air Force explained why we were not going to bomb Hanoi and Haiphong; at the end of June we began the strikes against the oil depots. The demilitarized zone between North and South Vietnam has been used by North Vietnam units for years, but suddenly we have begun to bomb it.

When such steps work no miracles —and it is safe to predict that escalation will be no more decisive in the future than it has been in the past—the demand will arise for "just one more step." Plenty of room remains for widening the war: the harbors of North Vietnam, the irrigation dikes, the steel plants, the factories, the power grid, the crops, the civilian population, the Chinese border. The fact that we excluded such steps yesterday is, alas, no guarantee that we will not pursue them tomorrow. And if bombing will not bring Ho Chi Minh to his knees or stop his support of the Vietcong in South Vietnam, there is always the last resort of invasion. General Ky has already told us that we must invade North Vietnam to win the war. In his recent press conference, the Secretary of State twice declined to rule out this possibility.

The theory, of course, is that widening the war will shorten it. This theory appears to be based on three convictions: first, that the war will be decided in North Vietnam; second, that the risk of Chinese or Soviet entry is negligible, and third, that military "victory" in some sense is possible. Perhaps these premises are correct, and in another year or two we may all be saluting the wisdom and statesmanship of the American Government. In so inscrutable a situation, no one can be confident about his doubt and disagreement. Nonetheless, to many Americans these propositions constitute a terribly shaky basis for action which has already carried the United States into a ground war in Asia and which may well carry the world to the brink of the third world war.

The illusion that the war in South Vietnam can be decided in North Vietnam is evidently a result of listening too long to our own propaganda. Our Government has insisted so often that the war in Vietnam is a clear-cut case of aggression across frontiers that it has come to believe itself that the war was started in Hanoi and can be stopped there. "The war," the Secretary of State has solemnly assured us, "is clearly an 'armed attack,' cynically and systematically mounted by the Hanoi regime against the people of South Vietnam."

Yet the best evidence is that the war began as an insurrection within South Vietnam which, as it has gathered momentum, has attracted increasing support and direction from the north. Even today the North Vietnamese regulars in South Vietnam amount to only a fraction of the total enemy force (and to an even smaller fraction of the American army in South Vietnam). We could follow the genial prescription of General LeMay and bomb North Vietnam back to the Stone Age—and the war would still go on in South Vietnam. To reduce this war to the simplification of a wicked regime molesting its neighbors, and to suppose that it can be ended by punishing the wicked regime, is surely to misconceive not only the political but even the military character of the problem.

As for the assurances that China will not enter, these will be less than totally satisfying to those whose memory stretches back to the Korean War. General MacArthur, another one of those military experts on Oriental psychology, when asked by President Truman on Wake Island in October, 1950, what the chances were of Chinese intervention, replied, "Very little. . . . Now that we have bases for our Air Force in Korea, if the Chinese tried to get down to Pyongyang, there would be the greatest slaughter." Such reasoning lay behind the decision (the Assistant Secretary of State for Far Eastern Affairs at that time is Secretary of State today) to send American troops across the 38th Parallel despite warnings from Peking that this would provoke a Chinese response. In a few weeks, China was actively in the war, and, while there was the greatest slaughter, it was not notably of the Chinese.

There seems little question that the Chinese have no great passion to enter the war in Vietnam. They do not want to put their nuclear plants in hazard; and, in any case, their foreign policy has typically been a compound of polemical ferocity and practical prudence. But the leaders in Peking are no doubt just as devoted students of Munich as the American Secretary of State. They are sure that we are out to bury them; they believe that appeasement invites further aggression; and, however deep their reluctance, at some point concern for national survival will make them fight.

When will that point be reached? Probably when they are confronted by a direct threat to their frontier, either through bombing or through an American decision to cross the 17th Parallel and invade North Vietnam. If a Communist regime barely established in Peking could take a decision to intervene against the only atomic power in the world in 1950, why does anyone suppose that a much stronger regime should flinch from that decision in 1966? Indeed, given the present discord in Peking, war may seem the best way to renew revolutionary discipline, stop the brawling and unite the nation.

It is true that the Chinese entry into the Korean War had at least the passive support of the Soviet Union; but it would be risky today to rely on the Sino-Soviet split to save us from everything, including Soviet aid to China in case of war with the United States or even direct Soviet entry into the war in Vietnam. For the Soviet Union is already extensively involved in Vietnam—more so in a sense than the Chinese—and it would be foolish to suppose that, given Moscow's competition with Peking for the leadership of the Communist world, Russia could afford to stand by and allow Communist North Vietnam or Communist China to be destroyed by the American imperialists.

As for the third premise (that military "victory" is in some sense possible): The Joint Chiefs of Staff, of course, by definition argue for military solutions. They are the most fervent apostles of "one more step." That is their business, and no one should be surprised that generals behave like generals. The fault lies not with those who give this advice but those who take it. Once, early in the Kennedy Administration, the then Chairman of the Joint Chiefs outlined the processes of escalation in Southeast Asia before the National Security Council, concluding, "If we are given the right to use nuclear weapons, we can guarantee victory." President Kennedy sat glumly rubbing an upper molar. After a moment someone said, "Mr. President, perhaps you would have the general explain to us what he means by victory." Kennedy grunted and dismissed the meeting. Later he said, "Since he couldn't think of any further escalation, he would have to promise us victory."

What is the purpose of bombing the north? It is hard to find out. According to Gen. Maxwell Taylor, "The objective of our air campaign is to change the will of the enemy leadership." Secretary McNamara, on the other hand, has said, "We never believed that bombing would destroy North Vietnam's will." Whatever the theory, the results would appear to support Secretary McNamara. The northern strategy, instead of driving Hanoi to the conference table, seems to have hardened the will of the regime, convinced it that its life is at stake, brought it closer to China and solidified the people of North Vietnam in its support.

"There is no indication," General Westmoreland said the other day, "that the resolve of the leadership in Hanoi has been reduced." In other words, bombing has had precisely the effect that the analyses of the United States Strategic Bombing Survey after the Second World War would have forecast. Under Secretary of State George Ball was a director of that survey; this may well be why he has been reported so unenthusiastic about the air assault on the North.

And, far from stopping infiltration across the 17th Parallel, bombing, if our own statistics are to be believed, has stimulated it. "It is perfectly clear," Secretary McNamara has said, "that the North Vietnamese have continued to increase their support of the Vietcong despite the increase in our effort. ... What has happened is that the North Vietnamese have continually increased the amount of resources, men and material that they have been willing to devote to their objective."

Nor can we easily match this infiltration by enlarging our own forces— from 300,000, for example, to 500,000 or 750,000. The ratio of superiority preferred by the Pentagon in guerrilla war is 10 to 1, which means that every time we send in 100,000 more men the enemy has only to send in 10,000 or so, and we are all even again. Reinforcement has not created a margin of American superiority; all it has done is to lift the stalemate to a higher and more explosive level. Indeed, there is reason to suppose that, in its own manner, the enemy can match our every step of escalation up to the point of nuclear war.

U. S. News & World Report says in its issue of Aug. 22: "It's clear now to military men: bombing will not win in Vietnam." This is a dispiriting item. Why had our military leaders not long ago freed themselves from the illusion of the omnipotence of air power, so cherished by civilians who think wars can be won on the cheap? The Korean war, as Gen. Matthew B. Ridgway has said, "taught that it is impossible to interdict the supply route of an Asian army by airpower alone. We had complete air mastery over North Korea, and we clobbered Chinese supply columns unmercifully . . . . But we did not halt their offensive nor materially diminish its strength." If air power was not decisive in Korea, where the warfare was conventional and the terrain relatively open and compact, how could anyone suppose that it would be decisive against guerrillas threading their way through the hills and jungles of Vietnam?

The bombing illusion applies, of course, to South as well as to North Vietnam. Tactical bombing—bombing in direct support of ground operations has its place; but the notion that strategic bombing can stop guerrillas runs contrary to experience. And we had it last winter, on the authority of the Secretary of State, that despite the entry of North Vietnamese regulars the war in South Vietnam "continues to be basically a guerrilla operation."

Sir Robert Thompson, who planned the successful British effort against the Malayan guerrillas and later served as head of the British advisory mission in Saigon, has emphasized that the defending force must operate "in the same element" as their adversaries. Counterinsurgency, he writes, "is like trying to deal with a tomcat in an alley. It is no good inserting a large, fierce dog. The dog may not find the tomcat; if he does, the tomcat will escape up a tree; and the dog will then chase the female cats. The answer is to put in a fiercer tomcat."

Alas, we have no fiercer tomcat. The counterinsurgency effort in Vietnam has languished, while our bombers roam over that hapless country, dumping more tonnage of explosives each month than we were dropping per month on all Europe and Africa during the Second World War. Just the other day our bombs killed or injured more than 100 civilians in a hamlet in the Mekong Delta—all on the suspicion that two Vietcong platoons numbering perhaps 60 men, were there. Even if the Vietcong had still been around, which they weren't, would the military gain have outweighed the human and political loss? Charles Mohr writes in The Times: "Almost every provincial hospital in Vietnam is crowded with civilian victims of the war. Some American doctors and other officials in the field say the majority are the victims of American air power and South Vietnamese artillery."

The trouble is that we are fighting one war, with our B-52's and our naval guns and our napalm, and the Vietcong are fighting another, with their machine guns and ambushes and forays in the dark. "If we can get the Vietcong to stand up and fight, we will blast him," General Westmoreland has plaintively said; and when they occasionally rise to the surface and try to fight our kind of war, we do blast them. But the fact that they then slide back into the shadows does not mean that we are on the verge of some final military triumph. It means simply that we are driving them underground—where they renew themselves and where our large, fierce dog cannot follow.

Saigon officials have been reporting that Vietcong morale is declining as long as I can remember; these reports need not be taken seriously now. I know of no convincing evidence that the Vietcong lack the political and emotional commitment to keep fighting underground for another 20 years.

Our strategy in Vietnam is rather like trying to weed a garden with a bulldozer. We occasionally dig up some weeds, but we dig up most of the turf, too. The effect of our policy is to pulverize the political and institutional fabric which alone can give a South Vietnamese state that hope of independent survival which is our presumed war aim. Our method, in other words, defeats our goal. Indeed, the most likely beneficiary of the smashed social structure of South Vietnam will be Communism. "My feeling," Gen. Wallace Greene, commandant of the Marine Corps, has wisely said, "is that you could kill every Vietcong and North Vietnamese in South Vietnam and still lose the war. Unless we can make a success of the civic-action program, we are not going to obtain the objectives we have set."

Much devotion and intelligence are at present going into the programs
of reconstruction, but prospects are precarious so long as the enemy can
slice through so much of South Vietnam with such apparent immunity;
and so long as genuine programs of social reform threaten the vested interests
of the Saigon Government and of large landholders. In any case, as claimants
on our resources, these programs of pacification are hopelessly outclassed
by the programs of destruction. Surely, the United States, with all its inge-
nuity, could have figured out a better way to combat guerrilla warfare than
the physical obliteration of the nation in which it is taking place. If this is
our best idea of "protecting" a country against "wars of national liberation,"
what other country, seeing the devastation we have wrought in Vietnam,
will wish American protection?

At the same time, our concentration on Vietnam is exacting a frightful
cost in other areas of national concern. In domestic policy, with Vietnam
gulping down a billion and a half dollars a month, everything is grinding to
a stop. Lyndon Johnson was on his way to a place in history as a great President for his vision of a Great Society; but the Great Society is now, except
for token gestures, dead. The fight for equal opportunity for the Negro, the
war against poverty, the struggle to save the cities, the improvement of our
schools—all must be starved for the sake of Vietnam. And war brings ugly
side-effects: inflation; frustration; angry protest; attack on dissenters on the
ground that they cheer the enemy (an attack often mounted by men who
led the dissent during the Korean war); premonitions of McCarthyism.

We also pay a cost abroad. Our allies naturally draw away as they see us
heading down the road toward war with China. When we began to bomb
the oil depots, James Reston wrote: "There is now not a single major nation
in the world that supports Mr. Johnson's latest adventure in Hanoi and
Haiphong." As nations seek to disengage themselves from the impending
conflict, the quasi-neutralism of leaders like de Gaulle gains new plausibility.

On any realistic assessment, Western Europe and Latin America are
far more significant to American security than South Asia; yet the Vietnam
obsession has stultified our policy and weakened our position in both these
vital areas. The war has clouded the hope, once mildly promising, of progress toward a *détente* with the Soviet Union. It has helped block agreements
to end underground nuclear testing and to stop the spread of nuclear weapons.
It has precipitated the decision of U Thant to resign as Secretary General
of the United Nations and condemns the U. N. itself to a time of declining
influence.

Our rejection of the views of our friends and allies—our conviction, as
Paul H. Smith has put it, "that we alone are qualified to be judge, jury
and executioner"—ignores Madison's solemn warning in the 63rd Federa-
list: "An attention to the judgment of other nations is important to every
government for two reasons: the one is that independently of the merits of
any particular plan or measure, it is desirable, on various accounts, that it

should appear to other nations as the offspring of a wise and honorable policy; the second is that in doubtful cases, particularly where the national councils may be warped by some strong passion or momentary interest, the presumed or known opinion of the impartial world may be the best guide that can be followed. What has not America lost by her want of character with foreign nations; and how many errors and follies would she not have avoided, if the justice and propriety of her measures had, in every instance, been previously tried by the light in which they would probably appear to the unbiased part of mankind."

The Administration has called the critics of its Vietnam policy "neo-isolationists." But surely the real neo-isolationists are those who have isolated the United States from its allies and raised the tattered standard, last flourished 15 years ago by Douglas MacArthur, of "going it alone."

How have we managed to imprison ourselves in this series of dilemmas? One reason surely is that we have somehow lost our understanding of the uses of power. Understanding of power implies above all precision in its application. We have moved away from the subtle strategy of "flexible response" under which the level of American force was graduated to meet the level of enemy threat. The triumph of this discriminate employment of power was, of course, the Cuban missile crisis (where the Joint Chiefs, as usual, urged an air assault on the missile bases). But President Johnson, for all his formidable abilities, has shown no knack for discrimination in his use of power. His technique is to try and overwhelm his adversary—as in the Dominican Republic and Vietnam—by piling on all forms of power without regard to the nature of the threat.

Given this weakness for the indiscriminate use of power, it is easy to see why the application of force in Vietnam has been surrendered to the workings of what an acute observer of the Johnson foreign policy, Philip Geyelin, calls "the escalation machine." This machine is, in effect, the momentum in the decision-making system which keeps enlarging the war "for reasons only marginally related to military need."

The very size and weight of the American military presence generate unceasing pressures to satisfy military demands. These may be demands to try out new weapons; the London Sunday Telegraph recently ran an informative article comparing the Vietnam war to the Spanish Civil War as a military testing ground and laboratory. Or they may be cries for "one more step," springing in part from suppressed rage over the fact that, with military power sufficient to blow up the world, we still cannot compel guerrilla bands in black pajamas to submit to our will. Whatever the reason, Sir Robert Thompson has noted of the American theory of the war: "There was a constant tendency in Vietnam to mount large-scale operations, which had little purpose or prospect of success, merely to indicate that something aggressive was being done."

The Administration has freely admitted that such operations, like the bombing of the North, are designed in part to prop up the morale of the Saigon Government. And the impression is growing now that they are also in part undertaken in order to smother doubts about the war in the United States and to reverse anti-Administration tendencies in the polls. Americans have become curiously insensitive to the use of military operations for domestic political purposes. A quarter-century ago President Roosevelt postponed the North African invasion so that it would not take place before the midterm elections of 1942; but today observers in Washington, without evidence of shock, predict a new venture in escalation before the midterm elections of 1966.

The triumph of the escalation machine has been assisted by the faultiness of the information on which our decisions are based. Nothing is phonier than the spurious exactitude of our statistics about the Vietnam war. No doubt a computerized military establishment demands numbers; but the "body count" of dead Vietcong, for example, includes heaven knows how many innocent bystanders and could hardly be more unreliable. The figures on enemy strength are totally baffling, at least to the ordinary citizen relying on the daily newspaper. The Times on Aug. 10 described "the latest intelligence reports" in Saigon as saying that the number of enemy troops in South Vietnam had increased 52,000 since Jan. 1 to a total of 282,000. Yet, "according to official figures," the enemy had suffered 31,571 killed in action in this period, and the infiltration estimate ranged from 35,000 as "definite" to 54,000 as "possible."

The only way to reconcile these figures is to conclude that the Vietcong have picked up from 30,000 to 50,000 local recruits in this period. Since this seems unlikely—especially in view of our confidence in the decline of Vietcong morale—a safer guess is to question the wonderful precision of the statistics. Even the rather vital problem of how many North Vietnamese troops are in South Vietnam is swathed in mystery. The Times reported on Aug. 7: "About 40,000 North Vietnamese troops are believed by allied intelligence to be in the South." According to an Associated Press dispatch from Saigon printed in The Christian Science Monitor of Aug. 15: "The South Vietnamese Government says 102,500 North Vietnamese combat troops and support battalions have infiltrated into South Vietnam.

"These figures are far in excess of United States intelligence estimates, which put the maximum number of North Vietnamese in the South at about 54,000."

But General Westmoreland told his Texas press conference on Aug. 14 that the enemy force included "about 110,000 main-force North Vietnamese regular army troops." Perhaps these statements are all reconcilable, but an apparent discrepancy of this magnitude on a question of such importance raises a twinge of doubt.

Nor is our ignorance confined to battle-order statistics. We have always lacked genuine knowledge of and insight into the political and cultural problems of Vietnam, and the more we press all problems into a military framework the worse off we are. The Administration in Washington was systematically misinformed by senior American officials in Saigon in 1962–63 regarding the progress of the war, the popularity of Diem, the effectiveness of the "strategic hamlet" program and other vital matters. It was not that these officials were deliberately deceiving their President; it was that they had deceived themselves first. Ordinary citizens restricted to reading the American press were better informed in 1963 than officials who took top-secret cables seriously.

The fact is that our Government just doesn't know a lot of things it pretends to know. It is not discreditable that it should not know them, for the facts are elusive and the judgments incredibly difficult. But it is surely inexcusable that it should pretend to know things it does not—and that it should pass its own ignorance on to the American people as certitude. And it is even less excusable that it should commit the nation to a policy involving the greatest dangers on a foundation so vague and precarious.

So now we are set on the course of widening the war—even at the cost of multiplying American casualties in Vietnam and deepening American troubles at home and abroad; even at the risk of miring our nation in a hopeless and endless conflict on the mainland of Asia beyond the effective employment of our national power and beyond the range of our primary interests; even at the risk of nuclear war.

Why does the Administration feel that these costs must be paid and these risks run? Hovering behind our policy is a larger idea—the idea that the war in Vietnam is not just a local conflict between Vietnamese but a fateful test of wills between China and the United States.

Our political and rhetorical escalation of the war has been almost as perilous as our military escalation. President Kennedy's effort was to pull Laos out of the context of greatpower conflict and reduce the Laotian civil war to rational proportions. As he told Khrushchev at Vienna in 1961, Laos was just not important enough to entangle two great nations. President Johnson, on the other hand, has systematically inflated the significance of the war in Vietnam. "We have tried to make it clear over and over again," as the Secretary of State has put it, "that although Hanoi is the prime actor in this situation, that it is the policy of Peking that has greatly stimulated Hanoi. . . . It is Ho Chi Minh's war. Maybe it is Mao Tse-tung's war."

"In the forties and fifties," President Johnson has said, "we took our stand in Europe to protect the freedom of those threatened by aggression. Now the center of attention has shifted to another part of the world where aggression is on the march. Our stand must be as firm as ever." Given this view, it is presumably necessary to pay the greatest costs and run the greatest risks—or else invite the greatest defeat.

Given this view, too, there is no reason not to Americanize the war. President Kennedy did not believe that the war in Vietnam could succeed as a war of white men against Asians. It could not be won, he said a few weeks before his death, "unless the people [of South Vietnam] support the effort. . . . We can help them, we can give them equipment, we can send our men out there as advisers, but they have to win it, the people of Vietnam." We have now junked this doctrine. Instead, we have enlarged our military presence until it is the only thing that matters in South Vietnam, and we plan now to make it still larger; we have summoned the Saigon leaders, like tribal chieftains on a retainer, to a conference in an American state; we crowd the streets of Saigon with American generals (58 at last count) and visiting stateside dignitaries. In short, we have seized every opportunity to make clear to the world that this is an *American* war—and, in doing this, we have surely gone far to make the war unwinnable.

The proposition that our real enemy in Vietnam is China is basic to the policy of widening the war. It is the vital element in the Administration case. Yet the proof our leaders have adduced for this proposition has been exceedingly sketchy and almost perfunctory. It has been proof by ideology and proof by analogy. It has not been proof by reasoned argument or by concrete illustration.

The proof by ideology has relied on the syllogism that the Vietcong, North Vietnam and China are all Communist states and *therefore* must be part of the same conspiracy, and that, since the Vietcong are the weakest of the three, they must *therefore* be the spearhead of a coordinated Chinese plan of expansion. The Department of State, in spite of what has struck most people as a rather evident fragmentation of the Communist world, has hated to abandon the cozy old clichés about a centralized Communist conspiracy aimed at monolithic world revolution.

As late as May 9, 1965, after half a dozen years of public Russo-Chinese quarreling, Thomas C. Mann, then No. 3 man in the department, could talk about "instruments of Sino-Soviet power" and "orders from the Sino-Soviet military bloc." As late as Jan. 28, 1966, the Secretary of State could still run on about "their world revolution," and again, on Feb. 18, about "the Communists" and their "larger design." While the department may have accepted the reality of the Russo-Chinese schism by September, 1966, the predominant tone is still to regard Asian Communism as a homogenous system of aggression. The premise of our policy has been that the Vietcong equal Hanoi and Hanoi equals Peking.

Obviously, the Vietcong, Hanoi and Peking have interests in common and strong ideological affinities. Obviously, Peking would rejoice in a Hanoi–Vietcong victory. But they also have divergent interests and purposes—and the divergencies may prove in the end to be stronger than the affinities. Recent developments in North Korea are instructive. If any country was bound to Peking by ties of gratitude, it was North Korea, which was preserved as an independent state by Chinese intervention 15 years ago. If any country today is at the mercy of Peking, it is again North Korea. When North Korea now declares in vigorous language its independence of China, does anyone suppose that North Vietnam, imbued with historic mistrust of China and led by that veteran Russian agent Ho Chi Minh, would have been more slavish in its attitude toward Peking?

The other part of the Administration case has been proof by analogy, especially the good old Munich analogy. "I'm not the village idiot," the Secretary of State recently confided to Stewart Alsop. "I know Hitler was an Austrian and Mao is a Chinese. . . . But what is common between the two situations is the phenomenon of aggression." The Vietnam war, President Johnson recently told the American Legion, "is meant to be the opening salvo in a series of bombardments or, as they are called in Peking, 'wars of liberation.' " If this technique works this week in Vietnam, the Administration suggests, it will be tried next week in Uganda and Peru. But, if it is defeated in Vietnam, the Chinese will know that we will not let it succeed elsewhere.

"What happens in South Vietnam," the President cried at Omaha, "will determine—yes, it will determine—whether ambitions and aggressive nations can use guerrilla warfare to conquer their weaker neighbors." The Secretary of State even described an exhortation made last year by the Chinese Defense Minister, Marshal Lin Piao, as a blueprint for world conquest comparable to Hitler's "Mein Kampf."

One thing is sure about the Vietnam riddle: it will not be solved by bad historical analogies. It seems a trifle forced, for example, to equate a civil war in what was for hundreds of years the entity of Vietnam (Marshal Ky, after all, is a North Vietnamese himself) with Hitler's invasion of Austria and Czechoslovakia across old and well-established lines of national division; even the village idiot might grasp that difference.

When President Eisenhower invoked the Munich analogy in 1954 in an effort to involve the British in Indochina, Prime Minister Churchill, a pretty close student of Munich in his day, was unmoved. The Chinese have neither the overwhelmingly military power nor the timetable of aggression nor, apparently, the pent-up mania for instant expansion which would justify the Hitler parallel. As for the Lin Piao document, the Rand Corporation, which evidently read it with more care than the State Department bothered to do, concluded that, far from being Mao's "Mein Kampf," it was a message to the Vietcong that they could win "only if they rely primarily on their own resources and their own revolutionary spirit," and that it revealed "the lack, rather than the extent, of Peking's past and present control over Hanoi's actions."

In any case, guerrilla warfare is not a tactic to be mechanically applied by central headquarters to faraway countries. More than any other form of warfare, it is dependent on conditions and opportunities within the countries themselves. Whether there are wars of national liberation in Uganda and Peru will depend, not on what happens in Vietnam, but on what happens in Uganda and Peru.

One can agree that the containment of China will be a major problem for the next generation. But this does not mean that we must re-enact in Asia in the sixties the exact drama of Europe in the forties and fifties. The record thus far suggests that the force most likely to contain Chinese expansionism in Asia (and Africa, too) will be not Western intervention but local nationalism. Sometimes local nationalism may call on Western support—but not always. Countries like Burma and Cambodia preserve their autonomy without American assistance. The Africans have dealt with the Chinese on their own. The two heaviest blows recently suffered by Peking—the destruction of the Communist party in Indonesia and the declaration of independence by North Korea—took place without benefit of American patronage or rhetoric.

In the unpredictable decades ahead, the most effective bulwark against "international" Communism in some circumstances may well be national Communism. A rational policy of containing China could have recognized that a Communist Vietnam under Ho might be a better instrument of containment than a shaky Saigon regime led by right-wing mandarins or air force generals. Had Ho taken over all Vietnam in 1954, he might today be enlisting Soviet support to strengthen his resistance to Chinese pressure—and this situation, however appalling for the people of South Vietnam, would obviously be better for the United States than the one in which we are floundering today. And now, alas, it may be almost too late: the whole thrust of United States policy since 1954, and more than ever since the bombing of the North began, has been not to pry Peking and Hanoi apart but to drive them together.

Is there no way out? Are the only alternatives widening the war or disorderly and humiliating withdrawal? Surely, our statesmanship is not yet this bankrupt. I think a middle course is still possible if there were the will to pursue it. And this course must begin with a decision to stop widening and Americanizing the war—to limit our forces, actions, goals and rhetoric. Instead of bombing more places, sending in more troops, proclaiming ever more ardently that the fate of civilization will be settled in Vietnam, let us recover our cool and try to see the situation as it is: a horrid civil war in which Communist guerrillas, enthusiastically aided and now substantially directed from Hanoi, are trying to establish a Communist despotism in South Vietnam, not for the Chinese but for themselves. Let us understand that the ultimate problem here is not military but political. Let us adapt the means we employ to the end we seek.

Obviously, military action plays an indispensable role in the search for a political solution. Hanoi and the Vietcong will not negotiate so long as they think they can win. Since stalemate is a self-evident precondition to negotiation, we must have enough American armed force in South Vietnam to leave no doubt in the minds of our adversaries that they cannot hope for victory. They must also have no illusion about the prospect of an American withdrawal. The object of the serious opposition to the Johnson policy is to bring about not an American defeat but a negotiated settlement.

Therefore, holding the line in South Vietnam is essential. Surely, we already have enough American troops, firepower and installations in South Vietnam to make it clear that we cannot be beaten unless we choose to scuttle and run, which will not happen. The opponents of this strategy talk as if a holding action would put our forces under siege and relinquish all initiative to the enemy. This need not, of course, be so. It is possible to slow down a war without standing still; and, if our present generals can't figure out how to do this, then let us get generals who can. Generals Ridgway and Gavin could doubtless suggest some names. Moreover, there is a South Vietnamese army of some 600,000 men which can take all the initiative it wants. And if we are told that the South Vietnamese are unwilling or unable to fight the Vietcong, then we must wonder all the more about the political side of the war.

The object of our military policy, as observers like Henry Kissinger and James MacGregor Burns have proposed, should be the creation and stabilization of secure areas where the South Vietnamese might themselves undertake social and institutional development. Our resources should go, in the Vietnam jargon, more to clear-and-hold than to search-and-destroy (especially when search-and-destroy more often means search-and-drive-underground). We should get rid of those "one-star generals who," in the words of Sir Robert Thompson, "regard their tour in Vietnam as an opportunity to indulge in a year's big-game shooting from their helicopter howdash at Government expense."

At the same time we should induce the Saigon Government to institute generous amnesty provisions of the kind which worked so well in the Philippines. And we should further increase the incentive to come over by persuading the South Vietnamese to abandon the torture of prisoners—a practice not only horrible in itself but superbly calculated to make the enemy fight to the bitter end. In the meantime we must end our own shameful collaboration with this barbarism and stop turning Vietcong prisoners over to the South Vietnamese when we know that torture is probable.

As for bombing the North, let us taper this off as prudently as we can. Bombing is not likely to deter Hanoi any more in the future than it has in the past; and, given its limited military effect, the Administration's desire to gratify the Saigon Government and the American voter is surely not important enough to justify the risks of indefinite escalation. Moreover, so long as the bombing continues there is no chance of serious negotiation. Nor does the failure of the 37-day pause of last winter to produce a settlement refute this. Thirty-seven days were hardly enough to persuade our allies that we honestly wanted negotiation; so brief an interlude left no time for them to move on to the tricky job of persuading Hanoi. For Hanoi has substantial reasons for mistrusting negotiation—quite apart from Chinese pressure or its own hopes of victory. Ho has entered into negotiation with the West twice in the past—in 1946–47 and again in 1954—and each time, in his view, he lost at the conference table things he thought he had won on the battlefield.

For all our official talk about our readiness to go anywhere, talk to anyone, etc., it cannot be said that the Administration has pursued negotiation with a fraction of the zeal, imagination and perseverance with which it has pursued war. Indeed, some American scholars who have studied the matter believe that on a number of occasions when pressure for negotiation was mounting we have, for whatever reason, stepped up the war.

Nor can it be said that the Administration has laid fairly before the American people the occasional signals, however faint, which have come from Hanoi—as in the early winter of 1965, when U Thant's mediation reached the point of selecting the hotel in Rangoon where talks might take place, until we killed the idea by beginning the bombing of the North. Nor, for all our declarations about "unconditional" negotiations, have we refrained from setting conditions—such as, for example, that we won't talk to the Vietcong unless they come to the conference table disguised as North Vietnamese. Though the Vietcong constitute the great bulk of the enemy force, they have been given little reason to think we will negotiate about anything except their unconditional surrender.

It is hard to see why we should not follow the precedent of Laos, when we admitted the Pathet Lao to the peace talks, and offer the Vietcong the prospect of a say in the future political life of South Vietnam —conditioned on their laying down their arms, opening up their territories and abiding by the ground rules of free elections. Nor is there reason to see why we have been so reluctant again to follow the Laos model and declare neutralization, under international guarantee, our long-run objective for Vietnam. An imaginative diplomacy would long since have discussed the ways and means of such neutralization with Russia, France, Britain and other interested countries. Unsatisfactory as the situation in Laos may be today, it is still incomparably better than the situation in South Vietnam.

On the other hand, negotiation is not an exclusive, or even primary, American responsibility. Along with a military stalemate, the other precondition of a diplomatic settlement is surely a civilian government in Saigon. Marshal Ky is one of those Frankenstein's monsters we delight in creating in our "client" countries, very much like the egregious General Phoumi Nosavan, who single-handedly blocked a settlement in Laos for two years. Like Phoumi, Ky evidently feels that Washington has committed itself irrevocably to him—and why should he not after the laying on of hands at Honolulu?— and that, whatever he does, we cannot afford to abandon him.

Robert Shaplen, in the August 20 issue of The New Yorker, reported from Saigon that the atmosphere there "is being compared to the miasma that surrounded Diem and his tyrannical brother Ngo Dinh Nhu" and that "many Vietnamese believe that the Americans, having embraced Ky so wholeheartedly and supported him so long, are just as responsible as his Government for the recent repressive acts."

I am sure that President Johnson did not intend to turn over American policy and honor in Vietnam to Marshal Ky's gimcrack, bullyboy, get-rich-quick regime. The time is bound to come when Ky must learn the facts of life, as General Phoumi eventually and painfully learned them.

But why wait? In our whole time in Vietnam, there has never been a Government in Saigon which had the active loyalty of the countryside. It might be an agreeable experiment to encourage one to come into existence. Instead of identifying American interests with Ky and rebuffing the broader political impulses in South Vietnam, we should long since have welcomed a movement toward a civilian regime representing the significant political forces of the country and capable both of rallying the army and carrying forward programs of social reform. We should give such a Government all possible assistance in rebuilding and modernizing the political and institutional structures of South Vietnam. And if it should favor the neutralization of its country, if it should seek negotiation with the Vietcong, even if it should release us from our commitment to stay in Vietnam, we should not think that the world is coming to an end.

It is not too late to begin the de-escalation of the war; nor would the reduction of our military effort damage our international influence. "There is more respect to be won in the opinion of this world," George Kennan has written, "by a resolute and courageous liquidation of unsound positions than by the most stubborn pursuit of extravagant or unpromising objectives." France was stronger than ever after de Gaulle left Algeria, the Soviet Union suffered no lasting damage from pulling its nuclear missiles out of Cuba. And the policy of de-escalation recommended here is, of course, something a good deal less than withdrawal.

De-escalation *could* work, *if* there were the will to pursue it. . . . This is the hard question. The Administration, disposed to the indiscriminate use of power, enmeshed in the grinding cogs of the escalation machine, committed to the thesis that China is the enemy in Vietnam, obviously could not turn to de-escalation without considerable inner upheaval. The issue in the United States in the months to come will be whether President Johnson's leadership is sufficiently resilient and forbearing to permit a change in the direction of policy and arrest what is coming increasingly to seem an accelerating drift toward a great and unnecessary catastrophe.

Bibliography

Adams, M., *Suez and After*. Boston: Beacon Press, 1958.

Arnold, G. I., *The Pattern of World Conflict*. New York: The Dial Press, Inc., 1955.

Baker, Charles A., *Problems of World Disarmament*. Boston: Houghton Mifflin Company, 1963.

Barnet, Richard J., and Raskin, M. G., *After 20 Years: Alternatives to the Cold War in Europe*. New York: Random House, Inc., 1965.

Barnett, A. Doak, *Communist China and Asia; Challenge to American Policy*. New York: Harper & Row, Publishers, 1960.

———, *China on the Eve of Communist Takeover*. New York: Frederick A. Praeger, Inc., 1964.

———, *Communist China: The Early Years, 1949–55*. New York: Frederick A Praeger, Inc., 1966.

Bass, R. H., *The Soviet–Yugoslav Controversy, 1948–58*, New York: Prospect Books, 1959.

Bechhoefer, Bernard G., *Postwar Negotiations for Arms Control*. Washington, D. C.: The Brookings Institution, 1961.

Berle, A. A., Jr., *Tides of Crisis: A Primer of Foreign Relations*. New York: Reynal & Company, Inc., 1957.

Berman, Harold J., *The Trial of the U–2*. Chicago: Translation World Publications, 1960.

Bernstein, Barton J., ed., *The Truman Administration: A Documentary History*. New York: Harper & Row, Publishers, 1966.

Binder, Leonard, *Iran; Political Development in a Changing Society*. Berkeley, Calif.: University of California Press, 1962.

Boorman, H. L., *et al.*, *Moscow–Peking Axis, Strengths and Strains*. New York: Harper & Row, Publishers, 1957.

Bouscaren, Anthony Trawick, *Soviet Foreign Policy, A Pattern of Persistence*. New York: Fordham University Press, 1962.

Bowett, D. W., *United Nations Forces: A Legal Study*. New York: Frederick A. Praeger, Inc., 1964.

Brzezinski, Zbignieu, *The Soviet Bloc: Unity and Conflict*. Cambridge: Harvard University Press, 1960.

Burns, Arthur, and Heathcote, Nina, *Peace-keeping by UN Forces*. New York: Frederick A. Praeger, Inc., 1963.

Burton, John W., *Peace Theory: Preconditions of Disarmament*. New York: Alfred A. Knopf, Inc., 1962.

Buss, C. A., *The People's Republic of China*. Princeton, N.J.: D. Van Nostrand Co., Inc., 1962.

Butwell, Richard, *Southeast Asia Today and Tomorrow, A Political Analysis*. New York: Frederick A. Praeger, Inc., 1961.

Campbell, J. C., *Defense of the Middle East*. New York: Harper & Row, Publishers, 1960.

Chow, Ching-wen, *Ten Years of Storm; The True Story of the Communist Regime in China*. Translated and edited by Lai Ming. New York: Holt, Rinehart & Winston, Inc., 1960.

Clay, Lucius, *Decision in Germany*. Garden City, N. Y.: Doubleday & Company, Inc., 1950.

Cousins, Norman, *In Place of Folly*. New York: Harper & Row, Publishers, 1961.

Crankshaw, Edward, *The New Cold War: Moscow vs. Peking*. Baltimore, Md.: Penguin Books, Inc., 1963.

Dallin, Alexander, *Soviet Conduct in World Affairs, A Selection of Readings*. New York: Columbia University Press, 1960.

———, *The Soviet Union and the United Nations*. New York: Frederick A. Praeger, Inc., 1962.

Davison, Walter Phillips, *The Berlin Blockade: A Study in Cold War Politics*. Princeton, N. J.: Princeton University Press, 1958.

de Gramont, Sanche, *The Secret War*. New York: G. P. Putnam's Sons, 1962.

Deutscher, Isaac, *The Great Conflict: Russia and the West*. New York: Oxford University Press, Inc., 1960.

Donnelly, Desmond, *Struggle for the World: The Cold War, 1917–1965*. New York: St Martin's Press, Inc., 1965.

Doolin, Dennis J., *Territorial Claims in the Sino-Soviet Conflict; Documents and Analysis*. Stanford, Calif.: The Hoover Institution on War, Revolution, & Peace, 1965.

Dulles, Eleanor Lansing, *et al.*, eds., *Détente; Cold War Strategies in Transition*. New York: Frederick A. Praeger, Inc., 1965.

Eagleton, William, *The Kurdish Republic of 1946*. New York: Oxford University Press, Inc., 1963.

Eayrs, J. G., ed., *Commonwealth and Suez*. New York: Oxford University Press, Inc., 1964.

Eden, Anthony, *Full Circle*. Boston: Houghton Mifflin Company, 1960.

Fall, Bernard B., *The Two Viet-Nams; a Political and Military Analysis*. 2nd Rev. Ed. New York: Frederick A. Praeger, Inc., 1966.

——— *Viet-Nam Witness: 1953–66*. New York: (Frederick A. Praeger, Inc., 1966.

Fifield, Russell H., *Southeast Asia in United States Policy*. New York: Frederick A. Praeger, Inc., 1963.

Finer, H., *Dulles over Suez*. Chicago, Ill.: Quadrangle Books, Inc., 1964.

Fleming, D. F., *The Cold War and its Origins, 1917–1960*. 2 Vols. Garden City, N. Y.: Doubleday & Company, Inc., 1961.

Floyd, David, *Mao Against Khrushchev, A Short History of the Sino-Soviet Conflict*. New York: Frederick A. Praeger, Inc., 1964.

Foley, Charles, *Legacy of Strife: Cyprus from Rebellion to Civil War*. Baltimore, Md.: Penguin Books, Inc., 1964.

Franck, Thomas, and Carrey, John, *The Legal Aspects of the United Nations in the Congo*. Dobbs Ferry, N. Y.: Oceana Publications, Inc., 1963.

Garthoff, Raymond L., *The Soviet Image of Future War*. Washington, D. C.: Public Affairs Press, 1959.

———, *Soviet Strategy in the Nuclear Age*. New York: Frederick A. Praeger, Inc., 1962.

———, ed., *Sino-Soviet Military Relations*. New York: Frederick A. Praeger, Inc., 1966.

Giap, Vo-nguyen, *Dien Bien Phu*. Rev. and Enlarged Ed. Hanoi: Foreign Languages Publication House, 1964.

Goebel, Dorothy, ed., *American Policy, A Documentary Survey, 1776–1960*. New York: Holt, Rinehart & Winston, Inc., 1961.

Goodman, Elliot R., *The Soviet Design for a World State*. New York: Columbia University Press, 1960.

Gordon, King, *The United Nations in the Congo*. New York: Carnegie Endowment for International Peace, 1962.

Gottlieb, Manuel, *The German Peace Settlement and the Berlin Cirsis*. New York: Paine-Whitman Publishers, 1960.

Graebner, Norman A., *Cold War Diplomacy, 1945–1960*. Princeton, N. J.: D. Van Nostrand Co., Inc., 1962.

Griffith, William E., *The Sino-Soviet Rift*. Cambridge: The Massachusetts Institute of Technology Press, 1964.

Hadley, Arthur T., *The Nation's Safety and Arms Control*. New York: The Viking Press, Inc., 1961.

Halperin, Morton H., *China and the Bomb*. New York: Frederick A. Praeger, Inc., 1965.

Hammer, Ellen, *The Struggle for Indochina*. Stanford, Calif.: Stanford University Press, 1954.

Hammond, Thomas Taylor., ed., *Soviet Foreign Relations and World Communism*. Princeton, N.J.: Princeton University Press, 1965.

Hennessy, Maurice N., *The Congo*. New York: Frederick A. Praeger, Inc., 1962.

Hinton, Harold C., *Communist China in World Politics*. Boston: Houghton Mifflin Company, 1966.

Home, Gordon C., *Cyprus, Then and Now*. London: J. M. Dent & Sons, Ltd., 1960.

Hsieh, A. L., *Communist China's Strategy in the Nuclear Age*. Englewood Cliffs, N.J.: Prentice-Hall, Inc., 1962.

Hudson, G. F., *The Hard and Bitter Peace, World Politics Since 1945*. New York: Frederick A. Praeger, Inc., 1966.

———, *et al.*, eds., *The Sino-Soviet Dispute*. New York: Frederick A. Praeger, Inc., 1961.

Ingram, Kenneth, *History of the Cold War*. New York: Philosophical Library, Inc., 1955.

Jackson, J. Hampden, *The World of the Postwar Decade: 1945–1955*. Boston: Houghton Mifflin Company, 1956.

Jackson, W. A. D., *Russo-Chinese Borderlands*. Princeton, N.J.: D. Van Nostrand Co., Inc., 1962.

Johnson, Paul., *Suez War*. London: Macgibbon & Kee, Ltd., 1957.

Jones, J. M., *The Fifteen Weeks*. New York: The Viking Press, Inc., 1955.

Kecskemeti, Paul, *The Unexpected Revolution*. Stanford, Calif.: Stanford University Press, 1961.

Kertesz, Stephen D., ed., *The Fate of East Central Europe*. Notre Dame, Ind.: University of Notre Dame Press, 1956.

Kim, Young Hum, *East Asia's Turbulent Century*. New York: Appleton-Century-Crofts, 1966.

———, ed., *Patterns of Competitive Coexistence: USA vs. USSR*. New York: G. P. Putnam's Sons, 1966.

Koenig, Louis W., ed., *The Truman Administration, Its Principles and Practices*. New York: New York University Press, 1956.

Kuo, Ping-chia, *China: New Age and New Outlook*. New York: Alfred A. Knopf, Inc., 1956.

Lagedz, Leopold., ed., *The Sino-Soviet Conflict: Eleven Radio Discussions*. Chester Springs, Pa.: Dufour Editions, Inc., 1965.

Larson, David L., ed., *The Cuban Crisis of 1962*. Boston: Houghton Mifflin Company, 1963.

Lauterpacht, E., ed., *The Suez Canal Settlement*. London: Stevens and Sons, Limited, 1960.

Lefever, Ernest N., *Crisis in the Congo: A UN Force in Action*. Washington, D. C.: The Brookings Institution, 1965.

Legum, Colin, *Congo Disaster*. Baltimore, Md.: Penguin Books, Inc., 1961.

Lenczowski, George, *Russia and the West in Iran, 1918–1948; A Study in Big Power Rivalry*. Ithaca, N. Y.: Cornell University Press, 1949.

Lerche, Charles O., *The Cold War and After*. Englewood Cliffs, N.J.: Prentice-Hall, Inc., 1965.

Lewis, John Wilson, *Major Doctrines of Communist China*. New York: W. W. Norton & Company, Inc., 1964.

Lippmann, Walter, *The Cold War, A Study in U. S. Foreign Policy*. New York: Harper & Row, Publishers, 1947.

Longgood, W. F., *Suez Story: Key to the Middle East*. New York: Greenberg Press, 1957.

Luard, Evan, ed., *The Cold War, A Re-appraisal*. New York: Frederick A. Praeger, Inc., 1964.

Lukacs, John A., *A History of the Cold War*. Garden City, N. Y.: Anchor Books, 1962.

Luke, Sir Harry, *Cyprus, A Portrait and an Appreciation*. New York: Roy Publishers, Inc., 1958.

McAleavy, Henry, *The Modern History of China*. New York: Frederick A. Praeger, Inc., 1966.

Manley, Chesley, *The Twenty Years' Revolution; From Roosevelt to Eisenhower*. Chicago, Ill.: Henry Regnery Co., 1954.

Martin, Ralph G., *President from Missouri: Harry S Truman*. New York: Julian Messner, 1964.

Meray, Tibner, *Thirteen Days that Shook the Kremlin*. New York: Frederick A. Praeger, Inc., 1959.

Merriam, Allan P., *Congo, Background of Conflict*. Evanston, Ill.: Northwestern University Press, 1961.

Meyer, Karl E., and Szulc, Tad, *The Cuban Invasion, The Chronicle of Disaster*. New York: Frederick A. Praeger, Inc., 1962.

Mezerik, Abrahim, *U–2 and Open Skies*. New York: International Review Service, 1960.

———, *Cuba and the United States*. New York: International Review Service.

Millis, Walter, and Real, James, *The Abolition of War*. New York: The Macmillan Company, 1963.

Moorad, George, *Lost Peace in China*. New York: E. P. Dutton & Co., Inc., 1949.

Moraes, Frank Robert, *Report on Mao's China*. New York: The Macmillan Company, 1953.

Morray, Joseph P., *From Yalta to Disarmament: Cold War Debate*. New York: Monthly Review Press, 1961.

Nogee, Joseph L., *Soviet Policy Towards International Control of Atomic Energy*. New York: Frederick A. Praeger, Inc., 1965.

North, Robert Carver, *Moscow sand Chinese Communists*. Stanford, Calif.: Stanford University Press, 1963.

O'Conor, John F., *Cold War and Liberation*. New York: Vantage Press, 1961.

Osgood, Charles E., *An Alternative to War or Surrender*. Urbana, Ill.: University of Illinois Press, 1962.

Pachter, Henry M., *Collision Course: The Cuban Missile Crisis and Coexistence*. New York: Frederick A. Praeger, Inc., 1963.

Padelford, Norman J., and Goodrich, Leland M., *The United Nations in the Balance*. New York: Frederick A. Praeger, Inc., 1965.

Perla, Leo, *Can We End the Cold War?* New York: The Macmillan Company, 1960.

Price, Harry Bayard, *The Marshall Plan and its Meaning*. Ithaca, N. Y.: Cornell University Press, 1955.

Raskin, Marcus G., and Fall, Bernard B., eds., *The Viet-Nam Reader; Articles and Documents on American Foreign Policy and the Viet-Nam Crisis*. New York: Random House, Inc., 1965.

Ray, Sibnarayan, ed., *Vietnam: Seen from East and West.* An International Symposium. New York: Frederick A. Praeger, Inc., 1966.

Roberts, Henry L., *Russia and America: Dangers and Prospects.* New York: The New American Library, Inc., 1956.

Robertson, Terence, *Crisis.* New York: Atheneum Publishers, 1965.

Robson, C. B., ed., *Berlin—Pivot of German Destiny.* Chapel Hill, N. C.: University of North Carolina Press, 1960.

Ronchey, Alberto, *Two Red Giants, An Analysis of Sino-Soviet Relations.* Translated by Raymond Rosenthal. New York: W. W. Norton & Company, Inc., 1965.

Rondot, Pierre, *The Changing Patterns of the Middle East.* Rev. Ed. New York: Frederick A. Praeger, Inc., 1962.

Rosecrence, R. N., *The Dispersion of Nuclear Weapons.* New York: Columbia University Press, 1964.

Rosner, Gabriella, *The U. N. Emergency Force.* New York: Columbia University Press, 1963.

Sabel, Lester A., ed., *Cuba, the U. S. and Russia, 1960–1963.* New York: Facts on File, Inc., 1964.

Schnapper, M. B., ed., *The Truman Program; Addresses and Messages.* Washington, D. C.: Public Affairs Press, 1949.

Schonfield, Hugh J., *The Suez Canal in World Affairs.* Boston: Houghton Mifflin Company, 1952.

Schramm, Wilber, *One Day in the World's Press.* Stanford, Calif.: Stanford University Press, 1959.

Schuman, F. L., *The Cold War: Retrospect and Prospect.* Baton Rouge, La.: Louisiana State University Press, 1962.

Schwartz, Harry, *Tsars, Mandarins, and Commissars: A History of Chinese-Russian Relations.* Philadelphia, Pa.: J. B. Lippincott Co., 1964.

Scigliano, Robert. G., *South Vietnam: Nation Under Stress.* Boston: Houghton Mifflin Company, 1964.

Seton-Watson, Hugh, *The East-European Revolution.* New York: Frederick A. Praeger, Inc., 1956.

———, *Neither War Nor Peace: The Struggle for Power in the Postwar World.* Rev. Ed. New York: Frederick A. Praeger, Inc., 1962.

Singh, Nagendra, *Nuclear Weapons and International Law.* New York: Frederick A. Praeger, Inc., 1959.

Smith, Jean Edward, *The Defense of Berlin.* Baltimore, Md.: The Johns Hopkins Press, 1963.

Spanier, John W., *American Foreign Policy Since World War II.* New York: Frederick A. Praeger, Inc., 1965.

———, *World Politics in an Age of Revolution.* New York: Frederick A. Praeger, Inc., 1966.

Speier, Hans, *The Soviet Threat to Berlin.* New York: Frederick A. Praeger, Inc., 1960.

Stebbins, Richard P., *The United States in World Affairs, 1962*. New York: Harper & Row, Publishers, 1963.

Steinberg, Alfred, *Harry S Truman*. New York: G. P. Putnam's Sons, 1962.

Stephens, Robert, *Cyprus: A Place of Arms, Power Politics and Ethnic Conflict in the Eastern Mediterranean*. New York: Frederick A. Praeger, Inc., 1966.

Stillman, Edmund, and Pfaff, William, *The New Politics: America and the End of the Postwar World*. New York: Coward-McCann, Inc., 1961.

Stoessinger, John G., *et al.*, *Financing the United Nations System*. Washington, D.C.: The Brookings Institution, 1964.

Strachey, John, *On the Prevention of War*. New York: St Martin's Press, Inc., 1963.

Summers, Robert Edward, *Economic Aid to Europe: The Marshall Plan*. New York: H. W. Wilson Co., 1948.

Trager, Frank N., *Why Viet Nam?* New York: Frederick A. Praeger, Inc., 1966.

Trefousse, Hans Louis, ed., *The Cold War, A Book of Documents*. New York: G. P. Putnam's Sons, 1965.

Truman, Harry S, *Memoirs*. Garden City, N. Y.: Doubleday & Company, Inc., 1955.

Tsou, Tang, *America's Failure in China, 1941–50*. Chicago, Ill.: University of Chicago Press, 1963.

U. S. State Department, *U. S. Relations with China; with special reference to the period 1944–1949*. Washington, D.C.: U. S. Government Printing Office, 1949.

Upton, Joseph M., *The History of Modern Iran: An Interpretation*. Cambridge: Harvard University Press, 1960.

Vali, Ferenc A., *Rift and Revolt in Hungary*. Cambridge: Harvard University Press, 1961.

Varma, Shanti Prasad, *Struggle for the Himalayas; A Study in Sino-Indian Relations*. Jullundur: Universal Publishers, 1965.

Warth, Robert D., *Soviet Russia in World Politics*. New York: Twayne Publishers, Inc., 1963.

Whiting, A. S., *China Crosses the Yalu: The Decision to Enter the Korean War*. New York: The Macmillan Company, 1960.

Wilber, Donald Newton, *Iran, Past and Present*. Princeton, N. J.: Princeton University Press, 1958.

Wilson, Thomas W., Jr., *Cold War and Common Sense*. Greenwich, Conn.: New York Graphic Society Publishers, Ltd., 1962.

Windsor, Philip, *City on Leave, A History of Berlin, 1945–1962*. New York: Frederick A. Praeger, Inc., 1963.

Winks, Robin W., *The Cold War, from Yalta to Cuba*. New York: The Macmillan Company, 1964.

Wint, Guy, *Communist China's Crusade: Mao's Raod to Power and the New Campaign for World Revolution.* New York: Frederick A. Praeger, Inc., 1965.

————, and Calvocoressi, Peter, *Middle East Crisis.* Harmondsworth, England: Penguin Books Ltd., 1957.

Wise, David, and Ross, Thomas B., *The U–2 Affair.* New York: Random House, Inc., 1962.

Wolfers, Arnold., ed., *Alliance Policy in the Cold War.* Baltimore, Md.: The Johns Hopkins Press, 1959.

Wright, Quincy, *Preventing World War III: Some Proposals.* New York: Simon & Schuster, Inc., 1962.

Yale, William, *The Near East.* Ann Arbor, Mich.: The University of Michigan Press, 1958.

Zablocki, Clement J., ed., *The Sino-Soviet Rivalry: Implications for U. S. Policy.* New York: Frederick A. Praeger, Inc., 1966.

Zagoria, D. S., *The Sino-Soviet Conflict, 1956–1961.* Princeton, N. J.: Princeton University Press, 1962.

Zaehringer, Alfred J., *Soviet Space Technology.* New York: Harper & Row, Publishers, 1961.

Zinner, Paul E., *Revolution in Hungary.* New York: Columbia University Press, 1962.